Working With Excelerator Version 1.9

SYSTEMS ANALYSIS
AND
DESIGN

Working With Excelerator Version 1.9
Allen Schmidt

to accompany

SYSTEMS ANALYSIS AND DESIGN

Kenneth E. Kendall
George Mason University

Julie E. Kendall
George Mason University

second edition

PRENTICE HALL, ENGLEWOOD CLIFFS, NEW JERSEY 07632

Editorial/production supervision: *Elaine Price*
Supplements acquisitions editor: *David Scholder*
Manufacturing buyers: *Trudy Pisciotti/Robert Anderson*

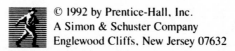
Printed in the United States of America

10 9 8 7 6 5 4 3 2 1

ISBN 0-13-855917-1

Prentice-Hall International (UK) Limited, *London*
Prentice-Hall of Australia Pty. Limited, *Sydney*
Prentice-Hall Canada Inc., *Toronto*
Prentice-Hall Hispanoamericana, S.A., *Mexico*
Prentice-Hall of India Private Limited, *New Delhi*
Prentice-Hall of Japan, Inc., *Tokyo*
Simon & Schuster Asia Pte. Ltd., *Singapore*
Editora Prentice-Hall do Brasil, Ltda., *Rio de Janeiro*

Dedicated to Donald J. and Lucille (Sue) Stadler

and to Oliver G. and June C. Schmidt

WORKING WITH EXCELERATOR - VERSION 1.9

TABLE OF CONTENTS

DETAILED TABLE OF CONTENTS

LIST OF FIGURES

LIST OF FIGURES

LIST OF FIGURES

LIST OF FIGURES

LIST OF FIGURES

Excelerator is located

In Building   _____

    Room   _____

On machines numbered:

_____   _____   _____   _____

_____   _____   _____   _____

_____   _____   _____   _____

_____   _____   _____   _____

Your user id is:

_____

Your password is:

_____

Your project name is:

_____

_____

Working With Excelerator Version 1.9

SYSTEMS ANALYSIS
AND
DESIGN

Introduction

Excelerator® by Intersolv (Cambridge, MA 02142), is a powerful, yet easy to use, microcomputer software package. It is a CASE (Computer Aided Software Engineering) tool used in the system analysis and design process to automate the development of computer systems.

Excelerator produces graphic representations of the system being designed, including data flow diagrams, structure charts, and others. The graphic products and data descriptions are stored on a microcomputer hard disk and may be created and modified with ease. Thus a complete system may be designed and updated as the development process evolves. Program language source code may be created from record layouts stored in the data dictionary.

Another powerful feature of Excelerator is the ability to perform comprehensive diagnostic checking of the system design, reporting errors and design flaws. This enables the analyst to detect errors in the early phases of system development, where they are easier and less costly to correct. A wealth of reports and cross-reference grids may easily be produced. Everything that Excelerator tracks, from graph objects and the connections between them to data dictionary entries, is stored in the XLDictionary. This dictionary is the information base for the variety of reports produced by Excelerator. The analyst has complete flexibility when creating report formats and sequences.

Excelerator has capabilities for the quick creation of screen and report prototypes. Prototype data fields are obtained directly from data elements described in the XLDictionary.   The prototype feature includes the ability to generate computer programming language data descriptions for screen designs.

Excelerator supports a variety of modeling techniques, accommodating many design philosophies.   Entity-Relationship diagrams and Data Model diagrams illustrate the relationship between data records. Data flow diagrams and structure charts and diagrams model processes and the data required by them. Prototyping allows the creation of screens and reports. Record and element data description entries may be generated directly from screen layouts. Data dictionary options allow data fields to be keyed directly into the system as they become available from interviews and JAD sessions. Elements not included on records may be easily identified using analysis options.

As data processing moves into the 1990's, we can be reasonably sure that the use of CASE tools will expand and encompass the data processing industry. Standards are being developed that will allow products to conveniently exchange data. Code generation will eventually replace applications programming.

This text is a thorough presentation of the features of Excelerator, version 1.9. The first two chapters provide an overview of the product. Major features of Excelerator are covered in separate chapters. Except the first two chapters, the text design has a flexible format allowing the student to use individual features of Excelerator without reading material in prior chapters. It is designed for use at a microcomputer workstation.
This text is for use by students and professionals in systems analysis and design. Appropriate courses are ACM course number IS5 Information Analysis and IS8 Systems Design, and DPMA course number CIS/86-5, System Development Methodologies: A Survey.

ACKNOWLEDGEMENTS

Many people have graciously contributed time and support for this text. I am deeply appreciative to them all.

I would like to give a special word of thanks and appreciation to many people at Index Technology. Judith Vanderkay has spent many long hours providing support for this text, including the production of high quality graphics and providing software. Her hard work and continual support is greatly appreciated. I would like to add another special thanks to Pamela Meyer, supplying information and answers to my continual questions. Susan Martin has provided an excellent, detailed technical review of this text. I greatly appreciate the comments and suggestions that she has made.

Richard Crisafulli at the Index Technology hotline deserves many thanks for the outstanding technical help that he and the hotline service group have provided. The support that the staff at Index Technology has given to the educational community is an outstanding example of the cooperation and assistance necessary for our society to continues its rapid technological advancement.

I would like to thank Ken and Julie Kendall for their many suggestions and kind words of encouragement. Their review of this text has been indispensable.

Mike McCandless of Micro Focus has my appreciation for support in the use of Micro Focus COBOL and the Micro Focus Excelerator Interface software. I would also like to thank Valerie Ashton at Prentice Hall for managing this project.

A SPECIAL NOTE FOR EDUCATORS

Index Technology has graciously given qualifying schools educational grants for Excelerator and all other Index Technology products. Schools may contact Judith Vanderkay or Pamela Meyer at Index Technology for further information.

Index Technology
One Main Street
Cambridge, MA 02142
Telephone: (617) 494-8200

Micro Focus has an educational grant program for Micro Focus COBOL, Assembler and the Excelerator Interface. The COBOL product may be used to create both microcomputer COBOL programs and mainframe COBOL programs, including code for CICS. For information on the grant program, contact: Barbara M. Bouldin, Manager, Academic Grant Program.

Micro Focus
Academic Grant Program
2465 E. Bayshore Rd.
Suite 400
Palo Alto, CA 94303
Telephone: (415) 856-6134

1

Getting Started With Excelerator

Chapter goals:

> Understanding Excelerator terminology
> Learning how to log onto Excelerator
> Knowing how to change Excelerator project defaults
> Understanding effective use of the graphics profile
> Know how to use the action keypad options
> Understand how to use selector lists

EXCELERATOR BASICS

Once the machine has been turned on, at the C:\> prompt type: **EXCEL**

The Excelerator logo screen will appear, press any key.

It is suggested that the User ID and password be entered in upper case. Excelerator is case sensitive, meaning that it distinguishes the difference between upper and lower case letters. If your user ID and password were originally setup in upper case letters and you enter them in lower case letters, a message will be displayed informing you that the user id is not found. It must then be re-keyed in upper case letters. A simple convention that you may want to use is to create user ids and passwords using all upper case letters and press the Caps Lock key.

Throughout this manual you will be told to select an option. This means to press or click the left button on the mouse. If the instructions tell you to press the cancel button or to cancel, press the right button. The cancel command is also used to exit some options. It may be used for escaping any operation that you have selected by mistake. The Esc key may also be used to cancel.

If an option is displayed in reverse video on the screen, you may press the Enter key to select the option. This may save time moving the mouse when several options are in a sequence and are displayed by default in reverse video. A third method of selecting options is to enter a single letter or number used as a selection choice for the option.

It is usually the first letter of the option.

Enter your user ID and password. A project list is displayed on the same screen. Select the one that you are working on. A main selection menu screen is presented, shown in Figure 1.1.

Excelerator maintains several defaults for the project you are working on as well as various graphics drawing screens. You may wish to change some of these defaults.

HOUSEKEEPING

The **HOUSEKEEPING** option allows you to alter defaults for your particular user ID. The first time you use Excelerator you should verify and, if necessary, modify any project defaults. You may want to select this option if you are working in a team environment to verify which printer or other defaults have been selected by previous team members.

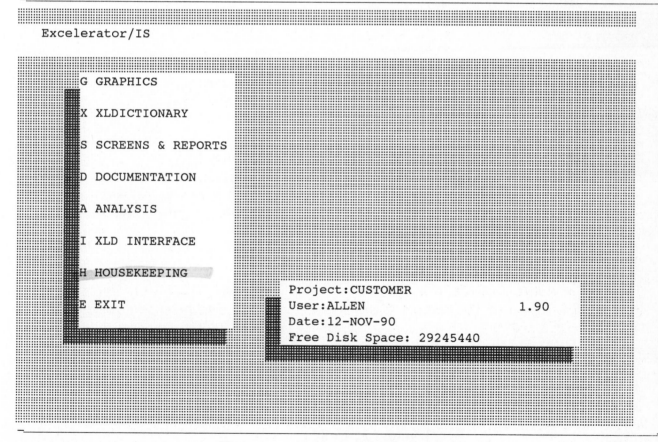

Figure 1.1 Excelerator Main Menu

Select **HOUSEKEEPING** (move the mouse so that the cursor is within the shaded area called HOUSEKEEPING and press the left button), then select **Profile**. Two options are available: Inspect or Modify. Inspect allows you to view the options but not to change them. Select **Modify** and the Profile screen, illustrated in Figure 1.2, is displayed.

Some of the settings may be altered. **Password** may be changed, but not without the mutual agreement of the other members, if you are in a group.

Hardcopy Device may be changed if more than one is displayed. This is especially useful if the PC is connected to a dot matrix printer and a laser printer is available, connected to another PC. The printed output may be stored on a diskette and transferred to the other PC for high-quality printing. The actual techniques of graphics printing will be covered in a Chapter 2. To change printers, select the desired hardcopy device. Note that this must be done before saving a print to diskette, since the Excelerator print routines must know how to format the print.

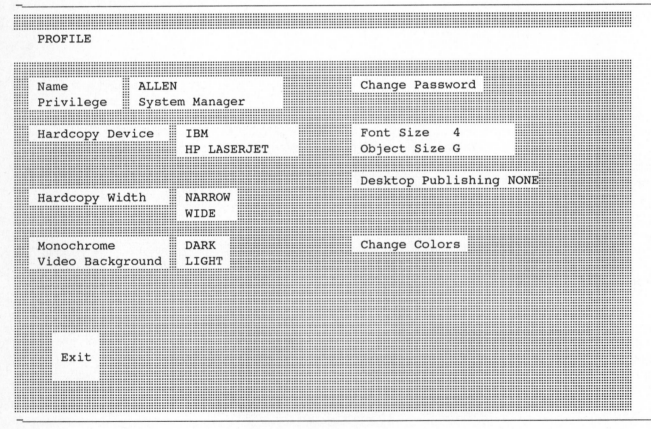

Figure 1.2 Profile Options

The font and object size may not be changed here. They may be temporarily altered when you are at the graphic print option. Details will be covered under printing in Chapter 2. Hardcopy width may be changed. **Narrow** will cause your print to be on 8½ X 11 paper, portrait style (8½ across, 11 down). **Wide** will print sideways (landscape mode) on 8½ X 11 paper or full width on a wide printer.

Monochrome Video Background may be changed <u>only</u> if the monitor is monochrome. Selecting **Dark** will make the background dark with white lines used for drawing.

For color monitors the default colors may be changed. Select **Change Colors**. Displayed are colors, numbered 0 through 15. Enter the color number desired for the various options available: Canvas (the background), Fields & Menus, Non-Graphic Text, Drawing Color (for graph objects, etc.) and a unique color to highlight which entities have an explosion path (covered in detail later). Dark colors for the drawing color and explosion path should be avoided unless you are using a light background and vice versa. It makes them difficult to see on the graphics orientation map. The Prompts & Highlights color is set to black and cannot be changed. Press F3 to save the color changes. Hit the Esc key (or the right mouse button) to abandon the changes.

Select Exit to return to the Profile menu and select Exit again to return to the Main Menu.

THE GRAPHICS PROFILE AND OTHER BASICS

Excelerator maintains defaults for the various drawings. Each time a new drawing (graph) is created, this profile will be set to the defaults for the particular graph (e.g. data flow diagram). They may be overridden and set to your individual taste. These profile options may be changed as needed when working on a drawing. Since defaults are used for all graphics, they will be presented in this introductory chapter.

Move the mouse so the arrow points to GRAPHICS and press the left button. This is called selecting GRAPHICS. The graphics menu screen is displayed, shown in Figure 1.3. Several choices are available:

Data Flow Diagram
Structure Chart
Data Model Diagram
Entity-Relationship Diagram
State Transition Diagram
Structure Diagram
Presentation Graph (used to draw system flowcharts and other pictorial representations of your system)

Work Breakdown Structure

Select the appropriate choice for the project you are working on or return to the main menu by selecting Exit.

When a selection is made, an action keypad appears with the following options:

Modify to change or work with an existing diagram.
Add to create a new diagram.
Delete to delete a diagram.
Copy to make a second copy of the diagram. This can be useful when creating new diagrams that are similar to already existing diagrams or to create a template for all diagrams. Simply copy and then modify.
Rename to change the name of the diagram.
List to display a list of the diagrams and their DOS filenames.

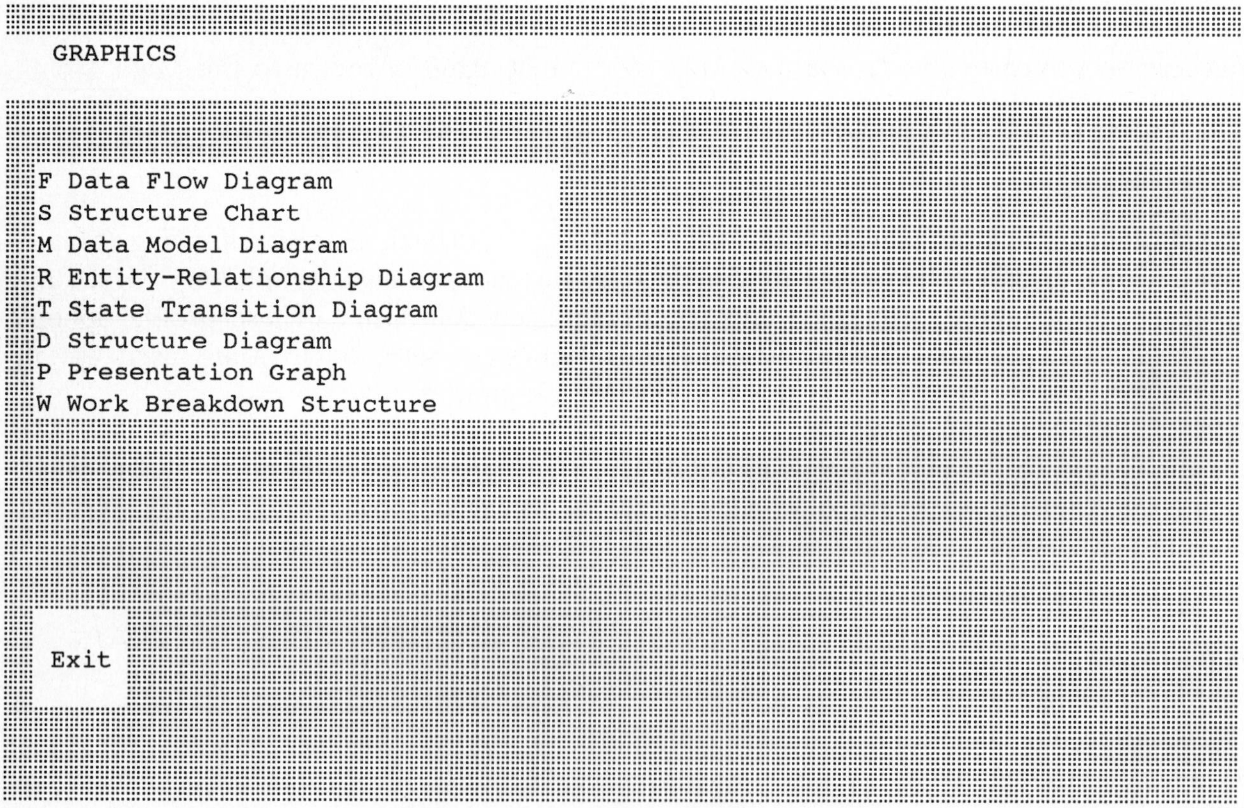

```
GRAPHICS

  F Data Flow Diagram
  S Structure Chart
  M Data Model Diagram
  R Entity-Relationship Diagram
  T State Transition Diagram
  D Structure Diagram
  P Presentation Graph
  W Work Breakdown Structure




  Exit
```

Figure 1.3 Graphics Menu Choices

Note: if the selection you want is already in reverse video you may simply press the Enter key instead of using the mouse. Example: Select **Data Flow Diagram**.

To create a new diagram, select Add, then type in the name you wish to call the diagram.

To modify a diagram, select Modify, and press the Enter key when prompted for a name. Excelerator will give you a list of diagrams already created. An example is shown in Figure 1.4. Use the mouse to select the diagram to be modified. You may also press the arrow keys to move the reverse video to the desired diagram and press the enter key. If there is more than one screenful of names on the selector list, select the plus sign at the bottom of the list (or PgDn) to display the next screenful. If you wish to return to the previous list, select the - sign from the top of the list (or PgUp). If the diagram is not in the list, cancel or press the Esc key.

```
Data Flow Diagram

   Entity name                          File

   ANNUAL SALES EXPANDED . . . . . . . .LJJY151.DFD
   BATCH ADD CUSTOMER...................LJKEZKU.DFD
   CONNECTION SAMPLES. . . . . . . . . .nqfsc2l.dfd
   CREATE BILLING STATEMENTS...........mek2stm.dfd
   CUSTOMER SYS HOLD . . . . . . . . .JQY4ADS.DFD
   CUSTOMER SYSTEM.....................JA1CDQ1.DFD
   DIAGRAM 0 . . . . . . . . . . . .JI1GOCN.DFD
   DIAGRAM 0 - LOGICAL.................LBLM4WG.DFD
   DIAGRAM 1 . . . . . . . . . . . .JQ0SAM1.DFD
   DIAGRAM 1.1.........................JQ0OBJU.DFD
   DIAGRAM 1.2 . . . . . . . . . .JQY0HQY.DFD
   DIAGRAM 1.2.NEW.....................lzjmwsv.dfd
   DIAGRAM 2 . . . . . . . . . . .JQ14EEF.DFD
   DIAGRAM 3...........................JQZWCPR.DFD
   DIAGRAM 4 . . . . . . . . . . .JQ00C0S.DFD
   DIAGRAM 5...........................JQ0CEFU.DFD
   DIAGRAM TEST 5. . . . . . . . . .KRKIWHM.DFD
   . . . . . . . . . . .  +  . . . . . . . . . . . . . . .
```

Figure 1.4 Example Of A Selector List

The selector list concept is used to retrieve information throughout Excelerator's various features. Use it any time you are prompted to enter the name of an object or other entity that has already been created.

Of course, you could also type in the name of the diagram when prompted instead of using the selector list. When modifying a diagram you will <u>not</u> have to set the profile that is described below. Excelerator remembers the previously initialized profile when the drawing is selected.

When you have selected a graphic, the drawing screen will be displayed, illustrated by Figure 1.5. For all diagrams, you will want to set the profile.
Select PROFILE. Figure 1.6 illustrates the options that are available.

Select GRID. For data flow diagrams, select FINE, which places fine tick marks around

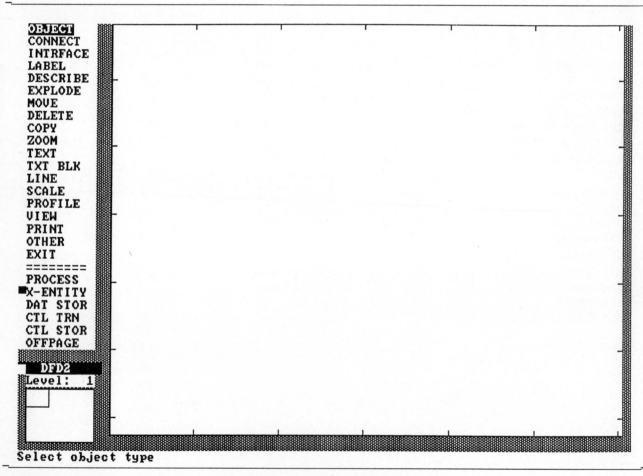

Figure 1.5 Drawing Screen

the drawing area. Excelerator lines up objects at the intersection of the tick marks, and the fine selection allows more control over object placement. For top to bottom alignment of system flow, medium works well. Click the right button (cancel) to save the options.

Select LABEL MD (Label Mode) to control how the label, the text within objects, will display. It is important to note that this option only takes effect when printing in the Draft Mode or on the drawing screen if the Zoom is set to Medium or Layout, where the text will crowd the diagram. COMPLETE will display a full label on the drawing area. Selecting WRAP will split label text between several lines, if it will not fit entirely on one line. CLIP will truncate text.

Select ALL TEXT, which gives the label and the ID. This is good for processes and data stores on the data flow diagram and processes on the structure chart. Some further instructions will have you select LAB ONLY. (ID ONLY could have also been selected but this would only show the object ID, not necessarily its graph label or name).

Press cancel (right button) to save the changes.

Select one of the following:

ONE WAY - used for one way arrows, generally on data flow diagrams.
TWO WAY - used for data flow diagrams or system flow charts for special conditions. If you need two way arrows, select PROFILE at any time when drawing. Change to TWO WAY, make the connection, then select PROFILE and change the connection type back to ONE WAY or NO ARROW.
NO ARROW - used for structure charts, entity-relationship diagrams, and system flowcharts.

Figure 1.7 demonstrates the effect of some PROFILE options. Select one of the following connections. They are used to connect objects, e.g. circles, rectangles, and so on.

PIPE - a bending connection used for data flow diagrams or structure charts.
STRAIGHT - no bend, used for system flow charts, entity relationship diagrams.
ARC - a curved connection used for data flow diagrams and screen flow diagrams.

See Figure 1.8 for examples of the three connection types.

Select one of the following: USERPORT, which allows you to control the location where the connection line touches the object, called the port, or SYSTPORT, which lets the system determine the location of connections. SYSTPORT is easier to work with but USERPORT gives you more control over connection locations. The details of using USERPORT and SYSTPORT are provided in Chapter 3 under the subheading Connecting Objects.

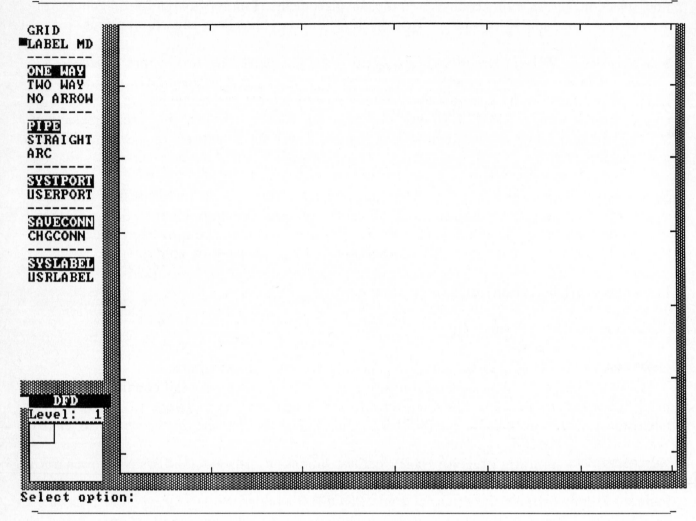

Figure 1.6   PROFILE Options menu

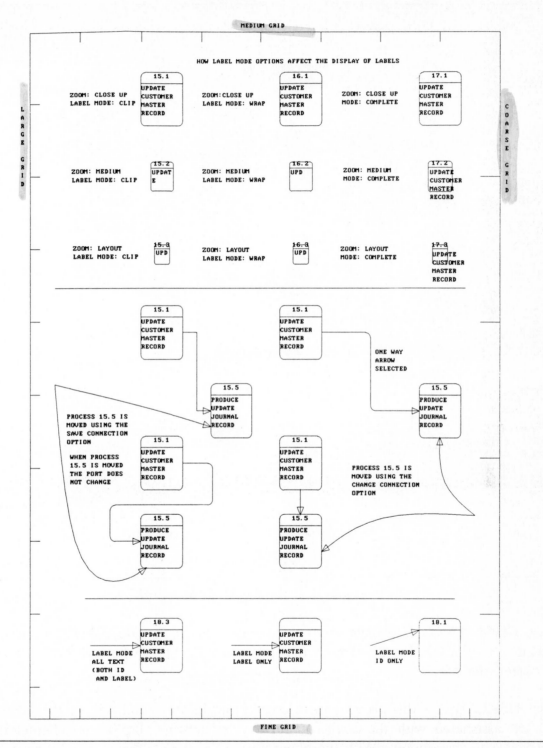

Figure 1.7   Effect of PROFILE Options

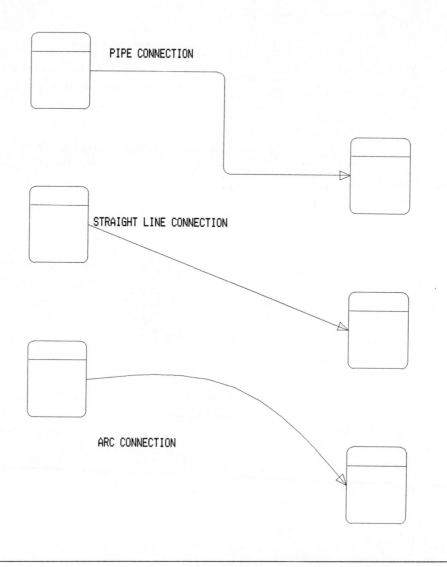

Figure 1.8 Types Of Connections

Select CHGCONN. If objects are moved, the connection side changes to give the best drawing. SAVECONN is the default that retains the location where the connection touches the object, the port.

Select USRLABEL - this allows you to control the location and size of the label or words that are associated with the *connections* on your drawing. Up to 60 characters may be displayed with this option. With the alternative, SYSLABEL, Excelerator determines where to display the connection label. Only 48 characters may be displayed when using the

SYSLABEL option.

Press Cancel (right button) to save changes.

TIP: Since it takes time to select the profile necessary for each graph, a template graph containing the profile but not any objects may be created. The template may be copied for each new graph, automatically including the profile. This method also creates a uniform standard for all project graphs of the same type.

Select PRINT followed by FULL GRAPH, then press Cancel. This places lines on the screen showing the boundaries of printed pages. At this time the drawing may be roughed out (perhaps objects only) and then zoomed in for a closer view later. The reason for roughing out the graph at this time is so that objects will not be split between two printed pages.

Later, when the graph is enlarged with the zoom feature, connections and descriptions may be conveniently added with a clearer picture of graph details. An alternative strategy is to use the line drawing feature to draw horizontal and vertical lines overlaying the page boundaries. Refer to Chapter 5 for details. When the graph is viewed at other than LAYOUT, the page boundaries disappear but the lines remain. The lines may be deleted after the drawing has been completed.

Select ZOOM, then MEDIUM for a good balance between displaying a sizable amount of drawing area and the ability to clearly determine where connections, descriptions and text should be placed. Notice that the printed page boundaries set under PRINT/FULL GRAPH have been erased.

Move the arrow to the orientation map (small square map on the bottom left of the screen). Click on the upper left corner of the map. This area is now displayed on the drawing screen. The orientation map may be used at anytime to scroll the drawing screen to a new area. This is necessary since the full drawing may be larger than the physical computer screen. Objects appear on the orientation map as dots, and give a perspective of your drawing.

When ZOOM is selected, you may also choose an area on the drawing screen. That area will be shifted to the center of the screen.

You may select CLOSE UP for a detailed view of your work or LAYOUT to see the whole drawing. When CLOSE UP is used, the screen will show how the drawing will actually print. At layout, the text does not show within the boundaries of the object (this will change as you zoom to medium or close up).

FUNCTION KEYS AND SOME DEFINITIONS

Help may be obtained by pressing F2.

F3 saves description screens and returns to the previous screen.

F4 is the browse key. It allows you to relate several entities. Details will be provided later.

An *entity* is a basic piece of information maintained by Excelerator. You create entities as system design information is keyed into Excelerator. Each entity has a three letter abbreviation. Examples are records (REC), elements (ELE), data flow diagram (DFD), process (PRC), and many more. Appendix B provides a complete list of Excelerator entities.

A *relationship* is the link between two entities. Relationships are not keyed in but are built by Excelerator as the design is created. Relationships may be reported on and analyzed. They provide a tremendous amount of analytical power. Examples would be records containing elements, data flow diagrams containing processes, a structure chart containing a function, and many others. Appendix E provides a complete list of relationships.

Attributes are specific fields that describe an entity or relationship. For example, the element entity has a name, input picture, edit criteria, and other attributes.

Entities, relationships, and attributes will be used and discussed throughout the text.

EXERCISES

1. List three ways of selecting options within Excelerator.

2. What does being case sensitive mean?

3. How does the PROFILE option selected from the main menu differ from the PROFILE option selected from the graphics drawing screen?

4. What is an action keypad?

5. What does a selector list provide? How may it be used when an action (e.g. Modify) is selected?

6. What are PIPE, STRAIGHT and ARC used for?

7. What is the orientation map and how is it used?

8. How does the ZOOM feature change the view of the graph?

9. In your words, describe what an entity is. What is a relationship? An attribute?

2
Printing, Saving
Backup, and Exiting

Chapter goals:

> Learn how to print graphics drawings
> Know how to transfer printed output to a file
> Understand how to set print options
> Know how to save project work using the Backup feature
> Know how to transfer backup files into the project
> Understand how to use the Export feature for creating project backup
> Understand how to Import project backup
> Know how to exit Excelerator and the Exit options.

GRAPHICS PRINTING

Printing, saving, backup, and exiting Excelerator are common activities and are covered in this introductory chapter.

Graphics printing is invoked by using a graphics menu option. If you have made many changes to the drawing, it is a good precaution to save your work before printing. Select **Other** and then **Save**. From the drawing screen, select PRINT, which may be done on three levels.

To print the full graph or drawing, select FULL GRAPH. This gives a high quality print of the graph. The print may be spread over several pages, depending on the drawing size. Boundary lines for the page outlines will appear on the screen.

Select YES (or NO to cancel - especially if the page boundary lines pass through an object, text or other critical part of the diagram).
Select PRINTER or FILE.
PRINTER will generate the graphics and transmit the drawing to the printer. The screen will become dark with light lines and dots appearing as the print is generated. Pressing the

right mouse button (or Esc) during printing will cancel the print.

If you have selected **FILE** you will be prompted for a file name on the bottom of the screen. Since Excelerator will save drawings in your project subdirectory of C:\EXCEL, entering a filename will save it in that subdirectory also.   To save in the root directory, enter \filename.ext where filename is a 1 to 8 character DOS filename.   The extension may be 1 to 3 characters or omitted.

A good convention is to use your initials as the extension (unless they are COM, EXE, SYS, BAT, or any other standard DOS extension).   After printing the files, they may be easily deleted, since they take up unnecessary disk space.   To delete the files (be sure and print first), type **DEL *.ext** at the C:\ prompt, where ext represents your initials.   You may also enter A:filename.ext (or B:filename.ext) when prompted by Excelerator to save the print file on a diskette.

To print a graphics file, use the GPRINT utility program supplied with the Excelerator package.   At the C:\ prompt type **GPRINT filename.ext**.

To obtain a high quality print of only a portion of the screen or drawing, select WINDOW. Select the upper left corner, then select the lower right corner of the area that you want to print.   Boundary lines for the page outlines will appear on the screen.   Select YES (or NO if you wish to change the boundary lines).   Select PRINTER or FILE, as mentioned above.

To obtain a print of the full graph on one page, select DRAFT.   This print is not high quality and may seem cluttered but will show the entire graph on one page.   It can be reviewed for completeness, etc. and then printed using one of the above methods for the finished product.

The SETUP option allows you to verify which printer has been selected if more than one printer option is available and to change the printed size of the objects and the font (text). Select SETUP.   The print setup screen is displayed as in Figure 2.1.

The selected printer and printer defaults are shown at the top of the drawing screen.   A sample object and label are displayed to show how text (the shaded area) will appear within them.   The orientation map (lower left corner) shows page boundaries and how many pages will be needed to print the full drawing area.   The bottom of the screen shows what objects and fonts would be needed to display all the text within an object.

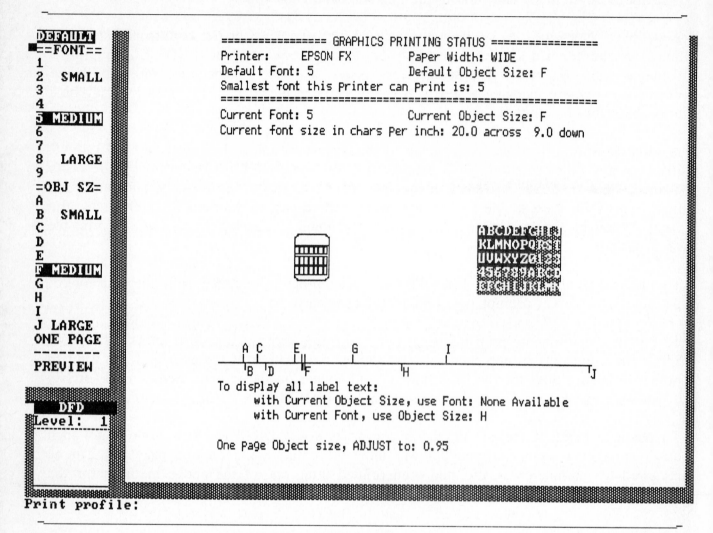

Figure 2.1 Print Setup Screen

The menu on the left is used to change font and object sizes. These may be selected, and the orientation map, sample object and sample label will reflect the changes. Reselect sizes as needed to obtain the right fit for your printer. Selecting **Preview** allows you to change which object is used for the sample. Press the right button (or Esc) to return to the sizing menu.

Object sizes may also be selected that are between the preset values (A through J). This is accomplished by selecting an area on the horizontal line shown on the drawing screen. The short vertical double line indicates the object setting. A good strategy is to set the font size that is optimal for your printer (small but still clear). Then select the object size from the line that just allows all text to be visible in the object and label area.

Try experimenting with different sizes using the line and observing how much text will display. Selecting ONE PAGE will set object sizes that will print the graph on one page. Selecting DEFAULT from the top of the menu will use the values set in the Housekeeping option. Press the right button (Esc) to return to the drawing menu.

A good technique is to create your drawing and then zoom to close up. Review your text labels for completeness and to verify that all of the text will print. If any text is clipped, use the Setup option to change the object or font size. Again review the drawing close up before printing.

SAVING YOUR WORK & EXITING GRAPHICS

There are two ways to save your graphic work. If you wish to make a periodic backup without exiting, select OTHER and then SAVE.

Once the graph is complete, select EXIT. You will be prompted to save or not save. Select SAVE if you have made any changes to your drawing. Select NO SAVE if you do not wish to save your changes or if you have not made any changes to the drawing. When a graph is saved, the Analysis Prep option must be invoked (at a later time) to update the extensive relationships that are maintained for your drawing. This can be a time consuming process.

Selecting EXIT returns control to the graphics menu screen. You may work on a different graph or select EXIT again to return to the main menu screen.

Note that your work has been saved on drive C (the hard disk) in a project subdirectory. It is a good practice to backup your work onto a diskette in drive A.

BACKING UP YOUR WORK TO A DISKETTE

There are two methods to backup your project data within Excelerator. One method is the Backup option, which will save all files within your project subdirectory (including graphics and text print files). The other uses the XLD Interface facility which will copy all or selected Excelerator files.

THE BACKUP FEATURE

From the main menu screen, select HOUSEKEEPING, BACKUP/RESTORE and then BACKUP. Insert your diskette into drive A.

NOTE THAT THE BACKUP OPTION DESTROYS ALL DATA ON THE DISKETTE IN DRIVE A. THE DISKETTE IS ERASED BEFORE THE BACKUP PROCESS STARTS. MAKE SURE THAT YOU HAVE A DISKETTE RESERVED FOR EXCELERATOR BACKUP ONLY.

Press the Enter key for the date prompt on the screen. Enter your project name (the one selected when you first logged on to Excelerator). Excelerator assumes that you are using several diskettes, but the 3.5 inch size can usually store all of your project files on one diskette (for smaller projects). If your work needs to be saved on several disks, insert new disks as prompted by Excelerator. Carefully label the order in which the disks have been inserted for backup because you must restore them in the exact order in which they were backed up. Select EXIT to return to the main menu.

RESTORING DATA FROM A DISKETTE

Restore is the reverse of Backup; the data from a diskette is uncompressed. To restore data from a diskette back into the Excelerator subdirectories, select HOUSEKEEPING. Select BACKUP/RESTORE, then select RESTORE. Enter your logon project name when prompted for a PROJECT NAME. Respond to the screen prompts by pressing any key. When finished restoring, select EXIT.

EXPORTING AND IMPORTING

Another method of saving project data is to use the XLD Interface feature of Excelerator. This allows data to be stored on diskette and to be input into the same or other projects. The advantage of using the Export and Import feature is that project data and graphics are stored as individual files on the backup diskette. The diskette is not completely erased as with the Backup feature. This is a good method for student projects since they are typically small in size. It may also be used for larger projects but the data is not compressed as in the backup feature, thus taking more diskette space.

```
┌─────────────────────────────────────────────────────────────────────────────┐
│                                                                               │
│  DICTIONARY INTERFACE                                                         │
│                                                                               │
│  1 Export                    All                        Preview              │
│                                                                               │
│  2 Import                    Via Entity List            Detailed Preview     │
│                                                                               │
│  3 Lock                      Via Selection              Execute              │
│                                                                               │
│  4 Unlock                                                                     │
│                                                                               │
│  5 Export & Lock                                                              │
│                                                                               │
│  6 Import & Unlock                                                            │
│                                                                               │
│  Exit                                                                         │
│                                                                               │
│                                                                               │
│                                                                               │
│  Transfer file:A:FULLPROJ                                                     │
│                                                                               │
│  Enter full path and filename, e.g. abc  \excel\demo\abc  a:abc  k:\share\abc │
│                                                                               │
└─────────────────────────────────────────────────────────────────────────────┘
```

Figure 2.2 Dictionary Interface Screen

To use this feature, select XLD INTERFACE from the main menu. The Dictionary Interface
screen is displayed as illustrated in Figure 2.2. This option has many features which will be
discussed later in this text. The discussion here will focus on exporting (saving) all the project
data and importing (retrieving) all the diskette data.

To save project data, select **Export, All** and then **Execute**. If you wish to see a count of the
entities being exported, Preview may be selected. Excelerator prompts you for a transfer
format. Press enter to accept the default. Then key in a full path and file name for where
the copied files should reside. Examples are A:PROJBACK or C:\XLBACK\PROJECT1.
Write down the path and file name on a piece of paper, since the Import feature will request
these. Press the enter key. After the export has completed, a count of the exported entities
will be displayed. Press any key to view the second page of totals and again to return to the
selection screen. Select Exit to return to the main menu.

To retrieve diskette data saved under the export feature, select **Import**. Excelerator will prompt you for a transfer file name. Enter the path and file name for the data saved with the Export feature. Options will be presented for the possibilities of collisions, that is, the data being imported already exists in the XLDictionary. At this time, press **A** to override all previously existing data in the project. Select **All** and then **Execute**. The data will be transferred into the project. Again there will be several screens of import information. Press any key to view the second page and again for the Dictionary Interface menu. Select Exit to return to the main menu.

EXITING EXCELERATOR

Select EXIT and then one of following four choices:

1.   **Return to DOS** to exit to DOS.

2.   **Change Projects** if you wish to work on a different project.

3.   **Change Users** if another person wants to use Excelerator.

4.   **Analysis Prep & Exit.** This option will run the Analysis Prep feature, which updates the relationships maintained by Excelerator and then exit.

EXERCISES

1.   What is the difference between printing a full graph, window, and draft?

2.   How does printed output that is placed on a disk file become printed?

3.   What does the print SETUP option do? Why is this valuable to use before printing a graph for the first time?

4.   What is the importance of backing up project files?

5.   What is the difference between the BACKUP and the EXPORT option for creating a copy of your Excelerator work?

6.   Should the BACKUP option be used to save project information on a disk containing other important files? Why or why not?

7.   When you are working on a large diagram, why should the drawing be periodically saved?

3

DATA FLOW DIAGRAMS

The data flow diagram is one of the most commonly used techniques to model a system. It provides a picture of both the data and processes that operate on and transform the input data to output information. This chapter will cover the basics of creating data flow diagrams and Chapter 4 will explain the creation of child diagrams and the concept of exploding processes and records.

Data flow diagram modeling may be approached by creating a high level context or environmental diagram. Then the central process is exploded or decomposed to create a child diagram. Each process in the child diagram may be further exploded until it is not feasible to create any further diagrams. These processes are called functional primitives, and their logic may be described using Excelerator's Primitive Process Specification. This top-down approach is easily performed with Excelerator's Explode option.

An alternate approach for creating data flow diagram levels is to create lower level diagrams based on business events and then link these diagrams to higher level processes grouped by task. This bottom-up strategy is also easy to create using Excelerator's return option. Details of creating data flow diagrams are covered in this chapter while the linking together of several diagrams is presented in the next chapter.

Chapter goals:

> Learn how to create data flow diagrams.
> Understand the various methods of connecting objects on the data flow
>   diagram.
> Know how to create labels and data dictionary descriptions for the graph
>   components.
> Learn how to add control transforms and control flow to the data flow diagram.

CREATING THE DATA FLOW DIAGRAM

From the main menu, select **GRAPHICS**, then **Data Flow Diagram**. Choose ADD or MODIFY (if the data flow already exists).

Type in the name of your chart. If you are modifying a chart, press ENTER in the name area and Excelerator will give you a list of charts previously drawn. Select one or press the right button (or the ESC key) to cancel.

If you are adding a new data flow diagram, set the profile (refer to Chapter 2). The connection type may be straight, pipe, or arc. Select print to place page boundaries on the drawing screen.

PLACING OBJECTS ON THE SCREEN

Select OBJECT and a list of objects is displayed at the bottom of the selection menu, illustrated in Figure 3.1. Select a specific object from the list. Object types are:

PROCESS A process
X-ENTITY The external entity
DAT STORE A data store
CTL TRN Control transform, a process symbol made of dashes
CTL STOR Control store, a data store made of dashes.

A good technique is to add the external entities, processes and data stores. Then add the control transforms and flow lines. Select the location for the object on the screen by moving the mouse and pressing the left button.

Repeat for all objects. A good strategy is to put all the objects of the same type on the screen, since you do not have to keep reselecting the type of object from the list at the bottom of the selection area. Simply move the mouse so the arrow points to the region on the screen and press the left button. When all objects of the same type are on the drawing, reselect a different object and place it on the screen as described above.

Note that dots appear on the orientation map in the lower left corner of the screen. These represent objects on the main drawing screen.

If you do not like the location of the objects, use the MOVE command (See Chapter 5) to change their location. The size of the objects may be changed by using the SCALE command. Refer to Chapter 6 for SCALE details.

CONNECTING OBJECTS

To connect objects with lines, select CONNECT. Choose either DAT FLOW for a data flow or CTL FLOW for control flow, a dashed line.

If you have selected SYSTPORT under the profile option, select the first object to be connected, then select the second object. If a line crosses an object, use the MOVE command (Chapter 5) to change the path of the connection.

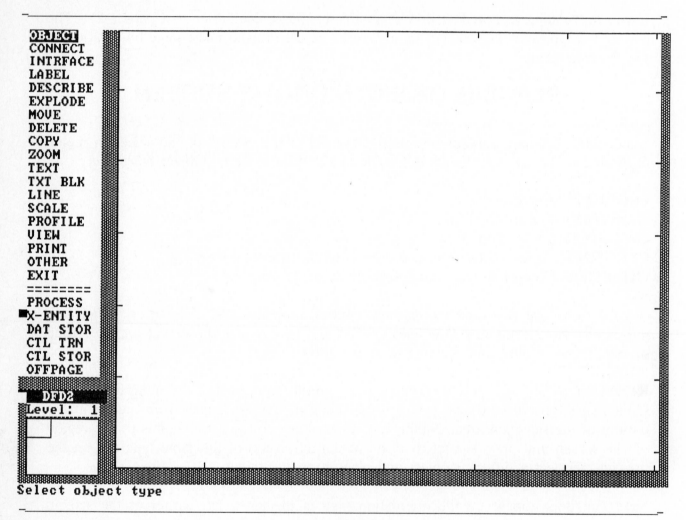

Figure 3.1 Data Flow Diagram Drawing Screen

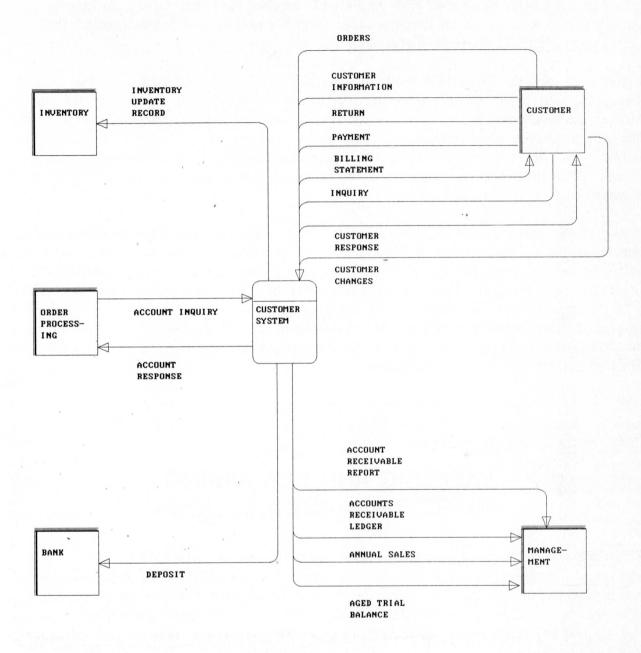

ORDERS

CUSTOMER
INFORMATION

RETURN

PAYMENT

BILLING
STATEMENT

INQUIRY

CUSTOMER
RESPONSE

CUSTOMER
CHANGES

INVENTORY

INVENTORY
UPDATE
RECORD

CUSTOMER

CUSTOMER
SYSTEM

ORDER
PROCESS-
ING

ACCOUNT INQUIRY

ACCOUNT
RESPONSE

ACCOUNT
RECEIVABLE
REPORT

ACCOUNTS
RECEIVABLE
LEDGER

ANNUAL SALES

MANAGE-
MENT

BANK

DEPOSIT

AGED TRIAL
BALANCE

CONTEXT LEVEL

Figure 3.2 Sample Context Level Data Flow Diagram

You may create diverging data flow streams by selecting the point where an existing flow already connects and then connect the other end of a flow to a different object. Refer to the Context Diagram shown in Figure 3.2.

If you have used the **USERPORT** option under PROFILE, the following procedure is used. Touch the first object to be connected. An arrow will appear on the side of the object. Moving the mouse will cause the arrow to move around the object. The location where the line will touch the object, called the port, will appear on the bottom of the screen (eg. RIGHT -2). Move the arrow to the side where you want the connection line to touch the object. Press the left button, then move the mouse so the arrow moves to the object to be connected to.

You may also move the cursor arrow to a place in the drawing area that you would like the line to extend to and then bend from, putting corners in the connecting line. Move the cursor arrow and press the left button. This gives a line segment. Repeat until the final object has been reached. Then press the left button and the small arrow reappears. Move it to the desired spot (eg. top left side) and press the left button. If the ARC connection type has been selected, the final arc will approximate the line segments. Pressing the right button will delete the last line segment and provides for an easy method of controlling the exact places that the lines should appear.

See Figures 3.3 and 3.4 for examples of line segments used to make connections. If the final line is not what you want it to be, you can move or delete the line (See Chapter 5). Continue connecting all the objects.

LABELING AND DESCRIBING OBJECTS AND CONNECTIONS

There are two methods for placing descriptive text into objects. The LABEL option creates text inside the object but not a data dictionary link. Using LABEL is the fastest method of placing text in the drawing area, since the drawing screen does not have to be redisplayed after each label has been created. LABEL also allows you to control exactly how you would like the text to appear within the object or beside the connection. Objects that are labeled may later be described and the label will be included automatically in the description.

The DESCRIBE feature allows you to place text in the object or by the connection and provides a link to the data dictionary as well. Label should be used first, but it is important to describe all objects and connections in the XLDictionary. Only then may you perform analysis and generate reports for the data and processes represented. The DESCRIBE option should also be used to create an explosion path and link child diagrams and records to the data flow diagram.

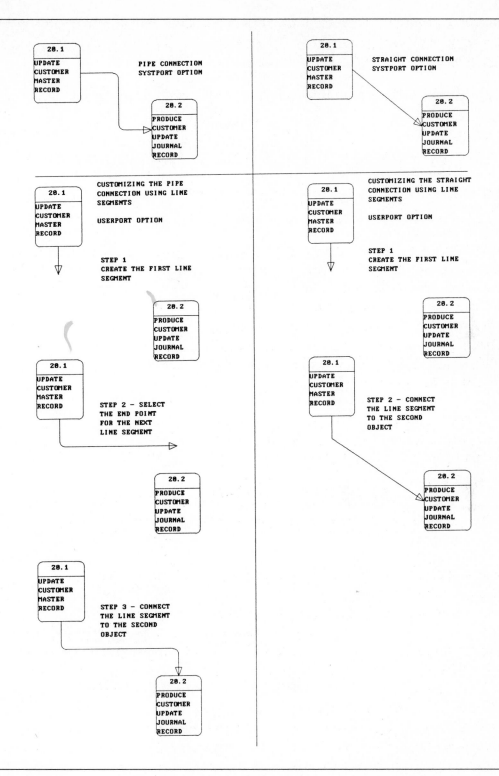

Figure 3.3 Connection Type Examples - Straight and Pipe

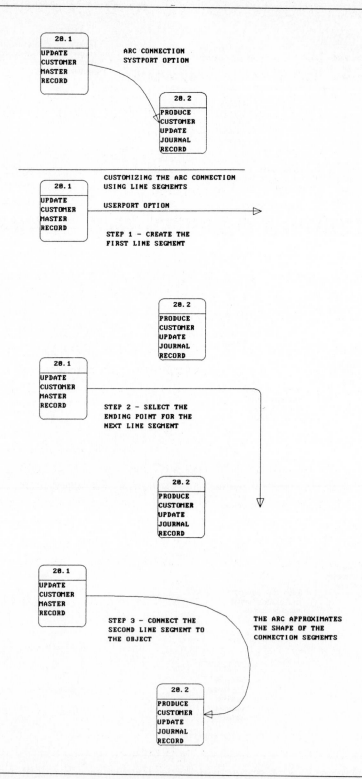

Figure 3.4   Connection Type Examples - Arc Connection

LABELING OBJECTS AND CONNECTIONS

To create a label within an object, select LABEL and then select the object for the label. Enter the text in the pop-up window that appears. Press the tab key to move to the next line in the label area. If any errors have been keyed, use insert, delete, or overtype the text. Press the Enter key when completed. Process labels should describe the work being done.

For connections, select the data handle, the small square on the line. If the user label has been chosen via the PROFILE option, select the upper left and lower right hand corners for the size of the label. Key in the label and press the enter key.

DESCRIBING OBJECTS AND CONNECTIONS

To put a description in the objects or alongside a connection and create a XLDictionary entry, select DESCRIBE. Then select the object you wish to describe. (Move the arrow to the object and click the left button).

On the bottom of the screen you are prompted to ENTER ID. For processes, a default ID is presented. Press Enter to accept or overtype it with your choice of ID. The default is the graph name and a suffix of .1, .2, .3, etc. depending on which order the objects have been selected for description.

If the object or data flow has already been described in a previous process, the data dictionary maintained by Excelerator will contain the description. Delete the default ID (press F1 and the **Del** key simultaneously), and press the enter key. A list of objects already described will be displayed. Select the object or data flow from the list (press the left button). The description screen is displayed. You may make any changes to the description screen at this time. Press F3 to save and return to the drawing screen. If the desired object or data flow is not on the list, press the Esc key or click the right button to cancel.

If the object does not already exist, key in a new name for the objects or data flow and press the enter key. Some suggested IDs are:

For an external entity, enter EE1, EE2, EE3, EE4. . .

For data stores, enter DD1, DD2, DD3, DD4. . . or D1, D2, D3, D4. . .

For data flow, enter an abbreviated name or the actual name of the data flow. If a label has been created for the data flow, it is presented as an ID. Press Enter to accept or overtype to change.

It is a good practice to form naming standards for IDs. Excelerator allows selection of diagrams and other entities using the wildcard concept. The first few letters are entered followed by an asterisk representing the remaining characters of the name, eg. CUST*. This is used to select all entities starting with the characters for producing reports, deleting entities and so on.

A description screen is displayed. Figure 3.5 is an example of a process description. If a label has been previously created for the object, it will appear on the description screen in the **Label** area. Otherwise enter the text that you would like to appear as the label on the drawing. Pressing the enter or arrow keys will take you to the next line in the label area. Each unique type of object will have a different procedure for completing description screens.

For external entities, press F3 at this time to save the entry in the XLDictionary and return to the drawing screen. Optionally, you may wish to enter a description of the entity, such as which person, what organization, etc.

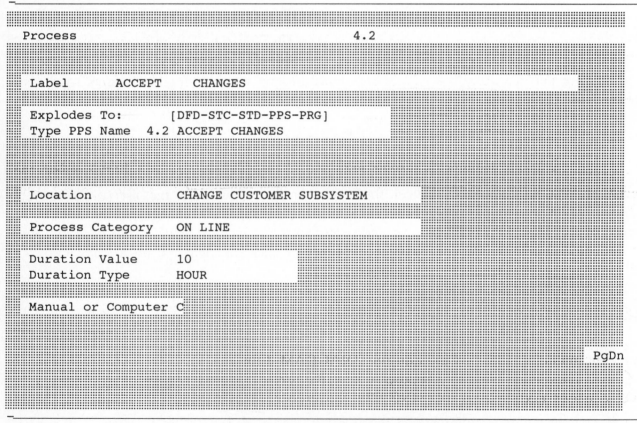

Figure 3.5 Process Description Example - Screen 1

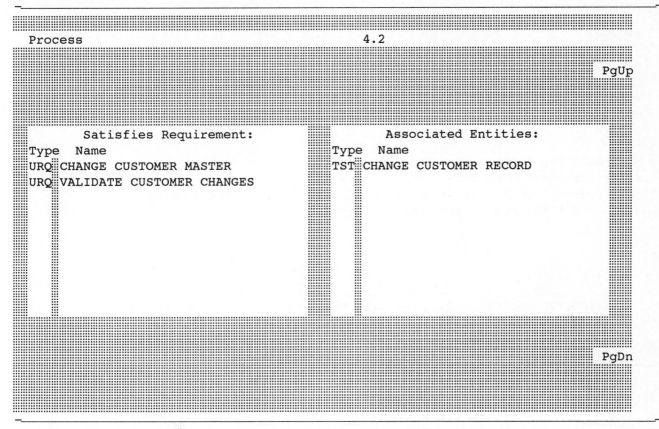

```
                                                              PgUp




          Satisfies Requirement:              Associated Entities:
Type   Name                            Type   Name
URQ CHANGE CUSTOMER MASTER             TST CHANGE CUSTOMER RECORD
URQ VALIDATE CUSTOMER CHANGES






                                                              PgDn
```

Figure 3.5   Process Description Example - Screen 2

For Processes which explode to further data flow diagrams (or structure charts), move the mouse so the cursor is in the first character of the area called **Type** found in the **Explodes To:** region and press the left button.   Enter one of the following:

DFD for data flow diagram.
STC for structure chart.
STD for structure diagram.
PPS for primitive process specifications (or minispecs).
PRG for presentation graph.

Enter the name of the child diagram (eg. **DIAGRAM 2** for Process 2 on a chart).   For data flow or a data store, move the mouse so that the arrow is pointing to the first character of **Record** under **EXPLODES TO ONE OF:** and press the left button.   Then enter the name of the record, usually the same name used in the label.   This will explode to a data dictionary entry and a complete description of the data may be entered at that time.   The record may be created at this time by pressing F4, the Browse key.   Details of this process will be covered in Chapter 4.   Presentation graphs are a good way of representing manual processes.

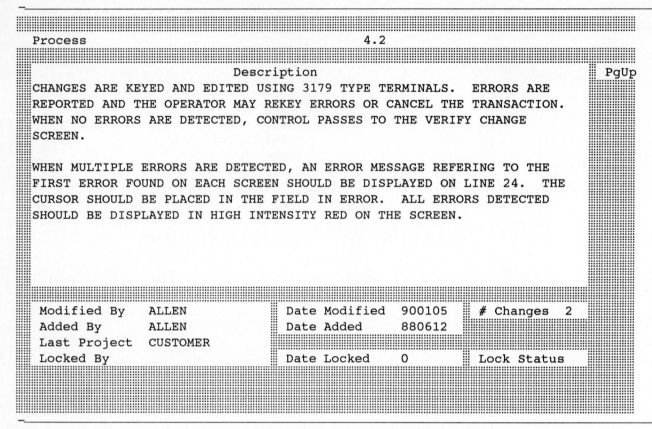

```
Process                                       4.2

                     Description                                  PgUp
CHANGES ARE KEYED AND EDITED USING 3179 TYPE TERMINALS.  ERRORS ARE
REPORTED AND THE OPERATOR MAY REKEY ERRORS OR CANCEL THE TRANSACTION.
WHEN NO ERRORS ARE DETECTED, CONTROL PASSES TO THE VERIFY CHANGE
SCREEN.

WHEN MULTIPLE ERRORS ARE DETECTED, AN ERROR MESSAGE REFERING TO THE
FIRST ERROR FOUND ON EACH SCREEN SHOULD BE DISPLAYED ON LINE 24.  THE
CURSOR SHOULD BE PLACED IN THE FIELD IN ERROR.  ALL ERRORS DETECTED
SHOULD BE DISPLAYED IN HIGH INTENSITY RED ON THE SCREEN.




Modified By      ALLEN        Date Modified  900105     # Changes  2
Added By         ALLEN        Date Added     880612
Last Project     CUSTOMER
Locked By                     Date Locked    0          Lock Status
```

Figure 3.5   Process Description Example - Screen 3

The **Location** refers to the system, subsystem, or program which contains this process. **Process category** is usually batch or on-line. The **Duration Value** and **Duration Type** refer to how often this process would execute per unit time. For example, 12 customers keyed per hour.

If the system problems have been defined as slow response time or inadequate throughput, fill in the duration value and type for all processes on the data flow diagram. After the entries have been completed, use the Report Writer feature to list all duration values and types, sorted by type. This will provide concise information on which processes are slowest, causing the entire operation to experience problems. The Report Writer feature is presented in Chapter 13.

Most of the graphic description screens have areas for entering user and engineering requirements and project documentation. Press PgDn to display a screen for linking the process, data store, etc. to requirements and associated entities.

To enter a requirement, select the area called **Type** under requirements and enter URQ for user or ERQ for engineering requirement. Then enter the name of the requirement or, if the requirement or associated entity has already been created, press F4 (Browse) to display a selector list or these entities. Select the name from the list. The description screen will be redisplayed with the name included. If desired, press F4 again to view the requirement, then press F3 to save and return to the previous description screen. Refer to the the second screen example in Figure 3.5.

Associated entities are a series of project documentation entities that may be linked to the description screen. Select the area titled **Entity type** and enter the 3 letter code for the entity followed by it's name. Entities codes are Category (CAT), Change Request (CHG), Entity List (ELS), Issue (ISS), Note (NTE), Reference Document (REF), and Test (TST). A detailed explanation of the associated entities is provided in Chapter 15.

If an associated entity has already been created, press F4 (Browse) to display a selector list of names. Choose a name from the list and the description screen will be redisplayed with the name included. Press F4 again to view the associated entity, then press F3 to save and return to the previous description screen.

Press PgDn again for a longer description screen for the selected entity. For a data store, enter filename information, physical file size, type of file (VSAM, sequential, database, etc.), and perhaps a comprehensive definition of the file. For a process, a brief description of the logic may be entered. The description area for a data flow might include how the data flow exists physically, such as a screen or report, a source document (form) related to the data flow, and any other relevant information. Refer to the third screen shown in Figure 3.5

Press F3 to save the description and return to the drawing screen. Repeat the process for all objects and data flow.

ADDING CONTROL INFORMATION

Control information such as signals and messages from direct file processing or database operations, control operations, and control stores may be added to the data flow diagram. This produces a complete view of the data, the processes that transform the data, and the underlying control that trigger the processes to be executed. Figure 3.6 shows a data flow diagram with control information added.

A control transform may be added. This is the control equivalent of a process. Use this symbol to show which processes are executed and the flow of signals and prompts between the control transform and the processes. Prompts control the execution of other processes, similar to a DO statement or a PERFORM in the COBOL language. Signals report on what

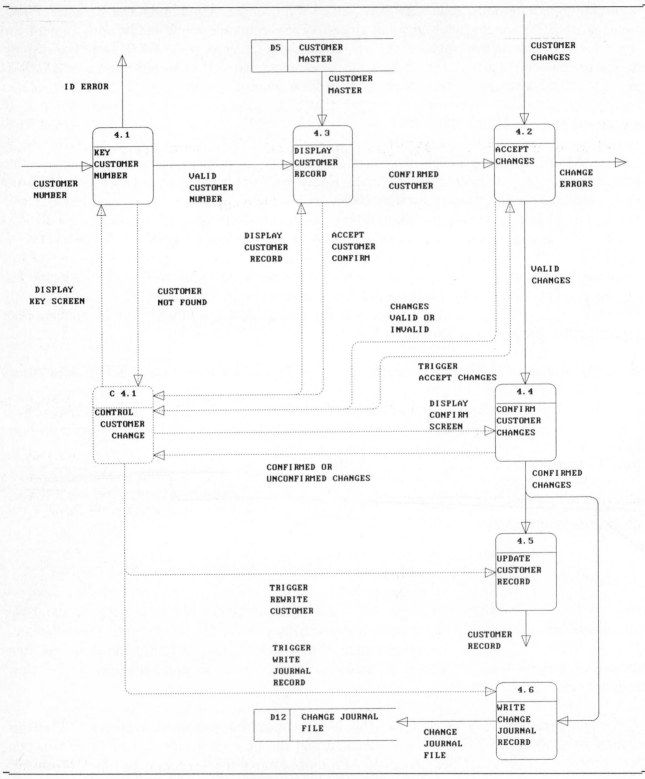

Figure 3.6 Example Data Flow Diagram With Control Added

conditions are found within processes, and would correspond to switches and flags in a computer program.

Select **OBJECT** and then **CTL TRN**. Choose the area on the screen where the control transform is to be located. This should ideally be a location that is central to the processes that are controlled by the transform.

You may use the LABEL or DESCRIBE options to label the control transform. To describe the control transform, select DESCRIBE and the transform. A default name is provided for you, similar to describing a process. Press the enter key to accept the name, overtype it, or delete the name and press Enter for a selector list. The control transform description screen is displayed, illustrated in Figure 3.7.

Enter the label if not previously created. The control transform may explode to either a State Transition Diagram (TRD) or a Structured Decision Table (SDT). Enter either TRD or SDT in the **Type** entry followed by the appropriate name. If the Control Transform explodes to a Structured Decision Table, you may create it at this time. Key in a name for

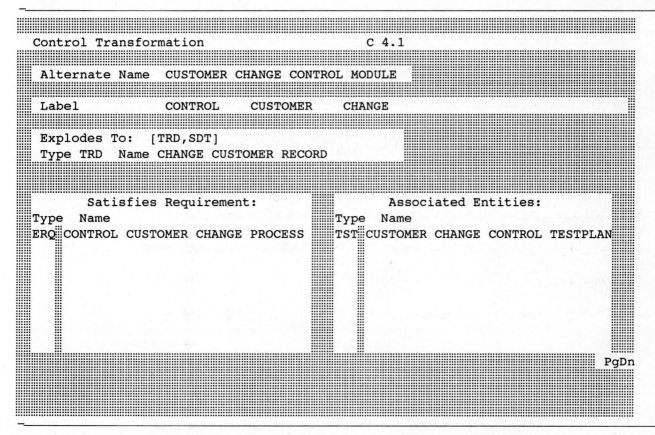

Figure 3.7 First Control Transform Description Screen

the decision table and press F4 with the cursor in the name area. The decision table description screen is displayed and may be filled in with values. Details will be presented in Chapter 4.

Enter any requirements that the control transform satisfies and related associated entities. Press PgDn to complete a longer description of the control logic. The second screen of Figure 3.7 illustrates control logic for Changing Customer Records interactively. Press F3 to save and return to the drawing screen.

If the explosion path is to a state transition diagram, you may select **EXPLODE** and create the diagram at this time. State transition diagrams will be explained in detail in Chapter 10.

Select **CTL STOR** to place a control store on the drawing. This would be a temporary holding area for control information until a process is ready to receive it. Enter an ID for the control store (generally it's name) and press the enter key. Complete the label and any explosion path. A control store may explode to a Signal or a Control Table.

```
 Control Transformation                      C 4.1

                        Description                          PgUp
 THIS CONTROL TRANSFORM TESTS WHETHER A VALID CUSTOMER ID WAS ENTERED.
 IF THE ID IS VALID, THE NAME AND ADDRESS IS DISPLAYED ON A CONFIRM
 SCREEN.  ACCEPT THE CUSTOMER CONFIRM.  IF CONFIRM IS Y CONTROL
 TRANSFERS TO THE ACCEPT CHANGES PROCESS.  OTHERWISE THE CUSTOMER ID
 ENTRY SCREEN IS REDISPLAYED.  THE ACCEPT CHANGES PROCESS WILL BE
 PERFORMED UNTIL ALL ENTRY FIELDS ARE VALID OR THE USER PRESSES THE
 CLEAR KEY TO CANCEL THE CHANGE TRANSACTION.  IF THE CHANGE IS
 CANCELLED, CONTROL RETURNS TO THE CUSTOMER ID ENTRY SCREEN.  IF ALL THE
 FIELDS ARE VALID, CONTROL TRANSFERS TO THE VISUAL CONFIRM SCREEN.  ALL
 ATTRIBUTE BYTES ARE SET TO PROTECTED.  IF THE ENTER KEY IS PRESSED,
 CONTROL PASSES TO THE REWRITE CUSTOMER MODULE.  THE RECORD IS TO BE
 LOCKED WHILE REWRITING.  IF PF1 IS PRESSED, ENTRY FIELDS ARE MADE
 UNPROTECTED AND CONTROL RETURNS TO THE ACCEPT CHANGES SCREEN.


 Modified By    ALLEN        Date Modified  900105     # Changes   4
 Added By       ALLEN        Date Added     891025
 Last Project   CUSTOMER
 Locked By                   Date Locked    0          Lock Status
```

Figure 3.7 Second Control Transform Description Screen

To connect the control transform or control store with other objects, select **CONNECT**, then **CTL FLOW** for Control Flow. Select the first object and then an intermediate location or the second object, as described under connecting objects. Control flow shows as a dashed line. To describe control flow, select DESCRIBE (or LABEL for text only). Select the control flow and enter an ID. The control flow description screen is displayed. Enter the label text and any explosion path. Control flow may explode to a Signal, Prompt, or a Control Table, described in Chapter 4. Press F3 to save and return to the drawing screen.

The **VIEW** option allows you to display either the full data flow diagram by selecting BOTH, which is the default. You may optionally show only the control elements or data elements. This is a useful feature for reviewing your data flow diagram, but before making any changes, deletions, or additions, it is best to view to the full diagram.

If you want to put text (the assignment number, your name, etc.) on the drawing, use the text feature described in Chapter 5. Excelerator will analyze your data flow diagram for syntax errors, presented in Chapter 4.

When finished, zoom to CLOSE UP to review how the graph will print and make any changes that are necessary. Check your print setup and print when ready. Save your work, backup and exit (see Chapter 2).

EXERCISES

1. Use Excelerator to produce the Student Registration System data flow diagram shown below.

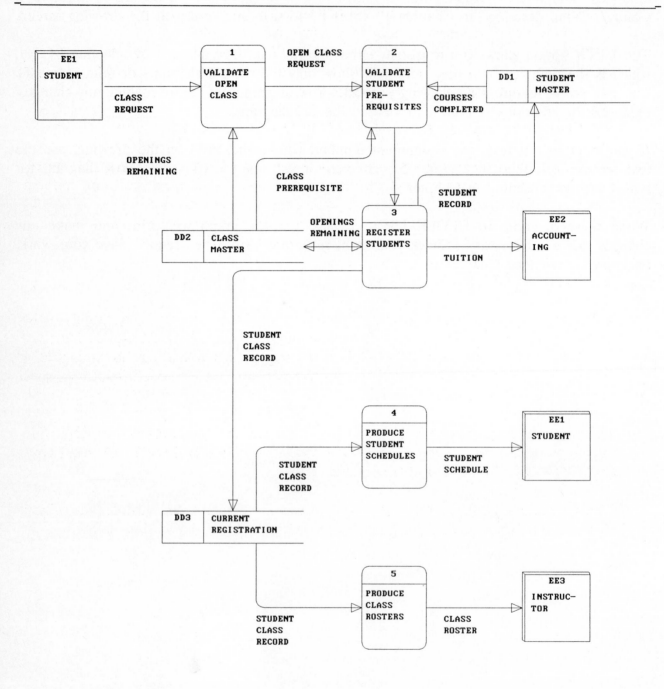

2. Produce a data flow diagram for the following description of an Order Processing System.

A customer order is received from the customer (external entity) and input into process 1, Validate Order. This process uses the Customer Master data store for validating the customer's credit rating. The Item data store is also input to determine if the items requested are available. Items not in stock are used to create a backorder data store. Unavailable credit is reported back to the customer.

Valid orders go to process 2, Produce Picking Slips. Picking slips are output which go to the Packaging and Shipping department.

Valid orders are also input to process 3, Create Order Summary.

The Order Summary record becomes input to process 4, Produce Customer Statement. Payment Summary records (from the Payment Summary data store) are also input to process 4. The Customer Statement is mailed to the customer.

3. Create a data flow diagram for the Employee Payroll System.

The employee fills out time slips that are input to a validation process.

Valid time slips are then input to the produce paycheck process. Also input to this process is the Payroll Deduction Table data store. The Employee Master file (data store) is updated with new year-to-date totals for gross pay and various withholding figures. Paychecks are produced by this process and distributed to employees. A payroll summary record is produced for each employee.

The payroll summary records are input into a process that produces two reports. The Payroll Report is sent to the various company Departments, and the Employee Payroll Listing is sent to the Payroll Department.

The payroll summary records are also input to a process to produce the Check Reconciliation records that are placed in the Check Reconciliation data store.

4. Exercise 4 is adapted from the case "There's No Business Like Flow Business" from the text <u>Systems Analysis And Design</u> by Kendall & Kendall, pp. 263-264, Prentice Hall.

The phone at Merman's rings, and Annie Oaklea, head of costume inventory, picks it up and answers a query by saying, "Let me take a look at my inventory cards. Sorry, it looks as if there are only two male bear suits in inventory - with extra growly expressions at that. We've had a great run on bears. When do you need them? Perhaps one will be returned. No, can't do it, sorry. Would you like these two sent, regardless? The name of your establishment? Theatre in the Square? Right. Delightful company! I see by your account card that you've rented from us before. And how long will you be needing the costumes?" Below is a data flow diagram that sets the stage for processing of costume rentals at Merman's. It shows rentals like the one Annie is doing for Theatre in the Square. After conversing for another few moments about shop policy on alterations, Annie concludes her conversation by saying, "You are very lucky to get the bears on such short notice. I've got another company reserving them for the first week in July. I'll put you down for the bear suits and they'll be taken to you directly by our courier. As always, prompt return will save enormous trouble for us all.

Modify the data flow diagram given below to include the rental <u>return</u> portion.

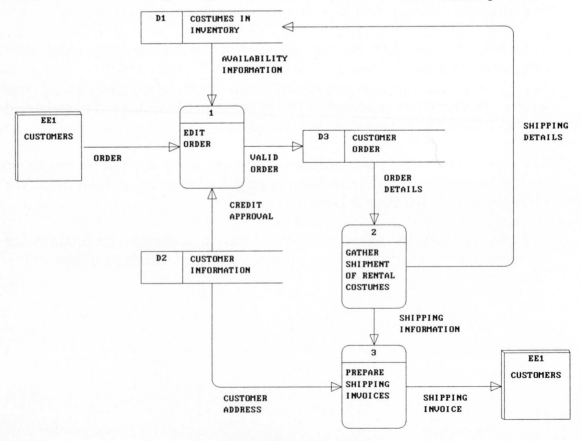

5. Create the data flow diagram shown in Figure 3.6 for the customer changes.

6. Add control information for the data flow diagram drawn in Exercise 1.

    The Validate Open Class process is triggered. If the class is open (a signal), the Validate Student Prerequisites process is triggered, otherwise control the Validate Open Class process is triggered. The Validate Student Prerequisites sends a signal (Prerequisites met) to the control transform. If the prerequisites have been met, the Register Students process is triggered. Otherwise the Validate Open Class process is triggered.

7. Add control information for the data flow diagram drawn in Exercise 3. The validate time slips process is triggered. If a time slip is valid, a signal reflecting that information is sent to the control process. If the time slip is valid, the produce payroll process is triggered, otherwise the validate employee time slip process is triggered.

8. Brainstorm and create user requirements that you think will be satisfied by one of the data flow diagrams that you have created. Add the TST associated entity for creating a test plan for the same data flow diagram.

4

EXPLODING THE DATA FLOW DIAGRAM INTO DETAILED COMPONENTS

Chapter goals:

>Understand how to link data flow diagram components to detailed drawings and descriptions.
>
>Learn how to create child data flow diagrams for   processes.
>
>Know how to describe process specifications (minispecs) for data flow diagram processes.
>
>Understand how to create a decision table for a control transform.
>
>Know how to describe the details of a control flow and control store.
>
>Know how to use the Analysis feature to validate data flow diagram syntax and level balancing.
>
>Understand how to produce summary reports for data flow diagrams.

All the components of a data flow diagram may be exploded to create detailed descriptions and (for processes and control transforms) child diagrams. This provides a method of ensuring that all the details of a system are accounted for giving a sense of closure. The analysis and reporting options of Excelerator can provide you with a list of explosion details that have not been described. Figure 4.1 is a graphical representation of the data and process components that may be exploded from a data flow diagram. In addition, control components: control transforms, control flow and control stores may explode to description screens and graphs.

If a data flow diagram object or connection has an entry in the **Explodes To:** area on any description screen (See Chapter 3, Describing objects), a detailed diagram or description may be created, linked to the parent data flow diagram. If the object or connection does not have an explosion path (shown by a change of color on the drawing screen), you may select DESCRIBE and the object or connection on the graph. When the description screen is displayed, add the explosion path. Figure 4.2 is an example of creating an explosion path from the process description screen.

DATA FLOW DIAGRAM

CONTAINS   CONTAINS

PROCESS   DATA STORE OR
                                         DATA FLOW

RETURN   DESCRIBE   F3   F3   E   F3   DESCRIBE   F3   E
                                  X   X
                                  P   P
                                  L   L
                                  O   O
                                  D   D
                                  E   E

PROCESS   DATA STORE OR
DESCRIPTION   FLOW DESCRIPTION

F4   F3   F4   D   F3   F4   F3   F3
                                 A
                                 T
PRIMITIVE PROCESS   A   RECORD
DESCRIPTION   F   DESCRIPTION
                                 L
                                 O
                                 W   F4   F3   F4   F3
DATA FLOW DIAGRAM   O
                                 N
                                 L   RECORD -
                                 Y   STRUCTURAL
PRESENTATION
GRAPH   F4   F3

STRUCTURE CHART   ELEMENT
OR DIAGRAM   DESCRIPTION

                                         ENTITY RELATION-
                                         SHIP DIAGRAM

                       RETURN
                                         DATA MODEL
                                         DIAGRAM

Figure 4.1 Explosion Paths for Data Flow Diagram Data Components

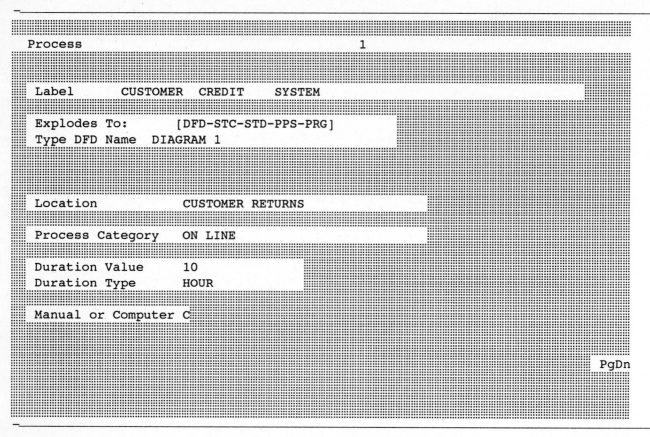

Figure 4.2 Process Description Screen

This chapter will provide the details for describing processes and descriptions of objects and connections on the data flow diagram. The exception is data flow explosions to records and elements, which will be covered in Chapter 8, Data Dictionary.

CREATING CHILD DATA FLOW DIAGRAMS

There are two approaches for creating data flow diagrams. One is to explode or decompose a higher level data flow diagram, creating detailed child diagrams (the top-down approach). The other is to create child diagrams based on events that occur in the business area. Then group these child diagrams together to create higher level data flow diagrams (the bottom-up approach). Excelerator supports both techniques but has a carry down feature that makes it easier to use the top-down explosion approach.

To create a child data flow diagram for a process, the **Type** area on the description screen should contain the code **DFD** and the name of the child diagram (eg. Diagram 1.1). Once the explosion path has been keyed in, press F3 to save and return to the drawing screen.

Select EXPLODE and then the parent process.

A fresh screen, with several default processes on it, is displayed with the name of the explosion graph. Even though this is a new graph, you do not need to set the profile. The profile is copied from the parent diagram. You may wish to alter the print setup and select print with the FULL GRAPH option to put page boundaries on the drawing screen. Then create the drawing as described in Chapter 3.

There are several additional techniques for drawing the child diagram.

INTERFACING

A child diagram process may contain connections that are not linked to an external entity, data store, or another process. These are input or output that match the parent process and are called *interface* data flow. Refer to examples in Figure 4.5. One of the rules for creating a child data flow diagram is that data flow in and out of a parent process must flow in and out of the child diagram.

Excelerator will automatically carry interface connections from the parent process to the child diagram. There will be one identical flow on the child for each on the parent. Since the size of the child diagram is unknown in carrying these connections down, processes are automatically placed on the extreme left and right sides of the drawing. Excelerator also has the output flowing backward, toward the center of the diagram. Thus some modification of the child diagram is in order.

Using print page boundaries as a reference, select the **MOVE** option to relocate the output flow processes from the far right of the full drawing screen. This is important for a smaller child diagram that does not use the full drawing area. Be sure to move these processes so that there is room for the output interface flows to print within page boundaries. Refer to Figure 4.3.

Next move the interface locations. Select the small square where the output interface ends. Then select a location near the process and going in the appropriate direction, usually to the right or down. You may want to move the input process or interface connection, since Excelerator provides a rather long interface. Finally, move the connection port, where the connection touches the object, to the desired location for a professional looking graph.

Additional interface connections may be created. Often the parent level will have a higher level flow, for example, a report, screen, record or source document (form). On the child diagram, the interface needed may be only a portion of the parent flow. For example, the child diagram may contain an element or smaller data structure found within the parent

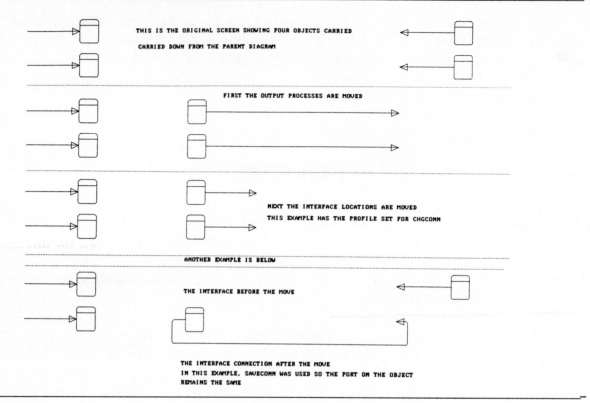

THIS IS THE ORIGINAL SCREEN SHOWING FOUR OBJECTS CARRIED
CARRIED DOWN FROM THE PARENT DIAGRAM

FIRST THE OUTPUT PROCESSES ARE MOVED

NEXT THE INTERFACE LOCATIONS ARE MOVED
THIS EXAMPLE HAS THE PROFILE SET FOR CHGCONN

ANOTHER EXAMPLE IS BELOW

THE INTERFACE BEFORE THE MOVE

THE INTERFACE CONNECTION AFTER THE MOVE
IN THIS EXAMPLE, SAVECONN WAS USED SO THE PORT ON THE OBJECT
REMAINS THE SAME

Figure 4.3   Moving The Interface Processes

diagram record. A single report line may be produced by the child diagram, where the parent contains several different report line formats. Thus several interface flows may be present on the child diagram for one flow on the parent process.

To create a new interface flow, select INTERFACE. Then select INPUT, OUTPUT or UPDATE (a double headed arrow) from the submenu that appears. Select the area on the screen where the line should terminate. Next select the object to connect with. Finally, select the side of the object (the port) where the connection should be made.

To change a connection description, select DESCRIBE and then the interface flow (not the ending square). Key in a new ID or delete the existing one and press the enter key for a selector list. The selector list is especially handy if you are changing from a record on the parent to an element (field) on the child diagram and the elements have already been added to the XLDictionary. Proceed with describing as presented in Chapter 3.

To change a label, select LABEL, then the interface flow. Touch opposite corners of where the label should be placed and key in the new label.

Proceed to describe or label the interface processes, then create the rest of the child diagram as explained in Chapter 3.

DESCRIBING OBJECTS PREVIOUSLY DESCRIBED

If an object has already been described, usually a data store or an external entity, select DESCRIBE and the object. Delete the ID and press Enter.

Excelerator presents a list of objects (Figure 4.4). Select an object from the list. If there is more than one screenful of choices, press PgDn or select the + sign on the bottom of the selector list. Pressing PgUp or selecting a minus sign from the top of the selector list will display the previous page. Alternatively (since the + sign is already in reverse video) you may press the enter key to view the next screenful. If the object is not on any list, Cancel or press Esc, then key in the new entry.

```
Process

  Entity name                        Label


. . . . . . . . . . . .    -    . . . . . . . . . .
 3.1.................................KEY NEW      CUSTOMER
 3.2 . . . . . . . . . . . . . . . .EDIT         CUSTOMER     DETAILS
 3.3.................................CREATE       CUSTOMER     RECORD
 4 . . . . . . . . . . . . . . . . .CHANGE       CUSTOMER     RECORD
 4.1.................................KEY          CUSTOMER     NUMBER
 4.2 . . . . . . . . . . . . . . . .ACCEPT       CHANGES
 4.3.................................DISPLAY      CUSTOMER     RECORD
 4.4 . . . . . . . . . . . . . . . .CONFIRM      CUSTOMER     CHANGES
 4.5.................................UPDATE       CUSTOMER     RECORD
 5 . . . . . . . . . . . . . . . . .PRODUCE      ANNUAL       SALES RPT
 5.1.................................PRINT        CUSTOMER     SALES
 5.2 . . . . . . . . . . . . . . . .PRINT        SALES        LINES
 6...................................POST         CUSTOMER     MASTER
 7 . . . . . . . . . . . . . . . . .CREATE       BILLING      STATEMENT
 8...................................PRODUCE      ACCOUNTS     RECEIVABLELEDGER
CONTEXT . . . . . . . . . . . . . . .CUSTOMER     SYSTEM
. . . . . . . . . . .    +    . . . . . . . . . . . . . . .
```

Figure 4.4   Object Selector List

The object description screen is displayed. Make any changes that may be necessary. Note that changes made at this time will be reflected on other diagrams using the same ID and description. Press F3 to save the description and return to the drawing screen.

CHANGING LEVELS

You may return to the previous parent level by selecting OTHER and RETURN from the submenu that appears on the bottom of the selection area. To return to the top level select OTHER, then RETRNTOP.

When finished, zoom to close up, review and modify where necessary, print, save, backup and exit (see chapter 2). Several example parent and child data flow diagrams are shown in Figure 4.5.

Excelerator provides analysis options for verifying that the parent and the child diagrams have matching input and output flows. Details are provided later in this chapter.

PROCESS SPECIFICATIONS (MINISPECS)

Processes which do not explode to further child diagrams are called *primitive processes*. The logic of these processes, called a minispec or process specification, may be described. The sum of the minispecs becomes the program specifications, used by the programmer to create program code.

To create a minispec, select DESCRIBE and the primitive process. In the description screen **Explodes To:** region enter **PPS** (for Primitive Process Specification) for the **Type** followed by a name for the minispec. A good standard is to use the process name as the minispec name, or a combination of process number and name. With the cursor on the **Name** line, press F4 (Browse) to display the Primitive Process Specification description screen. Refer to Figure 4.6.

An alternate approach may be used if the **Explodes To:** information has been previously entered. Select EXPLODE from the drawing screen, then choose the process.

The Primitive Process Description screen is displayed. Figure 4.7 is an example for Process 4.2, ACCEPT CHANGES. Enter the **Type** and names for input and output data. **Type** may be ELE for element or REC for record. Names may already exist in the XLDictionary or may be created.

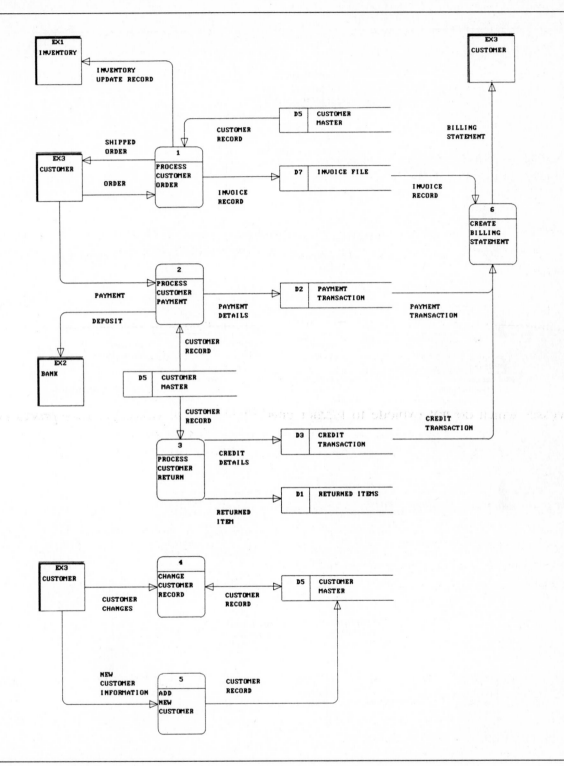

Figure 4.5 - Part 1   Diagram 0 For The Customer System

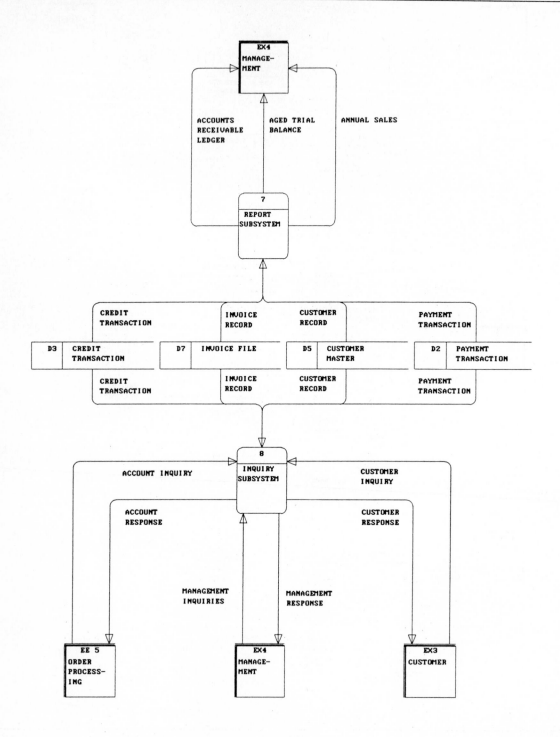

Figure 4.5 - Part 2 Diagram 0 For The Customer System

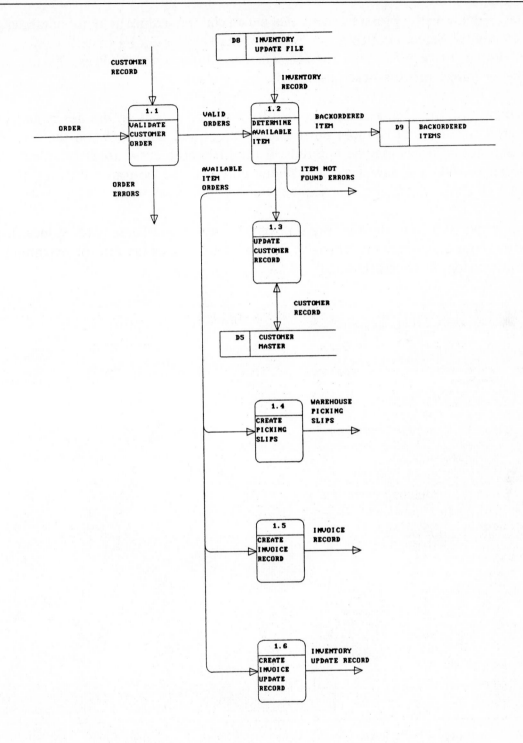

Figure 4.5 Part 3   Diagram 1 for the Customer System

If the names already exist, press F4 with the cursor in the name field to obtain a list of records or elements. Select one from the list. You may also press F4 once a name has been obtained to display the actual record or element description screen. Press F3 to save and return to the primitive process description screen.

Notice that there are three entry areas provided for input or output on the description screen. These are scroll regions, that is, more entries may be entered than show on the screen. Up to 10 input and output areas may be entered. If the first three entry areas are filled, the top entry will scroll providing a new **Type** and **Name** entry on the bottom. Pressing the up or down arrows will show previous or subsequent entries that have been keyed.

Constants may be supplied on the bottom of the screen. These are values used in calculations which do not frequently change. For example, a sales tax rate or maximum hours worked before paying an overtime rate.

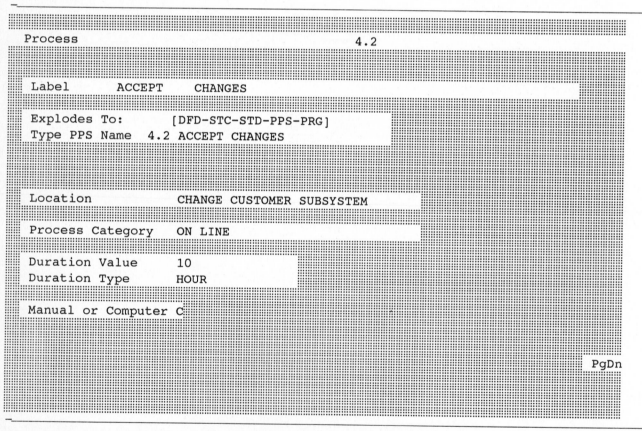

Figure 4.6 Process Description Area With Explosion Path

As explained above, press F4 to obtain a list of constant elements already existing in the system. You may press F4 after keying in a new constant name (with the cursor in the name field) to display a blank element screen. Since you are probably aware of values, etc. for the constant when describing the process specifications, this is a good time to complete the corresponding element entries. Press F3 to save.

Enter a description of the logic. This may be a formula, descriptive text or structured English (pseudocode). The description area is also a scroll region, allowing up to 25 lines of text. Press PgDn and complete any requirements or associated entities. When finished, press F3 to save and return to the previous description or drawing screen.

To print minispecs, select XLDictionary from the main menu, then PROCESS. Select Primitive Process Specification followed by Output. Press the enter key when prompted for a Name Range (or enter the name of the primitive process). Select a primitive process specification name from the list. Choose File, Screen, or Printer (refer to Chapter 12 for further details). Figure 4.8 shows an example of a primitive process print.

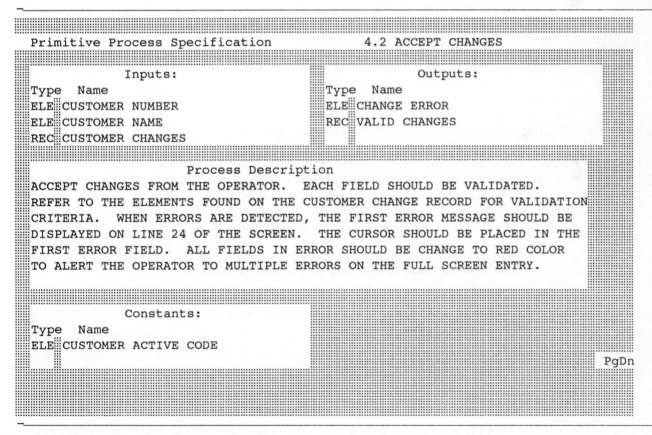

```
Primitive Process Specification              4.2 ACCEPT CHANGES

            Inputs:                              Outputs:
 Type   Name                          Type   Name
 ELE  CUSTOMER NUMBER                  ELE  CHANGE ERROR
 ELE  CUSTOMER NAME                    REC  VALID CHANGES
 REC  CUSTOMER CHANGES

                        Process Description
 ACCEPT CHANGES FROM THE OPERATOR.  EACH FIELD SHOULD BE VALIDATED.
 REFER TO THE ELEMENTS FOUND ON THE CUSTOMER CHANGE RECORD FOR VALIDATION
 CRITERIA.  WHEN ERRORS ARE DETECTED, THE FIRST ERROR MESSAGE SHOULD BE
 DISPLAYED ON LINE 24 OF THE SCREEN.  THE CURSOR SHOULD BE PLACED IN THE
 FIRST ERROR FIELD.  ALL FIELDS IN ERROR SHOULD BE CHANGE TO RED COLOR
 TO ALERT THE OPERATOR TO MULTIPLE ERRORS ON THE FULL SCREEN ENTRY.


            Constants:
 Type   Name
 ELE  CUSTOMER ACTIVE CODE
                                                                  PgDn
```

Figure 4.7 Primitive Process Description Screen

```
DATE: 9-NOV-89 PRIMITIVE PROCESS SPECIFICATION - OUTPUT
                        PAGE    1  TIME: 21:36    NAME: 4.2 ACCEPT CHANGES
Excelerator/IS
TYPE Primitive Process Specification
NAME 4.2 ACCEPT CHANGES


Inputs:                                   Outputs:
Type  Name                                Type  Name
ELE CUSTOMER NUMBER                       ELE CHANGE ERROR
ELE CUSTOMER NAME                         REC VALID CHANGES
REC CUSTOMER CHANGES


                        Process Description
ACCEPT CHANGES FROM THE OPERATOR.  EACH FIELD SHOULD BE VALIDATED.  REFER TO THE
ELEMENTS FOUND ON THE CUSTOMER CHANGE RECORD FOR VALIDATION CRITERIA.  WHEN ERRORS
ARE DETECTED, THE FIRST ERROR MESSAGE SHOULD BE DISPLAYED ON LINE 24 OF THE SCREEN.
THE CURSOR SHOULD BE PLACED IN THE FIRST ERROR FIELD.  ALL FIELDS IN ERROR SHOULD BE
CHANGE TO RED COLOR TO ALERT THE OPERATOR TO MULTIPLE ERRORS ON THE FULL SCREEN
ENTRY.


            Constants:
Type  Name
ELE CUSTOMER ACTIVE CODE


Satisfies Requirement:                    Associated Entities:
Type  Name                                Type  Name
ERQ PROVIDE ON-LINE CUSTOMER CHANGES TST CUSTOMER CHANGE


Modified By ALLEN   Date Modified   891031  # Changes  0
Added By    ALLEN   Date Added      891031  Last Project
DFD Locked By       Date Locked     0       Lock Status
```

Figure 4.8 Example Of A Primitive Process Print

DESCRIBING DATA STORES

Data stores may be described in detail. Select DESCRIBE, then the data store. On the description screen, enter the location of the data store. This may be a manual location or a specific computer system. An example would be an IBM PS2 Model 80 or IBM 3381. Enter the total and average number of records the data store will hold.

These entry areas may be used by the Report Writer feature as report data or for selectively printing data stores. For example, listing all the files to be stored on a specific microcomputer may help to plan local area networks. Refer to the example illustrated in Figure 4.9.

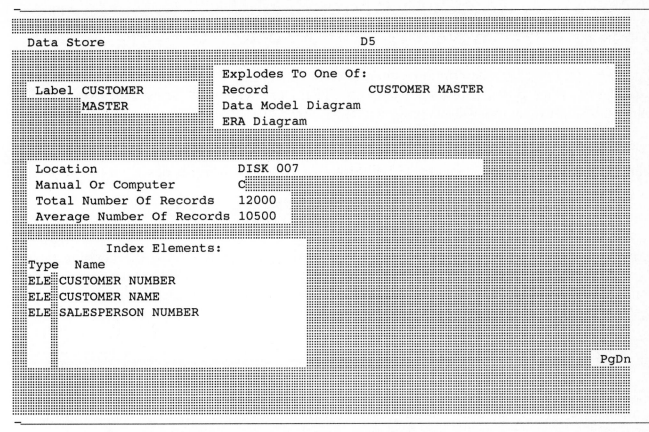

Figure 4.9   Data Store Description Screen

In the **Explodes To:** area, enter a record, data model diagram or ERA (entity-relationship) diagram name. When the EXPLODE option is used, the Data Model or ERA Diagram may be created. The Record description may be created by using EXPLODE and selecting the data store or by using the Browse (F4) key with the cursor at the record name entry.

Key fields may be entered in the Index Elements area. These are used for analysis and reporting. Enter ELE for the type and the name of the index or record key. If the index element has already been created, move the cursor into the name entry field. Press F4, the Browse key, to select from a list of names. Press F4 again if you wish to view the actual element description. Press F3 to save and return to the data store description screen.

Press PgDn to enter any requirements or associated entities. Press F3 to save and return to the drawing screen. Record descriptions will be covered in Chapter 8, Data Model and Entity-Relationship diagrams in Chapter 9.

DESCRIBING CONTROL TRANSFORMS

The Control Transform description screen is shown in Figure 4.10. Control transforms may explode to either State Transition Diagrams (TRD) or Structured Decision Tables (SDT). State transition diagrams will be presented in Chapter 10.

Complete any requirements or associated entities. Press PgDn to add a description of the control transform process. Figure 4.11 illustrates a control transform description.

CREATING DECISION TABLES

A decision table may be created to describe control logic. Before keying the decision table, it is a good idea to create it on paper and optimize the table. Thus only the essential conditions and actions will be entered. A good text to review for creating decision tables is Systems Analysis and Design by Kendall & Kendall, Prentice Hall.

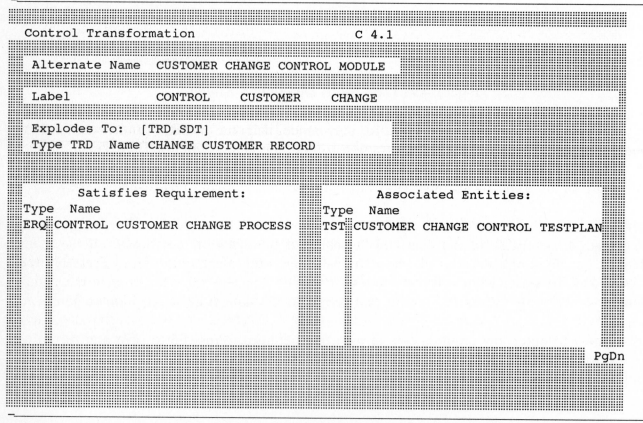

Figure 4.10 Control Transform Description Screen

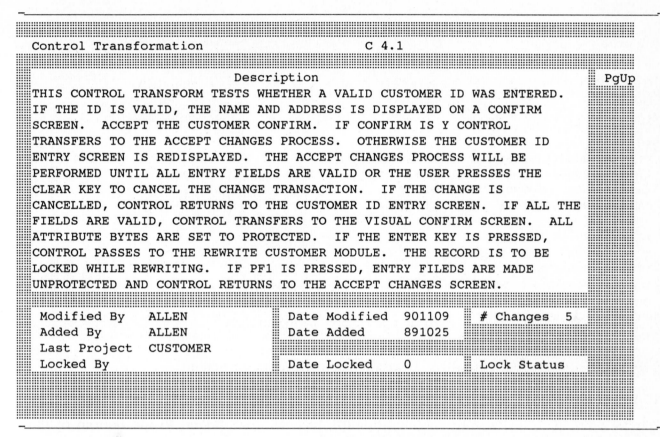

Description   PgUp

THIS CONTROL TRANSFORM TESTS WHETHER A VALID CUSTOMER ID WAS ENTERED.
IF THE ID IS VALID, THE NAME AND ADDRESS IS DISPLAYED ON A CONFIRM
SCREEN. ACCEPT THE CUSTOMER CONFIRM. IF CONFIRM IS Y CONTROL
TRANSFERS TO THE ACCEPT CHANGES PROCESS. OTHERWISE THE CUSTOMER ID
ENTRY SCREEN IS REDISPLAYED. THE ACCEPT CHANGES PROCESS WILL BE
PERFORMED UNTIL ALL ENTRY FIELDS ARE VALID OR THE USER PRESSES THE
CLEAR KEY TO CANCEL THE CHANGE TRANSACTION. IF THE CHANGE IS
CANCELLED, CONTROL RETURNS TO THE CUSTOMER ID ENTRY SCREEN. IF ALL THE
FIELDS ARE VALID, CONTROL TRANSFERS TO THE VISUAL CONFIRM SCREEN. ALL
ATTRIBUTE BYTES ARE SET TO PROTECTED. IF THE ENTER KEY IS PRESSED,
CONTROL PASSES TO THE REWRITE CUSTOMER MODULE. THE RECORD IS TO BE
LOCKED WHILE REWRITING. IF PF1 IS PRESSED, ENTRY FILEDS ARE MADE
UNPROTECTED AND CONTROL RETURNS TO THE ACCEPT CHANGES SCREEN.

Modified By ALLEN	Date Modified 901109	# Changes 5
Added By ALLEN	Date Added 891025	
Last Project CUSTOMER		
Locked By	Date Locked 0	Lock Status

Figure 4.11   Control Transform Description

Select DESCRIBE and the control transform. In the **Explodes To:** area enter SDT for the **Type** and enter the decision table name. With the cursor in the name area, press F4. The Decision Table description screen is displayed. Figure 4.12 is an example describing the logic used for a batch update program containing add, delete and change transactions.

Enter any initial condition that is known before the decision table logic is executed. Under the **Cond/Act** column enter **C** for condition or **A** for action. Key in the condition statement and press enter to place a one letter code for each condition value. Typically condition values are Y (yes), N (no), T (true), F (false), < > or =, or a single letter representing the value (eg. A for an add record, D for a delete record, and C for a change record). Each vertical column is called a <u>rule</u> and they are numbered 0 through 15. Press Enter to move to the next rule.

When all the conditions are entered, leave a blank row (space permitting) and enter an A followed by a description of the action. Place an X in each column where the conditions determine that this action should be executed.

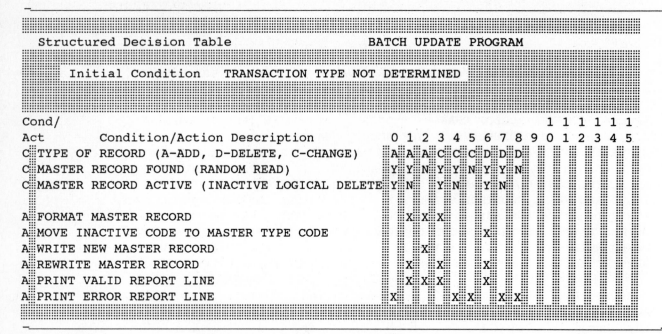

Figure 4.12 Decision Table Description Screen

The entry area allows 10 rows to be keyed, but this area is a scroll region. Up to 25 rows may be entered, with the rows scrolling upward and new rows added to the bottom of the region. To return to the top of the scroll region, press PgUp or the up arrow. To move to the bottom of the region, press the down arrow. Pressing F1 and the down arrow will move the cursor to the last field within the region shown. Use the mouse to select any entry row and column.

To insert a row, place the cursor on the line where the new row should be located. The row containing the cursor position will be moved lower. Press F1 and the insert keys simultaneously. F1 and the delete key will delete a row.

Press PgDn to enter any requirements and associated entities. Pressing PgDn again provides a description entry area. Use this to enter a legend for any codes used in the decision table and any other notes that may be meaningful. Press F3 to save the decision table and return.

A decision table may be created by using the XLDictionary option. A brief description of this process will be included here with further details provided in Chapters 8 and 12. Select **XLDICTIONARY** from the main menu. Then select CONTROL, Structured Decision Table, and Add. The decision table description screen is displayed and may be completed as described above. Press F3 to save.

You may use this method to create a decision table for a process, for example, calculating the amount of discount for a customer's order. Processes or Primitive Process Specifications may not explode directly to a decision table, but they may refer to a decision table created using the XLDictionary. Create a note (entity type NTE) in the Associated Entities area of the Process or Primitive Process Specification that makes a reference to the decision table. Alternatively refer to the decision table and it's name using the Process or Primitive Process Specification Associated Entities or Description areas.

To print the decision table, Select XLDICTIONARY, CONTROL, and Structured Decision Table as described above. Then select Output. Enter a name or press enter for a selector list and choose a decision table. Respond Y or N to the prompt for underlining fields. Select whether the output should go to the screen, printer or a file. IF file has been selected, key in a meaningful name and press enter. Select EXIT to return to the main menu.

DESCRIBING CONTROL FLOW

Control flow can be described in detail. It may be exploded into a signal, control table, or a prompt.

A signal is a simple message sent from one process or control transform to another. In a computer program, a signal would be a switch or flag. A control table is a group of signals similar to a record being a group of elements or fields. Usually it is used to simplify the data flow diagram. A prompt is used to start and stop a process or control transform. It is used to control which processes execute and the sequence of execution.

Select DESCRIBE and then the control flow. Enter an ID. If a label has been created, it will be presented as a default ID. Press enter to accept the default or overtype to change.

The Control Flow description screen is displayed, shown by the example in Figure 4.13. Enter an alternate name, if desired, and a label. Under **Explodes To:** enter either SIG for signal, PRM for prompt, or CTT for control table. Enter a name for the explosion. Complete any requirements or associated entities. With the cursor in the **Name** area, press F4 (browse) to explode the control flow.

If **SIG** for signal was entered as the type, the signal description screen is displayed, illustrated in Figure 4.14. Enter an alternate name and a definition. Signal values may be entered, such as specific return codes set by a process. Press F3 to save and return.

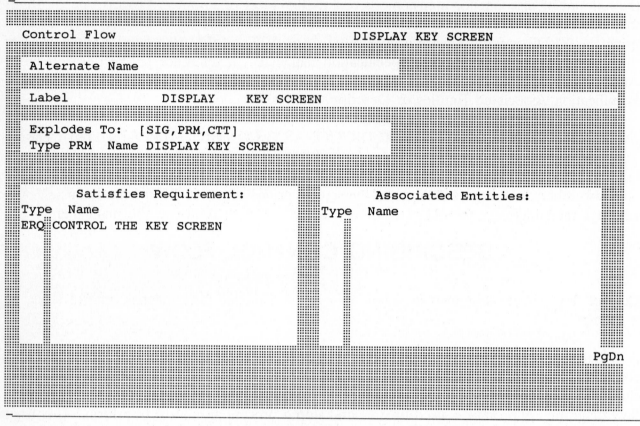

Figure 4.13 Control Flow Description

If **CTT** for control table was selected as the type, the control table description screen will be displayed when browsed (Press F4 is with the cursor in the name area). Refer to Figure 4.15 for an example of a control table. Enter an alternate name and definition. The **Contained Entity** area allows up to 100 entries (within a scroll region on the screen) for defining the signals or other control tables. These are the detailed expansions of the control table. They may be described by placing the cursor in the name area and pressing F4. Press F3 to save and return to the previous screen.

When **PRM** for prompt has been entered for the explosion **Type**, and the name field is browsed (press F4), the Prompt description screen is displayed, shown in Figure 4.16. The only area that is different from the previous two screens is the **Prompt Type** area. This contains a two letter code representing the type of prompt. These are listed on the next page.

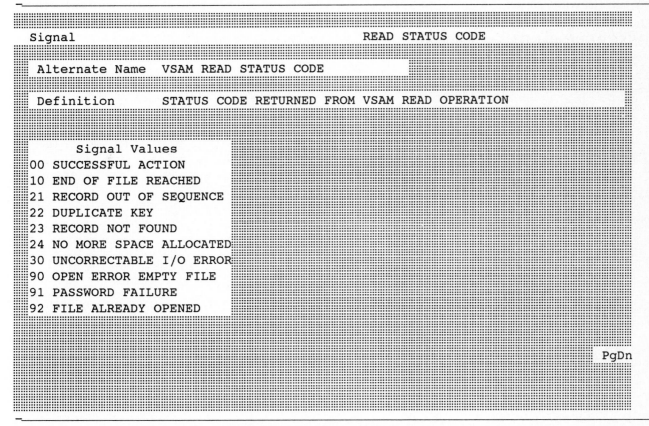

Figure 4.14 Signal Description

EN   Enable - to start a process or control transform.
DS   Disable - stop a process control transform.
ED   A combination of enable and disable.
TR   Trigger - for enabling and disabling a process that has a well-defined starting and
          ending point.
ST   Set - sets an initial value for a signal.
RS   Resets the signal to it's initial value.
CL   Clears the signal from all values.
SS   Suspend - pause a process or control transform.
RM   Resumes after suspension.
PS   A suspend and resume combination.

Press F3 to save and return to the Control Flow description screen. Press F3 again to return
to the drawing screen. Once explosion paths have been established on a description screen,
the EXPLODE command may be used to view signals and prompts, rather than using the
DESCRIBE and Browse method.

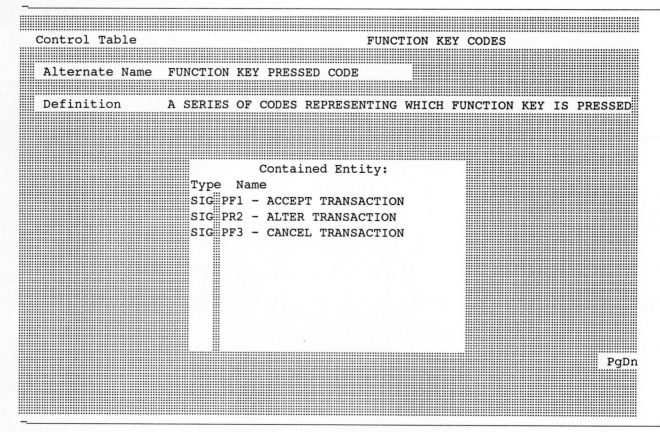

Control Table   FUNCTION KEY CODES

Alternate Name   FUNCTION KEY PRESSED CODE

Definition   A SERIES OF CODES REPRESENTING WHICH FUNCTION KEY IS PRESSED

                        Contained Entity:
                Type   Name
                SIG PF1 - ACCEPT TRANSACTION
                SIG PR2 - ALTER TRANSACTION
                SIG PF3 - CANCEL TRANSACTION

                                                              PgDn

Figure 4.15 Control Table Description

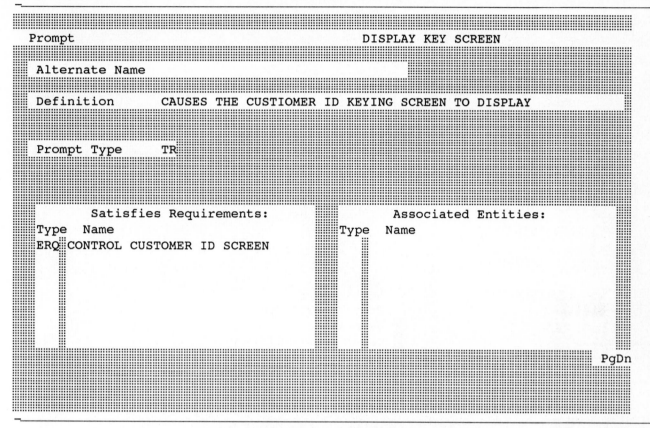

```
┌──────────────────────────────────────────────────────────────────────┐
│  Prompt                              DISPLAY KEY SCREEN                 │
│  ┌─────────────────────────────────────────────────────┐              │
│  │ Alternate Name                                        │              │
│  └─────────────────────────────────────────────────────┘              │
│  ┌─────────────────────────────────────────────────────────────────┐  │
│  │ Definition      CAUSES THE CUSTIOMER ID KEYING SCREEN TO DISPLAY  │  │
│  └─────────────────────────────────────────────────────────────────┘  │
│                                                                        │
│  Prompt Type       TR                                                  │
│                                                                        │
│  ┌──────────────────────────────────┐  ┌────────────────────────────┐ │
│  │     Satisfies Requirements:      │  │   Associated Entities:     │ │
│  │  Type  Name                      │  │ Type  Name                 │ │
│  │  ERQ CONTROL CUSTOMER ID SCREEN  │  │                            │ │
│  │                                  │  │                            │ │
│  │                                  │  │                            │ │
│  │                                  │  │                            │ │
│  │                                  │  │                            │ │
│  │                                  │  │                            │ │
│  └──────────────────────────────────┘  └────────────────────────────┘ │
│                                                                  PgDn  │
│                                                                        │
└──────────────────────────────────────────────────────────────────────┘
```

Figure 4.16 Prompt Description Screen

DATA FLOW DIAGRAM ANALYSIS

The analysis feature of Excelerator provides comprehensive analysis validation and reporting for graphs and entities. Data Flow Diagram analysis provides several important features for validating data flow diagram syntax, explosion diagrams, and descriptions of objects and connections. Select ANALYSIS from the main menu, then Graph Verification. Refer to the analysis menu shown in Figure 4.17.

DATA FLOW DIAGRAM SYNTAX VALIDATION

A menu for the Graph Verification options is displayed, shown in Figure 4.18. Select Data Flow Diagram. Each specified data flow diagram is analyzed. The report produced shows data flow diagram syntax errors such as objects with no connections or invalid connections, control flow problems, and many other errors, listed in Figure 4.19.

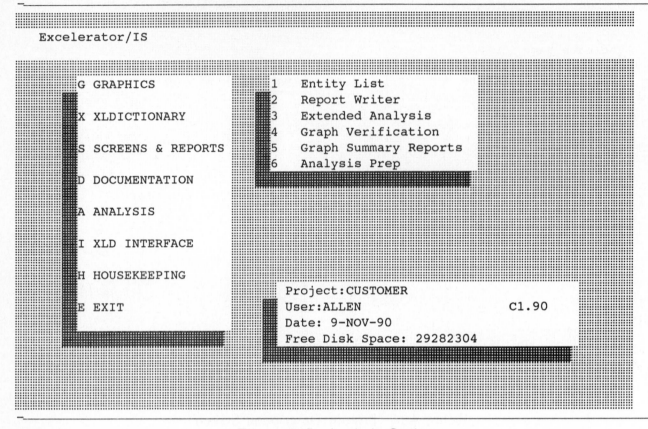

Figure 4.17 Analysis Options

Figure 4.20 shows a sample parent and child data flow diagram that contain many of these errors. The analysis report is shown in Figure 4.21.

When prompted for a Graph Name, press the enter key and choose a diagram from the selector list that is displayed. Select Screen, Printer, or the file name in reverse video.

If the file name is selected, overtype the default name. The data is stored in a print file with the DOS extension of PRN and can be printed later. Write down the name of the print file. After exiting Excelerator, change to the project subdirectory (via the DOS CD command, for example, CD EXCEL\CLASSPRJ). Type **PRINT filename.PRN** at the C:\> prompt (where filename is the name the print file was saved under). If you did not write down the filename, you can type **DIR *.PRN** at the DOS prompt to get a list of all print files. Within Excelerator, you may overtype the name with **A:filename.PRN** or **C:\filename.PRN** if you would like the file to go on drive A or the root directory of drive C.

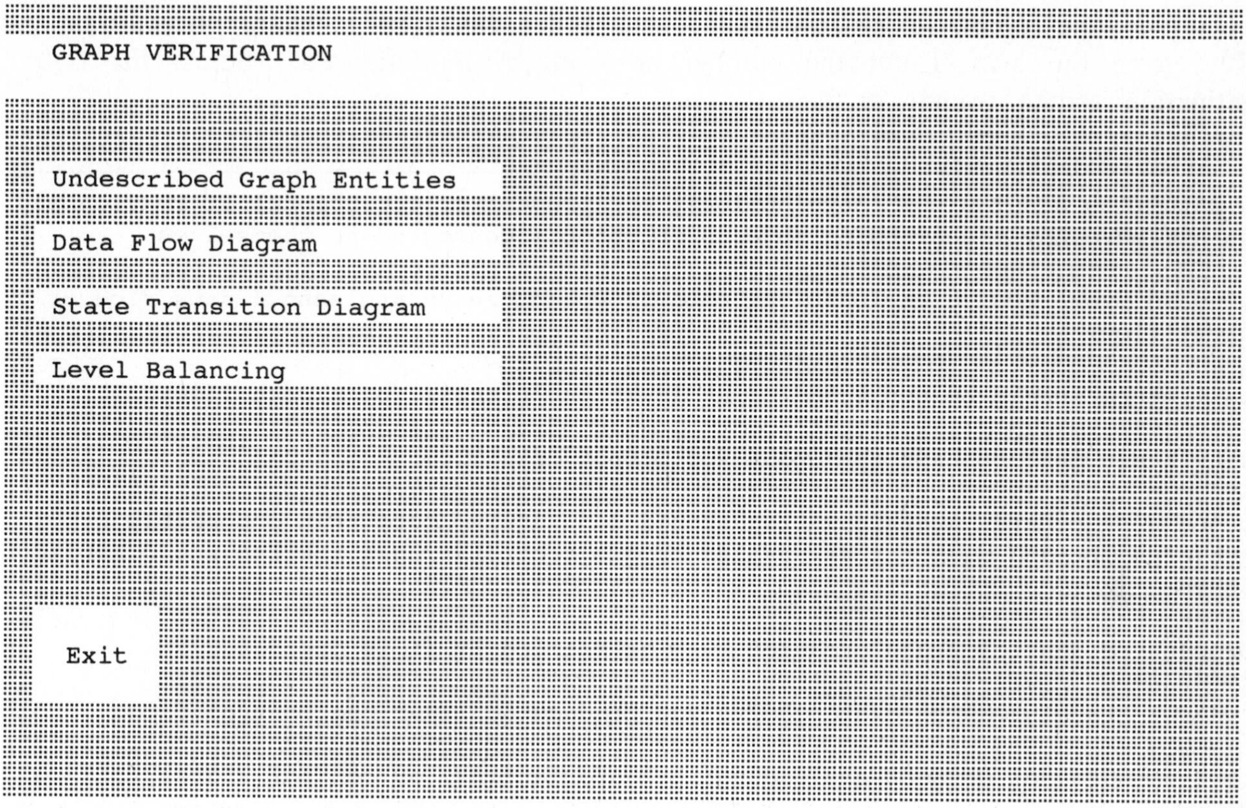

```
┌─────────────────────────────┐
│ Undescribed Graph Entities  │
├─────────────────────────────┤
│ Data Flow Diagram           │
├─────────────────────────────┤
│ State Transition Diagram    │
├─────────────────────────────┤
│ Level Balancing             │
└─────────────────────────────┘




┌──────────┐
│ Exit     │
└──────────┘
```

Figure 4.18 Graph Verification Options

It is suggested that you put the reports on the screen first, rather than printing what may not be needed. If you select screen, the report (depending on the type selected) may scroll. Press the pause key (or CTRL-Num Lock or CTRL-S if not using an IBM model PS2). Press any key to continue the scroll.

LEVEL BALANCING

The Level Balancing report shows which data flow and control flow on the child diagram do not match those on the parent diagram. If the data flow on the child process is an elementary field (element), which has been defined in a data structure (record) on the parent, the data flow will be in balance. In is necessary to describe the records and elements in the XLDictionary before producing this report. Details are provided in Chapter 8. Refer to Figure 4.22 for the report produced by the parent and child data flow diagrams shown in Figure 4.20.

To product the report, select Level Balancing. Enter the graph name or press Enter and select from the list. Enter the number of levels to be balanced. Select the output destination: screen, printer, or file.

The data flow diagram must have at least one process or control transformation and must not have any freestanding objects or objects connected to themselves.

A process must receive at least one data flow and create at least a data flow or control flow.

A data store should be connected to at least one process, by a data flow.

A data store must contain the input and output data flow.

A process or control transformation should not receive more than one enable or disable prompt and must not be enabled by one control transformation and disabled by another.

A process or control transformation must be enabled if it is disabled.

A control transformation must receive and produce at least one control flow.

Data flow must not connect any control transformations, or control stores.

A signal must not connect to a data store, or connect an external entity to another external entity.

When a signal flows out from a control store, it may only be to a control transformation.

A signal may not be an interface flow to a control store or data store.

A prompt may only flow from a control transformation.

A prompt may only connect to a process, control store, or control transformation.

A prompt may not disable a control store.

A prompt may not interface to a data store, control store, or external entity.

Figure 4.19 Data Flow Diagram Syntax Errors

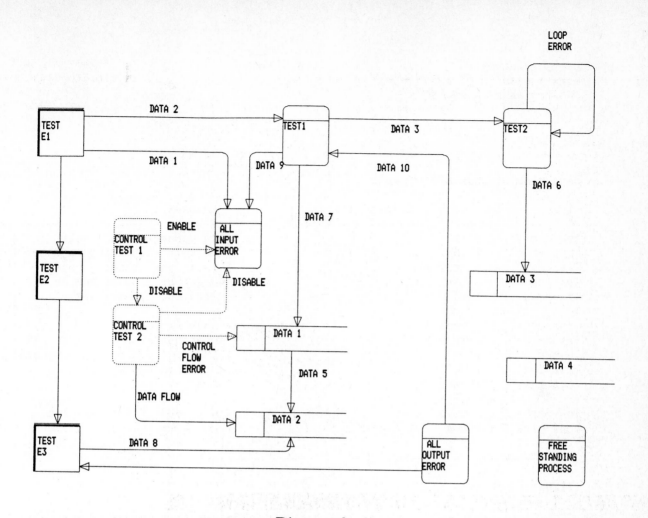

Diagram 0

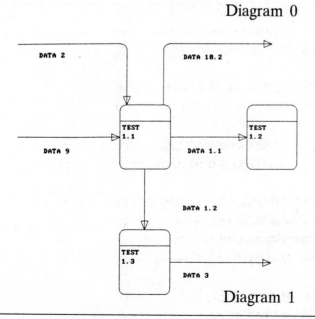

Diagram 1

Figure 4.20 Sample Data Flow Diagram With Errors

DATE: 15-MAR-91   DATA FLOW DIAGRAM   PAGE   1
TIME: 16:30   Excelerator/IS
PROJECT NAME: CUSTOMER

GRAPH NAME: TEST

Data Flow Diagram Exceptions:

```
TYPE        I/L   OBJECT ID OR LABEL              MESSAGE
-----------------------------------------------------------------------
|PROCESS  | I | T2                             | Is connected to itself     |
|DAT STOR | I | DD4                            | Is a free standing object  |
|PROCESS  | I | TEST 5                         | Is a free standing object  |
|PROCESS  | I | T3                             | Does not produce DAF or CTF |
|PROCESS  | I | T4                             | Does not receive DAF        |
|                                                                           |
|PROCESS  | I | TEST 5                         | Does not receive DAF        |
|PROCESS  | I | TEST 5                         | Does not produce DAF or CTF |
|PROCESS  | I | T3                             | EN & DS by different objects|
|CTL TRN  | L | CONTROL TEST 2                 | Disabled but not Enabled    |
|CTL TRN  | I | TEST.1                         | Does not receive a CTF      |
|                                                                           |
|DAT STOR | I | DD 2                           | Not connected to any PRC    |
|DAT STOR | I | DD4                            | Not connected to any PRC    |
|                                                                           |
    -------------------------------------------------------------------
```

Illegal Connections:

```
CONN        ----------------------------ENDPOINTS-----------------------------
TYPE     OBJ TYPE I/L OBJECT ID OR LABEL
-----------------------------------------------------------------------
|                                                                           |
|DATA     |X-ENTITY| I |TEST E1                                             |
|         |X-ENTITY| I |TEST E2                                             |
|                                                                           |
|DATA     |X-ENTITY| I |TEST E2                                             |
|         |X-ENTITY| I |TEST E3                                             |
|                                                                           |
|DATA     |DAT STOR| I |DD1                                                 |
|         |DAT STOR| I |DD 2                                                |
|                                                                           |
|DATA     |CTL TRN | L |CONTROL TEST 2                                      |
|         |DAT STOR| I |DD 2                                                |
|                                                                           |
|CONTROL  |CTL TRN | L |CONTROL TEST 2                                      |
|         |DAT STOR| I |DD1                                                 |
|                                                                           |
    -------------------------------------------------------------------
```

Figure 4.21 Sample Verification Report

```
LEVEL NUMBER: 1
PARENT GRAPH NAME:  TEST
```

Graph Object Summary

OBJECT TYPE	I/L	ID OR LABEL	NOT DESCRIBED	CHILD TYPE N/A	CHILD NOT FOUND	IN BALANCE
PROCESS	I	T1				X
PROCESS	I	T3		X		
PROCESS	I	T4		X		
PROCESS	I	T2			X	
PROCESS	I	TEST 5		X		
CON TRAN	I	TEST.1		X		
CON TRAN	L	CONTROL TEST	X			

```
LEVEL NUMBER: 2
PARENT GRAPH NAME:  TEST 1.1
```

Graph Object Summary

OBJECT TYPE	I/L	ID OR LABEL	NOT DESCRIBED	CHILD TYPE N/A	CHILD NOT FOUND	IN BALANCE
PROCESS	I	TEST 1.2		X		
PROCESS	I	TEST 1.1		X		
PROCESS	I	TEST 1.3		X		

Figure 4.22   Sample Level Balancing Report

The two major types of errors that can occur are shown on the report shown in Figure 4.22.

Process errors, which include inputs or outputs not matched between the parent and child levels. The I/L column indicates whether the ID or label is used as a name in the third column. IDs are used unless the object has not been described in the XLDictionary.

Control transformation errors, which include:

Signal inputs on the parent that do not match conditions on the child State Transition Diagram.

Control outputs on the parent control transform that do not match actions on the child State Transition Diagram.

UNDESCRIBED GRAPH ENTITIES REPORT

The **Undescribed Graph Entities** report shows entities: data stores, processes, control transformations, data flow, control flow, and so on, which are found on a diagram but are not described in the XLDictionary. This report should be produced after the analyst has finished describing all objects and connections to list omissions. It may also be used to determine which portions of the system need describing as work on the project continues.

Select **Undescribed Graph Entities** and Data Flow Diagram. Press the enter key when prompted for a name and select one from the list. Select a destination for the report: a file, the screen or printer. An example is shown in Figure 4.23.

DATA FLOW DIAGRAM SUMMARY REPORTS

Another analysis option is Graph Summary Reports. This provides a Data Flow Diagram analysis report and a graph explosion report which shows all explosion entities for a given graph. These reports should be produced after the diagrams are complete, the analysis reports have been run to detect errors and the corrections have been made.

Select **Graph Summary Reports** from the ANALYSIS menu, then **Analysis Report.** Enter the name of the graph to be analyzed and the maximum number of lines to be printed per page. Since each line contains 132 characters, select Wide from the HOUSEKEEPING PROFILE options. Select a destination for the report: file, screen or printer.

The report lists the input and the output data flows for each Process and Data Store on the graph, including the ID, the label, and the records and elements that they explode to. Processes and data stores are shown with the entities they explode to.

The report is an excellent tool for analyzing the data flow diagram to ensure that the output of a process may be obtained from the input and that the data being extracted from a data store is available within the data store.

```
 ┌                                                                              ┐
 │ DATE: 25-JAN-90    UNDESCRIBED GRAPH OBJECTS AND CONNECTIONS    PAGE  1
 │ TIME: 10:58                                              Excelerator/IS
 │ PROJECT NAME: DFD
 │
 │ GRAPH TYPE:  Data Flow Diagram
 │ GRAPH NAME:  TEST
 │
 │ The following objects are not described:
 │
 │  OBJ TYPE    LABEL
 │  ----------------------------------------------------------------------
 │ |CTL TRN  |  CONTROL TEST 2                                             |
 │ |                                                                      |
 │  ----------------------------------------------------------------------
 │
 │ The following connections are labeled but not described:
 │
 │  CONN TYPE   LABEL
 │  ----------------------------------------------------------------------
 │ |CTL FLOW |  CONTROL FLOW ERROR                                         |
 │ |DAT FLOW |  DATA FLOW ERROR                                            |
 │ |                                                                      |
 │  ----------------------------------------------------------------------
 │
 │ The following connections are not labeled or described:
 │
 │  CONN          -------------------- ENDPOINTS ----------------------------
 │  TYPE       OBJ TYPE I/L  OBJECT ID OR LABEL
 │  ----------------------------------------------------------------------
 │ |                                                                      |
 │ |DAT FLOW|  X-ENTITY|  I  |TEST E1                                      |
 │ |        |  X-ENTITY|  I  |TEST E2                                      |
 │ |                                                                      |
 │ |DAT FLOW|  X-ENTITY|  I  |TEST E2                                      |
 │ |        |  X-ENTITY|  I  |TEST E3                                      |
 │ |                                                                      |
 │  ----------------------------------------------------------------------
 └                                                                              ┘
```

Figure 4.23 Undescribed Graph Entities Report Example

A second report is the Graph Explosion report. This report shows all the explosion entities
for a particular graph. It lists the entity type, the name and label, and a section number that
the entity explodes to. The referenced section is included later in the report. This is a
comprehensive, lengthy report, 132 characters wide. Select **Graph Explosion,** then Data Flow
Diagram. Press the enter key when prompted for a name and select one from the list.
Again select a destination for the report: a file, the screen or printer. Key in the Explosion
depth, the number of levels (parent, child, etc.) to report on.

EXERCISES

1.   Use Excelerator to produce a child diagram for Process 1, Validate Order, presented in Exercise 2 of Chapter 3. The diagram is shown below.

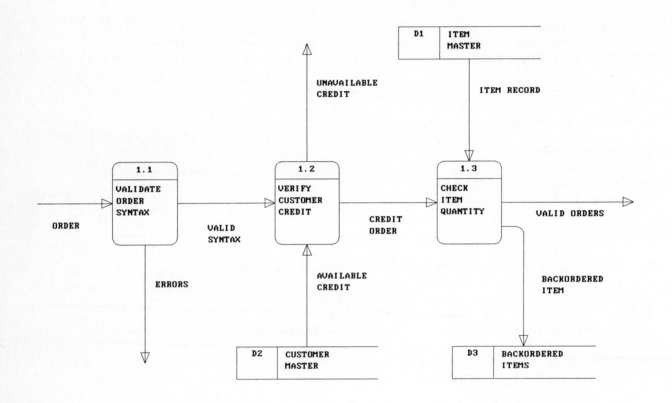

DIAGRAM 1

2. Produce a child diagram for Process 2, Produce Paycheck, found in Chapter 3, Exercise 3.

The Valid Time Slip is input to process 2.1, Calculate Gross Pay.

The Employee Master and the Payroll Deduction Tables are input to process 2.2, Calculate Federal, State and FICA deductions.

The Deductions and the Gross Pay are input into process 2.3, Compute Net Pay.

The Gross Pay, Deductions, Net Pay and Employee Master are input to process 2.4, Update YTD Totals. The Employee Master year to date totals are updated and the Employee Record is rewritten.

The Gross Pay, Deductions, Net Pay and Employee Master are input to process 2.5, Print Employee Paycheck.

The Gross Pay, Deductions, Net Pay and Employee Master are input to process 2.6, Produce Payroll Summary. The output is the Payroll Summary record.

3. Create Diagram 2.2, the child of process 2.2 in Exercise 2. The input to processes 2.2.1, 2.2.2 and 2.2.3 are the Number Of Deductions from the Employee Master file, and the Federal, State, and FICA rates from the Payroll Deduction Tables. Output is the Federal Deduction, State Deduction, and FICA Deduction.

Process 2.2.1 is Calculate Federal Deduction
Process 2.2.2 is Calculate State Deduction
Process 2.2.3 is Calculate FICA Deduction

4. Create a minispec entry for Process 1.3 of Exercise 1, Check Item Quantity.

Subtract the Order Quantity from the Quantity On Hand on the Item Master giving the Quantity Remaining. If the Quantity Remaining is less than zero, move the Quantity Remaining to the Backorder Quantity. Move the Quantity On Hand to Quantity Shipped. Otherwise move the Order Quantity to the Quantity Shipped.

5.   Create a minispec entry for Process 2.1 (in Exercise   2 above), Calculate Gross Pay.

If Hours is greater than 60
        Gross Pay is Rate X 40 + Rate X 20 X 1.5 + Rate X (Hours - 60) X 2.

Otherwise if Hours is greater than 40
        Gross Pay is Rate X 40 + Rate X (Hours - 40) X 1.5

Otherwise Gross Pay is Rate X Hours.

6.   Write a minispec for Process 1.2, Verify Customer Credit found in Exercise 1.

Add the Order Total to the Current Balance on the Customer Master record.

If the New Balance is less than the Credit Limit on the Customer Master, then the order is valid.

If the New Balance is less than $100 over the Credit Limit and the Net Purchases YTD is over $2000, the order is a valid credit order.

All other conditions result in a rejected credit order.

7.   Describe the signals created in Chapter 3 for one of the data flow diagrams which includes control.

8.   Describe the prompts for a data flow diagram with control that you have created in Chapter 3.

9.   Create descriptions for the data stores on the data flow diagrams that you have created. Brainstorm with team members (if you are on a team). Include the keys that you feel should be included as indexes for the file.

10.   Describe the control transforms on one of the data flow diagrams that you have created. Include the simple logic of the control in the description screen.

11.   Create the decision table shown in Figure 4.12.

12.   Create a decision table for the following control logic of a batch Item Maintenance (add, delete, and change) program. The Maintenance Transaction record is read. There are three maintenance types: Add, Delete, and Change. These would modify the Item master file. Read the Item master file. If the record is found, check the master file record code to determine if the record is active, that is, one currently selling, or inactive, one that is on the file for statistical and historical reports. A valid Add transaction record is when the master record is not found or if the master record is found and the record code indicates an inactive record. An inactive record may be re-activated. A valid delete or change record is one in which the master record is found and the record code is active. All other cases are errors.

If the transaction record is an add and the master record is not found, format and write the new record. For an add with an inactive master record, change the record code to active and rewrite the record. If the transaction record is a valid delete, change the record code to inactive and rewrite the record. For a valid change transaction, format the changes and rewrite the record.

13.   Choose a data flow diagram that you have created and run the Data Flow Diagram option of Graph Verification analysis. Review the report and check your diagram for syntax errors.

14.   Execute the Level Balancing option to verify the parent and child diagrams for one of the sets of data flow diagrams that you have created.

15.   Run the Undescribed Graph Entities report for any of the data flow diagrams that you have created.

16.   Produce the Analysis Report for a data flow diagram that you have created. Review the report. What information is being shown?

17.   Execute the Graph Explosion report for one of the sets of data flow diagrams that you have created. What information is this report providing?

5
GENERAL DRAWING TECHNIQUES

Chapter Goals:

Learn how to move objects, connections, text and other drawing components.
Know how to copy objects.
Know how to delete objects and other graph components.
Understand the screen refresh option.
Learn how to center the drawing.
Know how to add a line or a block of text to the drawing.
Learn how to add lines and boxes to the drawing.
Understand how to disconnect an object from it's XLDictionary ID.
Know how to create and delete a drawing title.

MOVING OBJECTS

To change the location of objects on the drawing screen, select MOVE. You may move as many objects as necessary without reselecting MOVE. Select the object. Move the arrow to the location that the object is to be moved to and click the left button. Connections will move with the object.

MOVING CONNECTION

If the connections cross or you don't like where they connect to the object (called the entry/exit port) you can change the connection. Select MOVE and then move the mouse so that the cursor arrow touches the handle, the little square that overlaps the line. Refer to the example in Figure 5.1.

Select the handle and two new handles appear at either end of the connection. Click the left button on the handle at the connection end to be moved. Now touch the object where you want the end of the connection moved to. This may be the same object or a different one.

A small arrow appears on the outside of the object. Use the mouse to move this arrow around until the desired location is indicated. The location where the line will connect to the object, or *port* is indicated by a number on the status line on the bottom of the screen. Press the left button. If both ends are to be moved, move first one end, then the other.

You may also move the label for a <u>connection</u>. Select any location within the label text and then the location where the upper left corner of the label should be placed. This is a fine technique for polishing finished graphs. Zoom to CLOSE UP and align connection labels for a pleasing effect.

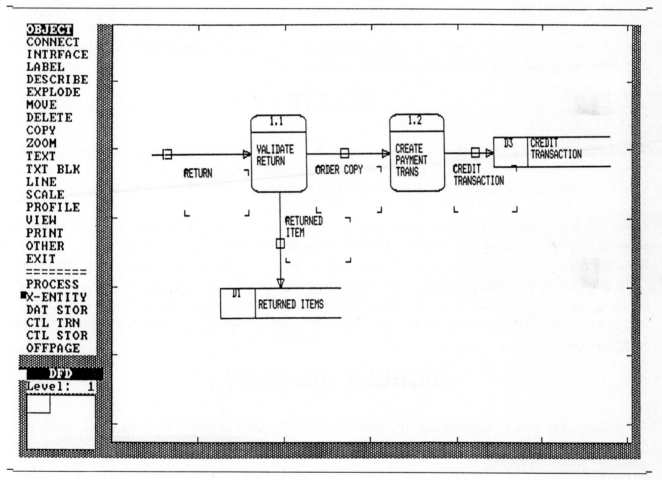

Figure 5.1 Move Screen

MOVE TEXT OR LINE

To move text, select an area within the text you wish to move. Then select an area on the drawing screen where you want the upper left corner of the text block or the left side of a line of text to appear. For a line, select the handle on the line.

COPY

Objects may be copied from one location to another. Select COPY and the object to be copied. Choose the location for the object to be placed and press the left button. Copy is best used <u>after</u> the object has been described, or at least the label placed in the object. If the size of the object has been changed with the SCALE option, use copy only after the size has been changed. This insures uniformly sized objects.

DELETE

To remove objects, text, lines or connections, select DELETE. Choose the object or the connection handle to be deleted. If the connections and objects are close to each other, zoom to CLOSE UP first, avoiding the accidental deletion of a wrong object.

Once the left button has been pressed the object will be deleted. You will be asked whether to delete connections to the object. Answer appropriately for each situation. You will also be prompted whether or not you wish to delete descriptions of the object from the data dictionary. It is best NOT to delete the data dictionary entries for the objects, since they may be used elsewhere or may be used later in the design. To verify where objects or connections are used, run Where Used from the XLDictionary feature. Details are provided in Chapter 12.

SCREEN REFRESH

As objects are moved or deleted, the screen may become cluttered with small dots, pieces of drawings or missing line segments. To clean up the screen and restore lines on the drawing, select OTHER.

Select REFRESH from the menu on the bottom of the selection area. As long as this menu remains on the bottom, REFRESH may be selected, even if OTHER is not in reverse video. It is a good practice to put the OTHER submenu on the bottom before doing extensive moving and deleting.

CENTERING

The screen may be centered in the full drawing area by selecting OTHER and then CENTER. This can be useful for moving a whole drawing to a different section of the full drawing area. Place an object in the corner of the drawing area opposite of the way you want the whole drawing moved. Select Center. Then use the Move option to move the object back to the corner and repeat. When the drawing is positioned where you want it, delete the extra object used for shifting.

LINES OF TEXT

To place a single line of text on the screen (a diagram name, comments, etc.) select TEXT. Select the SIZE: small, medium, or large. The actual size of the text also depends on the print font size setting. See Chapter 2 for details. Select the area on the screen where you want the text to appear. Key in the text and press enter.

To put a block of text on the screen (eg. your name, date, assignment number), select TXT BLK. Move the mouse to select the upper left corner of the text area, then repeat for the lower right corner. Key in the text. The tab key will advance to the next line. Use up and down arrows to move around the block. Home and End keys give the first and last characters of each line. The maximum size is 30 lines of 60 characters each.

The size of the block and text may be changed. To view the full text, zoom to CLOSE UP first. Select TXT BLK and then an existing block on the screen. To change the size, select corners outside (or inside for reduction) the existing block. Rekey any existing text as needed. Text may be moved, copied, or deleted in the same manner as objects.

LINES

Lines on the screen are created by selecting LINE. The final line can consist of many shorter segments and may be drawn horizontal, vertical, or at a 45 degree angle. Examples include underlining a diagram name or drawing a box around text.

Select solid or dashed, then the area on the screen. Select one end of the line and then the other end. Continue selecting endpoints if a box or other angle is to be drawn. To finish drawing the line, select another menu option. Lines can be moved, copied, or deleted in the same manner as objects or text.

CLEARING THE GRAPH ID

The ID of an object or connection provides the link to the XLDictionary. Selecting OTHER and then CLEAR ID will sever this connection. The XLDictionary entry will remain and the object or connection will retain it's label. A new ID may be created or a different ID from the data dictionary may be selected. Select DESCRIBE and key the ID or press enter for a selector list.

TITLE

A title block may be placed on the screen. Select OTHER, then TITLE. The title may be moved or deleted.

EXERCISES

1.   How do the move and the copy commands differ?

2.   Describe the technique of moving an entire graph to a new location on the drawing screen.

3.   When a connection line is to be moved, the line is selected and small squares are placed on each end of the line to determine which end is to be moved. When an end is selected and a connection object is chosen, an arrow appears that moves around the object. What is the small arrow used for? What do the numbers (Bottom -1, 4, etc.) mean?

4.   What does screen refresh accomplish?

5.   How do you indicate to Excelerator that you have finished drawing lines?

6.   How are lines or blocks of text moved?

6
STRUCTURE CHARTS

Chapter goals:

Understand how to create a structure chart and structure diagrams.
Know how to describe functions.
Understand how to link a function to a module description.
Know how to associate a function to user, engineering or other management documentation.
Understand how to add iteration, data coupling and control coupling to the structure chart.

CREATING STRUCTURE CHARTS

To create structure charts select GRAPHICS and then STRUCTURE CHART. Select Add (or Modify to change a previously drawn chart). Select PROFILE and set options as described in Chapter 1, including PIPE and SYSTPORT.

There is one additional PROFILE option, MOVEHRHY, which works with the move command. When moving a function within the drawing area (Chapter 5), all the subordinate functions, those directly below the higher level one, are moved with the function. This is the recommended selection. MOVEONE only moves the selected function. This is useful to align higher level functions without moving related subordinate ones.

Select OBJECT, then FUNCTION from the lower submenu. Move the mouse so that the arrow on the screen moves to the place you want the rectangle to appear. Press the left button. Repeat for all the functions. For an external subroutine (a CALLED subroutine), select DEF FUNC (predefined function). Refer to Figure 6.1 for an example of a structure chart.

You may wish to use the ZOOM feature to view the screen close up. Select ZOOM, then CLOSE UP. Select either an area on the orientation map or the screen to view. There is a tendency for beginning users of Excelerator to place objects too far apart creating a large print with long connecting lines.

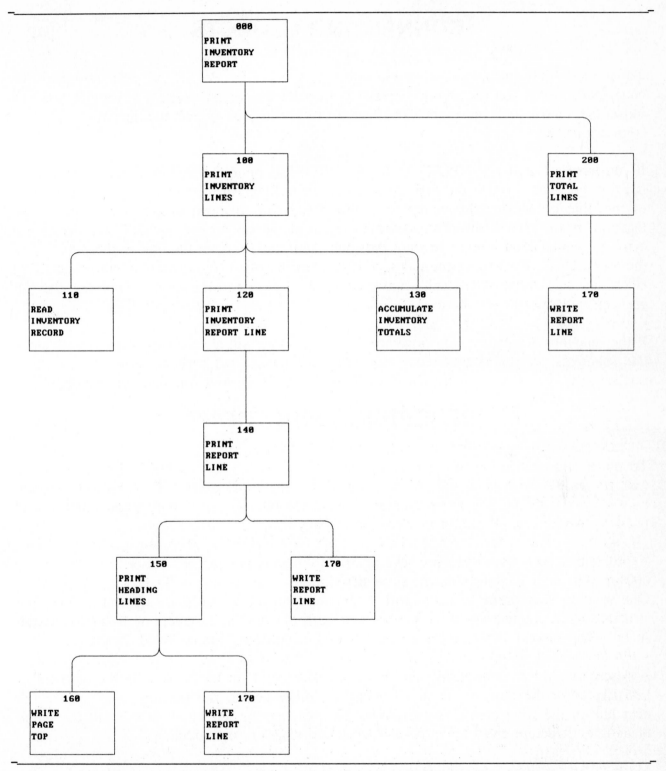

Figure 6.1 Structure Chart Example

CONNECTING OBJECTS

To connect the functions with lines, select CONNECT. Select the first object to be connected, then select the second object. If the final line is not where you want it, you can move the entire line, move individual ends of the line, or delete the line and redo the connection (see Chapter 5).

If you have selected USERPORT under the PROFILE option, a slightly different procedure is to be followed. Touch the first object to be connected. An arrow will appear on the side of the object. Moving the mouse will cause the arrow to move around the object. The location on the object will appear on the bottom of the screen (eg. RIGHT -2). Move the arrow to the location where you want the connection line to touch the object, the port. Click the left button. Then move the mouse so the arrow moves to the object to be connected to. Click the left button. The small arrow reappears. Move it to the desired spot (eg. top left corner) and click the left button.

If the functions are placed close together, the connections will have square corners with small line segments protruding upward. To produce nicely rounded corners, move the functions further apart vertically. Figure 6.6 is an example of square and rounded connections.

DESCRIBING FUNCTIONS

To put a text description in the function, select DESCRIBE. Then select the function you wish to describe, that is, move the arrow to the rectangle and press the left button. On the bottom of the screen you are prompted to ENTER ID. Key in the function number and press the enter key. Function numbers are usually 000, 100, etc.

A problem occurs when there are several structure charts per project. Each one cannot use 000 or 100 for a module number, since descriptions with the same ID replace each other. One solution is to prefix functions with a number referring to the structure chart. The first structure chart created would be number one, with function ID numbers of 1-000, 1-100 and so on. The second structure chart would have function numbers of 2-000, 2-100, etc.

A description screen is displayed, illustrated by the example in Figure 6.2. In the area called LABEL, enter the function name. Pressing the enter key or the tab key takes you to the next line in the label area. The **Explodes To** area may be left blank or contain the name of another structure chart (subprogram), structure diagram, or module.

Most of the graphic description screens have areas for entering user and engineering requirements as well as project documentation. To enter a requirement, select the area called

Type under requirements and enter URQ for user or ERQ for engineering requirements. Then enter the name of the requirement, which may be created at this time or later.

If the requirement or associated entity has already been created, press F4 (Browse) to display a selector list or these entities. Select the name from the list. The description screen will redisplay with the name included. Press F4 again to view the requirement or associated entity. Press F3 to save and return.

If the requirement or associated entity has not been created, enter the name for the entity and press F4 (Browse) to display the requirement or associated entity description screen. The description screen for the entity may be completed. Press F3 to save and return to the previous description screen.

Associated entities are a series of project documentation entities that may be linked to the description screen. To link this documentation to the description screen, select the area titled **Entity type** and enter the 3 letter code for the entity and it's name. These entities and their codes are Category (CAT), Change Request (CHG), Entity List (ELS), Issue (ISS), Note

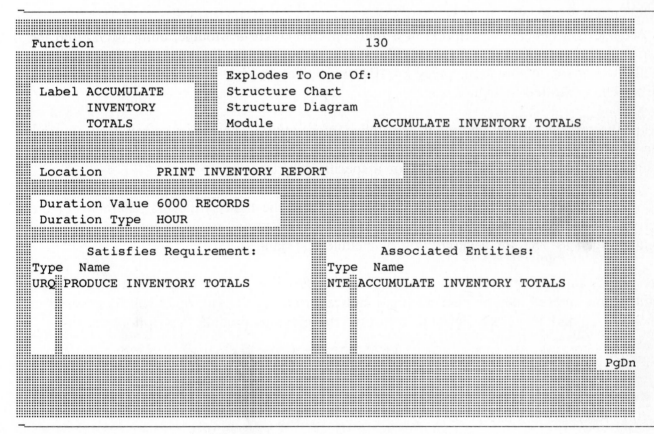

Figure 6.2 Function Description Screen

(NTE), Reference Document (REF), and Test (TST). A detailed explanation is provided in Chapter 15. Function logic written in COBOL code may be used to generate Microfocus COBOL utilizing the Microfocus interface. The logic is entered on the second Function description screen (press PgDn).

Often a good top-down strategy is to create the function descriptions providing only a label, then return to the drawing screen, providing descriptive details later. When the function description is complete, press F3 to save and return to the drawing screen. Repeat for all rectangles.

A function used in several places on the structure chart is called a common function. The easiest way of describing second and third occurrences of a function is to COPY one previously described. Alternately, select DESCRIBE and type the module number. Press enter and Excelerator will display the description for the function. Review, make any changes and press F3 to save and return.

DESCRIBING MODULES

A Module is a detailed description of a function. To create a Module, enter MOD and the name of the module in the **Explodes To** section found on the <u>Function</u> description screen. With the cursor in this area, press F4 (Browse). The module description entry screen is displayed, illustrated in Figure 6.3.

Enter the project, author, and other descriptive information. These may be reported on using the Report Writer feature. For example, listing all Modules created by a specific author or totaling the number of lines of code for a specific project.

Complete the input and return fields by selecting (with the mouse) the first character of the entry area and keying the information. Press PgDn to enter any requirements and associated entities, such as TST for a description of module test data.

Pressing PgDn again provides an area for the description of the module and it's logic. The information entered may be later analyzed and reported on. These topics will be covered in Chapters 12 and 15. Press PgUp to return to the previous module description screens.

Press F3 (Save) to save the module description and return to the function description screen.

If you want to put text (the assignment number, your name, etc.) on the drawing, use the text feature described in Chapter 5.

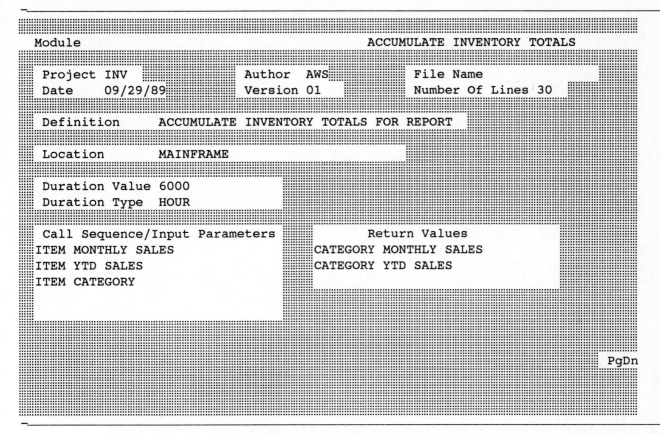

Module		ACCUMULATE INVENTORY TOTALS

Project INV   Author AWS   File Name
Date   09/29/89   Version 01   Number Of Lines 30

Definition   ACCUMULATE INVENTORY TOTALS FOR REPORT

Location   MAINFRAME

Duration Value 6000
Duration Type HOUR

Call Sequence/Input Parameters   Return Values
ITEM MONTHLY SALES   CATEGORY MONTHLY SALES
ITEM YTD SALES   CATEGORY YTD SALES
ITEM CATEGORY

                                 PgDn

Figure 6.3 Module Description Screen

DESCRIBING THE STRUCTURE CHART

The entire structure chart may be described in the XLDictionary. Select **DESCRIBE** and then select the structure chart graph name located directly above the orientation map.

The structure chart description screen is displayed. Refer to the example in Figure 6.4. Enter a new description, if desired, and the percent complete of the diagram. Enter the requirements satisfied by the structure chart and any associated entities. Press PgDn for a longer description area. This might include strategies for control of coding and other suggestions. Press F3 to save.

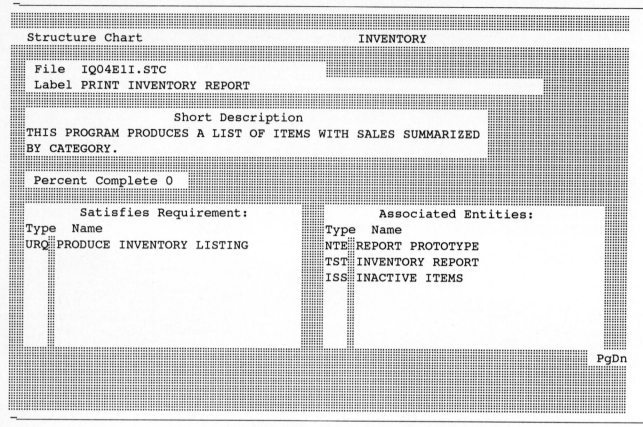

```
Structure Chart                       INVENTORY

  File  IQ04E1I.STC
  Label PRINT INVENTORY REPORT

                Short Description
 THIS PROGRAM PRODUCES A LIST OF ITEMS WITH SALES SUMMARIZED
 BY CATEGORY.

  Percent Complete 0

        Satisfies Requirement:               Associated Entities:
 Type  Name                          Type  Name
 URQ  PRODUCE INVENTORY LISTING      NTE  REPORT PROTOTYPE
                                     TST  INVENTORY REPORT
                                     ISS  INACTIVE ITEMS


                                                                  PgDn
```

Figure 6.4   Structure Chart Description Screen

DATA COUPLING, ITERATION

Data coupling, control coupling and iteration symbols may be placed on the structure chart. Select SYMBOL.

To put a repetition loop, select REP LOOP. Select a module (rectangle) to have the loop under (eg. Print Inventory Report). Select the starting and then the ending location for the loop.

For data passed up the structure chart, select DATA UP. Select the connection by moving the arrow to the small box on the line (the data handle) and pressing the left mouse button. The same procedure is used for data passed down the structure (DATA DOWN), control up (CTRL UP), and control down (CTRL DWN).

To add the data names to the symbols, select LABEL, then the symbol circle. Type in the text and press enter. See Figure 6.5 for a sample structure chart with coupling shown.

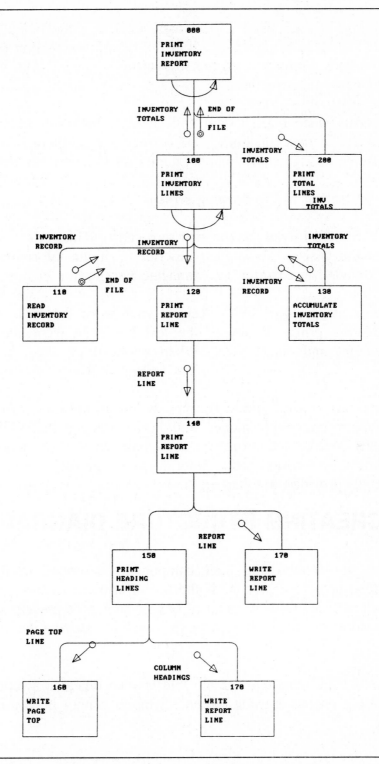

Figure 6.5 Sample Structure Chart With Coupling

Data and control may be described in the data dictionary and used for further analysis. Select DESCRIBE and then a connection. On the description screen complete entity types of REC (record) or ELE (element) and the respective names for both control and data that are passed up and down the structure.

A problem that occurs when placing data and control symbols is label text often overlays function rectangles and connection lines. To correct this problem, move functions further apart vertically. Refer to Figure 6.6 for an example of function placement.

Press F3 to save and return to the drawing screen.

You may include a System Device on the structure chart. This reflects a piece of hardware used to implement the design. A detailed description of the information available for the System Device is included in Chapter 15, Managing Excelerator Projects.

When finished, zoom to CLOSE UP. Review your work for style, and to ensure that complete label text will print. If any of the text has been truncated select PRINT and SETUP to review font and object size. When ready, print, save, backup and exit (see Chapter 2).

A final note on structure charts. Index Technology has an interface product that will create the procedure division paragraph names and corresponding PERFORM statements for Microfocus COBOL Workbench from the structure chart. Function descriptions are transferred into Procedure Division code. Data division code for records and screens may be generated with details provided in Chapters 8, 11 and 17.

CREATING STRUCTURE DIAGRAMS

Structure Diagrams are created and their components described in the same fashion as structure charts. One notable difference is the use of symbols to show procedure logic. To include symbols, select SYMBOL. A menu of symbol choices is presented. Choose one, and then select the function rectangle to receive the symbol. Repeat for all objects using the same symbol.

Select the next symbol and continue for all objects. To delete a symbol, select DELETE, then the actual symbol on the drawing screen. Symbols cannot be moved or copied.

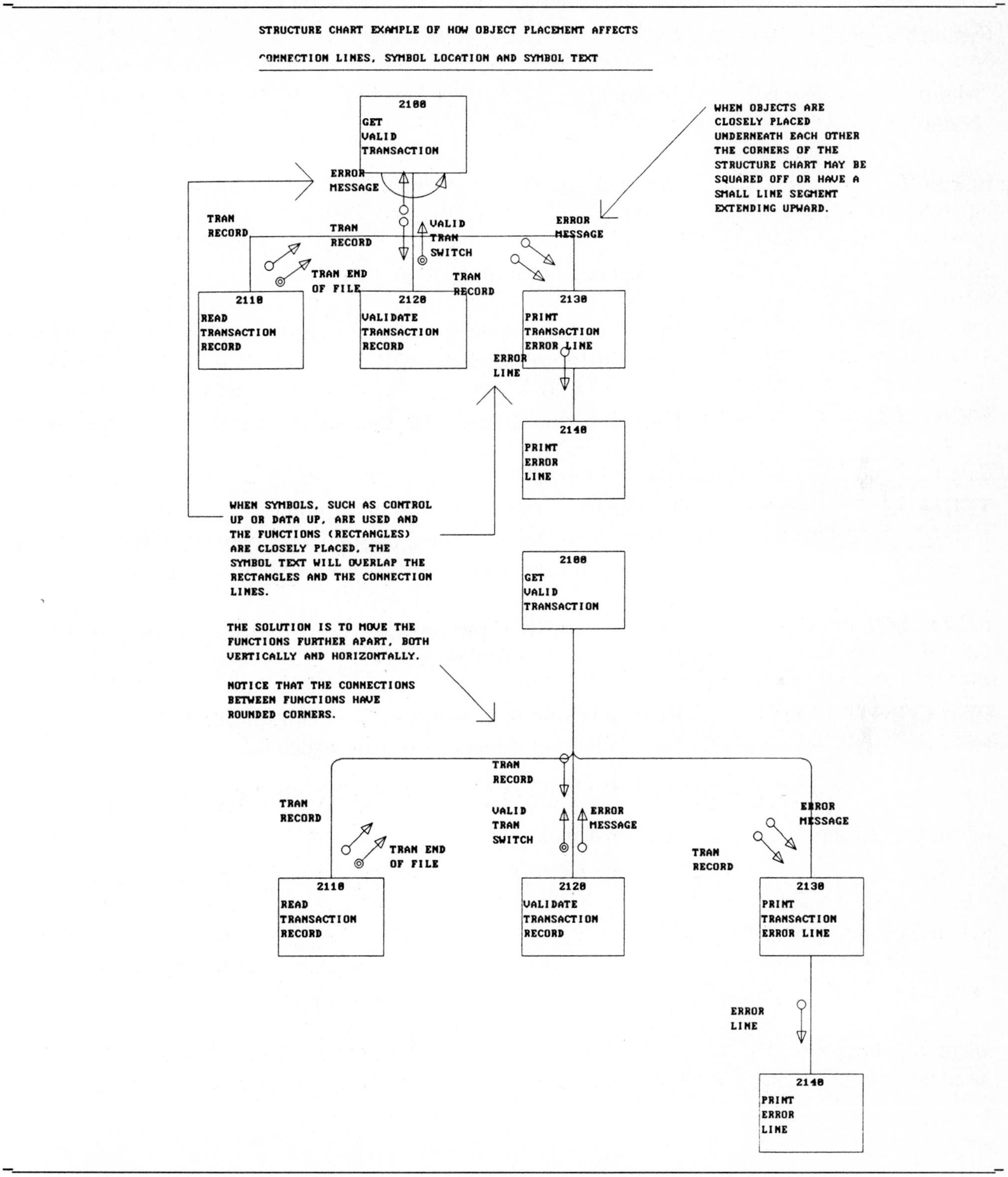

STRUCTURE CHART EXAMPLE OF HOW OBJECT PLACEMENT AFFECTS

CONNECTION LINES, SYMBOL LOCATION AND SYMBOL TEXT

2100
GET
VALID
TRANSACTION

ERROR
MESSAGE

WHEN OBJECTS ARE
CLOSELY PLACED
UNDERNEATH EACH OTHER
THE CORNERS OF THE
STRUCTURE CHART MAY BE
SQUARED OFF OR HAVE A
SMALL LINE SEGMENT
EXTENDING UPWARD.

TRAN
RECORD

TRAN
RECORD

VALID
TRAN
SWITCH

ERROR
MESSAGE

TRAN END
OF FILE

TRAN
RECORD

2110
READ
TRANSACTION
RECORD

2120
VALIDATE
TRANSACTION
RECORD

2130
PRINT
TRANSACTION
ERROR LINE

ERROR
LINE

2140
PRINT
ERROR
LINE

WHEN SYMBOLS, SUCH AS CONTROL
UP OR DATA UP, ARE USED AND
THE FUNCTIONS (RECTANGLES)
ARE CLOSELY PLACED, THE
SYMBOL TEXT WILL OVERLAP THE
RECTANGLES AND THE CONNECTION
LINES.

THE SOLUTION IS TO MOVE THE
FUNCTIONS FURTHER APART, BOTH
VERTICALLY AND HORIZONTALLY.

NOTICE THAT THE CONNECTIONS
BETWEEN FUNCTIONS HAVE
ROUNDED CORNERS.

2100
GET
VALID
TRANSACTION

TRAN
RECORD

TRAN
RECORD

VALID
TRAN
SWITCH

ERROR
MESSAGE

ERROR
MESSAGE

TRAN END
OF FILE

TRAN
RECORD

2110
READ
TRANSACTION
RECORD

2120
VALIDATE
TRANSACTION
RECORD

2130
PRINT
TRANSACTION
ERROR LINE

ERROR
LINE

2140
PRINT
ERROR
LINE

Figure 6.6   Effect of Function Placement On Symbol Labels and Connections

Symbols and their meanings are:

Menu Name	Symbol	Meaning
SELECT	o	Shows a condition that must be satisfied before a function may be executed.
REPEAT	*	Indicates a repetition or looping activity.
INCL ALT	?	Inclusive Alternative shows when either one or the other of two functions is to be performed.
EXPL SEQ	>	Explicit Sequence indicates that an order must be followed when performing the functions.
TERM ACT	⊥	Terminating Activity shows a terminal activity or endpoint in the diagram that is not a normal occurrence. This would be an early termination, such as a VSAM open file error.
PARA ACT	‖	Parallel Activity shows two functions that are on the same level but do not occur in sequence.
REL COND	#	Release Condition indicates a condition that must be filled before another function may be executed.

A sample Structure Diagram is shown in Figure 6.7.

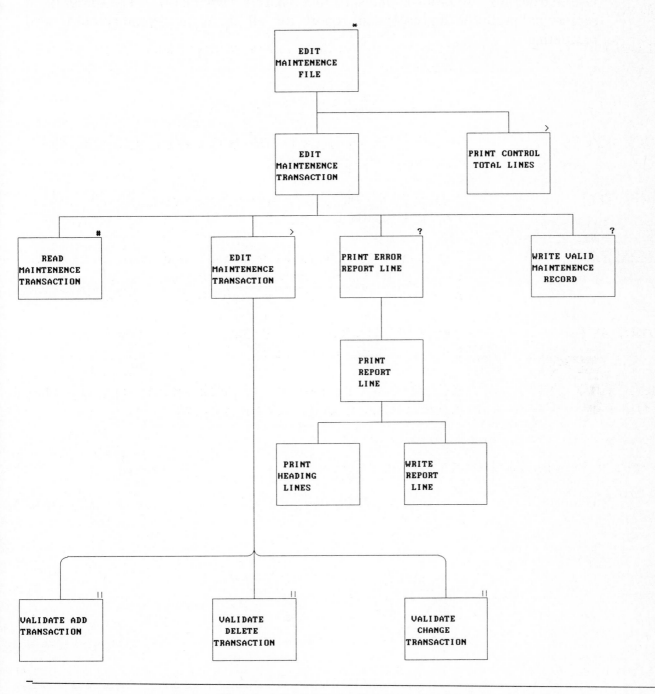

Figure 6.7   Sample Structure Diagram

EXERCISES

1. Use Excelerator to produce the structure chart shown below. The program it represents produces an exception report for all items in inventory that need reordering.

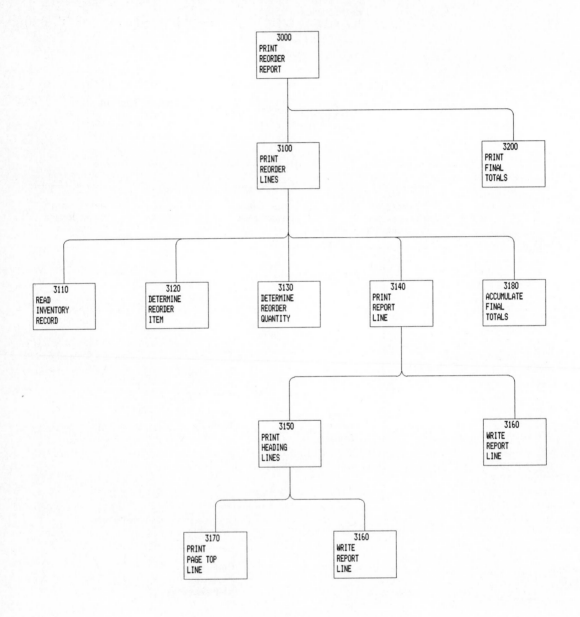

Inventory Reorder Report Program

2.   The structure chart shown below represents a program to calculate the employee payroll. Modify the structure chart to include the following modules.

   A.   <u>Calculate Regular Pay</u> and <u>Calculate Overtime Pay</u> (under the module Calculate Gross Pay).

   B.   <u>Calculate Federal Withholding</u>, <u>Calculate State Withholding</u>, and <u>Calculate Social Security Withholding</u>, (under the module Calculate Withholding Pay).

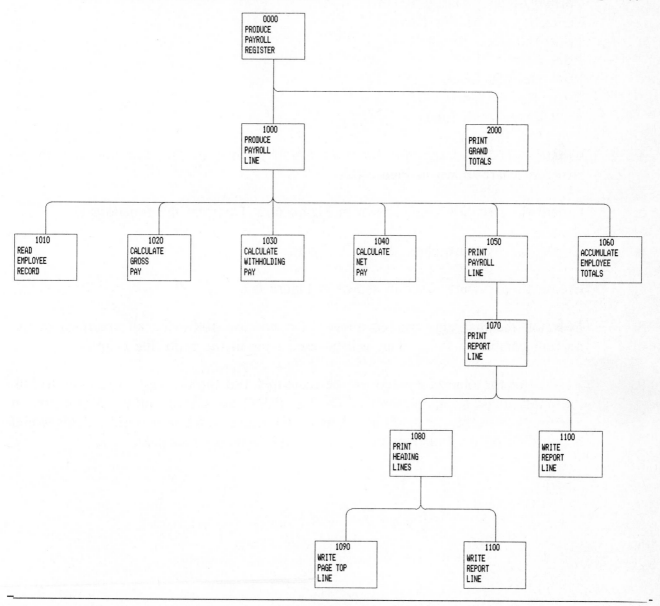

Produce Employee Payroll Program

3.   Create a structure chart to add a new student to the Student Master File. The necessary modules are listed below:

      Add Student Records (Control module)
      Add Student Record (Main loop module)
      Read Add Transaction Record
      Edit Add Transaction Record
      Format Student Master Record
      Write Student Master Record
      Print Validation Report Line
      Print Report Line
      Print Heading Lines
      Write Report Line
      Print Final Totals Line

4.   Create a module description for the functions numbered 110, 120, and 130 on the structure chart shown in Figure 6.5.

5.   Create the structure chart shown in Figure 6.1. Describe the functions.

6.   Create the structure chart shown in Figure 6.5.

7.   Create the structure diagram shown in Figure 6.7.

8.   Describe the diagrams created above. Do not use 100% for all diagrams in the percent completed field. This will be used later in the reporting chapter.

9.   For any of the objects created on the diagrams, use the description screens to link the entity to user requirements or the test (TST) associated entity. If you are on a team, brainstorm with team members to determine which user requirements would be satisfied by the functions or what test types would be needed.

7

SYSTEM FLOWCHARTS & OTHER PRESENTATION GRAPHICS

Chapter goals:

> Know how to create a presentation graph.
> Learn how to describe objects on the graph.
> Understand how to link an object to the XLDictionary.
> Know how to link a process to user, engineering or other management
>   documentation.
> Understand how to create an explosion path for presentation graph objects.
> Know how to view presentation graph object explosions.
> Learn how to create a system flowchart using Excelerator
> Know how to create a screen flow diagram using Excelerator.

Presentation graphics allow you to create drawings that pictorially represent your system, program, or other project. Objects on the graph may be exploded to provide a detailed view. Several uses for Presentation Graphics will be discussed in this chapter but many more may be created using the objects available, for example a module flowchart or a picture of the users and their interaction with microcomputers.

Select Presentation Graph from the graphics menu, then Add, or Modify to change a previously drawn chart. Type in the name of your chart. If you are modifying a chart, press ENTER with the cursor in the name area and Excelerator will give you a list of previously drawn charts. Select one or press the right button (or the ESC key) to cancel.

SYSTEM FLOWCHARTS

The first topic is system flowcharts. These provide a pictorial view of the system and its components. The Presentation Graphics drawing screen is shown in Figure 7.1. Under PROFILE select NO ARROW, STRAIGHT and the others as in Chapter 1.

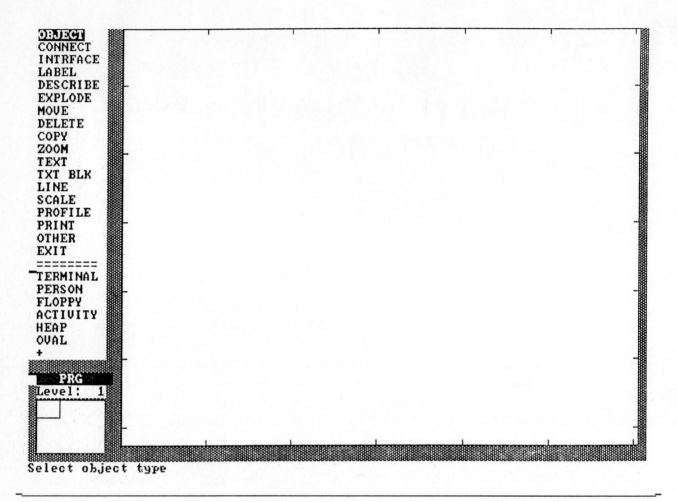

Figure 7.1 Presentation Graphics Drawing Screen

Select OBJECT. A list of icons is displayed at the bottom of the menu. There are two ways to place an object on the screen.

One method is to select the object name with the mouse. Selecting the + sign gives additional objects (or the top + gives previous objects).

For example, select +, then select RECTANGLE, the process symbol (or select Activity if you are using the Gane and Sarson convention). Select the area on the screen where you want the object to appear by moving the mouse to the location and pressing the left button. A complete list of objects is shown in Figure 7.2.

The other method for selecting objects is to press the letter or number that represents the object. Most objects can be selected by typing their first letter. Exceptions are summarized as follows:

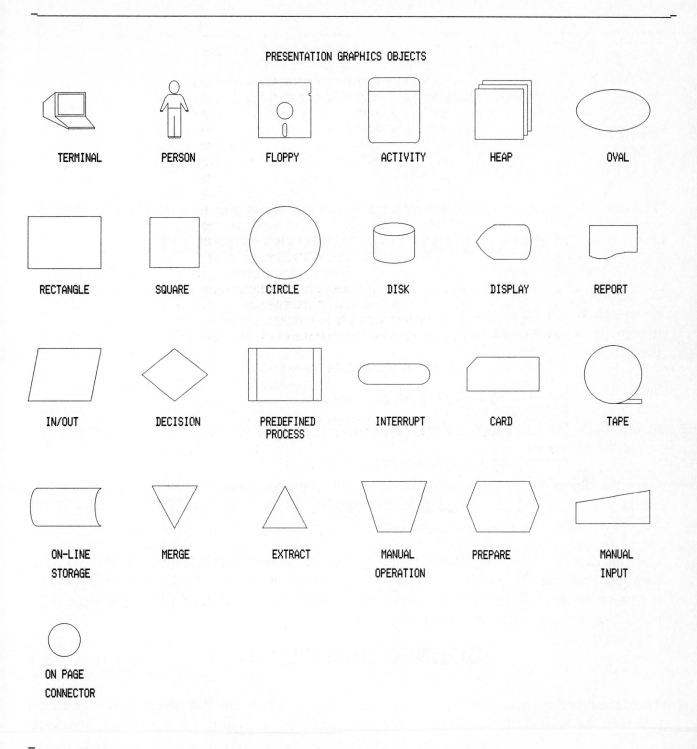

Figure 7.2 Presentation Graphics Objects

E RECTANGLE
I DISPLAY
4 TAPE
5 ON-LINE STORAGE (DISK)
6 MANUAL OPERATION
7 PREPARATION
8 MANUAL INPUT
9 ONPAGE CONNECTOR

Then use the mouse to select the area on the screen where you want to place the object.

CHANGING THE SIZE OF OBJECTS

If the objects are too small or too large for your diagrams, relative to each other (not just zoom), they may be enlarged or reduced using the scale feature. SCALE changes the text within the object as well as the size of the object. Use it before describing or labeling the object.

Select SCALE. Choose BOTH to change the object uniformly, X-AXIS to change horizontally and Y-AXIS to change vertically. Touch the outer size that the object should be expanded to and click the left button. To shrink an object repeat the process but move the arrow inside the object.

Once the object has been changed, use the COPY option to place the same object elsewhere on the drawing screen and maintain a uniform size. Refer to Figure 7.3 for examples of the SCALE feature.

Use the ZOOM feature to view the screen close up. Select ZOOM, then CLOSE UP, and then an area on the orientation map or the screen to view. There is a tendency for beginning users or Excelerator to place objects too far apart and thus create a large print instead of a neatly presented diagram.

CONNECTING OBJECTS

To connect the symbols with lines, select CONNECT. Touch the first object to be connected and then the second object. Refer to the example shown in Figure 7.4 of a system flowchart.

The connection procedure is modified if you have selected USERPORT under the PROFILE option. Select the first object to be connected. An arrow will appear on the side of the

USING THE SCALE FEATURE TO CHANGE OBJECT SIZES

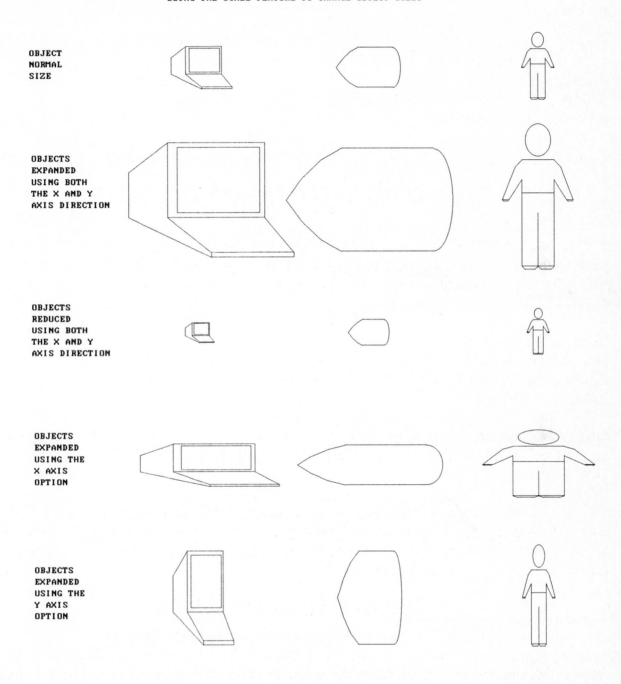

OBJECT
NORMAL
SIZE

OBJECTS
EXPANDED
USING BOTH
THE X AND Y
AXIS DIRECTION

OBJECTS
REDUCED
USING BOTH
THE X AND Y
AXIS DIRECTION

OBJECTS
EXPANDED
USING THE
X AXIS
OPTION

OBJECTS
EXPANDED
USING THE
Y AXIS
OPTION

Figure 7.3   Effects of the Scale Feature

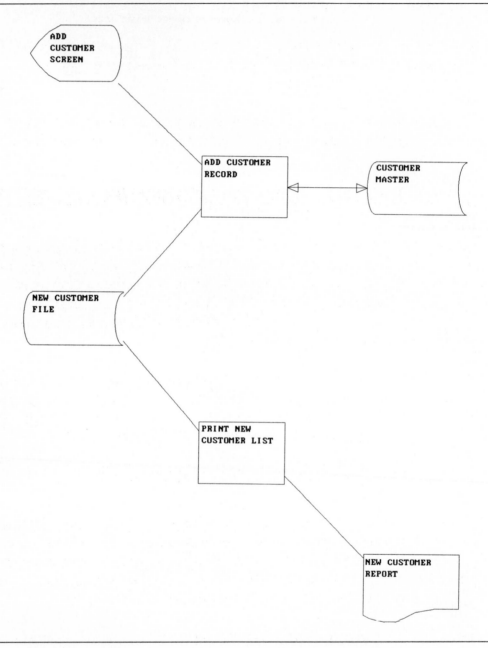

Figure 7.4 System Flowchart for Adding New Customers

object. Moving the mouse will cause the arrow to move around the object. The port location on the object will appear on the bottom of the screen (eg. RIGHT -2). Move the arrow to the corner where you want the connection line to touch the object. Click the left button. Then move the mouse so the arrow moves to the object to be connected to. Again, press the left button and the small arrow reappears. Move it to the desired spot (eg. top left corner) and press the left button. Repeat for all objects.

If a part of the line you are working on is not straight or to your liking, you can cancel (right button) and redo the connection. If the final line is not what you want it to be, you can move or delete the line (see Chapter 5).

For two way arrows (eg. a read and rewrite of an indexed file record) select PROFILE, then TWO WAY. Make the connection as described above. Then reset the connection profile to NO ARROW.

LABELING AND DESCRIBING OBJECTS

There are two methods for placing descriptive text into objects. The LABEL option creates text inside the object but does not provide an XLDictionary link. Using LABEL is the fastest method of placing text on the diagram, since the drawing screen does not have to be redisplayed after entering each label. LABEL also allows precise placement of the text within the object or along the connection. Objects that are labeled may be described and the label will automatically be included in the description.

The DESCRIBE feature allows you to place text in the object and provides a link to the XLDictionary as well. This is important for performing analysis and reporting on the various components of your system. DESCRIBE further allows you to create an explosion path for the graph object and then view the explosion graph or text.

LABELING OBJECTS

Labeling objects is the simplest method of providing text. Select LABEL and then select the object that the label should appear within. Enter the text in the pop-up window that appears. Press the tab key or a combination of the down arrow and the home key for the next line. Up to sixty characters may be entered. Correct errors using insert, delete, or by overtyping the text. Press the enter key when finished. Repeat for all objects.

To label a connection (eg. R for an indexed file random read or listing a key field), select the connection by moving the mouse arrow to the box on the line and pressing the left button. Select first the upper left corner, then the lower right corner for the label and key the text.

DESCRIBING OBJECTS

When **DESCRIBE** is chosen, Excelerator will provide you with a suggested ID. This is the presentation graph name with a .1, .2, etc. added as a suffix. You may press enter to accept this default ID or you may overtype it with an ID to your liking or specific standards. Since the ID provides a link to the XLDictionary and does not show on the screen (unless chosen via the PROFILE) the easy choice is to press enter.

The description screen for Presentation Graph Objects is displayed. Refer to the example in Figure 7.5. In the area called Label, enter the text that you would like to appear in the object. At this point you may wish to return to the drawing screen (press F3 to save) and add details to the description screen later. Alternately, if details are known, they may be entered on the description screen.

In the area labeled **Explodes To:** enter any XLDictionary entity that you would like linked to the object. Key in the entity type code (see Appendix B for a complete list) and the name of the entity. If you wish to link to an existing entity, key in the entity type code and press F4 for a selector list. Select from the list of names displayed for the particular entity type.

In the example shown, the Add Customer Screen explodes to the screen design prototype called Add Cust Screen. The entity **Type** is SCD for **SC**reen **D**esign. Other entity types could be another presentation graph (PRG), structure chart (STC), record layout for a file (REC), data flow diagram (DFD), or <u>any</u> of Excelerator's 53 entity types.

Fill in any requirements, either user or engineering which the object being described satisfies. Add any associated entities for managing the project. Refer to Chapter 3 for a description of this process. When the description is complete, press F3 to save and return to the drawing screen.

EXPLODING OBJECTS

If an explosion path has been created (an entry is in the **Explodes To:** area on the description screen) the color of the object will change. This allows you to easily view which objects and connections have an explosion path defined.

To view the explosion graph or text, select **EXPLODE** and then select the object or connection. For example, explode the screen display symbol for Add Customer Screen. The actual screen will be displayed for review. This is a great method for viewing the system flowchart and seeing the underlying screens, reports, data structures, structure charts, etc.

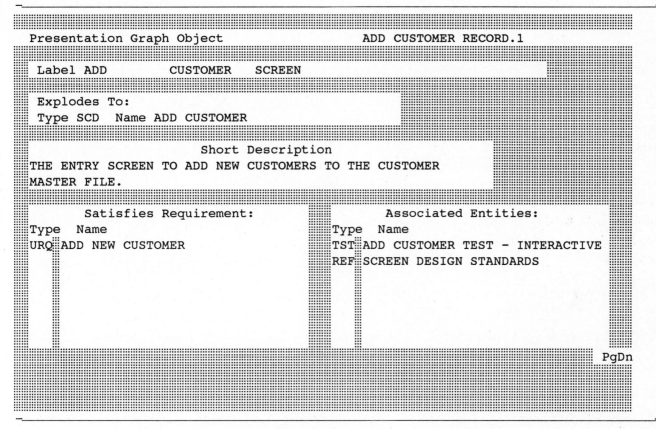

Figure 7.5   Presentation Graph Object Description Screen

After viewing the exploded object, press the enter key to return to the Presentation Graph. Refer to Figure 7.6 for an example of the NEW CUSTOMER ENTRY screen design, exploded from the system flowchart. The explosion path may be listed using the XLDictionary reporting features described in Chapter 12.

To place text on the diagram, see Chapter 5. When finished, zoom to CLOSE UP to review how the graph will print and make any changes that are necessary. Check your print setup and print when ready. Save your work, backup and exit (refer to Chapter 2).

SCREEN FLOW DIAGRAMS

Screen flow diagrams (in the style of Murach and Lowe) are used to show screens and the actions taken when function keys, editing, and other major decision making events occur. These diagrams give the programmer a picture of an interactive program from the control view and may be created using the Presentation Graphics feature.

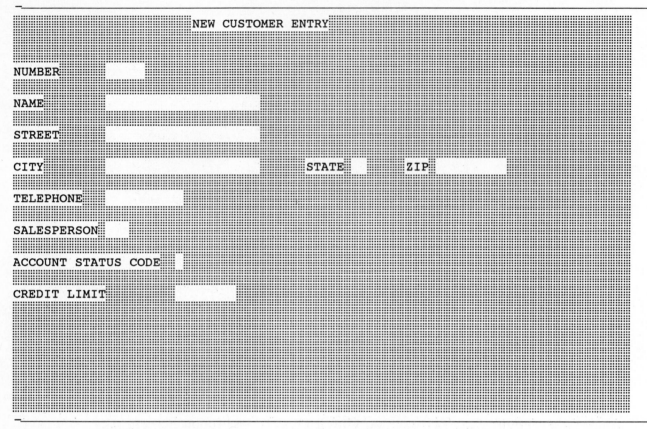

Figure 7.6 Presentation Graph Object Explosion Add Customer Screen

Select GRAPHICS, then Presentation Graph. Select Add or Modify to change a previously drawn screen flow diagram. Type in the name of your diagram. If you are modifying a diagram press enter for the name and Excelerator will give you a list of diagrams previously drawn. Select one or press the right button (or the ESC key) to cancel.

Under PROFILE select ONE WAY, ARC and the others as in Chapter 1.

Select OBJECT and the + sign for a list of additional objects. Select the SQUARE. Optionally you could use the rectangle symbol. Select the area on the top of the screen where you want the screen symbol (square) to appear. Refer to the example shown in Figure 7.7. Repeat for other screens and for major processes, such as editing, input/output operations, etc.

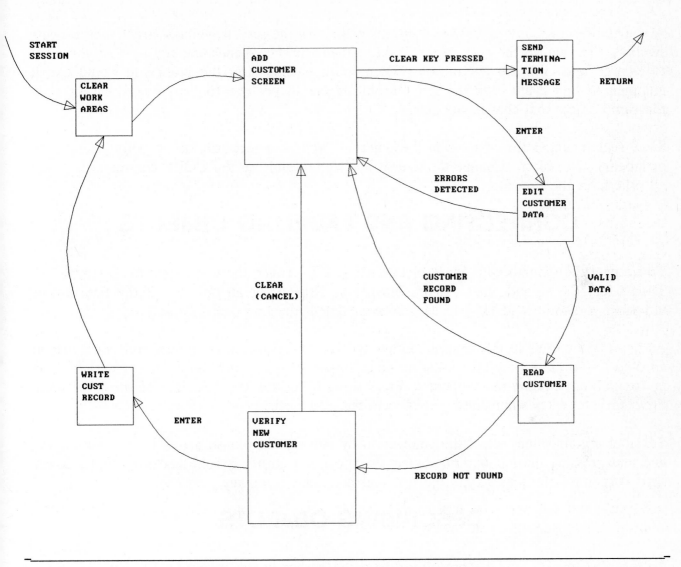

Figure 7.7 Sample Screen Flow Diagram

ENLARGING THE SCREEN SYMBOLS

A convention used on screen flow diagrams is to show the screen symbols larger than process symbols. To change the size, select SCALE, then BOTH. Touch the square that you want to enlarge and click the left button. Then touch outside it at the point you would like it enlarged to and again click the left button. If the shapes are too large or small, reselect the same object and change the size.

Since scale changes the text within the object as well as object size, use it <u>before</u> describing or labeling the object. Change the size of one square and use the COPY command to place all others on the drawing.

CONNECTING AND LABELING OBJECTS

To connect the symbols with lines, select CONNECT. Touch the first object to be connected. Then select the second object to be connected. Repeat for all objects. If the final line is not what you want it to be, you can move or delete the line (see Chapter 5).

As described earlier in this chapter, either the label or describe command will place text in an object. To place only text inside an object, select LABEL and the object. Enter the text in the pop-up window that appears. Press the tab key for the next line of the label area. Press the enter key when finished. Repeat for all objects.

To label a connection, select the connection by moving the mouse arrow to the box on the line and pressing the left button. Select an upper left corner for the text area and a lower right corner for the text. Type the text and press the enter key.

DESCRIBING OBJECTS

To describe objects, use the procedure discussed earlier in this chapter. For screens, enter any user or engineering requirements that may be appropriate. You may wish to create an explosion path to the actual screen design. The entity type is SCD for **SC**reen Design.

When the description is complete, press F3 to save and return to the drawing screen.

If an explosion path has been created and you wish to view the screen design, select **EXPLODE** and then the square on the Presentation Graph. The prototype screen will be displayed. Press the enter key to return to the Presentation Graph.

When finished, zoom to CLOSE UP, review your drawing and modify the print setup if necessary. Print, save, backup and exit (see Chapter 2).

CREATING DECISION TREES

Presentation Graphics may be used to create decision trees, used to depict control and other logical choices. Select PROFILE and the following settings: LABEL MD, COMPLETE, LAB ONLY, then press the right button. Select PIPE, SYSTPORT (the default), and USRLABEL. Select PRINT, then SETUP. Choose Object Size A and press the right button. This is to make the objects as small as possible while retaining a larger font size.

Select OBJECT and C for circle. Alternatively select the plus sign and then select CIRCLE. Use the mouse to place the circle on the left side of the screen, where the decision tree would start. Select SCALE and the circle. When prompted to select a location to change the size of the circle, select the center, thus making it as small as possible.

Use COPY to replicate this small circle to the junction and end points of the tree diagram. Select CONNECT, touch the first and then the second small circles. Repeat for all branches of the decision tree.

Use ZOOM to show the drawing screen close up and choose the area where the tree begins. Select LABEL, then a connection. Choose an upper left corner and a lower right corner. If the label size, shown in the pop-up window is too small, press the right button to cancel and reselect the label size corners. Key in the label and press enter. If the label is not where you want it (often they are not exactly lined up), use MOVE to move the label to the right location. When using move, select the corner of the screen that you want the upper left corner of the label to start at. Repeat for all decision tree line text.

Figure 7.8 shows an example of a decision tree. When finished, review your drawing and modify if necessary. Print, save, backup and exit.

MAINTENENCE DECISION TREE
ADD, DELETE, CHANGE
ASSUMPTION IS THAT A MATCHING
MASTER RECORD EXISTS

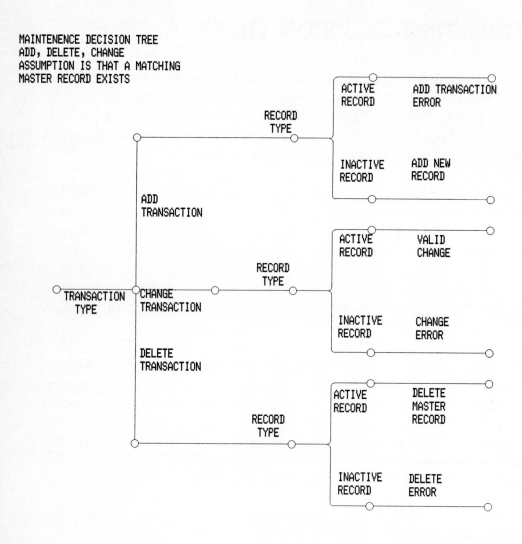

Figure 7.8   Decision Tree Example

EXERCISES

1. Draw the system flow shown below. This depicts customer orders keyed onto an order entry screen. The orders update the Customer Master, Item Master, and Salesperson Master files. An Order Summary record is produced. The Order Summary record is input to an inquiry program to display order information.

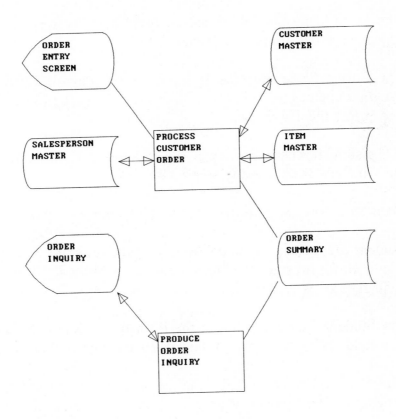

2. Create the systems flowchart shown in Figure 7.4, Add New Customer.

3.   Produce a system flowchart for the Payroll Processing System, containing the following processing steps:

A.   Data entry keys and verifies the Employee Time slips, creating the Time Slip transaction file.

B.   An edit program verifies the data on the Time Slip transaction file. Valid records are written onto the Valid Time Slip file. All records, whether valid or not, are printed on a Validation report.

C.   The Valid Time Slip file is sorted using a utility sort program. The major sequence is by Employee Number.

D.   The Sorted Time Slip file is input to the Payroll Program. The Payroll Program updates the Employee Master, produces the Check Reconciliation file, and prints the Paychecks.

4.   Produce a system flowchart to depict the processing of student grades at the end of a term. Include the following steps:

A.   Data entry keys and verifies the student grades at the end of the term.

B.   Student grades are validated using an edit program. A validation report is produced for all student grades entered. A Student Grade transaction file of valid records is created.

C.   The Student Grade transaction file is sorted by Student Number as the major sort field. This is accomplished using the Sort utility program.

D.   The Sorted Student Grade file is input to the Update Student Master program. The Student Master is updated. A Student Grade Summary file is created containing all the grades for a specific student, the grade point average, and name and address information.

E.   The Student Grade Summary file is sorted by Zip using the Sort utility program.

F.   The Sorted Grade Summary file is input to a program that produces the Grade Reports that are mailed to students.

5.   Create the screen flow diagram for the Add Customer screen, shown in Figure 7.5.

6.   Draw a screen flow diagram for changing an employee. The Employee Number entry screen is displayed. An Employee Number is keyed in and the Enter key pressed or the operator may press the Clear key to exit. If the Enter key is pressed, the Employee Record is read. If the Employee Record is not found, control returns to the Employee Number key screen. If the record is found, the change screen is displayed with the current employee values on it. If the Clear key is pressed, control returns to the Employee Number key screen, otherwise changes are keyed in and the enter key is pressed. Changes are edited. If errors occur control is returned to the change screen. If no errors occur, a protected verification screen is displayed. If PF1 is pressed, control returns to the change screen. If the enter key is pressed, the record is rewritten and control returns to the Employee Number key screen.

7.   Draw the screen flow diagram for the student inquiry. An entry screen is displayed which allows the first three letters of the student's last name to be keyed in. If the Clear key is pressed, the program is exited. If the enter key is pressed, the Student Master file is read using the first three letters entered as a start key. If no students are found matching the first three letters, control returns to the entry screen. If a match is found, a list is displayed of all students whose last names start with the three letters entered. If PF2 is pressed, the next page of names is displayed. Pressing the Clear key returns control to the key screen. The student names are displayed with a number in front of them. If a number is entered, that individual student record is read and displayed. Pressing PF1 gives a display of the courses completed by the student. Pressing the Clear key returns control to the entry screen.

8.   Describe the diagrams created above. Do not use 100% for all of the diagrams in the percent completed field. This will be used later in the reporting chapters.

9.   For any of the objects created on the diagrams, use the description screens to link the entity to user requirements or the test (TST) associated entity. If you are on a team, brainstorm with team members to determine which user requirements would be satisfied by the processes or what test types are needed.

8

DATA DICTIONARY

Chapter Goals:

> Learn how to create data dictionary record structures and elements from description screens.
>
> Know how to use the XLDictionary feature for creating record structures and elements.
>
> Understand how to create a record description and record type codes.
>
> Know what to include in the element description areas.
>
> Understand the meaning and use of edit rules.
>
> Learn how to create a table of codes for edit purposes and project documentation.
>
> Learn how to print data dictionary entries.
>
> Understand how to delete, copy, and rename data dictionary entries.
>
> Know how to list and inspect the data dictionary entities.
>
> Know how to generate computer program code using the data record and element definitions.

Data dictionary entries may be created for data structures (records) and for elements (fields). These may be modified, printed and analyzed using Excelerator's extensive analysis capabilities. Program code may be easily generated.

There are two methods used to create a data dictionary entry. The technique of creating the entries is the same for both, but the path for getting to the data dictionary entry screen is different. One method is to explode a data flow or data store. The advantage to this method is that entries are linked to the data flow diagram. The disadvantage is that the drawing screen must be redrawn after describing each data store or connection.

A second method is to use the XLDictionary feature of Excelerator, presented later in this chapter. The advantage of this method is that the drawing screen does not have to be redisplayed after each entry is created. The XLDictionary may also be used to enter record structures and elements (fields) gathered in a series of interviews or JAD (Joint Application Development) sessions. These may later be grouped into higher level records or exploded into more detail. Excelerator conveniently provides a report that shows all elements not included within record structures. This analysis option will be described in Chapter 12, Project Analysis.

CREATING DATA DICTIONARY ENTRIES FROM GRAPHICS

Retrieve a previously created data flow diagram following the procedure described in Chapter 3. Select DESCRIBE from the data flow diagram screen. Select a data store or data flow connection. Create an ID if necessary and press the enter key to display the description screen.

On the description screen, the **EXPLODES TO ONE OF:** area must contain a name. If an explosion name is not present, enter the name at this time. If possible, use the name entered in the label area. Refer to the example for the CUSTOMER MASTER Data Store description screen in Figure 8.1.

With the cursor in the name field, press F4. The record description screen is displayed. Refer to the CUSTOMER MASTER example in Figure 8.2. Alternately you could select EXPLODE on the drawing screen and then select the data flow or data store.

Complete the Alternate Name field if there is an alias for the data, perhaps another name the data is referred to by users. It may be left blank. The Definition area contains a brief description of the record.

Normalized refers to whether the data is normalized or not, (Y/N). The default value is N and may be changed to Y if the data is in the third normal form. This field determines if the record will be selected for normalization analysis. Chapter 12 provides further details.

For each data element (field) or data structure (group of fields) there are five areas to complete.

1.   The **Name of Element or Record.** If this area contains a data structure, it can be exploded to another record. An element may be exploded to a detailed element description, explained later in this chapter.

2.   **Occ** is for occurrences, normally 1. If a table or other repeating field is on the record (eg. day of the week - occurs 7 times) fill in the number of times the data repeats.

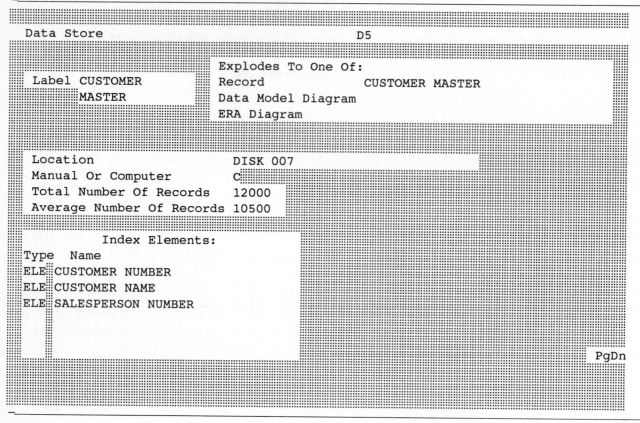

Figure 8.1 Data Store Description Screen

3.　　　**Seq** is for a sequence number. This can be left to the default of 0 (No sequencing) or can contain numbers which will allow new entries to be placed in sequence. For example Seq can have numbers of 10, 20, 30, 40, and 50. A new entry to be placed in sequence between the second and the third entry can be added to the next blank entry on the screen. It can given the number 25 and Excelerator will put the entry into sequence. Use this feature to re-sequence entries for a final description or before generating program language code.

4.　　　**Type** is a coded entry for the type of data. The codes are summarized below:

　　　E　　　Elemental - not further subdivided.

　　　R　　　Record - a data structure, one containing several elements or records.

　　　K　　　Key - the primary key for the record. This key may not be subdivided.

```
┌─────────────────────────────────────────────────────────────────────────┐
│ Record                                    CUSTOMER MASTER                 │
│                                                                           │
│   Alternate Name                                                          │
│   Definition      MASTER FILE OF ALL CUSTOMERS                            │
│   Normalized      Y                                                       │
│            Name of Element or Record        Occ  Seq  Type  Sec-Keys      │
│            BRANCH NUMBER                      1    10   E                  │
│            CUSTOMER NUMBER                    1    15   K                  │
│            CUSTOMER NAME                      1    20   E                  │
│            CUSTOMER ADDRESS                   1    30   R                  │
│            CUSTOMER TELEPHONE                 1    40   E                  │
│            SALESPERSON NUMBER                 1    50   7                  │
│            ACCOUNT STATUS CODE                1    60   E                  │
│            DATE OF LAST PURCHASE              1    62   E                  │
│            DATE OF LAST PAYMENT               1    64   E                  │
│            FINANCIAL INFORMATION              1    70   R                  │
│                                               1    0    e                  │
│                                               1    0    e                  │
│                                               1    0    e                  │
│                                               1    0    e                  │
│                                                                    PgDn    │
└─────────────────────────────────────────────────────────────────────────┘
```

Figure 8.2 Data Dictionary Screen

5.   **Sec-Keys** are two entry columns to denote alternate or secondary keys. The values that may be entered are

S   Secondary key that is not subdivided.

1-9   These numbers are for keys which are composed of several elementary items, that is, a <u>concatenated</u> key. The first field that makes up a <u>single key</u> should have the number 1, the second field number 2, etc.

To add fields to an existing data dictionary entry, select the first available character of a blank **Name of Element or Record** or use the arrow keys to move the cursor to the same area. The Tab (or Shift-Tab) keys will move forward (or backward) across the entry fields one at a time.

To insert a row <u>above</u> the one containing the cursor, press F1 and the Ins key simultaneously. To delete an entire row, press F1 and the Del key simultaneously. Press PgDn to enter a record length and any user requirements or associated entities.

DESCRIBING DATA STRUCTURES

A data structure is a record which consists of several elementary fields and has a **Type** of **R**. To describe the data structure, select the data structure name (move the cursor to the record name and press the left button), then press F4, the Browse key.

A new data dictionary entry screen appears for the data structure. Key in the entries for the structural record as previously described. Refer to Figure 8.3, the description screen for the CUSTOMER ADDRESS. Press F3 to save the entry and return to the previous screen.

Continue describing other data structures until completed.

Press F3 to save the data dictionary entry and return to the drawing screen.

Record				CUSTOMER ADDRESS	

Alternate Name					
Definition	ADDRESS OF THE CUSTOMER				
Normalized	Y				
Name of Element or Record	Occ	Seq	Type	Sec-Keys	
STREET	1	0	E		
CITY	1	0	E		
STATE	1	0	E		
ZIP	1	0	E		
ZIP EXPANSION	1	0	E		
	1	0	e		
	1	0	e		
	1	0	e		
	1	0	e		
	1	0	e		
	1	0	e		
	1	0	e		
	1	0	e		
	1	0	e		
					PgDn

Figure 8.3 Customer Address Data Dictionary Entry

REC/ELE	R Record		Modify	Add	Delete
	E Element				
DATA					
			Copy	Rename	List
PROCESS					
GRAPHS			Inspect	Generate	Analysis
					Prep (P)
SCR/REPS					
CONTROL			Output	Summary	Audit
					(U)
MANAGE					
			Expanded	Where	
OTHER			(N)	Used	
	Relationships				
	(T)		Name		
Exit					

Figure 8.4 XLDictionary Options For Records And Elements

CREATING DATA DICTIONARY ENTRIES FROM WITHIN THE XLDICTIONARY

Another method of creating data dictionary entries is to select XLDICTIONARY from the main menu. An introduction to this powerful feature will be discussed in this chapter, with complete coverage in Chapter 12. The advantage of using the XLDictionary to create data dictionary entries is speed. It is faster than returning to the drawing screen after completing each entry. The XLDictionary may also be used to enter data which does not yet exist on data flow diagrams.

The XLDICTIONARY menu is shown in Figure 8.4. Select **REC/ELE** for records and/or elements. Select **Record,** then Add or Modify. If Add has been selected, key in the name of the entry. If Modify is chosen, press the enter key and select a name from the list (or press Cancel or the Esc key if not found on the list). Describe the record data dictionary entries as explained earlier.

DESCRIBING DATA ELEMENTS

The data elements of a system may be described in detail. This includes edit rules, defaults, pictures and other information. This information is used to determine how prototype screens accept their data, the layout of report prototypes and the content of program record layouts. Analysis and reporting may be performed on elements.

Select a record and display it on the description screen. This may be accomplished in one of two ways.

1.   Exploding a data store or a data structure from a data flow diagram, or

```
Element                              CUSTOMER NUMBER

   Alternate Names CUSTOMER-NUMBER



   Definition      CUSTOMER NUMBER - UNIQUE FOR EACH CUSTOMER

   Input Format    X(5)
   Output Format   X(5)
   Edit Rules      VALUES ARE "00019" THRU "99998"
   Storage Type    C
   Characters left of decimal 5   Characters right of decimal   0

   Default
   Prompt          CUSTOMER NUMBER
   Column Header   CUSTOMER NUMBER
   Short Header    NUMBER
   Base or Derived B
   Data Class      CUSTOMER
   Source          NEW CUSTOMER FORM                          PgDn
```

Figure 8.5   Part 1
Data Dictionary - Element Description Screen

2. Selecting a record from the XLDictionary.
    Select **XLDICTIONARY** from the main menu.
    Select REC/ELE.
    Select Record.
    Select Modify.
    Press Enter to get a selector list and choose a record from the list. This method may be used for data structures, or records within higher level records.

Once a record has been chosen, select an element from the record. This is any entry that is not further subdivided, that is, does not contain an **R** in the type entry. To select an element, use the mouse (or cursor keys) to move the cursor to the first character of the element name and press the left button. Then press F4, the Browse key.

```
Element                              STATE

  Alternate Names STATE ABBREVIATION


  Definition      THE TWO CHARACTER STATE ABBREVIATION

  Input Format    XX
  Output Format   XX
  Edit Rules      FROM "STATE TABLE"
  Storage Type    C
  Characters left of decimal 2   Characters right of decimal   0

  Default
  Prompt          STATE ABBREVIATION
  Column Header   STATE
  Short Header    STATE
  Base or Derived B
  Data Class
  Source          NEW CUSTOMER FORM                          PgDn
```

Figure 8.5 Part 2
Data Dictionary - Element Description Screen

You may also select an element directly from the XLDictionary. Then add, modify, print, etc. by choosing an action. The procedure is:

Select XLDICTIONARY from the main menu.
Select REC/ELE.
Select Element.
Select Add or Modify.
Key in a name or press Enter to list elements and choose one.

An element description screen is displayed. Figure 8.5 illustrates several examples. Complete the screen areas or leave them blank, depending on the element. Select the area or press the enter key to move the cursor (reverse video square) to the desired area. The entries are described below.

1. **Alternate Names.** These lines describe other names for the element. An example would be another name commonly used by the user to refer to the element. It could include program language code names such as COBOL - CM-CUSTOMER-NUMBER or a data base language name eg. DBASE III - C_NUMBER.

2. **Definition.** A brief definition. This is used by the prototyping feature for a help message.

3. **Input Picture.** Used for prototyping data entry screens. The following codes are available, similar to COBOL edit characters. Pictures may contain parenthesis and the number of characters inside eg. X(9) for 9 alphanumeric characters.

   X   Alphanumeric - any letter, number or special character.
   9   Numeric - a field arithmetic may be performed on.
   A   Alphabetic
   B   Blank
   S   Sign
   .   Period
   ,   Comma
   M   Month
   D   Day
   Y   Year

If the input picture contains 9's, an error message will appear on prototype screens if the data entered is not numeric. If dollars and cents are to be entered on a prototyping screen, the decimal point should be included.

The maximum length of a picture is 80 characters, eg. X(80). This is the maximum length of a screen line and the pictures are used for creating prototype data fields.

4.	**Output Picture.** Used for prototyping printed reports. The following codes are used, similar to COBOL editing characters.

X	Alphanumeric
9	Numeric
Z	Zero suppression - display leading zeros as spaces.
$	Dollar sign
A	Alphabetic
B	Blank
S	Sign
.	Period
,	Comma
+	Plus sign
-	Minus sign
M	Month
D	Day
Y	Year

5.	**Edit rules.** These define the allowable values the element can have. There are several formats:

A.	VALUE IS followed by either characters in double quotes or numbers for numeric fields (without quotation marks).

Examples:	VALUE IS 0	(No quote marks)
		VALUE IS "PART-TIME"	(Need quote marks)
		VALUE IS > 15	(age for driver's license)
		VALUE IS < 6	(pre-school age)

Wildcards, or asterisks (*), may be used before or after data.

Example:	VALUE IS "A*" for Item Number, where all active item numbers start with an "A".

B.	VALUES ARE with several numbers or character strings separated by commas.

Examples:	VALUES ARE 0, 1, 2, 3
		VALUES ARE "A", "B", "C", "D", "F" for valid classroom grades.

C. A range of values. VALUES ARE separated by the word THRU.

Examples: VALUES ARE 94 THRU 100 (for a letter grade of an "A").
             VALUES ARE "A" THRU "D" (for a passing grade).
             VALUES ARE "A" THRU "D", "F", "W". "I" (for a valid final grade).

The words VALUE IS and VALUES ARE are optional, for readability.

NOT (or the word EXCLUDE(D)) can be used before any condition.

OPT means an optional entry. It can be combined with the VALUES ARE/IS by placing it at the end, for Example: VALUES ARE "A" THRU "Z" OPT (for a person's Middle Initial). For optional numeric fields, use a zero (0) instead of optional as part of the criteria.

```
Element                                    CUSTOMER TELEPHONE

  Alternate Names  CUSTOMER-TELEPHONE
                   PHONE NUMBER
                   TELEPHONE

  Definition       TELEPHONE NUMBER INCLUDING AREA CODE

  Input Format     9(10)
  Output Format    999B999-9999
  Edit Rules
  Storage Type     C
  Characters left of decimal 10  Characters right of decimal    0

  Default
  Prompt           CUSTOMER TELEPHONE
  Column Header    CUSTOMER TELEPHONE
  Short Header     TELEPHONE
  Base or Derived  B
  Data Class       CUSTOMER
  Source           NEW CUSTOMER FORM                              PgDn
```

Figure 8.5 Part 3
Data Dictionary - Element Description Screen

D. FROM "tablename" or NOT FROM "tablename". The values must be stored in an Excelerator table. Table definition will be discussed later.

Example: FROM "STATETABLE"

6. **Storage Type.** The following codes are available.

    C   Character
    P   Packed decimal
    B   Binary
    D   Date (avoid using this for COBOL applications)
    F   Floating point
    I   Bit (C and PL/1)
    R   Picture (use for PL/1)
    M   Time (avoid with COBOL)
    V   Variable (avoid with COBOL)

```
Element                                    CURRENT BALANCE

   Alternate Names  CUSTOMER AMOUNT DUE
                    CUSTOMER CURRENT BALANCE


   Definition       THE CUSTOMER'S CURRENT BALANCE

   Input Format     9(7)V99
   Output Format    ZZZ,ZZ9.99
   Edit Rules       VALUES ARE 0 THRU 50000
   Storage Type     C
   Characters left of decimal 6    Characters right of decimal    2

   Default
   Prompt           CURRENT BALANCE
   Column Header    CURRENT BALANCE
   Short Header     BALANCE DUE
   Base or Derived  D
   Data Class       CUSTOMER
   Source           CUSTOMER INVOICE RECORD                        PgDn
```

Figure 8.5   Part 4
Data Dictionary - Element Description Screen

7.   **Characters left/right of the decimal** is self explanatory. Characters to the right needs to be filled in <u>only</u> when the data is packed or picture. For all other types, leave this field set to zero. Binary fields must have a length of 1, 2 or 4.

8.   **Prompt** is for documentation and describes the caption to be used for this element.

9.   **Column Header/Short Header** are used for documentation and for reports.

10.   **Base or Derived** - use the following values:

        B - Base, an input field, one originally keyed.
        D - Derived, a calculated field, produced by a process.

        Base or derived information is used to generate valuable analysis reports on the system design.

11.   **Data Class.** For grouping user data. This is for documentation only, eg. Payment information. This entry is very useful for producing reports on element groups.

12.   **Source.** The original source of the data. Again, an important entry for producing documentation. Enter the source document or the input <u>form</u> containing the element. Later, produce a report (using the Report Writer feature) to show all the fields which should be included on the form.

13.   **Default.** Fill in a default value if there is one. This will appear on the prototyping screen and may be overtyped by the data entry operator.

Pressing PgDn provides an area to enter user requirements and associated entities. Pressing PgDn again gives an additional description area, if needed. This can be used for meanings of simple codes, intricate editing specifications, how account numbers are assigned, and other notation on specific data fields.

Press F3 to save and return to the record description screen or the XLDictionary. Repeat for all elements.

TABLE DEFINITION

Tables may be defined using Excelerator. These may be used as edit criteria when prototyping and for documentation, providing a concise store of codes used in the system. Use the following procedure to define entries in a table. Refer to the illustration in

Figure 8.6.

> Select XLDICTIONARY.
> Select DATA.
> Select Table Of Codes.
> Select Add (or Modify to change).

Enter the name of the table. This should be the same name used in the <u>FROM</u> option of the Element edit criteria. A table of codes entry screen is displayed. Refer to the example in Figure 8.7, the State Abbreviation table.

Key in an alternate name or leave blank. Enter a definition (or leave blank if desired). The total number of codes that may be entered is 100. If there are more than 100 codes, link this table of codes to another by entering the continuation table name in the **Next Table of Codes** entry area. Press F4 with the cursor in the name area to create (or view, if already created) the continuation table. Pressing F4 with the name area blank presents a selector list of available Table Of Codes.

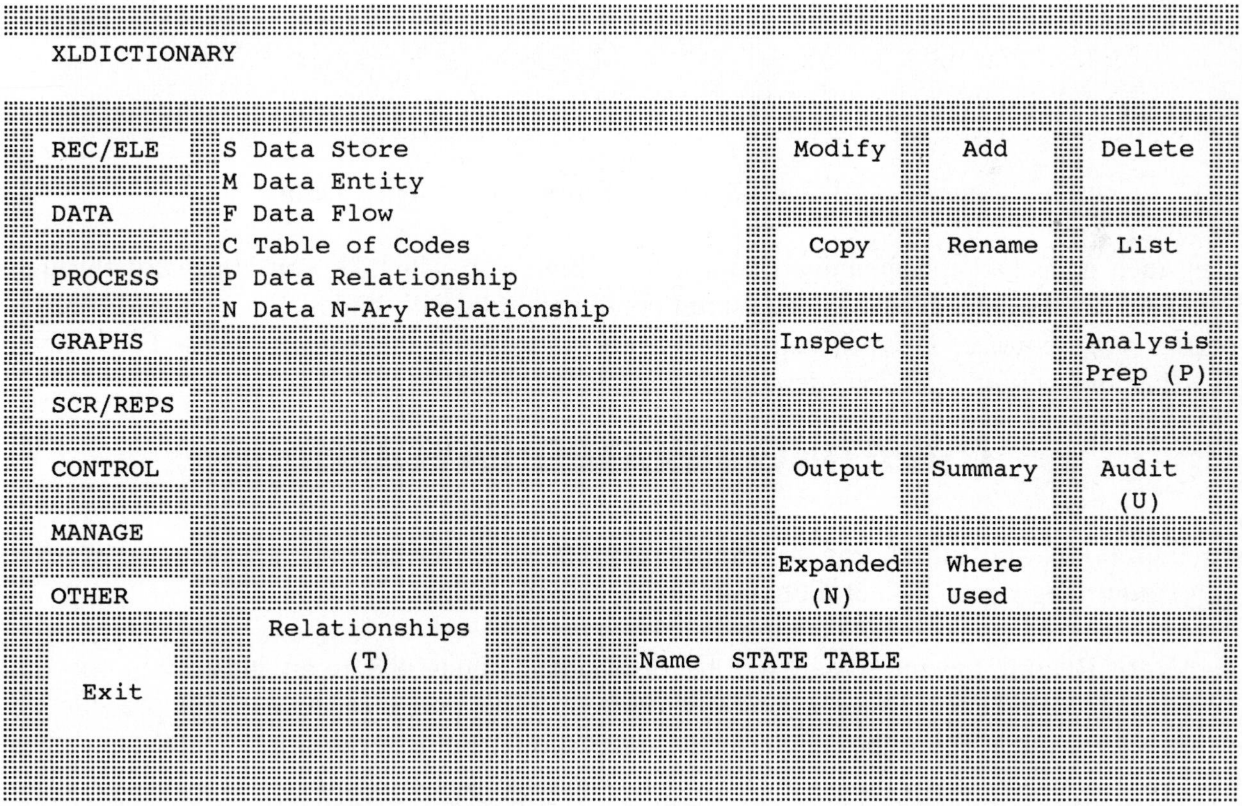

```
XLDICTIONARY

  REC/ELE      S Data Store               Modify    Add      Delete
               M Data Entity
  DATA         F Data Flow
               C Table of Codes           Copy    Rename     List
  PROCESS      P Data Relationship
               N Data N-Ary Relationship

  GRAPHS                                  Inspect          Analysis
                                                           Prep (P)
  SCR/REPS

  CONTROL                                 Output  Summary   Audit
                                                             (U)
  MANAGE
                                          Expanded  Where
  OTHER                                     (N)     Used

            Relationships
                (T)            Name  STATE TABLE
   Exit
```

Figure 8.6 Menu Options - Table Of Codes

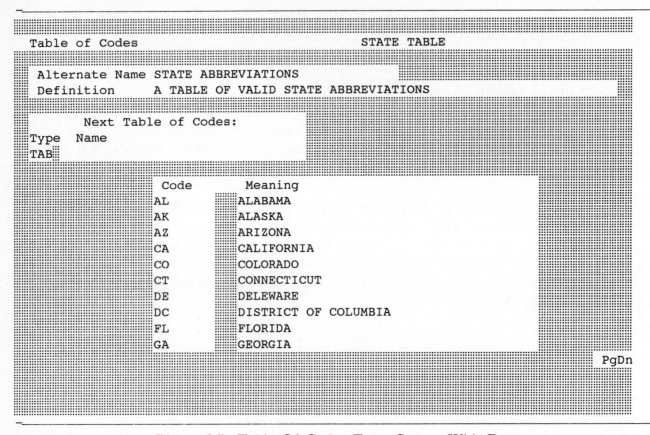

```
┌──────────────────────────────────────────────────────────────────────────┐
│ Table of Codes                              STATE TABLE                     │
│                                                                            │
│  ┌────────────────────────────────────────────┐                           │
│  │ Alternate Name STATE ABBREVIATIONS          │                           │
│  │ Definition     A TABLE OF VALID STATE ABBREVIATIONS                      │
│  └────────────────────────────────────────────┘                           │
│                                                                            │
│  ┌──────────────────────────────────┐                                     │
│  │      Next Table of Codes:         │                                     │
│  │ Type   Name                       │                                     │
│  │ TAB                               │                                     │
│  └──────────────────────────────────┘                                     │
│                                                                            │
│            Code        Meaning                                             │
│            AL          ALABAMA                                             │
│            AK          ALASKA                                              │
│            AZ          ARIZONA                                             │
│            CA          CALIFORNIA                                          │
│            CO          COLORADO                                           │
│            CT          CONNECTICUT                                         │
│            DE          DELEWARE                                            │
│            DC          DISTRICT OF COLUMBIA                                │
│            FL          FLORIDA                                             │
│            GA          GEORGIA                                             │
│                                                                     PgDn   │
└──────────────────────────────────────────────────────────────────────────┘
```

Figure 8.7   Table Of Codes Entry Screen With Data

Key in each code and the meaning of the code. Shift-Tab will take you backward through the entries. If the entry block on the screen completely fills with codes, the region will scroll to permit more entries. Press the up or down arrows to scroll the entries. Press F3 to save. Print using the output selection, described later in this chapter.

CREATING RECORD LAYOUTS

The generate feature allows you to create program code for record structures in several programming languages. Select **Generate** and a screen design.

A Generate Record Layout screen will be displayed. Figure 8.8 is an illustration for the CUSTOMER MASTER. Enter a prefix if desired. The prefix (eg CM-) will precede all fields on the layout. Enter the language the code should be generated in. Valid languages are BASIC, C, COBOL and PL/1. For COBOL language, select whether you want the input or the output picture to be used to generate the program code. Press F3 when finished.

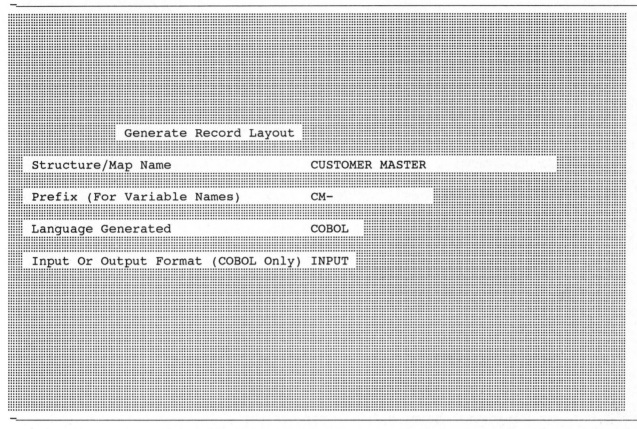

```
┌─────────────────────────────┐
│  Generate Record Layout     │
└─────────────────────────────┘

Structure/Map Name            CUSTOMER MASTER

Prefix (For Variable Names)   CM-

Language Generated            COBOL

Input Or Output Format (COBOL Only) INPUT
```

Figure 8.8 Generate Record Layout Entry Screen

Select a file, the screen, or the printer for the output destination. Figure 8.9 illustrates COBOL code generated for the Customer Master file.

Tip: If you have several related repeating fields on one record, define these as a single record (**Type** of **R**) and then define the structural record. An example is item number, item description and quantity purchased on an order record. When code is generated for the record, the table items will be treated as a group.

Figure 8.10 illustrates the point. Record descriptions and COBOL code illustrate Order Items that repeat on the Order Record. Figure 8.10, Part B and C show the repeating fields defined as a group on the order record. Individual fields are defined on the line item record. The fields on the line item record occur only once, since the repeat factor is on the <u>Order</u> record. This second method provides a better COBOL layout.

```
*Record CUSTOMER-MASTER Generated:  9-NOV-90
 01  CUSTOMER-MASTER.
     05  CM-BRANCH-NUMBER              PIC X.
     05  CM-CUSTOMER-NUMBER            PIC X(5).
     05  CM-CUSTOMER-NAME              PIC X(20).
     05  CM-CUSTOMER-ADDRESS.
         10  CM-STREET                 PIC X(20).
         10  CM-CITY                   PIC X(20).
         10  CM-STATE                  PIC XX.
         10  CM-ZIP                    PIC XXXXX.
         10  CM-ZIP-EXPANSION          PIC XXXX.
     05  CM-CUSTOMER-TELEPHONE         PIC 9(10).
     05  CM-SALESPERSON-NUMBER         PIC XXX.
     05  CM-ACCOUNT-STATUS-CODE        PIC X
                                       VALUE '0'.
     05  CM-DATE-OF-LAST-PURCHASE      PIC 9(6).
     05  CM-DATE-OF-LAST-PAYMENT       PIC 9(6).
     05  CM-FINANCIAL-INFORMATION.
         10  CM-CURRENT-BALANCE        PIC 9(6)V99
                                       COMP-3.
         10  CM-NET-PURCHASES-YTD      PIC 9(6)V99
                                       COMP-3.
         10  CM-MONTH-CHARGES          PIC 9(5)V99
                                       COMP-3.
         10  CM-MONTH-CREDITS          PIC 9(5)V99
                                       COMP-3.
         10  CM-CREDIT-LIMIT           PIC 9(5)V99
                                       COMP-3
                                       VALUE 1000.
```

Figure 8.9 Sample Of Generated Code - COBOL Language

```
Record                              ORDER RECORD

   Alternate Name CUSTOMER ORDER
   Definition     ONE RECORD PER CUSTOMER ORDER
   Normalized     N
                  Name of Element or Record    Occ  Seq  Type  Sec-Keys
                  CUSTOMER NUMBER               1    0    E
                  SALESPERSON NUMBER            1    0    E
                  ORDER DATE                    1    0    E
                  ORDER NUMBER                  1    0    E
                  QUANTITY ORDERED              10   0    E
                  QUANTITY SHIPPED              10   0    E
                  ITEM NUMBER                   10   0    E
                                                1    0    e
                                                1    0    e
                                                1    0    e
                                                1    0    e
                                                1    0    e
                                                1    0    e
                                                1    0    e
                                                                    PgDn
```

```
*Record ORDER-RECORD  Generated: 26-DEC-90
01   ORDER-RECORD.
     05   OR-CUSTOMER-NUMBER        PIC XXXXX.
     05   OR-SALESPERSON-NUMBER     PIC XXX.
     05   OR-ORDER-DATE             PIC X(6).
     05   OR-ORDER-NUMBER           PIC X(7).
     05   OR-QUANTITY-ORDERED       PIC 9(5)
                       COMP-3       OCCURS 10 TIMES.
     05   OR-QUANTITY-SHIPPED       PIC 9(5)
                                    OCCURS 10 TIMES.
     05   OR-ITEM-NUMBER            PIC 9(8)
                                    OCCURS 10 TIMES.
```

Figure 8.10   Part A
Single Repeating Fields and Resulting COBOL Language Code

```
Record                                    ORDER RECORD NEW

Alternate Name  CUSTOMER ORDER
Definition      ONE RECORD PER CUSTOMER ORDER
Normalized      N
                Name of Element or Record     Occ  Seq  Type  Sec-Keys
                CUSTOMER NUMBER                1    0    E
                SALESPERSON NUMBER             1    0    E
                ORDER DATE                     1    0    E
                ORDER NUMBER                   1    0    E
                ORDER ITEMS                    10   0    R
                                               1    0    e
                                               1    0    e
                                               1    0    e
                                               1    0    e
                                               1    0    e
                                               1    0    e
                                               1    0    e
                                               1    0    e
                                                                 PgDn
```

Figure 8.10 Part B
Group Repeating Fields and Resulting COBOL Language Code

PRINTING DATA DICTIONARY ENTRIES

To print data dictionary entries, select Output. When prompted for a Name Range, key in a name or press the enter key. When using a selector list, choose the data dictionary entry that you want to print. If you want to print all the entries, select the first entry on the list: **..All Entries on Selector List...**

When prompted for where the output should go, select Screen if you wish to view the output on the monitor. Note that if you have selected the all entries option, the screen will scroll rapidly. Press the pause key (PS2 models) or CTRL-S or CTRL-NumLock to suspend scrolling. Press any key to continue. Press any non-arrow key to return to the data dictionary menu when finished.

Select Print if you wish to receive printed output.

```
Record                                    ORDER ITEMS

  Alternate Name  ITEMS PLACED ON ORDER
  Definition      UP TO TEN ITEMS PER CUSTOMER ORDER
  Normalized      N
                    Name of Element or Record    Occ  Seq  Type  Sec-Keys
                    QUANTITY ORDERED              1    0    E
                    QUANTITY SHIPPED              1    0    E
                    ITEM NUMBER                   1    0    E
                                                  1    0    e
                                                  1    0    e
                                                  1    0    e
                                                  1    0    e
                                                  1    0    e
                                                  1    0    e
                                                  1    0    e
                                                  1    0    e
                                                  1    0    e
                                                  1    0    e
                                                                      PgDn
```

```
*Record ORDER-RECORD-NEW Generated: 26-DEC-90
01   ORDER-RECORD-NEW.
     05   OR-CUSTOMER-NUMBER        PIC XXXXX.
     05   OR-SALESPERSON-NUMBER     PIC XXX.
     05   OR-ORDER-DATE             PIC X(6).
     05   OR-ORDER-NUMBER           PIC X(7).
     05   OR-ORDER-ITEMS            OCCURS 10 TIMES.
          10   OR-QUANTITY-ORDERED  PIC 9(5)
                                    COMP-3.
          10   OR-QUANTITY-SHIPPED  PIC 9(5).
          10   OR-ITEM-NUMBER       PIC 9(8).
```

Figure 8.10   Part C
Group Repeating Fields and Resulting COBOL Language Code

Select File (the default) if you wish to route the print to a file. A default file name is displayed and should be overtyped. Write down the name of the file (it has an extension of PRN). The file can be printed after exiting Excelerator using the DOS PRINT utility. At the DOS prompt change to the project subdirectory and enter PRINT filename.PRN. You may change the default drive for a print by entering A:filename.PRN. This will place the print on drive A.

To print a summary list of data dictionary records, select Summary Output. When prompted for a Name Range, press the enter key for all entries. Enter a name or a partial name followed by an asterisk (*) for all names beginning with the characters. Press any non-arrow key to return to the data dictionary menu.

Sample output is illustrated in Figure 8.11, Record Output; Figure 8.12, Record Summary Output and Figure 8.13, Sample Element Output.

DELETING, COPYING, RENAMING, LISTING, AND INSPECTING

The data dictionary menu screen may be used to delete, make copies of or rename any data dictionary entry.

Select: XLDICTIONARY from the main menu.
REC/ELE (or DATA for Table Of Codes).
Record for data structures or Element for elementary fields.
The appropriate function from the menu action pad. (Copy, Rename, etc.).
Key in the names as prompted or press the enter key for a selector list.

Choosing **List** will provide an on-screen list of the data dictionary entries. Press enter when prompted for a **Name Range** to obtain a list of all entries. Press any key (keyboard or mouse) to return to the menu screen.

Inspect allows you to view at a data dictionary entry without changing it. Select Inspect. Press enter when prompted for a **Name Range** to get a selector list, then choose the entry you wish to view. You may obtain a more specific list to select from. When prompted for a Name Range, enter the starting letters of the data you wish to view followed by an asterisk (*). For example, enter **CUST***, and a list of all entries starting with CUST will appear. Select the one you wish to view. Press Cancel to return to the main menu.

There are many other features of the XLDICTIONARY that will be discussed later. When finished, perform backup and exit (refer to Chapter 2).

```
NAME:                   CUSTOMER MASTER          DEFINITION:
ALIAS:                                           MASTER FILE OF ALL CUSTOMERS              Y


ELEMENT/RECORD                      OFF  OCC  TYPE  LEN  DEFINITION
----------------------------------  ---  ---  ----  ---  ------------------------------------------------------------


BRANCH NUMBER                       000  001  E     001  BRANCH NUMBER FROM O THROUGH 9


CUSTOMER NUMBER                     001  001  K     005  CUSTOMER NUMBER - UNIQUE FOR EACH CUSTOMER


CUSTOMER NAME                       006  001  E     020  CUSTOMER NAME


CUSTOMER ADDRESS                    026  001  R          ADDRESS OF THE CUSTOMER                            Y
  STREET                            026  001  E     020  THE STREET ADDRESS OF THE CUSTOMER
  CITY                              046  001  E     020  CUSTOMER CITY
  STATE                             066  001  E     002  THE TWO CHARACTER STATE ABBREVIATION
  ZIP                               068  001  E     005  ZIP CODE FOR THE CUSTOMER
  ZIP EXPANSION                     073  001  E     004  OPTIONAL ZIP EXPANSION AREA


CUSTOMER TELEPHONE                  077  001  E     010  TELEPHONE NUMBER INCLUDING AREA CODE


SALESPERSON NUMBER                  087  001  7     003  SALESPERSON NUMBER - UNIQUE FOR EACH SALESPERSON


ACCOUNT STATUS CODE                 090  001  E     001  A ONE DIGIT CODE TO REFLECT THE CUSTOMER'S STATUS


DATE OF LAST PURCHASE               091  001  E     006  THE DATE OF THE CUSTOMER'S LAST PURCHASE


DATE OF LAST PAYMENT                097  001  E     006  THE DATE OF THE CUSTOMER'S LAST PAYMENT


FINANCIAL INFORMATION               103  001  R                                                            Y
  CURRENT BALANCE                   103  001  E     005  THE CUSTOMER'S CURRENT BALANCE
  NET PURCHASES YTD                 108  001  E     005  CUSTOMER NET PURCHASES YEAR TO DATE
  MONTH CHARGES                     113  001  E     004  THE CUSTOMER'S CHARGES FOR THE MONTH
  MONTH CREDITS                     117  001  E     004  THE AMOUNT CREDITED TO THE CUSTOMER ACCOUNT THIS MONTH
  CREDIT LIMIT                      121  001  E     004  CUSTOMER'S CREDIT LIMIT


Record length is 125.
```

Figure 8.11 Sample Record Output

```
DATE: 15-MAR-91                        RECORD - SUMMARY OUTPUT                              PAGE     1
TIME: 16:28                            NAME: *                                              Excelerator/IS


RECORD NAME                       ALTERNATE NAME                  DEFINITION
-----------------------------     -----------------------------   ------------------------------------------------
ADD ORDER                         NEW ORDER RECORD TRANSACTION
BILLING FILE                                                      A RECORD FOR EACH CUSTOMER WITH AN OUTSTANDING BALANCE
CREDIT TRANSACTION                RETURNED ITEM TRANSACTION       PAYMENT INFORMATION FOR A PARTICULAR INVOICE
CUSTOMER ADDRESS                                                  ADDRESS OF THE CUSTOMER
CUSTOMER MASTER                   CLIENT MASTER                   MASTER FILE OF ALL CUSTOMERS
FINANCIAL INFORMATION             CUSTOMER FINANCIAL DATA
INSTRUCTOR COURSES                COURSES TAUGHT
INVENTORY RECORD                  INVENTORY RECORD - CODE GENERATE %IR-%
INVOICE RECORD                    CUSTOMER ORDER SUMMARY          RECORD OF A PARTICULAR SALE MADE TO A CUSTOMER
LINE ITEM                         ITEMS ON THE ORDER RECORD
ORDER ITEM RECORD
ORDER ITEMS                       ITEMS PLACED ON ORDER           UP TO TEN ITEMS PER CUSTOMER ORDER
ORDER RECORD                      CUSTOMER ORDER                  ONE RECORD PER CUSTOMER ORDER
PAYMENT TRANSACTION               CUSTOMER PAYMENT                PAYMENT INFORMATION FOR A PARTICULAR INVOICE
PRINT FIELDS                      PRINT FIELDS - CODE GENERATION  A GROUP OF FIELDS FOR CONTROLLING REPORT PRINTING
REPORT TOTALS                     REPORT TOTALS - CODE GENERATION A GROUP OF REPORT TOTALS - INVENTORY REPORT
SALESPERSON                       SALES REPRESENTATIVE            A RECORD FOR EACH SALES REPRESENTATIVE
STUDENT COURSES                   STUDENT ENROLLMENT
STUDENT GRADES                    SEMESTER GRADES
SWITCHES                          PROGRAM SWITCHES - CODE GENERATE A LIST OF SWITCHES USED IN PROGRAMS
```

Figure 8.12 Sample Record Summary Output

```
DATE:   9-NOV-90              ELEMENT - OUTPUT          PAGE      1
TIME: 21:33                     NAME: STATE             Excelerator/IS
TYPE Element            NAME STATE


Alternate Names CUSTOMER-STATE


Definition       THE TWO CHARACTER STATE ABBREVIATION FOR THE CUSTOMER


Input Format     XX
Output Format    XX
Edit Rules       FROM "STATE TABLE"
Storage Type     C
Characters left of decimal 2  Characters right of decimal 0
Default
Prompt           STATE
Column Header    STATE
Short Header
Base or Derived B
Data Class
Source           NEW CUSTOMER FORM


     Satisfies Requirement:              Associated Entities:
Type  Name                        Type  Name



                     Description



Modified By   ALLEN   Date Modified   891109   # Changes 2
Added By      ALLEN   Date Added      880719   Last Project CUSTOMER
Locked By             Date Locked     0        Lock Status
```

Figure 8.13 Sample Element Output Part 1

```
DATE:  9-NOV-90              ELEMENT - OUTPUT                PAGE     2
TIME: 21:34                   NAME: CUST*                    Excelerator/IS
TYPE Element         NAME CUSTOMER NUMBER


Alternate Names CUSTOMER-NUMBER


Definition         CUSTOMER NUMBER - UNIQUE FOR EACH CUSTOMER


Input Format    X(5)
Output Format   X(5)
Edit Rules      VALUES ARE "00019" THRU "99998"
Storage Type    C
Characters left of decimal 5  Characters right of decimal 0
Default
Prompt          CUSTOMER NUMBER
Column Header   CUSTOMER NUMBER
Short Header
Base or Derived B
Data Class
Source          NEW CUSTOMER FORM


    Satisfies Requirement:              Associated Entities:
Type  Name                          Type  Name
URQ PROVIDE A UNIQUE CUSTOMER NUMBER   TST ADD CUSTOMER


                        Description
THE CUSTOMER NUMBER SHOULD BE UNIQUE.  THE ADD CUSTOMER PROGRAM SHOULD ASSIGN THE
CUSTOMER NUMBERS SEQUENTIALLY.

THE CUSTOMER NUMBER IS THE PRIMARY KEY FOR THE CUSTOMER MASTER.


Modified By     ALLEN  Date Modified  891109  # Changes  2
Added By        ALLEN  Date Added     880719  Last Project CUSTOMER
Locked By              Date Locked    0       Lock Status
```

Figure 8.13 Sample Element Output Part 2

```
DATE:  9-NOV-89   ELEMENT - OUTPUT        PAGE      3
TIME: 21:34       NAME: CUST*             Excelerator/IS

TYPE Element      NAME CUSTOMER TELEPHONE

Alternate Names CUSTOMER-TELEPHONE

Definition      TELEPHONE NUMBER INCLUDING AREA CODE

Input Format    9(10)
Output Format   (999)B999-9999
Edit Rules      > 0
Storage Type    C
Characters left of decimal 10 Characters right of decimal 0
Default
Prompt          CUSTOMER TELEPHONE
Column Header   CUSTOMER TELEPHONE
Short Header
Base or Derived B
Data Class
Source          NEW CUSTOMER FORM

    Satisfies Requirement:                Associated Entities:
Type  Name                            Type  Name


                            Description


Modified By  ALLEN  Date Modified  891109  # Changes  2
Added By     ALLEN  Date Added     880630  Last Project DFD Locked By          Date
Locked    0        Lock Status
```

Figure 8.13 Sample Element Output Part 3

EXERCISES

1.   Create a data dictionary record entry for the Employee Master record. The entries are summarized below.

Field Name	Rec/Ele	Stor	Len	Dec	Occ
Number	E	C	5		1
Name	R	C	30		1
Date Hired	E	C	6		1
Social Security No	E	C	9		1
Department Code	E	C	2		1
Job Class. Code	E	C	2		1
Rate Of Pay	E	P	5	2	1
Num. Of Dependents	E	C	2		1
Vacation Hrs.	E	P	3	0	1
Sick Leave Accum.	E	P	3	0	1
Current Gross Pay	E	P	7	2	1
YTD Gross Pay	E	P	9	2	1
YTD Federal Ded	E	P	9	2	1
YTD State Deduct.	E	P	9	2	1
YTD FICA Deduct.	E	P	9	2	1

Key: **Rec/Ele** R is for record, E for Element.
         Stor represents storage, C for character, P for packed decimal.
         Len is for the length of the field or the whole number for packed data.
         Dec represents the number of decimal digits, used in the packed format.
         Occ for occurrences, lists how many times the field repeats.

2.   Create a data dictionary entry for the Order Record. Entries are:

Field Name	Rec/Ele	Stor	Len	Dec	Occ
Customer Number	E	C	7		1
Salesperson Number	E	C	5		1
Order Number	E	C	5		1
Order Date	E	C	6		1
Number Of Items	E	P	3	0	1
Items	R	C	10		15
Order Total Amount	E	P	7	2	1

3.   Create a data dictionary entry for the Student Master record. Entries are:

Field Name	Rec/Ele	Stor	Len	Dec	Occ
Student Number	E	C	9		1
Last Name	E	C	17		1
First Name	E	C	12		1
Middle Initial	E	C	1		1
Address	R	C	71		1
Grade Point Ave.	E	P	3	2	1
Credits Earned	E	P	3	0	1
Major Program Code	E	C	3		1
Courses Completed	R	C	14		50

4.   Create the data dictionary entry for the Student Address. Entries are:

Field Name	Rec/Ele	Stor	Len	Dec	Occ
Street	E	C	20		1
Apartment	E	C	20		1
City	E	C	20		1
State	E	C	2		1
Zip	E	C	9		1

5.   Create the data dictionary entry for the order items.

Field Name	Rec/Ele	Stor	Len	Dec	Occ
Item Number	E	C	6		1
Item Quantity	E	P	4	0	1

6.   Create a data dictionary for the Student Courses Completed. The entries are:

Field Name	Rec/Ele	Stor	Len	Dec	Occ
Course Number	E	C	6		1
Section Number	E	C	3		1
Term Completed	E	C	3		1
Grade Received	E	C	2		1

7. Create data dictionary elements for the Employee Master file. Create reasonable edit criteria and help messages. The following fields should have the **Source** entry of <u>New Employee Form</u>: Number, Name, Date Hired, Social Security No., Department Code, Job Class. Code, Rate Of Pay, Num. Of Dependents, and Vacation Hrs. The Sick Leave Accumulated, Current Gross Pay and YTD fields are derived. The other fields are base.

8. Create data dictionary elements for the Order Record. Create reasonable edit criteria and help messages (definitions).

9. Create data dictionary elements for the Student Master file. Include reasonable edit criteria and help messages. The Grade Point Average, Credits Earned and Courses Completed are derived. The rest of the fields are base fields, found on the <u>Student Registration Form</u>.

10. Create a table of codes for the Employee Departments. The values for the codes are:

    02 Personal
    04 Marketing
    06 Sales
    08 Accounting
    10 Manufacturing
    12 Shipping
    14 Data Processing
    16 Order Processing
    18 Customer Service
    20 Advertising

11. Create a table of codes for the Major Program Codes used in your school. Use a school catalog for numbers and departments.

12. Generate a COBOL record layout for the Employee Master File.

13. Generate a COBOL record layout for the Order Record.

14. Generate a COBOL record layout for the Student Master File.

9
DATA MODELING

ENTITY-RELATIONSHIP AND DATA MODEL DIAGRAMS

Chapter Goals:

> Learn how to use Excelerator for data modeling.
> Understand the basic differences between the Entity-Relationship and Data Model Diagrams.
> Learn how to create Entity-Relationship diagrams.
> Learn how to describe Data Entities.
> Know how to describe Data N-Ary Relationships.
> Learn how to create a Data Model Diagram.
> Know how to describe the Data Relationship.
> Understand how to use analysis options to validate the Entity-Relationship Diagram and the Data Model Diagram.

Data modeling is a very important part of building the system model. The data flow diagram and the structure chart are *process oriented*, and reflect the processes that transform input data to output information. Data modeling is the other side of the picture. It shows how data records and structures are linked to other records. In interactive systems and creating data base structures, data modeling shows how to find related records from a given record. For example, given an order, find the Customer record, the Salesperson record for the sales representative who serviced the order, and the Item record for all items sold.

The Entity-Relationship diagram is used when a relationship may involve more than two entities. This diagram may be used to model a system using a series of Indexed files or a data base structure.

The Data Model Diagram shows only *binary* relationships, between only two data entities or record structures. This is usually used to model data base design. Excelerator provides normalization analysis for this model only.

CREATING ENTITY-RELATIONSHIP DIAGRAMS

From the main menu, select **GRAPHICS**, then Entity-relationship diagram. Select ADD or MODIFY (if the entity-relationship diagram already exists). Type in the name of your chart. If you are modifying a diagram, press the enter key for the name and Excelerator will give you a list of charts previously drawn. Select one or press the right button (or the ESC key) to cancel.

Select the following options:
Use the PROFILE settings described in Chapter 1 with the following changes:

LABEL MD.
LAB ONLY. (Press the right mouse button to save your selection.
NO ARROW.
STRAIGHT or PIPE.
Press the right button to save the settings.

A sample Entity-Relationship diagram is shown in Figure 9.1

Select OBJECT. The submenu at the bottom of the selection area shows two objects. Select ENTITY, a rectangle, then the location on the drawing screen. Repeat for all entities. Select RELATION, the diamond shape, and the location on the drawing area. Repeat for all Relations.

CONNECTING OBJECTS

To connect the objects with lines, select CONNECT. Touch the first object to be connected. Then move the mouse so the cursor arrow moves to the object to be connected <u>to</u>. Press the left button. Repeat for all objects. If the final line is not where you want it, move or delete the line (refer to Chapter 5).

LABELING ENTITIES AND RELATIONS

Select LABEL to place text into the entity or relation. Select the object to be labeled and enter text in the pop-up window. Press the tab key to move to the second line of the label. Use the insert key to center the text. When finished, press enter. Repeat for all entities and relations.

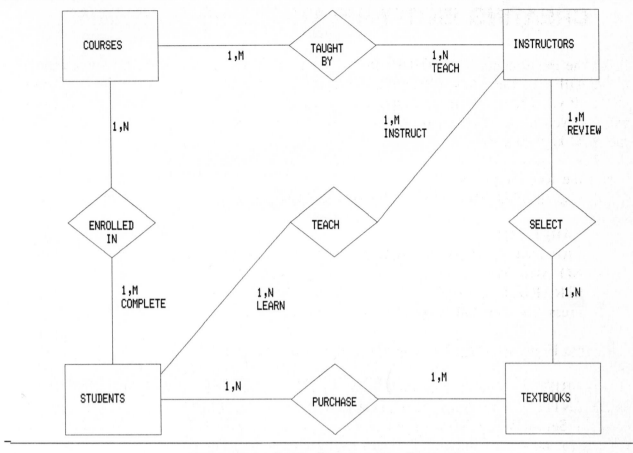

Figure 9.1   Entity-Relationship Example

DESCRIBING DATA ENTITIES

A <u>Data</u> Entity is a high level portrayal of an entity, a person, company, item, etc. that your system is storing information on. They may be described in the XLDictionary. Data entities should not be confused with external entities on a data flow diagram. External entities supply or receive information to or from the system, but a file may not be stored on them. An example would be a bank receiving a deposit. A file is not kept for banks.

Select DESCRIBE, then select the corresponding data entity (rectangle). The label is presented as a default ID. Press enter to accept it, or overtype it with the entity name (eg. Customer). If the ID field is blank, you may press the enter key for a selector list and choose a data entity.

The Data Entity description screen is displayed, illustrated in Figure 9.2. Enter the Label text, if it has not been created.

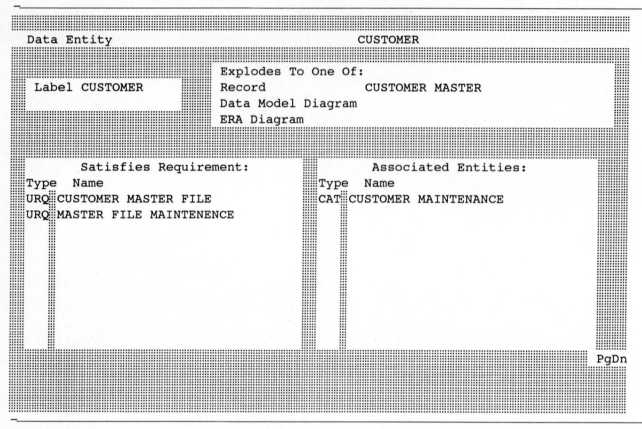

```
┌────────────────────────────────────────────────────────────────────┐
│ Data Entity                              CUSTOMER                    │
│  ┌──────────────────────┐    Explodes To One Of:                     │
│  │                      │    Record              CUSTOMER MASTER     │
│  │  Label CUSTOMER      │    Data Model Diagram                      │
│  │                      │    ERA Diagram                             │
│  └──────────────────────┘                                           │
│                                                                      │
│  ┌──── Satisfies Requirement: ────┐  ┌──── Associated Entities: ───┐ │
│  │ Type  Name                     │  │ Type  Name                  │ │
│  │ URQ CUSTOMER MASTER FILE       │  │ CAT CUSTOMER MAINTENANCE     │ │
│  │ URQ MASTER FILE MAINTENENCE    │  │                             │ │
│  │                                │  │                             │ │
│  │                                │  │                             │ │
│  │                                │  │                             │ │
│  │                                │  │                             │ │
│  │                                │  │                             │ │
│  │                                │  │                             │ │
│  └────────────────────────────────┘  └─────────────────────────────┘ │
│                                                                 PgDn │
└────────────────────────────────────────────────────────────────────┘
```

Figure 9.2   Data Entity Description Screen

Under the **Explodes to one of:** area, enter a record name. It is suggested that you press F4 to obtain a selector list of records already created and choose one. This provides consistency between the records and the data entities. Alternatively, you could enter a data model Diagram or an entity-relationship diagram (ERA). Normally the data entity would explode to records but, for higher level data, it may explode to further diagrams.

Enter any requirements and associated entities. Refer to Chapter 3 for details. Press PgDn for a more detailed description, which might include any special definitions or peculiarities of this data entity. Press F3 to save and return to the drawing screen. Repeat the process for all entities.

DESCRIBE THE RELATIONSHIPS

The relationships on an entity-relationship diagram are called **Data N-Ary** (pronounced data en-ary) relationships since they may link more than two data entities.

Select DESCRIBE, then the data N-ary relationship, a diamond. Enter an ID. If a label has been created, it is presented as a default ID. The Data N-Ary relationship description screen is displayed, illustrated in Figure 9.3.

Fill in an alternate name, if appropriate, and a label. If this data N-ary relationship explodes to a record, enter the record name or press F4 for a selector list. An example of a record would be student grades, linking students and courses. The courses could be shown either as a table on the Student Master or as a separate record, when data is normalized (no tables allowed).

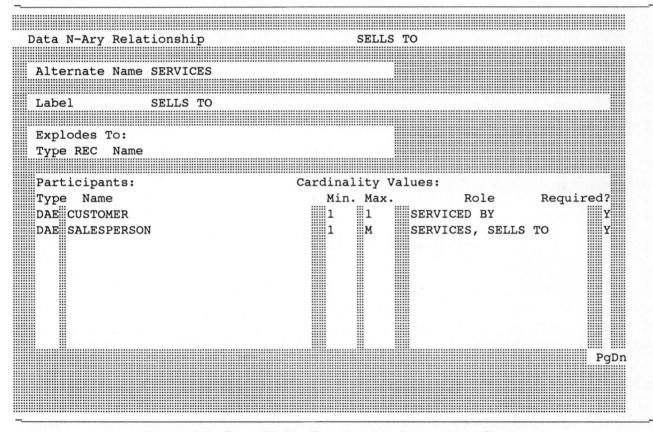

Figure 9.3 Data N-Ary Relationship Description Screen

The **Participants:** area is used to capture information on the type of relationship or *cardinality*. This is either 1 to 1 (each course registered receives one grade), 1 to many (one sales representative services many customers), or many to many (each order contains many items, each item is sold on many orders).

Enter the type of entity - either DAE for data entity, or DNR for data N-ary relationship. Type in a name of the data entity or data N-ary relationship or press F4 for a selector list. Fill in the cardinality values. Use **M** or **N** for many. The **Role** field shows how the entity is involved in the relationship. It may be left blank. Lastly, enter a Y or N for whether the entity is required in the relationship. An example of <u>not</u> required would be a text used for a course, since some courses may not have texts.

An important feature of the Excelerator Entity-Relationship diagram analysis options is that the cardinality and role can be automatically filled for you on these screens. The information is derived from the connection label. To automatically include these values, place a Y in the required field and leave the cardinality and role fields blank. The connection line label must have the two cardinality values (minimum and maximum) separated by a comma, colon or other non-alphabetic character. If a role is on the line, it will also be copied.

Press PgDn for a second screen. Enter any requirements and associated entities. Pressing PgDn again provides a description area to enter any comments or text on the relationship. Press F3 to save and return to the drawing screen. Repeat for all relationships.

You may explode the entities into record descriptions if desired. See Chapter 8 and repeat the process that was described for exploding data stores or data flow.

LABELING CONNECTIONS

The connections cannot be described in the XLDICTIONARY but they may be labelled to show cardinality: the one-to-one, one-to-many or many-to-many relationships between entities. If this label is correctly created, the label information may be used to create the relationship information in the XLDictionary, as described above.

Select LABEL, then a connection (the small box or *handle* on the line). Choose the upper left hand corner of the area where you want the label to appear (press left button). Touch the lower right hand corner of the same area. Enter the label text in the window that has appeared on the screen. If the window is not large enough, cancel (press right button or the Esc key) and re-do the process.

Key in the cardinality, separated by a colon or comma. Press the tab key and enter the role, that is, how the entity participates in the relationship; what it does. The role may be left blank. Repeat for all connections.

Additional text entities, relationships, or connections may be added using the text command. Select TEXT, then SMALL. Position the arrow where the text should start and press the left mouse button. Key in the text and press the enter key. To underline key fields, select LINE, then SOLID. Choose an area on the screen (under the text) to start the line, then the ending location. Select any menu option to exit the line drawing process.

DESCRIBING THE ENTITY-RELATIONSHIP DIAGRAM

To describe the Entity-Relationship diagram in the XLDictionary select DESCRIBE and the name of the Entity-Relationship diagram found directly above the orientation map. An example is shown in Figure 9.4.

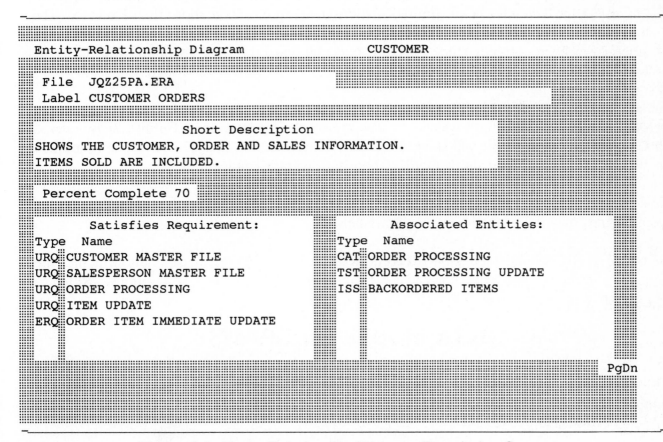

```
Entity-Relationship Diagram              CUSTOMER

   File  JQZ25PA.ERA
   Label CUSTOMER ORDERS

                   Short Description
 SHOWS THE CUSTOMER, ORDER AND SALES INFORMATION.
 ITEMS SOLD ARE INCLUDED.


  Percent Complete 70

        Satisfies Requirement:              Associated Entities:
 Type   Name                          Type   Name
 URQ CUSTOMER MASTER FILE             CAT ORDER PROCESSING
 URQ SALESPERSON MASTER FILE          TST ORDER PROCESSING UPDATE
 URQ ORDER PROCESSING                 ISS BACKORDERED ITEMS
 URQ ITEM UPDATE
 ERQ ORDER ITEM IMMEDIATE UPDATE

                                                                PgDn
```

Figure 9.4 Entity-Relationship Diagram Description Screen

On the description screen, enter the diagram label and a short description. Fill in the percent complete, the requirements it satisfies and any Associated Entities. Press PgDn to enter a longer description. When finished, press F3 to save and return.

When the diagram is completed, zoom to close up to review how the graph will print and make any necessary changes. Check your print setup and print when ready. Save your work, backup and exit (see Chapter 2).

ENTITY-RELATIONSHIP DIAGRAM GRAPH ANALYSIS

There are several analysis options available for the Entity-Relationship diagram. One will be covered here and the others will be presented at the end of the chapter, along with the Data Model Diagram graph analysis.

Select **ANALYSIS** from the main menu, then **Extended Analysis**. From the Extended Analysis menu, select the seventh option, **Entity-Relationship Diagram Validation**, then Execute. The output information is generated and may be displayed in either a Matrix or Report format. If labels have been correctly made on the connecting lines, this analysis option will fill in the relationship description with cardinality information, as previously described.

Select **Reports** and then **Modified Data N-Ary Relationships**. Select a destination: a file, the screen, printer, or Entity List, which will save the results for later use. Entity List is covered in Chapter 14. This report will show the Data N-Ary Relationships that have been modified in the XLDictionary using the Entity-Relationship diagram connections.

Selecting **ERA/DNR Exceptions** will show all Cardinality contradictions between Data N-Ary relationships and those on the connection labels.

Select **MATRICES** and then **DNR/Record Relationships**. Choose a destination: a file, the screen, or printer. This grid shows which Data Entities have record descriptions. Refer to Figure 9.5 for an Example.

DATA MODEL DIAGRAMS

The data model diagram is used to show binary relationships, that is, the relationship between only two Data Entities. Thus there is no actual symbol for the relationship - it is shown using the connection line.

```
                            ----------------
                            |R  |R  |R  |R  |
                            |E  |E  |E  |E  |
                            |C  |C  |C  |C  |
                            |   |   |   |   |
                            |OR |S  |S  |IC |
                            |RE |T  |T  |NO |
                            |DC |U  |U  |SU |
                            |EO |D  |D  |TR |
                            |RR |E  |E  |RS |
                            | D |N  |N  |UE |
                            |I  |T  |T  |CS |
                            |T  |   |   |T  |
                            |E  |G  |C  |O  |
                            |M  |R  |O  |R  |
                            |   |A  |U  |   |
                            |   |D  |R  |   |
                            |   |E  |S  |   |
                            |   |S  |E  |   |
                            |   |   |S  |   |
                            ----------------
----------------------------   ----------------
|DNR CONTAIN                |   | E |   |   |   |
|---------------------------|   |---+---+---+---|
|DNR GRADED                 |   |   | E |   |   |
|---------------------------|   |---+---+---+---|
|DNR TAKES                  |   |   |   | E |   |
|---------------------------|   |---+---+---+---|
|DNR TEACHES                |   |   |   |   | E |
----------------------------   ----------------
```

Figure 9.5   Example DNR/Record Relationships Matrix

CREATING THE DATA MODEL DIAGRAM

Select **GRAPHICS** from the main menu, then Data Model Diagram. Select Add or Modify.
Enter the name of the diagram. If you are modifying a diagram, press enter for a name
and Excelerator will give you a list of Data Model Diagrams previously drawn. Choose one
or press the right button (or the Esc key) to cancel.

Select PROFILE. Use the settings described in Chapter 1 with the following changes:
Leave the GRID set to medium.
Select LABEL MD, then Select COMPLETE and LAB ONLY. Press the right mouse button to save your selection.
Select USRLABEL.
Select STRAIGHT.

Select NO ARROW if a *trident* symbol is being used to connect to the ovals. Alternatively, select TWO WAY if arrowheads are being used as the connection symbol. Normally you would use only one type of connection symbol but, in the example shown in Figure 9.6, both types of connection symbols have been used for the purpose of explanation.

Press the right button to save the settings.

Select OBJECT. There is only one object type, the oval, representing a data entity. Choose locations to place the data entities. Select CONNECT and the first object to be connected followed by the second. Repeat for all connections.

To place the trident or double headed arrows, indicating a *many* connection, select **SYMBOL**. Then choose either ARROW or TRIDENT. Select the connection, the small box on the line, and then the end which will receive the symbol. Repeat for all connections, as necessary.

LABELING DATA ENTITIES
AND RELATIONSHIPS

Select LABEL, then the oval representing the data entity. Enter the text in the pop-up window. Use the insert key and spaces to center the text in the window. Use the Tab key to move to a new line. Press enter when completed. Repeat for all data entities.

Select the relationship, the connecting line. Choose the upper left and lower right corners. Key the relationship in the pop-up window. Repeat for all relationships.

DESCRIBING THE DATA ENTITIES

Select DESCRIBE, then a data entity. The label is presented as a default ID. Press enter to accept or overtype. Press the enter key with a blank ID for a selector list. Describe the data entity as presented under the entity-relationship diagram section.

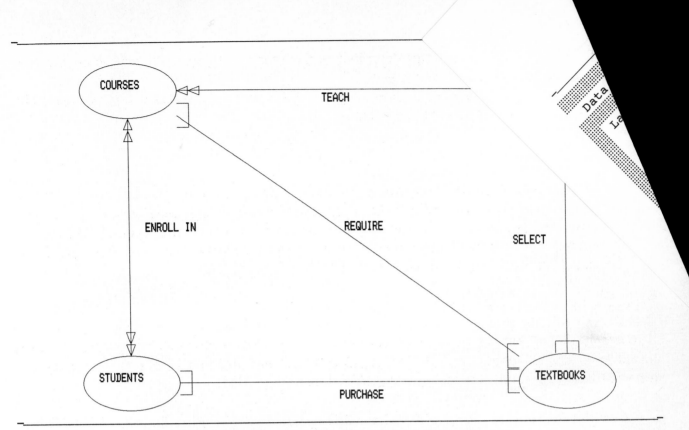

Figure 9.6 Sample Data Model Diagram

DESCRIBING RELATIONSHIPS

Select DESCRIBE and the data relationship, the connection between data entities. The label is presented as an ID. Press enter to accept or overtype if desired. The Data Relationship description screen is displayed, illustrated in Figure 9.7.

Enter a label, if not previously created. Excelerator will automatically create the entity name entries from the Analysis feature, if desired. This ensures consistency with data from the graph components. Alternatively, you may use the following procedure to create the relationship description: Enter the name of the first entity. The best strategy is to press F4 for a selector list and choose one. This provides correct naming and project consistency. Enter the cardinality, how many of the second entity exist. Use a number or **M** for many. Key in a Y/N response to the prompt **Must the SECOND Entity exist for this Entity to exist?**. Repeat these steps for the second entity.

Press PgDn and enter any requirements or associated entities. Pressing PgDn again will provide an area to enter a description of the relationship. Press F3 to save and return to the drawing screen. Repeat for all relationships.

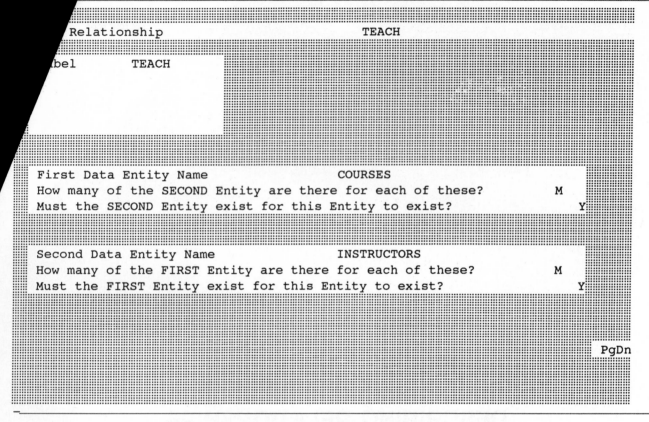

Figure 9.7 Data Relationship Description Screen

DESCRIBING THE DATA MODEL DIAGRAM

To describe the Data Model Diagram in the XLDictionary select DESCRIBE and the name of the Data Model Diagram found directly above the orientation map. Refer to Figure 9.8.

On the description screen, enter a label to be placed on the diagram and a short description. Fill in the percent complete, the requirements it satisfies and any Associated Entities. Press PgDn to enter a longer description. When finished, press F3 to save and return.

When the diagram is complete, zoom to close up to review how the graph will print and make any changes that are necessary. Check your print setup and print when ready. Save your work, backup and exit (see Chapter 2).

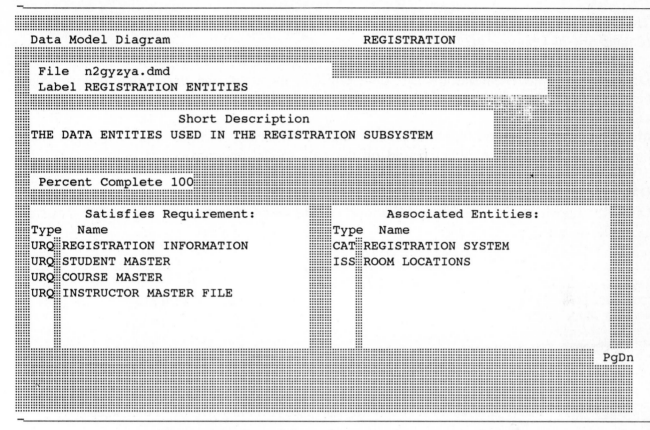

```
Data Model Diagram                          REGISTRATION

 File   n2gyzya.dmd
 Label REGISTRATION ENTITIES

                    Short Description
 THE DATA ENTITIES USED IN THE REGISTRATION SUBSYSTEM


 Percent Complete 100

        Satisfies Requirement:              Associated Entities:
 Type   Name                          Type   Name
 URQ  REGISTRATION INFORMATION        CAT  REGISTRATION SYSTEM
 URQ  STUDENT MASTER                  ISS  ROOM LOCATIONS
 URQ  COURSE MASTER
 URQ  INSTRUCTOR MASTER FILE

                                                                    PgDn
```

Figure 9.8 Data Model Diagram Description Screen

DATA MODEL DIAGRAM ANALYSIS

Data Model Diagram analysis checks for errors and inconsistencies in the data model diagram and the data relationships. The connections on the data model diagram are analyzed against those described for the corresponding data relationships. If the data relationship description does not have the names of the data entities and the cardinality, the analysis feature will complete these entries and update the XLDictionary.   Select **ANALYSIS** and **Extended Analysis.** Then choose **Data Model Validation Analysis.**

There are four report options available:

Undescribed Data Relationships
Modified Data Relationships
DMD/DAR Exceptions
ALL REPORTS

The reports may be sent to a file, displayed on the screen, printed or saved in an entity list (details are in Chapter 14).

Undescribed Data Relationships lists data entity connections, the data relationships, which have not been described in the XLDictionary.

Modified Data Relationships shows the data relationship entities whose XLDictionary descriptions have been modified based on the data model diagram connections.

DMD/DAR Exceptions shows cardinality inconsistencies between the graph connections of Data Relationships and the cardinality shown on the description screen. Figure 9.9 shows an example of this report.

```
 ───────────────────────────────────────────────────────────────────── ─
 DATE: 18-JAN-90          DMD/DAR EXCEPTIONS              PAGE     1
 TIME: 00:11                                          Excelerator/IS
 PROJECT NAME: DFD

 DESCRIPTION:    This report identifies naming and cardinality inconsistencies between
                 Data Relationships as drawn on a Data Model Diagram and described in
                 the XLDictionary. For each Data Relationship, the report shows the
                 Data Entity names and quantities as drawn on the graph (left-hand
                 side) and as described in the XLDictionary (right-hand side).

 DMD:REGISTRATION
 DAR:ENROLL IN
    GRAPH VIEW                          |XLD VIEW
 --------------------------------+-----------------------------------
 |FM:COURSES                     |M|FM:COURSES                    |1|
 |TO:STUDENTS                    |M|TO:STUDENTS                   |M|
 ¦                               ¦                                 ¦
 --------------------------------------------------------------------
 ───────────────────────────────────────────────────────────────────── ─
```

Figure 9.9   DMD/DAR Exception Report Example

There is one matrix available for printing or viewing. Select MATRICES and **Data Relationships**, showing how each data entity is related, either one or many. Refer to the example in Figure 9.10.

The Data Model Diagram is also used to verify that the data records are normalized. This information is presented in Chapter 12, Project Analysis.

```
                        Jan18 90 00:13:59  A-1


                          --------------------
                         |D  |D  |D  |D  |
                         |A  |A  |A  |A  |
                         |E  |E  |E  |E  |
                         |   |   |   |   |
                         |C  |I  |S  |T  |
                         |O  |N  |T  |E  |
                         |U  |S  |U  |X  |
                         |R  |T  |D  |T  |
                         |S  |R  |E  |B  |
                         |E  |U  |N  |O  |
                         |S  |C  |T  |O  |
                         |   |T  |S  |K  |
                         |   |O  |   |S  |
                         |   |R  |   |   |
                         |   |S  |   |   |
                          --------------------

 ------------------------       --------------------
|DAE COURSES             |     |   | M | M | M |
|------------------------|     |---+---+---+---|
|DAE INSTRUCTORS         |     | M |   |   | M |
|------------------------|     |---+---+---+---|
|DAE STUDENTS            |     | M |   |   | M |
|------------------------|     |---+---+---+---|
|DAE TEXTBOOKS           |     | M | M | M |   |
 ------------------------       --------------------
```

Figure 9.10 Data Relationships Matrix Example

ENTITY-RELATIONSHIP AND
DATA MODEL DIAGRAM ANALYSIS

Both data model graphs have some common analysis options. Select ANALYSIS, **Graph Verification** and **Undescribed Graph Entities**. This report shows the entities, either Data Entities or relationships, which are found on a diagram but are not described in the XLDictionary.

Select the graph to be verified, either Entity-Relationship Diagram or Data Model Diagram. Press the enter key when prompted for a name and choose one from the list. Select a destination for the report: a file, the screen or printer.

Another analysis option is the Graph Summary Report. This shows all explosion entities for a chosen graph. Select **Graph Summary Reports**, then **Graph Explosion**. Select either Entity-Relationship Diagram or Data Model Diagram. Press the enter key when prompted for a name and select one from the list. Again select a destination for the report: a file, the screen or printer. Key in the Explosion depth, the number of levels (parent, child, etc.) to report on.

EXERCISES

1.   Create the Entity Relationship diagram shown in Figure 9.1.

2.   Create an Entity Relationship diagram for the Student System.

        Students take classes.
        Instructors teach students.
        Instructors develop courses.
        Instructors advise students
        Instructors teach classes.

3.   Create the Data Model Diagram shown in Figure 9.6.

4.   Create the corresponding Data Model Diagram for the Entity-Relationship Diagram shown in Figure 9.1.

5.   Create an Entity-Relationship Diagram for the Data Processing Analyst Project System.

        Analysts work in departments. Each department may have several analysts.

        Analysts work on projects. One analyst may work on several projects and one project may have many analysts working on it.

        Each project may have several users. Each user may be involved in several projects.

        An analyst may or may not be a user contact person. One analyst may be the contact for several users and one user may have several analysts they are in contact with.

6.   Create the Data Model Diagram for the Data Processing Analyst Project System explained in Exercise 5.

7.   Create a Data Model Diagram for the Manufacturing system. Vendors supply parts to be used in manufacturing products. Each vendor may supply many different parts and each part may be purchased from several vendors. The manufactured products are made from several parts and each part may be included in several products. Finished products are stored in a number of regional warehouses. Each warehouse may hold many products. Create Data Relationship and Data Entity descriptions for all graph components.

---

8.   Create an Entity-Relationship diagram for the situation described in Exercise 7.

9.   For any diagram that you have created, explode the data entities to records. Describe the record structures with the fields you feel would be on the records. If you are on a team, brainstorm with team members.

10.   Execute the Undescribed Graph Entities for either an Entity-Relationship diagram or a Data Model Diagram that you have created.

11.   Run the Entity-Relationship Diagram Validation from the Extended Analysis feature. Select Reports, then All Reports. Produce the only matrix. What information are the reports and matrix presenting to you?

12.   Produce the Data Model Diagram Validation from the Extended Analysis feature. Select Reports, then All Reports. Produce the only matrix. What information are the reports and matrix presenting to you?

13.   Run the Graph Explosion report. Select either an Entity-Relationship Diagram or Data Model Diagram that you have created.

14.   Describe the graphs you have created. Enter some as 100 percent complete and some as less than 100 percent. These will be used for reporting in a later chapter.

10
CONTROL MODELING WITH THE STATE TRANSITION DIAGRAM

Chapter goals:

> Learn how to create State transition diagrams.
> Understand <u>states</u> and how to describe them.
> Understand and describe transition vectors.
> Know how to validate the state transition diagram for completeness and
> accuracy.

The State Transition Diagram provides a model of control activities within a system or a program. The logic is depicted by a series of rectangles representing states of the system. Arrows represent transitions between two states. These are labeled with conditions that initiate and actions that accompany the transition. State Transition Diagrams may be created from the Graphics menu or from exploding a Control Transform found on a data flow diagram.

CREATING STATE TRANSITION DIAGRAMS

From the main menu select **GRAPHICS** and then **State Transition Diagram.** Choose Add to create or Modify to change. Enter a meaningful name for the diagram.

Alternatively, select a Control Transform on a data flow diagram. Select Describe and enter **TRD** for the **Type** in the **Explodes To:** area. Enter the name of the diagram and press F3 to save and return to the drawing screen. Select Explode and the Control Transform. Refer to Figure 10.1 for a sample state transition diagram showing the control of an on-line customer change process.

Set the following profile options: LABEL MD - COMPLETE, LAB ONLY, press Esc or the right mouse button. Select SYSTPORT for the straight line connections between states. Select PIPE, and be sure to select USRLABEL so that all the text will fit for connection labels. Press Esc or the right mouse button.

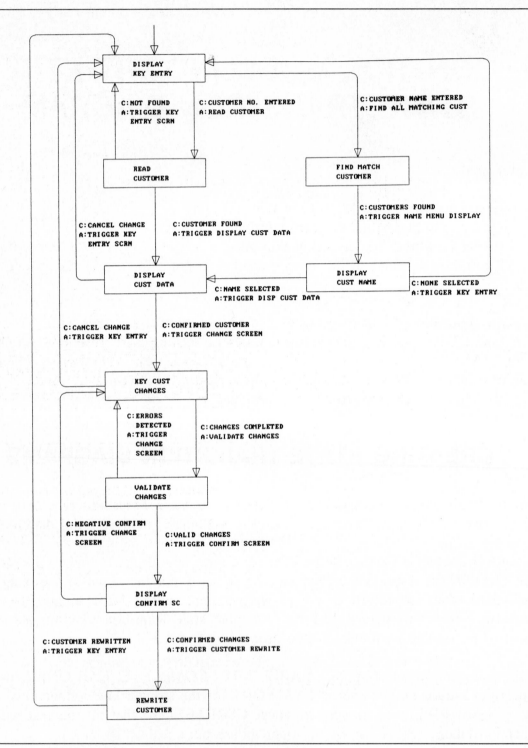

Figure 10.1 Customer Change State Transition Diagram

Select OBJECT and, since the only object is the state, select the areas on the screen for states to be placed. When all the states are placed on the diagram, select INTERFACE and INPUT. Create the initial transition vector to the first state by selecting the point above (or to the left) of the initial state and then select the state to be connected with.

CONNECTING STATES

Then select the PROFILE option and change to USERPORT. This gives better control of where the connecting lines are drawn. Select CONNECT. Choose the first state (the start of the transition arrow) and then the second. Repeat for all straight line connections. Select CONNECT and create all bending connections. If two states have arrows both up and down between them, a good idea is to place the arrows at the ends of the rectangles.

LABELING STATES AND THE CONNECTIONS

To enter text in the states, use LABEL first and later describe in the XLDictionary. This lets you create neatly aligned text. Select LABEL, then the state. Key in the text and press enter. Remember to use the tab key to move to the second line of the label. The default State label only allows two short lines to be placed within the rectangle. If more text is necessary, use the scale feature to increase the length, or the height, of the state rectangles.

Label the connections by selecting LABEL and the connection handle. Define the label area by selecting an upper right and lower left corner. Be sure to give yourself a long enough label to include the condition and the action being described. A condition corresponds to an input control flow on the data flow diagram and is stored as a signal in the XLDictionary. An action is an output flow on the data flow diagram and is a trigger or other type of prompt. Key in the text, placing conditions first and actions last. Press the enter key when completed. If the label line is not long enough, select the label text area and then reselect the corners. The text will remain with the re-sized label.

DESCRIBING THE
STATE TRANSITION DIAGRAM

To describe the State Transition Diagram in the XLDictionary select DESCRIBE and the name of the state transition diagram found above the orientation map.

On the description screen, enter a label to be placed on the diagram and a short description. Fill in the percent complete, the requirements satisfied and any Associated Entities. Press PgDn to enter a longer description. When finished, press F3 to save and return. Refer to Figure 10.2 for an example.

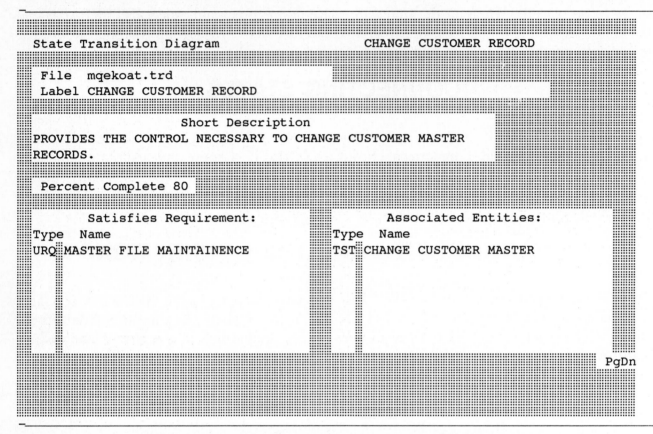

```
State Transition Diagram                    CHANGE  CUSTOMER  RECORD

  File  mqekoat.trd
  Label CHANGE CUSTOMER RECORD

                  Short Description
PROVIDES THE CONTROL NECESSARY TO CHANGE CUSTOMER MASTER
RECORDS.

  Percent Complete 80

      Satisfies Requirement:                Associated Entities:
Type   Name                          Type   Name
URQ MASTER FILE MAINTAINENCE         TST CHANGE  CUSTOMER  MASTER




                                                                  PgDn
```

Figure 10.2 State Transition Diagram Description Screen

DESCRIBING STATES

States are the times when the system or program is performing a well defined activity. Examples would be processing data, accepting keying activity, random reading file records, editing input data, searching a file, or just waiting (paused). Events, or activities, change the system from one state to another, for example, pressing a function key, or a program that has finished running.

To describe a state, select DESCRIBE and the rectangle representing the desired state. A default ID of the State Transition Diagram name followed by an incremental number is presented. Press enter to accept or overtype. It's a good practice to overtype the default ID with a meaningful one if the state is on more than one State Transition Diagram. The default ID is rather meaningless when used on a selector list. Another good strategy is to enter an alternate name. This is important if you are using the standard Excelerator default ID, since the alternate name will also show on selector lists.

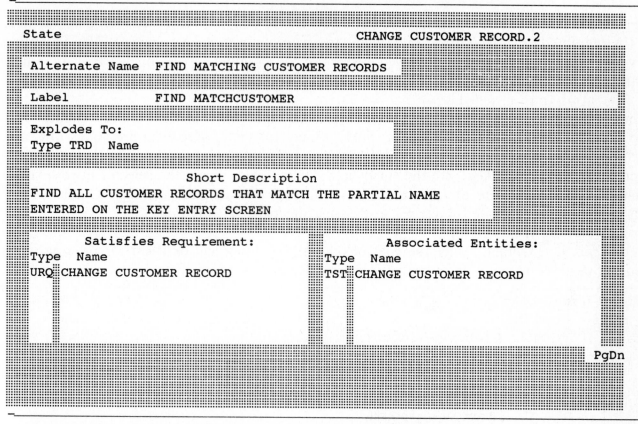

```
 State                                CHANGE CUSTOMER RECORD.2

   Alternate Name   FIND MATCHING CUSTOMER RECORDS

   Label             FIND MATCHCUSTOMER

   Explodes To:
   Type TRD   Name

                        Short Description
 FIND ALL CUSTOMER RECORDS THAT MATCH THE PARTIAL NAME
 ENTERED ON THE KEY ENTRY SCREEN

        Satisfies Requirement:                Associated Entities:
 Type   Name                            Type   Name
 URQ  CHANGE CUSTOMER RECORD            TST  CHANGE CUSTOMER RECORD

                                                                  PgDn
```

Figure 10.3   State Description Screen

The State may explode to a further State Transition Diagram. If so, enter the name of the child diagram in the **Explodes To:** area. An example would be a menu, with each option exploding to a state transition diagram. Fill in a short description, any requirements satisfied, and any associated entities. Press PgDn to enter a longer description. When finished, press F3 to save and return to the drawing screen.

DESCRIBING TRANSITION VECTORS

A transition vector represents an event that changes the system from one state to another. This is typically depicted as a condition and an action. As mentioned previously, a condition corresponds to an input control flow on the data flow diagram and is stored as a signal in the XLDictionary. An action is an output flow on the data flow diagram and is a trigger or other type of prompt. Transition vectors control which processes are performed under what conditions.

Select DESCRIBE and a transition vector arrow on the diagram. If a label has been created, it is presented as a default id. Press enter to accept or overtype to change. The Transition Vector description screen is displayed. Refer to the example shown in Figure 10.4. Fill in any alternate name and label, if not previously created. Key in a short description.

In the **Transition Inputs** area, enter the name of the input signal and any logical operator that connects several signals in the **LogOp** field. Values for the LogOp field are AND, OR, and NOT. If the signal has been previously described (for example, on the data flow diagram), press F4, the Browse key, with the cursor in the name field. From the selector list displayed, choose the signal. This ensures consistency with data flow diagram naming. Otherwise key in a name and, if desired, press F4 to describe the signal at this time.

For Transition Outputs, enter the type of output: **SIG** for signal or **PRM** for prompt. Key in the corresponding name or press F4 for a selector list.

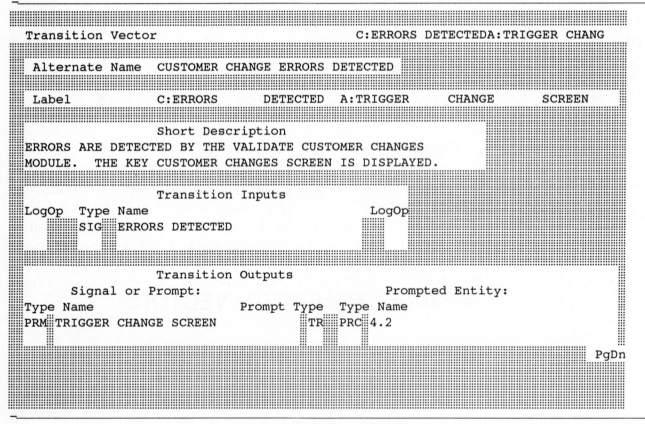

Figure 10.4 Transition Vector Description Screen

For the prompt type, use the following values:

EN - Enable   DS - Disable   ED - Enable/disable
TR - Trigger   ST - Set   RS - Reset
CL - Clear   SS - Suspend   RM - Resume
PS - Pause.

For a more detailed description of prompts, see Chapter 3.

Under the **Prompted Entity** area, enter the **Type** and **Name** of the process (PRC) or control transform (CTA) that is activated as a result of the prompting. Enter a name or, if the entity has been previously described, press F4 for a selector list and choose the name.

Complete any requirements satisfied and associated entities. Press PgDn to enter a longer description. When finished, press F3 to save and return to the drawing screen.

When the diagram is complete, zoom to close up to review how the graph will print and make any necessary changes. Check your print setup and print when ready. Save your work, backup and exit (see Chapter 2).

STATE TRANSITION DIAGRAM VALIDATION

Several reports are available to help validate the syntax and contents of the state transition diagram. Select **ANALYSIS** from the main menu, then **Graph Verification**. Three reporting options are available for the state transition diagram. Refer to Figure 10.5.

Select the State Transition Diagram verification option. Enter a name or press enter to use a selector list. Select a file, the screen, or printer for the report destination.

The report will show syntactical errors on the state transition diagram. There are three types of errors represented by the following report codes:

G   Graph
S   State
T   Transition Vector.

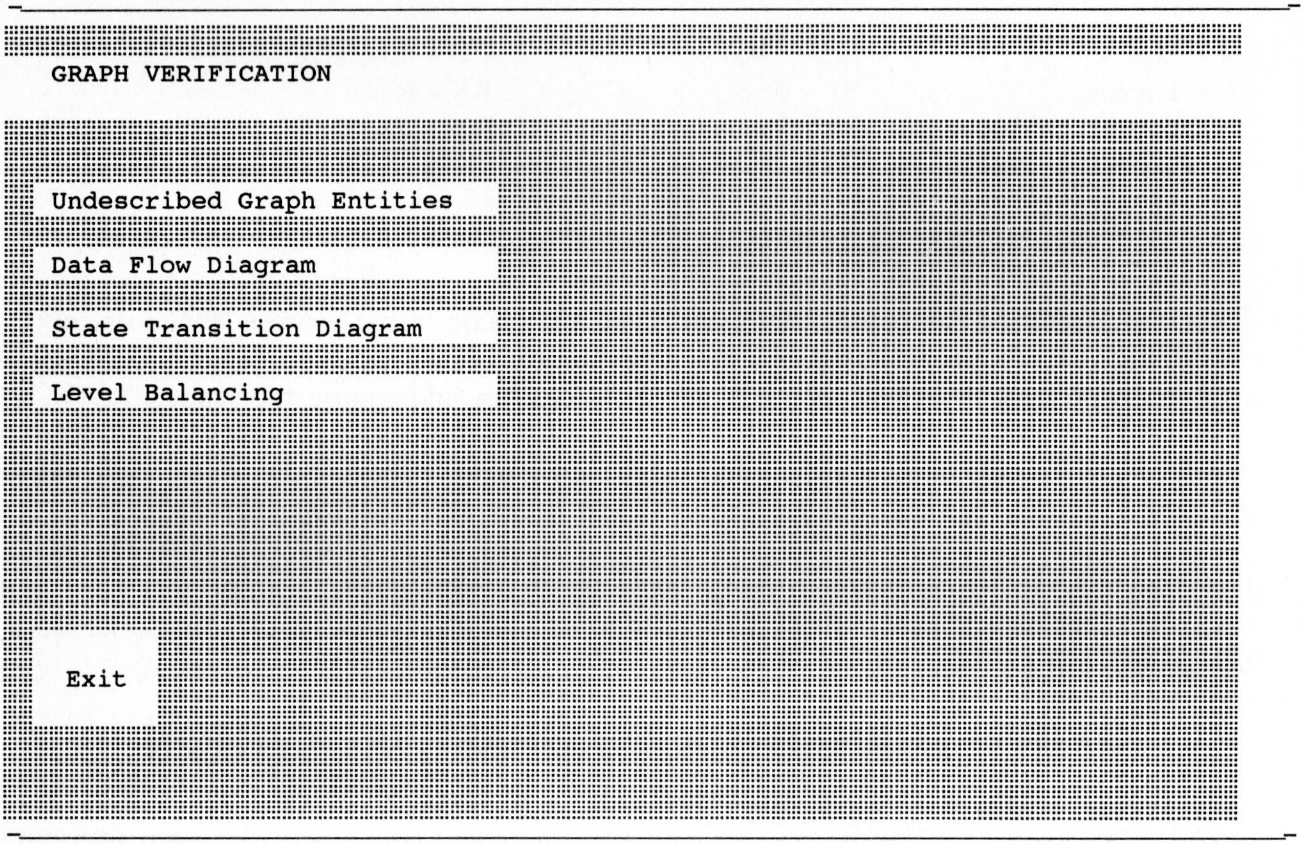

```
GRAPH VERIFICATION


  ┌──────────────────────────┐
  │ Undescribed Graph Entities │
  └──────────────────────────┘
  ┌──────────────────────────┐
  │ Data Flow Diagram          │
  └──────────────────────────┘
  ┌──────────────────────────┐
  │ State Transition Diagram   │
  └──────────────────────────┘
  ┌──────────────────────────┐
  │ Level Balancing            │
  └──────────────────────────┘




  ┌────────┐
  │  Exit  │
  └────────┘
```

Figure 10.5 Graph Verification Options

The possible errors are summarized below.

Type	Error
G	Only one initial (or interface) transition vector is allowed, the one that starts the diagram.
G	The diagram needs at least one transition vector other than the starting one.
G	There must be at least one state.
S	There must be at least one input transition vector.
S	A State is not described.
S	Cannot produce more than one transition vector with the same condition from the same state.
T	The initial transition vector must not have a condition on it.
T	Transition vector information can be in only one direction.
T	Transition vector not described.
T	Only one condition allowed.
T	Transition vector must end in a state.

Refer to Figure 10.6 for a sample state transition diagram with errors on it and to Figure 10.7 for the verification report.

UNDESCRIBED GRAPH ENTITIES

Selecting Undescribed Graph Entities produces a report of State Transition Diagram objects and connections which are not described in the XLDictionary. This report should be run late in analysis, after the design work is assumed complete.

Select the Graph Verification and Undescribed Graph Entities. From the menu presented, select State Transition Diagram and enter a name or use a selector list. The report detects errors for the following conditions:

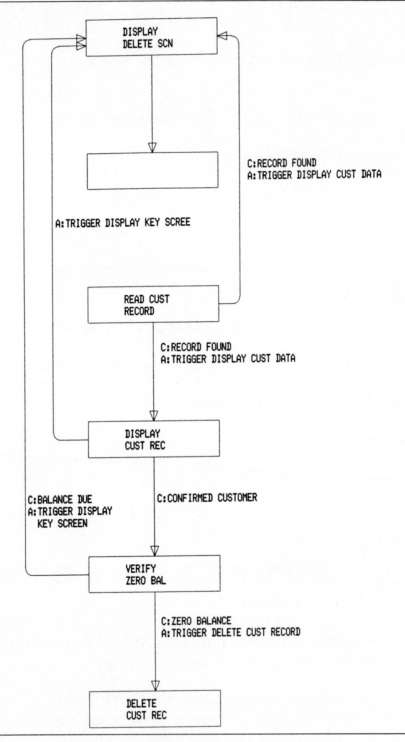

DISPLAY
DELETE SCN

C:RECORD FOUND
A:TRIGGER DISPLAY CUST DATA

A:TRIGGER DISPLAY KEY SCREE

READ CUST
RECORD

C:RECORD FOUND
A:TRIGGER DISPLAY CUST DATA

DISPLAY
CUST REC

C:BALANCE DUE
A:TRIGGER DISPLAY
  KEY SCREEN

C:CONFIRMED CUSTOMER

VERIFY
ZERO BAL

C:ZERO BALANCE
A:TRIGGER DELETE CUST RECORD

DELETE
CUST REC

Figure 10.6 State Transition Diagram With Errors

```
DATE: 05-JAN-90 STATE TRANSITION DIAGRAM VERIFICATION PAGE 1
TIME: 10:54                                    Excelerator/IS
PROJECT NAME: DFD

GRAPH NAME:  SAMPLE WITH ERRORS

            Graph (G), State (S), or Transition (T) Exceptions

------------------------------------------------------------
ID OR LABEL                   MESSAGE
|S|DISPLAY DELETE SCN         | Is not described
|S|      ** not labeled **    | Is not described
|S|DISPLAY CUST REC           | Is not described
|S|VERIFY ZERO BAL            | Is not described
|S|DELETE CUST REC            | Is not described
| |                           |
|T|       ** not labeled **   | Is not described
|T|C:CONFIRMED CUSTOMER       | Is not described
|T|A:TRIGGER DISPLAY KEY SCREEN | Is not described
|T|C:BALANCE DUE A:TRIGGER DISPL| Is not described
|G|                           | Does not receive an
                              | initial transition      |
| |                           |
|T|       ** not labeled **   | Does not have a condition
|T|C:CONFIRMED CUSTOMER       | Does not have a condition
|T|A:TRIGGER DISPLAY KEY SCREEN | Does not have a condition
|T|C:BALANCE DUE A:TRIGGER DISPL| Does not have a condition
|S|READ CUSTOMER RECORD       | Does not receive an input
                              | transition   |
|S|READ CUSTOMER RECORD       | Condition appears on >1
                              | output transition       |
```

Figure 10.7   State Transition Diagram Verification Report

Unlabeled objects
Undescribed objects
Undescribed connections
Unlabeled and undescribed connections.

Refer to Figure 10.8 for the report run against the state transition diagram shown in Figure
10.6.

```
DATE: 05-JAN-90      UNDESCRIBED GRAPH OBJECTS          PAGE 1
                         AND CONNECTIONS
TIME: 10:53                           Excelerator/IS   PROJECT NAME: DFD

GRAPH TYPE:   State Transition Diagram
GRAPH NAME:   SAMPLE WITH ERRORS

The following objects are not described:

 OBJ TYPE     LABEL
 -------------------------------------------------
|STATE      | DISPLAY DELETE SCN
|STATE      |    ** not labeled **
|STATE      | DISPLAY CUST REC
|STATE      | VERIFY ZERO BAL
|STATE      | DELETE CUST REC
 -------------------------------------------------
The following connections are labeled but not described:

 CONN TYPE    LABEL
 -------------------------------------------------
|TRN VEC    | C:CONFIRMED CUSTOMER
|TRN VEC    | A:TRIGGER DISPLAY KEY SCREEN
|TRN VEC    | C:BALANCE DUE A:TRIGGER DISPLAY KEY SCREEN
 -------------------------------------------------
The following connections are not labeled or described:

 CONN          ---------------------- ENDPOINTS -----------
 TYPE          OBJ TYPE I/L  OBJECT ID OR LABEL
 -------------------------------------------------
|TRN VEC   | STATE    | L  |DISPLAY DELETE SCN
|          | STATE    |    |    ** not labeled **
 -------------------------------------------------
```

Figure 10.8 Undescribed Graph Entities Report

LEVEL BALANCING VERIFICATION

The Level Balancing Verification report analyzes all Control Transforms on a data flow
diagram and checks the signals and prompts against those on a matching State Transition
Diagram. Inputs to the control transform are checked against the state transition diagram's
conditions and outputs from the control transform are checked against the state transition
diagram's actions. Any missing (label only, not defined in the XLDictionary), or wrongly
defined conditions or inconsistent entries (perhaps different names used, etc.) between the
control transform and the state transition diagram are reported.

EXERCISES

1. Create the state transition diagram shown in Figure 10.1. Describe the states and the transition vectors.

2. Create the following state transition diagram for the Delete Customer program. Describe all states and transition vectors.

Opening state:	Display delete key screen
Condition:	Customer number entered
Action:	Trigger Obtain customer record
Condition:	Clear key pressed
Action:	Exit program - return to menu
State:	Obtain customer record
Condition:	Record found
Action:	Trigger Display customer information
Condition:	Record not found
Action:	Trigger Display delete key screen
State:	Display customer information
Condition:	Record accepted
Action:	Trigger Verify customer balance
Condition:	Record rejected
Action:	Trigger Display delete key screen
State:	Verify customer balance
Condition:	Balance is zero
Action:	Trigger Delete customer record
Condition:	Balance is greater than zero
Action:	Trigger Display delete key screen
State:	Delete customer record
Condition:	Record deleted
Action:	Trigger Display delete key screen

3.   Create a state transition diagram for the following scenario. Describe all states and transition vectors.

An on-line grade book is being used to manage student grades. Students are sorted alphabetically within each class. On a Course Entry screen, instructors key in a class number. The Class Record is read and, if found, a Grade Update screen is displayed with a line (up to 15 per screen) for each student in the class. If no record is found, control returns to the Course Entry screen.

The program waits for grades to be entered. When the enter key is pressed, visual confirmation of the grades is requested. If the Grade Entry screen is cancelled, by pressing the clear key, control returns to the Course Entry screen.

If the operator presses the enter key to confirm the grades (from the Visual Confirmation screen) they are updated on the Class Master file. If rejected, control returns to the Grade entry screen.

If the enter key has been pressed, and there are more students than are displayed on the screen, control is passed to the Grade Entry screen and the next screenful of students is displayed. If there are on more students to be displayed, control returns to the Key Course Number screen.

4.   Describe the State Transition Diagrams that have been created. Make some 100 percent complete and some less than 100 percent complete.

5.   Produce the State Transition Diagram verification report for each diagram.

6.   Produce the Undescribed Graph Entities report for each diagram.

11
PROTOTYPING

Chapter Goals:

Understand how to create report prototypes.
Know how to create screen prototypes.
Learn how to link a series of screen prototypes.
Understand how to test prototype screens.
Know how to create a test data file for saving screen prototypes and test data.
Learn how to convert a screen design directly into XLDictionary records and
elements.
Know how to generate program language code from screen designs.

The prototyping feature of Excelerator allows you to design screens and reports. Screens
may be tested, entering data and displaying error messages. The Transform feature
allows you to create XLDictionary record and element descriptions. Screen designs may
be used to generate program source code in several programming languages.

Select **SCREENS & REPORTS** from the main menu. Five options are displayed on the
right hand side of the screen. The Report Design, Screen Design, Screen Data Entry
and the Transform feature will be covered in this chapter. Screen Data Reporting will
be covered in Chapter 13.

REPORT DESIGN

The simplest type of prototyping is report design. Select Report Design, then Add or
Modify to change. Enter a report design name and the Report Description screen is
displayed. Enter a description for the report. Change any of the physical report
parameters if desired (starting/ending line or column). To move from one field to the
next, use the Tab key (or Shift-Tab to move backward). Press F3 when finished.

The report drawing screen is displayed. Refer to Figure 11.1 for an example. Function
key definitions are located at the bottom of the screen. On the top and sides are
column and line reference numbers.

Key in the heading lines. If you reach the right hand side of the screen, it will scroll to the left, allowing additional report columns.   Press and hold F1 and then simultaneously press the left arrow (or right arrow) key to move the screen left (or right) one full screen.

You need not press the space bar to create large blocks of spaces on the screen.   Just move the mouse so the underscore is where you want text, such as column headers to be placed and press the left button.   You can select any position on the screen and key in text or a field description.   If a field is not correctly aligned or has a missing character, press the Insert key to insert spaces or characters.

REPORT DATA FIELDS

After creating the heading lines, select an area on the screen for the first data field. Instead of keying the data field entry, press F10 or select the F10 area on the bottom of the screen.   When prompted for the field name (Related Data Element Name), enter the name of an element that has been previously stored in the data dictionary, or

```
1...+...10....+...20....+...30....+...40....+...50....+...60....+...70....+...
1DATE   7/19/88                 CUSTOMER FINANCIAL REPORT                    PAGE
|
|
|          CUSTOMER        CUSTOMER          SALESPERSON        YEAR-TO-DATE
|          NUMBER          NAME              NUMBER                SALES
+
|          XXXXX      XXXXXXXXXXXXXXXXXXXX        XXX             ZZZ,ZZ9.99
|          XXXXX      XXXXXXXXXXXXXXXXXXXX        XXX             ZZZ,ZZ9.99
|          XXXXX      XXXXXXXXXXXXXXXXXXXX        XXX             ZZZ,ZZ9.99
|          XXXXX      XXXXXXXXXXXXXXXXXXXX        XXX             ZZZ,ZZ9.99
10         XXXXX      XXXXXXXXXXXXXXXXXXXX        XXX             ZZZ,ZZ9.99
|          XXXXX      XXXXXXXXXXXXXXXXXXXX        XXX             ZZZ,ZZ9.99
|          XXXXX      XXXXXXXXXXXXXXXXXXXX        XXX             ZZZ,ZZ9.99
|          XXXXX      XXXXXXXXXXXXXXXXXXXX        XXX             ZZZ,ZZ9.99
|
+                         TOTAL YEAR-TO-DATE SALES   ZZZ,ZZZ,ZZ9.99
|
|
|
|
|
20
|
|
|


             3 EXIT      1,8COLUMN      8REPEAT      10FIELD
```

Figure 11.1 Report Design Drawing Screen

press F4 for a selector list and choose an entry. If you wish to view or modify the element, press F4 again. The element screen will be displayed. Press F3 to save the element screen and return.

```
Select   the data field location
Press    F10 - Field
Press    F4  - Selector list
Select   an element from the list
Press    F3  - transfer to drawing screen
```

Report Prototype Command Summary

The following characters may be used for data fields on the report prototype:

X	Alphanumeric character, representing letters, numbers or special characters
9	Number
A	Alphabetic character
Z	Zero suppress, leading zero are replaced with spaces
M	Month
D	Day
Y	Year
B	Blank
S	Sign, either + or -
,	Comma
.	Period
$	Dollar sign
+	Plus sign
-	Minus sign

Regardless of whether the element description screen has been viewed or not, press F3. The output picture from the element description will be placed on the screen. You may press cancel to return to the drawing screen without the creating the output picture. Repeat for all fields. Using fields from the XLDictionary provides project consistency.

To cause data fields to be repeated vertically down the page, creating columns and showing several lines on the report, use either of the following two procedures:

1.   To repeat a block of text: Select the first character of a field. Press and hold F1 and press F8 (or select the word COLUMN, displayed in reverse video on the bottom of the screen). Enter the number of times to repeat the column (eg. 7) and press the enter key. The data field is duplicated down the screen.

2.   To repeat a portion of the screen only one time, select the first character of a field. Then press F8 or select REPEAT from the bottom of the screen. The message 'Repeat key now refers to current field' is displayed. Select the location where the field is to be copied to and again press F8. The field is copied once. This technique is useful for copying total lines from one area to another, etc. and may be used to copy any text.

```
─                                                                        ─
                               Report Design


   Report Name    CUSTOMER REPORT

   Description    THIS REPORT LISTS THE CUSTOMERS AND THE TOTAL SALES
                  AMOUNT THEY HAVE PURCHASED.



   Date Created:  7 /19/88         Date Last Modified: 1 /7 /91

   Created By:    ALLEN            Last Modified By:    ALLEN

   Starting Line: 1                Starting Column:     1

   Ending Line:   66               Ending Column:       132


DATE   7/19/88            CUSTOMER FINANCIAL REPORT              PAGE   1

          CUSTOMER       CUSTOMER          SALESPERSON        YEAR-TO-DATE
           NUMBER          NAME              NUMBER              SALES

          XXXXX    XXXXXXXXXXXXXXXXXXX        XXX            ZZZ,ZZ9.99
          XXXXX    XXXXXXXXXXXXXXXXXXX        XXX            ZZZ,ZZ9.99
          XXXXX    XXXXXXXXXXXXXXXXXXX        XXX            ZZZ,ZZ9.99
          XXXXX    XXXXXXXXXXXXXXXXXXX        XXX            ZZZ,ZZ9.99
          XXXXX    XXXXXXXXXXXXXXXXXXX        XXX            ZZZ,ZZ9.99
          XXXXX    XXXXXXXXXXXXXXXXXXX        XXX            ZZZ,ZZ9.99
          XXXXX    XXXXXXXXXXXXXXXXXXX        XXX            ZZZ,ZZ9.99
          XXXXX    XXXXXXXXXXXXXXXXXXX        XXX            ZZZ,ZZ9.99

                    TOTAL YEAR-TO-DATE SALES   ZZZ,ZZZ,ZZ9.99
─                                                                        ─
```

Figure 11.2 Report Prototype Print

Add any total lines using the same method as the heading lines. If the report will not fit entirely on the drawing screen, press F1 and either a right, up, down, or left arrow to scroll the report prototype. Press F3 to save when finished.

PRINTING THE REPORT PROTOTYPE

Select OUTPUT to print the report prototype. Key in the report name or press the enter key for a selector list of reports. The print can be saved as a PRN file, displayed on the screen, or directed to the printer. A sample report output is shown in Figure 11.2.

PRODUCING A MOCKED UP REPORT

To produce a prototype containing actual data, copy the report prototype containing codes, the Xs, Zs and so on. Select SCREENS & REPORTS, then Report Design, followed by Copy. Press the enter key when prompted for a **From Name**. Enter a new name under the **To Name**. Choose the report name to be copied from the selector list that is displayed.

```
   1...+...10....+...20....+...30....+...40....+...50....+...60....+...70....+...
1DATE   7/19/88                 CUSTOMER FINANCIAL REPORT                   PAGE
i
i          CUSTOMER       CUSTOMER          SALESPERSON        YEAR-TO-DATE
i          NUMBER         NAME              NUMBER             SALES
+
i          00123    KATRINA KOSY KITCHEN       020                122.88
i          01044    PETER'S COMPUTER INC       191              2,101.00
i          09002    ZING SOFTWARE              020             25,258.89
i          12093    EASYSOFT, INC              307              4,101.00
10         29094    ORGANIC MERCHANTS          191                334.20
i          40887    DOWN TO EARTH HIKING       307              2,223.77
i          70055    COSMIC BOOKS               191             49,302.07
i          92880    GREAT BEAR ASTRONOMY       020              7,473.31
i
+                         TOTAL YEAR-TO-DATE SALES              90,917.12
i
i
i
i
20
i
i

          3 EXIT      1,8COLUMN     8REPEAT     10FIELD
```

Figure 11.3   Report Prototype With Sample Data

Select Modify, press the enter key and select the new report name. Make any changes desired in the description area and press F3. The report prototype screen is displayed. Select the first data field and overtype the Xs and Zs with actual data. Select each field (using the mouse) or use the space bar or arrow keys and repeat the process. See Figure 11.3 for an example. Press F3 to save the changes and exit.

SCREEN DESIGN

The screen design option allows you to design screens which may be demonstrated by entering data. There are two distinct parts of screen prototyping, represented by two separate choices on the **Screens and Reports** selection menu. First, the screen needs to be designed and then the design may be interactively tested, via the Screen Data Entry option. The Screen Data Entry option consists of two parts. First, create a data file to hold the screen input and then test the screen.

```
                        Screen Design


  Screen Name      ADD CUSTOMER              Next Screen Name

  Description      NEW CUSTOMER ENTRY SCREEN

  Date Created      7 /19/88                 Date Last Modified 1 /16/90

  Created By       ALLEN SCHMIDT             Last Modified By

  Starting Row      1                        Starting Column     1

  Ending Row       24                        Ending Column      80
```

Figure 11.4 Screen Prototype Description Screen

Select SCREENS & REPORTS, Screen Design and Add or Modify to change. Enter a screen prototype name. A Screen Design Description screen is displayed, illustrated in Figure 11.4. If the screen you are designing controls the display of a second screen, enter that second screen name after the prompt **Next Screen Name**. This provides the means of linking several screens together. It is recommended not to link more than six screens since long chains will use up available memory.

Enter a description of the screen. Change any of the physical screen characteristics (starting/ending row or column) if desired. Press the enter key or the Tab (or Shift-Tab) key to move forward (or backward) through the fields displayed. Press F3 after making any changes. The Screen Design drawing screen is displayed, shown in Figure 11.5.

Enter the headings and captions - any fixed text to appear on the screen. Some useful techniques for modifying areas already keyed on the screen, either mistakes or user changes, are listed below.

1.   To insert a line, select (using the mouse) the line <u>below</u> the new line. Press and hold F1 and tap the Insert key.

2.   Pressing the Insert key in a blank area will insert a space on the line - no need to press the space bar.

3.   To delete a line, select the line and press (and hold) F1 and the Delete key simultaneously.

4.   To move fields and text, use the following cut and paste technique:

      To move a field on the screen, select the field with the mouse. Press F5 (Cut) and the field is removed from the screen. Select the location for the field to be moved to and press F6 (Paste). You may paste as often as needed to perform a copy operation.

5.   F9 deletes a field from the screen.

SCREEN DATA FIELDS

To enter data fields on the screen, select the area for the data to be placed. The first field or group of fields on the screen should be the <u>key</u> fields if you plan on entering data onto the screen using the Screen Data Entry feature.

```
 ┌─                                                                          ─┐
 │                          NEW CUSTOMER ENTRY                                │
 │                                                                            │
 │                                                                            │
 │  NUMBER                                                                    │
 │                                                                            │
 │  NAME                                                                      │
 │                                                                            │
 │  STREET                                                                    │
 │                                                                            │
 │  CITY                                      STATE        ZIP                │
 │                                                                            │
 │  TELEPHONE                                                                 │
 │                                                                            │
 │  SALESPERSON                                                               │
 │                                                                            │
 │  ACCOUNT STATUS CODE   O                                                   │
 │                                                                            │
 │  CREDIT LIMIT            01000.00                                          │
 │                                                                            │
 │                                                                            │
 │                                                                            │
 │                                                                            │
 │    3 EXIT    5 CUT    6PASTE    7REGION  8REPEAT  9DELETE  1,10BLOCK   10FIELD │
 └─                                                                          ─┘
```

Figure 11.5 Screen Design Drawing Screen

Press F10 and a field definition area is displayed on the bottom of the screen. Refer to Figure 11.6. Complete the following entries:

Field name: Type a name you want the field on the *screen* to be referred to and press enter. This name is stored separately from the data dictionary element. It may have a different Input Picture or other attribute and not change the corresponding XLDictionary element. You may enter the name of an XLDictionary element and press F10 and the element's attributes will be transferred to the field definition area.

Related ELE: Key in the name of an element and press F10 to transfer the element attributes from the XLDictionary to the field definition. You may also press F4 to display a selector list. This will list the elements (elementary data items) that have been defined in the data dictionary. Select an element from the list. If the element is not found, cancel using the right button or Esc key. If you need to view the element description in the XLDictionary, press F4. The data dictionary element description screen may be modified if necessary. Press F3 to save and return to the Field Definition Screen.

```
Select   the data field location
Press    F10 - Field
Enter    screen Field Name
Press    enter - place cursor in Related ELE
Either:
      Press   F4  - Selector list
      Select  an element from the list
 Or
      Key   in XLDictionary name
Press    F10 - transfer element attributes
Press    F3  - transfer to drawing screen
```

Screen Prototype Command Summary

```
                          NEW CUSTOMER ENTRY


NUMBER

NAME

STREET

CITY                                          STATE        ZIP

TELEPHONE

SALESPERSON
                              *FIELD DEFINITION SCREEN*
Field name:     NUMBER              Related ELE: CUSTOMER NUMBER
Length: 5   I/O/T:I  Required:N  Skip:Y  Bright:N  Reverse:Y Blink:N Underline:N
Storage type: C  Characters left of decimal: 5   Characters right of decimal: 0
Dflt:
Input format:   X(5)                      Output format:  X(5)
Edit rules:     VALUES ARE "00019" THRU "99999"
Help:CUSTOMER NUMBER - UNIQUE FOR EACH CUSTOMER
```

Figure 11.6 Field Definition Area

Once the XLDictionary element appears in the Related ELE entry, press F10 to copy the element attributes of the element to the Field Definition Screen. The attributes may be changed by typing over entries on the Field Definition Screen. If you have made any erroneous entries in the XLDictionary for the element, an error message will display on the bottom of the screen (for example, an invalid output picture or edit criteria).

The field definition attributes are:

Length: the length of the field on the screen, <u>including</u> any editing characters, such as commas or periods.

I/O/T: Whether the field is input, output, or text. The default is input and may be overridden as output for display information. **Text** displays prompts, captions and other fixed information.

Required: is the field a required field, Y/N. A value of **Y** means that a blank field is reported as an error. You must provide an edit rule of NOT " " (described below).

Skip: automatic skip to the next field if the field is completely filled, Y/N. If the value is **N** the enter key must be pressed to advance to the next field.

Bright: Y/N for a high intensity field display.

Reverse: Y/N to display the field in reverse video.

Blink: a blinking field, Y/N

Underline: Y/N for an underlined field.

Storage type: how the data is stored.

Values are: C - character, any letter, number or any special character.
                 P - packed, decimal format for arithmetic
                 D - date
                 B - binary, decimal format for arithmetic
                 F - floating point, scientific notation format.

                 You may not use Bit, Picture, Time, or Variable Character.

Characters to the left and the right of the decimal point. Length stored is characters to the left of the decimal. Characters right is for packed fields and is used to generate program code for the screen (details later).

Dflt: is the default entry, if any. This value will display when prototyping the screen.

Input format: Entries are the same as on the element description screen. A picture of 9's will edit for numeric data. If non-numeric data is entered, an error message will be displayed. Use M for month, D for day, and Y for year. **S** is for a + or - sign.

If a storage type of D for date is entered, the input format has a default of MM/DD/YY. This may be changed to DD-MM-YY, DD.MM.YY, and DD/MM/YY. If the length is changed, the format may be changed to MMDDYY or MM.DD.YYYY. If you plan on using the date as a sort field for screen data reporting, change the Storage Type to C for character and define the date as YYMMDD.

Output format. The output format is the same as the input format plus $, +, -, and Z for zero suppression.

Edit rules: the same as on the element description screen. Refer to chapter 8. These limit what may be entered by the operator. If data is entered that does not conform to the edit criteria, an error message is displays.

Help: a help message that is displayed when the user presses F2.

Press F3 when finished to save the field description. Repeat for all fields. To line up data entry fields, pick the starting character of the first field and use the up/down arrows to locate the starting character of other fields. Press F10 to define them.

REGIONS

A region may be defined containing multiple entries of the same field. An example would be DEPENDENTS on an Employee Master file. Individual entries will scroll if the screen region contains fewer table entry areas than are provided on the resulting file. When the entries are full, a new line is added to the bottom and previously keyed lines scroll upward.

To create a region, first create the fields that will be used as columns within the region. Select the first (leftmost) field of the column. Press F7 or select REGION from the bottom of the screen. Figure 11.7 provides an example of the region entry area.

Enter a name for the region, eg. LINE ITEMS. The starting line will be displayed. Enter the number of lines you want to be displayed as a part of the region. They must fit withing the screen. Key in the total number of lines that will scroll within the region (100 maximum). If the total lines are greater than the lines displayed, then the lines will scroll within the region. If the total lines equals the lines displayed, no scrolling will occur. For a user prototype, the latter would be more appropriate unless the final application is written with the intent of using scrolling lines.

```
                            ORDER SYSTEM
                            ADD NEW ORDER


CUSTOMER NUMBER:

SALESPERSON:

BRANCH:


QUANTITY      ITEM NUMBER          DESCRIPTION          UNIT PRICE      EXTENDED




                        *REGION DEFINITION SCREEN*
Region name: LINE ITEM
Start line:  13          Lines displayed: 8          Total lines: 8
Start column:3           Total columns:   78
```

Figure 11.7 Region Definition Screen

Overtype the **Total columns** entry (using the number of characters, not fields) if you do <u>not</u> want the entire screen width to be used as a region.

To change any of the field columns, select the region on the drawing screen and press F10 or select FIELD from the bottom of the screen.

To delete a region, select the region and change the lines displayed to zero.

REPEATING FIELDS

Fields may be copied across a row (or down columns). To copy one field to an adjacent location <u>across</u> a row, select the field to copy and press F8 or select REPEAT from the bottom of the screen. Select an adjacent location and press F8 again (or select REPEAT). The field is copied. Continue with as many fields as needed. A change to an individual field (select the field, press F10 and change attributes, etc.) changes all repeated fields. Single fields may be deleted by pressing F9. Text may be included between repeating fields, but other data fields may not.

TEXT BLOCKS

A text block may be defined.   This can be used as a text entry field for lengthy text descriptions.   Text keyed into the text block will scroll within the screen entry region if the amount of text keyed is greater than the region defined on the screen.   Press and hold F1 and press F10 (or select BLOCK from the bottom of the screen).   A Text Block Definition Screen is displayed, illustrated in Figure 11.8.

Fill in the text block name and press the enter key. Enter the number of characters wide and change any of the preset attributes.   You may link the block to an element as described for fields.   Remember to press F10 to transfer the XLDictionary attributes for the element to the screen.   Press F3 when finished.

To cut and paste text, first define it as a field or a text block.   Cut and paste as previously described.   Use F9 to delete a text block.   Press F3 when the screen prototype is finished to save and exit.

```
                              ORDER SYSTEM
                             ADD NEW ORDER


CUSTOMER NUMBER:

SALESPERSON:

BRANCH:


QUANTITY     ITEM NUMBER          DESCRIPTION          UNIT PRICE     EXTENDED




                      *TEXT BLOCK DEFINITION SCREEN*
Text block name: HOLD REASON        Related ELE:
Characters wide: 40    Lines displayed: 3    Total lines: 8
I/O: I   Required: N    Skip: Y   Bright: N   Reverse: Y   Blink: N  Underline: N
Help:ENTER THE REASON THAT THE ORDER WILL NOT BE SHIPPED (EG. NEEDS PREPAYMENT)
```

Figure 11.8 Text Block Definition Screen

PRINTING THE SCREEN DESIGN

To print a screen design, including summary screen information, select Output. Press enter when prompted for a "Name or Name Range' to display selector list of screens. Choose the screen to be printed from the list. Select the output destination (print file, screen, or printer). Three options are presented for the information available for printing. They are preset to default values that may be overtyped.

1.   Screen Header. Enter:
        S for summary information (name and description).
        D for detail (the default)
        N for none.

2.   Screen Image
        Y includes a screen image (the default)
        N does not include a screen image.

3.   Field description
        S for summary - the location, attributes, and region of the screen for each field (the default).
        D for a detailed description of each field (similar to the Field Definition Screen).
        N is for not included.

Make any changes to the defaults and press F3. Sample output is illustrated in Figure 11.9.

SCREEN PROTOTYPING

The data entry screen can be tested. Data may be entered, edited and help messages may be displayed. There are two methods for testing. One method (Inspect) is quick and easy and should be used for initial screen testing. A second method, Screen Data Entry, should be used after any screen changes and refinements have been made.

QUICK PROTOTYPING

To view and enter data onto a screen, select **Inspect**. Type the screen name or press enter for a list of names and select one.

Key in data, test edit rules by keying invalid data, and review help messages (press F2 for each field). Use the Tab key to move forward or press the shift key and Tab to move backward

```
-_____-
                              Screen Design

         Screen Name      ADD CUSTOMER            Next Screen Name

         Description      NEW CUSTOMER ENTRY SCREEN

         Date Created     7 /19/88                Date Last Modified 1 /7 /91

         Created By       ALLEN SCHMIDT            Last Modified By

         Starting Row     1                       Starting Column    1

         Ending Row       24                      Ending Column      80

   Nbr of groups:  0

   Total fields:  22

   Field descriptors by field type:
      Input fields:  11
      Output fields:  0
      Text fields:  11

   Form map size:    98

   Chain map size:   98

   Form <ADD CUSTOMER    > (as of  7-JAN-91)
   ------------------------------------------------------------------------
                              NEW CUSTOMER ENTRY

   NUMBER           _____

   NAME             _____

   STREET           _____

   CITY             _____        STATE __     ZIP _____

   TELEPHONE        _____

   SALESPERSON      ___

   ACCOUNT STATUS CODE   _

   CREDIT LIMIT          _____
-_____-
```

Figure 11.9 Sample Screen Output - Page 1

Field groups

   None

Field Descriptions

(row,col) ----- name ----- Req Skip Brt Rev Blnk Und len styp(s1,s2):sloc

Input Fields

(row,col)	name		Req	Skip	Brt	Rev	Blnk	Und	len	styp(s1,s2):	sloc
(4,13)	'NUMBER	'	N	Y	N	Y	N	N	5	C(5, 0):	0
(6,13)	'NAME	'	N	Y	N	Y	N	N	20	C(20, 0):	5
(8,13)	'STREET	'	N	Y	N	Y	N	N	20	C(20, 0):	25
(10,13)	'CITY	'	N	Y	N	Y	N	N	20	C(20, 0):	45
(10,45)	'STATE	'	N	Y	N	Y	N	N	2	C(2, 0):	65
(10,56)	'ZIP	'	N	Y	N	Y	N	N	5	C(5, 0):	67
(10,61)	'ZIP EXTENSION	'	N	Y	N	Y	N	N	4	C(4, 0):	72
(12,13)	'TELEPHONE	'	Y	Y	N	Y	N	N	10	C(10, 0):	76
(14,13)	'SALESPERSON	'	Y	Y	N	Y	N	N	3	C(3, 0):	86
(16,22)	'ACCOUNT STATUS	'	N	Y	N	Y	N	N	1	C(1, 0):	89
(18,22)	'CREDIT LIMIT	'	N	Y	N	Y	N	N	8	P(5, 2):	90

Output Fields

Text Fields

(row,col)	name		Req	Skip	Brt	Rev	Blnk	Und	len
(1,24)	'NEW CUSTOMER ENT'		N	N	N	N	N	N	18
(4, 1)	'NUMBER	'	N	N	N	N	N	N	6
(6, 1)	'NAME	'	N	N	N	N	N	N	4
(8, 1)	'STREET	'	N	N	N	N	N	N	6
(10, 1)	'CITY	'	N	N	N	N	N	N	4
(10,39)	'STATE	'	N	N	N	N	N	N	5
(10,52)	'ZIP	'	N	N	N	N	N	N	3
(12, 1)	'TELEPHONE	'	N	N	N	N	N	N	9
(14, 1)	'SALESPERSON	'	N	N	N	N	N	N	11
(16, 1)	'ACCOUNT STATUS C'		N	N	N	N	N	N	19
(18, 1)	'CREDIT LIMIT	'	N	N	N	N	N	N	12

Figure 11.9 Sample Screen Output - Page 2

through the entry fields. PgUp and PgDn allow you to view the next or prior screens within a screen chain. Press F3 or Esc to exit. Data entered will not be saved. Make any changes to your design by selecting **Modify** and when they are complete, re-test your screen.

SCREEN DATA ENTRY

CREATING THE SCREEN DATA ENTRY FILE STRUCTURE

The first step in full testing of screens is to create a file structure to hold the screen data. Select SCREENS & REPORTS, if you are working from the main menu. Select Screen Data Entry and select Add or Modify to change. This will create the data file or change an existing one. The data file holds data keyed on the prototype screen. Note that you may only modify a data file if entries have not already been stored on records within the file.

Enter a data file name (eg. CUSTOMER MASTER). If you are modifying, press the enter key to obtain a selector list of files previously created and select one from the list. A Screen Data Entry screen is displayed. Fill in the following three fields:

Screen Name: the name of a previously created screen (eg. ADD CUSTOMER).

Record length: the number of characters in the record (maximum length is 2047). If you do not wish to enter a value for the Record length, Excelerator will determine the length for you.

Key length: the length of the key. The key is the first data entry field on the screen. It is best to use a single, simple key, which may be shorter than the first field on the screen. The key may also be several of the first fields (a concatenated key) found on a screen or a chain of screens.

Review the above information, since once data records are created via the entry screen, these file characteristics may not be changed. Use PgDn if a more complete description is desired, and press F3.

PROTOTYPE THE SCREEN

Select Execute and enter the name of the data file created for the screen (eg. CUSTOMER MASTER). You may press enter for a selector list and choose a file. A new menu is displayed which allows you to add, modify, copy, etc. records in the data file created in the previous step. Select Add. Enter a record key (eg. 12345 for a customer number key).

The prototype screen is displayed. Refer to Figure 11.10, the ADD CUSTOMER Prototype Screen.

Key in values for the various fields. Press the enter key if the data entered does not completely fill the field. Keying invalid data will display an error message on line 23. These are from the edit rules entered on the element description screen of the data dictionary. If a field is defined with a picture of 9's, keying non-numeric data will display an error message.

Pressing F2 will display the help message on line 23. The Tab key (or Shift-Tab) will move the cursor forward (or backward) through the entry fields. If two screens are linked, press PgDn to display the second screen, then enter data as above. PgUp allows you to view prior screens in the chain. Press F3 to save the record and exit.

From the same Records menu (displayed by selecting Execute from the Screen Data Entry menu), other options are available.

```
                          NEW CUSTOMER ENTRY


    NUMBER        09288

    NAME          GREAT BEAR ASTRONOMY

    STREET        122 WOMBAT AVENUE

    CITY          URSA MAJOR              STATE        ZIP 12345

    TELEPHONE     9998887777

    SALESPERSON   123

    ACCOUNT STATUS CODE   3

    CREDIT LIMIT          1000.00
```

Figure 11.10 Add Customer Prototype Screen

Select **List** and press the enter key when prompted for a record key. The keys stored in the file are displayed.

Select **Inspect,** then press the enter key when prompted for a record key. The keys stored in the file are displayed on a selector list. Select any key and the screen with the corresponding data is displayed. This can be used for demonstrating inquiry programs: the key is entered and the matching record is displayed.

Copy lets you create duplicate records.

Rename changes the key for a record.

Modify lets you change records. Type a record key and press enter (or press enter to obtain a selector list). The prototype screen is displayed with the data on it. Overtype any data and press F3 to save. This can be a useful technique for prototyping change screens.

Delete removes records.

Output prints screens with data in the entry areas.

PROTOTYPING TECHNIQUES

To produce a realistic prototype of a system the technique of chaining screens together may be utilized. Suppose a prototype is needed to show a Customer System main menu which has options to update, perform inquiry, and produce reports. When Update is selected, a second menu with choices for add, change, and delete is displayed. Finally, the Add Customer screen should be prototyped. While Excelerator does not provide menus that actually execute within prototyping, the methodology described here will simulate menu actions.

The solution is to create a series of chained screens as shown in Figure 11.11. First, create the Main Menu screen and fill in the Next Screen Name with the name Update Menu. Press F3 and then design the Main Menu. Next create the Update Menu screen and enter Add Customer Screen in the Next Screen Name. Press F3 and design this screen.

The next step is to use the Screen Data Entry feature to create an ADD CUSTOMER master file. The key field would be 7 characters long. The first character would be the menu selection choice (the only entry field) on the Main Menu screen. The second character in the key would be the entry choice field (one character) on the Update Menu screen. The remaining five characters would be the ADD CUSTOMER key field, the Customer Number, found on the third screen.

The key field scheme would be: MUCCCCC

Where   **M** is the Main menu choice
                    U is the Update menu choice
                    CCCCC is the key for the Add Customer Screen.

Once the ADD CUSTOMER file has been created, select **Execute** to run the prototype. If the customer number should be 12345, enter 1112345 when prompted for the key to add. The first 1 would be filled in on the Main Menu, selecting the Update menu. The second 1 would be filled in on the Update Menu selecting the Add Customer option. Finally the remaining 12345 would appear in the CUSTOMER NUMBER field.

Enter the key, press enter and the Main Menu screen will be presented. Press PgDn for the next screen in the chain, the Update Menu. The entry choice field has a 1 in it indicating the selection of the Add Customer program. Press PgDn again and the Add Customer screen will be displayed showing Customer Number 12345 on the screen. The rest of the Add Customer screen fields may now be entered. Press F3 to save the record.

To show a change screen, copy the Main Menu to a second menu screen called Main Menu - Change. Modify this menu with the **Next Screen Name** field changed to Update Menu - Change. Press F3 and then press F3 again to save the Main Menu screen without any further changes.

Next copy the Update Menu to a new screen design called Update Menu - Change. Then modify the screen and change the Next Screen Name field to Customer Change Screen. Save the screen design and create a CUSTOMER MASTER record as described above and enter a key of 1212345. The 1 being the selection choice for the Update Menu, the 2 selecting the Change Customer Program and the 12345 for the Customer Number on the Change Customer screen.

CREATING RECORD LAYOUTS

Screen or screen chain record layouts may be generated from Excelerator. These can be printed, saved on a disk, or saved as an ASCII file for interfacing into a program. The Interface File may be used, with modification, to create CICS, IMS, or FMS code. A Data Map may be directly incorporated into program code (for example, BASIC language).

```
 ___                                                                       __
|
    03-04-91                    CUSTOMER SYSTEM                    4:18 PM
                                  MAIN MENU

    1.   UPDATE CUSTOMER RECORDS

    2.   CUSTOMER INQUIRY SUBSYSTEM

    3.   CUSTOMER REPORT SUBSYSTEM

    4.   EXIT

         CHOICE 1
 _____

    03-04-91                 UPDATE CUSTOMER MASTER                 4:18 PM

    1.   ADD NEW CUSTOMER

    2.   CHANGE CUSTOMER RECORD

    3.   DELETE CUSTOMER RECORD

    4.   EXIT

         CHOICE 1
 _____

    03-04-91                  NEW CUSTOMER ENTRY                    4:19 PM

    NUMBER        23445

    NAME          GREAT BEAR ASTRONOMY

    STREET        709 COMET

    CITY          URSA MAJOR              STATE         ZIP 53210

    TELEPHONE    6081112222

    SALESPERSON 019

    ACCOUNT STATUS CODE   5

    CREDIT LIMIT         1000.00




    PRESS F1 TO CANCEL, F3 TO SAVE
 _____
```

Figure 11.11 Chained Prototype Screens - Customer Maintenance

PROTOTYPING   199

Select SCREENS & REPORTS, Screen Design and Generate. Enter a screen name or press enter for a selector list and choose a name. Select either Data Map for code layout or Interface File to create an DOS ASCII file. A Generate Record Layout description screen is displayed, shown in Figure 11.12.

Press enter for the map name or change if necessary. Enter a prefix for the data names, if desired. An example is ACM- meaning Add Customer Map for COBOL data division entries. The prefix will precede each data field.

Choose the language: BASIC, C, COBOL, or PL/I. If COBOL has been selected, choose either Input or Output format to select whether **pictures** used for the map should come from screen input or output format definitions. Press F3 to execute. Select a file, the screen, or the printer for the output. See Figure 11.13 for a sample record output in the COBOL language.

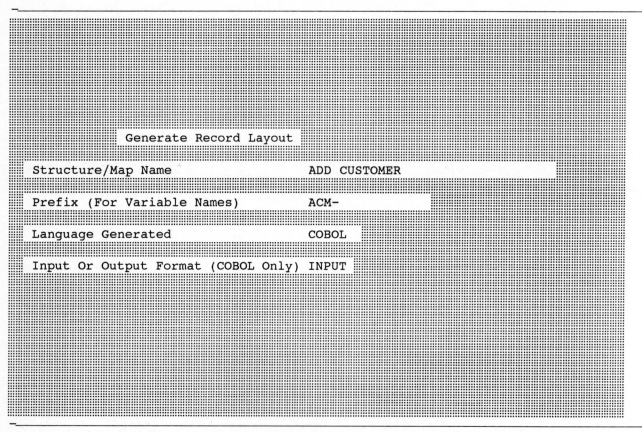

```
                 Generate Record Layout

  Structure/Map Name                  ADD CUSTOMER

  Prefix (For Variable Names)         ACM-

  Language Generated                  COBOL

  Input Or Output Format (COBOL Only) INPUT
```

Figure 11.12 Generate Record Layout Description Screen

```
*Record ADD-CUSTOMER Generated: 16-JAN-90
  01  ADD-CUSTOMER.
        05   ACM-NUMBER                     PIC X(5).
        05   ACM-NAME                       PIC X(20).
        05   ACM-STREET                     PIC X(20).
        05   ACM-CITY                       PIC X(20).
        05   ACM-STATE                      PIC XX.
        05   ACM-ZIP                        PIC X(5).
        05   ACM-ZIP-EXTENSION              PIC XXXX.
        05   ACM-TELEPHONE                  PIC X(10).
        05   ACM-SALESPERSON                PIC XXX.
        05   ACM-ACCOUNT-STATUS             PIC X
                                VALUE '0'.
        05   ACM-CREDIT-LIMIT               PIC 99999.99
                     COMP-3    VALUE 01000.00.
```

Figure 11.13   Sample Record Generation Output

TRANSFORM - THE POWER TO CREATE DATA STRUCTURES AND ELEMENTS FROM PROTOTYPE SCREENS

The Transform option gives you the power to create record and element descriptions from screens created via the Screen Design feature. This has a great advantage when the approach to analysis and design is to create prototypes based on interviews or JAD sessions. The prototypes may be reviewed by the users and modified until they have final approval. Then the record and element descriptions may be created with the expectation that they will not need significant modifications in the future.

Select **SCREENS & REPORTS** and **Transform**, followed by the only option, Execute. When prompted for a Screen Design, enter a name or press Enter for a selector list and choose a screen. The maximum number of elements that can be transformed per screen is 115. The Action By Item screen is displayed, illustrated in Figure 11.14. Press the enter key to move from name to action down the list. The actions are defined as follows:

Create   A new record or element will be created. Excelerator has determined that the record or element does not currently exist.

Update   The record or element does exist but will be updated with pictures, edit rules or other attributes defined within the screen design.

Locked The record or element does exist but is locked via the XLD Interface option.

To change an action, use the mouse, or press the enter key to place the cursor is in the action field. Then press the first letter of the action you would like for the field. Pressing **S** for Skip will cause Excelerator to ignore this field during the transformation process. Figure 11.14 shows the use of the Skip option. To change other actions, press the down arrow to move to the action and again change by pressing the first letter. You may also change the *name* of the record or element that will be created.

Press F3 (Save) to initiate the transform process. Progress is displayed at the bottom of the screen. After the records have been processed, a summary report is displayed. Press Esc to return to the Action Screen and transform another screen or select Exit to return to the main menu.

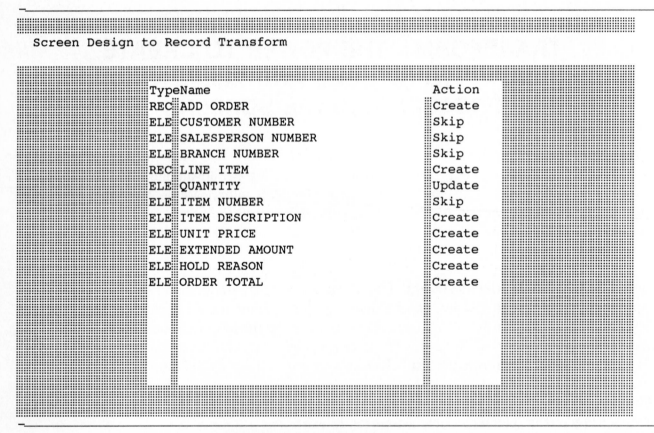

Screen Design to Record Transform

Type	Name	Action
REC	ADD ORDER	Create
ELE	CUSTOMER NUMBER	Skip
ELE	SALESPERSON NUMBER	Skip
ELE	BRANCH NUMBER	Skip
REC	LINE ITEM	Create
ELE	QUANTITY	Update
ELE	ITEM NUMBER	Skip
ELE	ITEM DESCRIPTION	Create
ELE	UNIT PRICE	Create
ELE	EXTENDED AMOUNT	Create
ELE	HOLD REASON	Create
ELE	ORDER TOTAL	Create

Figure 11.14   Action By Item Screen

EXERCISES

1.   Create a prototype report for the Weekly Payroll. Fields on the report would include:

Number
Name
Social Security No
Department Code
Rate Of Pay
Vacation Hours Remaining
Sick Leave Accumulated
Current Gross Pay
YTD Gross Pay

2.   Create the Order Entry prototype screen shown on page 191. Print the prototype. Demonstrate the prototype to your instructor using the Screen Data Entry feature.

3.   Create the Student Record Inquiry prototype screen. The data fields are:

Student Number
Last Name
First Name
Middle Initial
Grade Point Average
Credits Earned
Major Program Code
Courses Completed

Link this screen to a second screen to display the courses completed by the student. A single screen should display up to sixteen courses, defined as a region. The entries for each line are:

Course Number
Section Number
Term Completed
Grade Received

Print the prototype. Demonstrate it to your instructor.

4.   Create a prototype for the Add Customer screen shown in this chapter. Print the prototype and demonstrate to your instructor.

5.   Create a series of menu screens linked to the Add Customer screen. The first menu would be the Customer Main Menu with options to Update Customer, Produce Customer Inquiry, and Produce Customer Reports. A final selection would be Exit.

The first menu should be linked to the Update Menu with choices to Add Customer, Change Customer, Delete Customer, and Exit. This Update Menu should be linked to the Add Customer screen created in Exercise 4. Demonstrate the prototype for your instructor.

6.   Use the transform option to create records and elements for the Add Customer Screen.

7.   Use the transform option to create records and elements for the Add Order Screen.

8.   Exercise the transform option to create records and elements for the Student Record Inquiry.

12

PROJECT ANALYSIS

One of the finest features of Excelerator is the powerful analysis capabilities inherent in the XLDictionary. Entities are recorded, relationships automatically maintained, and a comprehensive series or reports and matrices may easily be obtained. Errors in the XLDictionary entries as well as missing and incomplete information in the system design as a whole may be determined.

Previous (and subsequent) chapters explain the use of diagram or graph analysis, which determines if the syntax and level balancing is correct. This chapter will focus on the XLDictionary analysis and reporting features and portions of the Extended Analysis feature. Subsequent chapters will present the Report Writer and Entity List features.

Chapter Goals:

>   Learn how to use the XLDictionary options for printing and analyzing
>   Excelerator entities.
>   Understand how to use XLDictionary relationships for analysis and reporting.
>   Know how to use the Extended Analysis options, and the nature of the
>   information presented.
>   Know how to analyze record and element entities.
>   Understand how to use Excelerator to determine if the data is in the third
>   normal form.

GENERAL PRINCIPLES

Throughout the analysis options, when prompted for a Name Range, three choices are available.

1.   You can enter a specific name (eg. Customer Master) to receive information on only that entity.

2.   A name can be followed by an asterisk (*) for a range of names. For example, CUST* would list all names starting with CUST.

3.   Press the enter key to obtain a selector list of all data names.

Reports and matrices can be output to a print file, the screen, or the printer. Many of the Extended Analysis options also allow you to create an Entity List to save the entity types and names.

XLDICTIONARY ANALYSIS AND REPORTING

Reporting on Excelerator entities is done by selecting XLDICTIONARY from the main menu. Many options are available and a few of the more useful will be described below. Concepts and the strategy of using the XLDictionary for reporting will be presented. You may explore many of the other options and relationships as needed.
Once XLDICTIONARY has been selected, the *Class* menu displays. Since there are 54 entities within Excelerator, they are grouped into eight broad classes or categories. Each class contains several entities.

To briefly review, an entity is any object that Excelerator allows you to create via the description screens. Each entity has numerous fields contained within it. These are the entity *attributes*. Appendix C summarizes XLDictionary classes and entities within them.

Select an XLDictionary class, for example, REC/ELE representing records and elements. Refer to Figure 12.1. Select an entity within the class, eg. Record. You can then obtain information about records in the XLDictionary. You may also select Relationships, which provide links this entity, eg. record has with other entities. Relationships will be covered later in this chapter.

XLDICTIONARY REPORTS

There are several reports that are available from the XLDictionary.

Output allows you to print XLDictionary entities. Details are in Chapter 8.

Summary prints the names of entities and several key attributes (entity fields). The report is 132 characters wide. The List option (described below) shows similar information, but only for display, not print. Summary reports provide a concise list of entities and help to determine redundant entities. Since the lists are sorted by the entity name, similar spellings should be investigated as possible redundant entries.

Audit prints information for project control. The persons and date created, modified, and locked, as well as the number of times modified. Since this is a 132 character report, select **wide** (housekeeping option) prior to executing Audit if you have an 8½ X 11 printer.

Expanded Output is an excellent means for determining how the entity relates to other entities, either directly or indirectly. An example of an indirect relation would be elements of a structural record contained within a higher level record. The report shows entities in a forward direction only, that is, only the entities that are expansions of the current entity. Refer to Figure 12.2 for an example.

The example above shows what the Customer Master record contains within it. This report lists entities that explode or are browsed from the selected entity. It may be used to determine how any changes you may make will affect other entities.

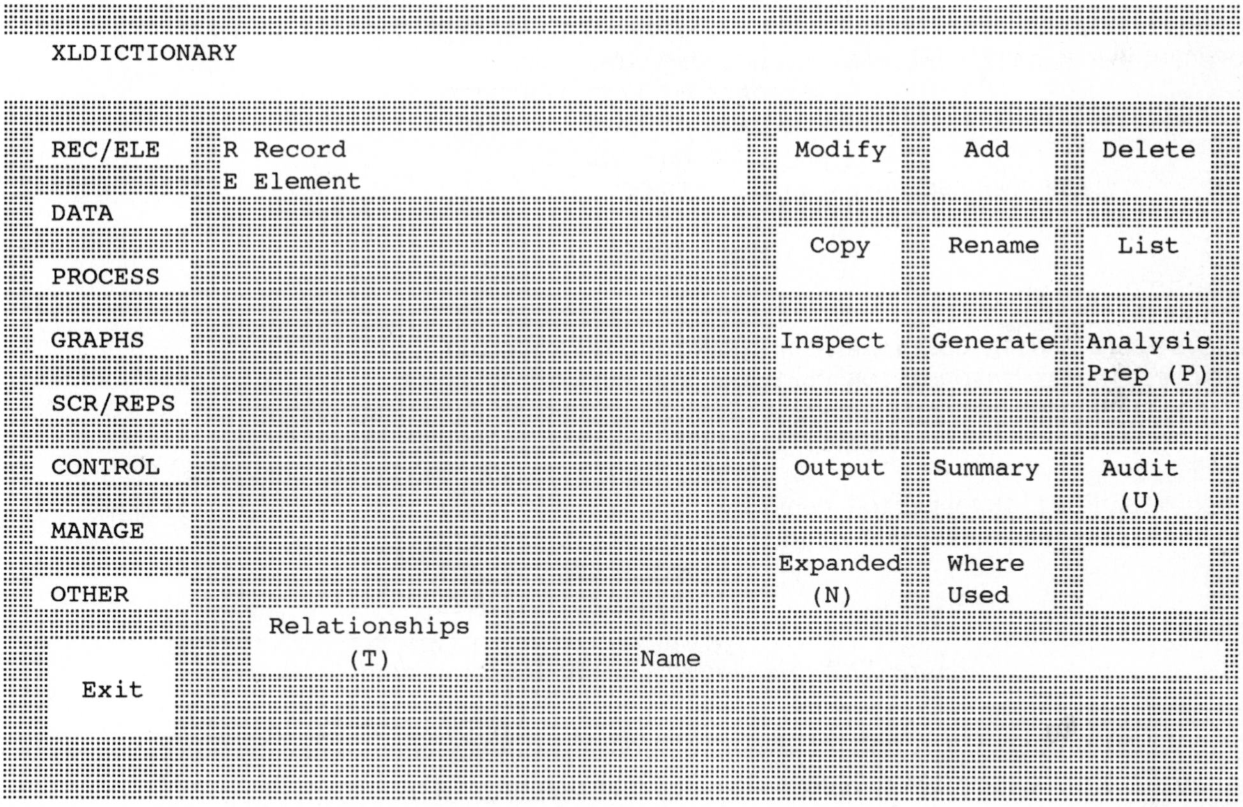

XLDICTIONARY

REC/ELE	R Record		Modify	Add	Delete
	E Element				
DATA					
			Copy	Rename	List
PROCESS					
GRAPHS			Inspect	Generate	Analysis Prep (P)
SCR/REPS					
CONTROL			Output	Summary	Audit (U)
MANAGE					
			Expanded (N)	Where Used	
OTHER					
	Relationships (T)	Name			
Exit					

Figure 12.1 XLDICTIONARY Menu Options

```
TYPE REC                                 NAME CUSTOMER MASTER

 REC CUSTOMER MASTER Contains ELE BRANCH NUMBER
                              ELE CUSTOMER NUMBER
                              ELE CUSTOMER NAME
                              ELE CUSTOMER TELEPHONE
      ELE CUSTOMER TELEPHONE Has-Associated REF SUBPROGRAM LISTINGS
                                            TST ADD CUSTOMER RECORDS
                         Satisfies URQ MAINTAIN CUSTOMER INFORMATION
 REC CUSTOMER MASTER Contains ELE SALESPERSON NUMBER
      ELE SALESPERSON NUMBER Has-Associated REF MODULUS 11 METHODOLOGY
                                            TST MODULUS 11 SUBPROGRAM
                         Satisfies URQ MAINTAIN LIST OF SALESPN NUMBERS
                                   URQ CROSS REFERENCE CUST TO SLSPN
 REC CUSTOMER MASTER Contains ELE ACCOUNT STATUS CODE
                              ELE DATE OF LAST PURCHASE
                              ELE DATE OF LAST PAYMENT
                              REC CUSTOMER ADDRESS
      REC CUSTOMER ADDRESS Contains ELE STREET
                                    ELE CITY
                                    ELE STATE
                                    ELE ZIP
                                    ELE ZIP EXPANSION
 REC CUSTOMER MASTER Contains REC FINANCIAL INFORMATION
      REC FINANCIAL INFORMATION Contains ELE CURRENT BALANCE
         ELE CURRENT BALANCE Has-Associated TST UPDATE CUSTOMER MASTER
                        Satisfies URQ MAINTAIN CUSTOMER AMOUNT OWED
                                  URQ UPDATE SALES, PAYMENTS, CREDITS
      REC FINANCIAL INFORMATION Contains ELE NET PURCHASES YTD
                                         ELE MONTH CHARGES
                                         ELE MONTH CREDITS
                                         ELE CREDIT LIMIT
```

Figure 12.2 Expanded Output Report Example

Where Used produces a report of every relationship directly maintained by Excelerator for this entity. Run Where Used before deleting or renaming. This report lists related entities going in a forward and backward direction. Figure 12.3 illustrates the Where Used report.

```
DATE:  7-JAN-91     ELEMENT - WHERE USED                    PAGE    1
TIME: 15:18         NAME: CUSTOMER NAME                 Excelerator/IS

TYPE ELE                                  NAME CUSTOMER NAME

ELE CUSTOMER NAME Contained-In REC BILLING FILE
                               REC CUSTOMER MASTER
                               ELS ADD SCREEN FIELDS
                               ELS ALL ELEMENTS
                               ELS BASE CUSTOMER ELEMENTS
                               ELS BASE ELEMENTS
                               ELS BASE ELEMENTS - NO DEFAULT VALUE
                               ELS DIFFERENCE EXAMPLE
                               ELS UNION MODIFY EXAMPLE
                               ELS ADD SCREEN FIELD ELEMENTS
                  Referenced-By SCD ADD CUSTOMER
                                SCD CUSTOMER INQUIRY
                                SCD ZZZ
                                RED CUSTOMER REPORT
                                RED NEW CUSTOMER REPORT
                  Access-Key-Of DAS D5
                  Input-To PPS 4.2 ACCEPT CHANGES
```

Figure 12.3   Where Used Report Example

DELETING, COPYING, RENAMING, LISTING, INSPECTING

The data dictionary menu screen may be used to delete, make copies of or rename any data dictionary entry. Select any category of XLDictionary entities. These are listed in Appendix C. Select the entity that is to be either inspected or any other XLDictionary action. For example, select Record for data structures or Element for elementary fields.

Select an action, described below, and key in the names as prompted. You may press enter without a name for a selector list.

LISTING XLDICTIONARY ENTITIES

Selecting **List** displays the name and one other attribute for an entity. It shows which items have been created for each entity. The attribute displayed varies from entity to entity. List information is for display only and cannot be printed. Press enter when prompted for a **Name Range** to get a simple list of all entries. You may also enter a partial name followed by an asterisk (eg. CUST*) to list a subset of entity names all starting with CUST. Press any key (keyboard or mouse) to return to the menu screen.

DELETING XLDICTIONARY ENTITIES

To remove entities, select Delete. To delete a group of records or other entity with a common prefix (eg. CUST), key in the prefix followed by an asterisk (*) when prompted for a name. A selector list will be displayed with only those entities starting with the prefix. Select the top line, **All Entries on Selector List**.

To delete a single entity, key in the name of the entity or press enter for a selector list and choose a name. Confirm Y to delete.

INSPECTING ENTITIES

Inspect allows you to look at a data dictionary entry without changing it. Select Inspect. Press enter when prompted for a **Name Range** to get a list of all entries and then select the entry you wish to view. Press Cancel to return to the main menu.

RENAMING

Rename gives a new name to an entity. This may lead to problems if the entity occurs in many different areas of the design. All the graphs will be automatically updated with the changed name but entity lists (covered in Chapter 14) will not be. A good strategy is to run the **Expanded Output** and **Where Used** reports before renaming to see the impact of the name change. You may be prompted to run Analysis Prep prior to the rename.

GENERATING RECORD STRUCTURES

Record structures or program code may be automatically generated for the Record entity only. This topic is covered in detail in Chapters 8 and 11.

ANALYSIS PREP

Analysis Prep updates the set of complex relationships maintained by Excelerator. These are used for reporting and analysis. Analysis Prep should be run whenever a new graph has been created or if changes have been made to existing graphs. Since it takes some time to execute, Analysis Prep may be run after a series of changes have been made. When producing a report using relationships, Excelerator will prompt you to run Analysis Prep, if necessary.

RELATIONSHIPS

The Relationships option provides access to the many relationships maintained automatically (as least after selecting Analysis Prep) by Excelerator for each entity. Select **Relationships** and a selector list showing all the relationships for this particular entity will be displayed. Figure 12.4 is an example of this list.

Choose the desired relationship. Select the plus sign for a next screenful of relationships, the minus sign for the previous screenful. As you can see, there are quite a few relationships maintained by Excelerator! Appendix E provides a complete list.

After a relationship has been chosen, the name displays on the XLDictionary menu screen, under the Relationships selection area. A new set of actions appears, illustrated in

```
XLD Relationship Type

    Entity name                         2nd Entity Type

    REC Constant-In PPS . . . . . . . . .Primitive Process Specification
    REC Contained-In REC.................Record
    REC Contains ANY. . . . . . . . . . .Any Entity Type
    REC Contains ELE....................Element
    REC Contains REC. . . . . . . . . . .Record
    REC Explodes-From ANY...............Any Entity Type
    REC Explodes-From DAE . . . . . . . .Data Entity
    REC Explodes-From DAF...............Data Flow
    REC Explodes-From DAS . . . . . . . .Data Store
    REC Explodes-From DNR...............Data N-Ary Relationship
    REC Explodes-From SGC . . . . . . . .Structure Graph Connection
    REC Has-Associated ANY..............Any Entity Type
    REC Has-Associated CAT. . . . . . . .Category
    REC Has-Associated CHG..............Change Request
    REC Has-Associated ELS. . . . . . . .Entity List
    REC Has-Associated ISS..............Issue
    REC Has-Associated NTE. . . . . . . .Note
    . . . . . . . . . . .   +   . . . . . . . . . . . . . . . . . .
```

Figure 12.4 XLDictionary Relationship Selector List

Figure 12.5. These are:

Analysis Prep, as described above.

Summary output produces a report showing the first entity and the entities related to it. In the example above, the record selected will be displayed with all the elements contained in the record.

List provides the same information as summary, except for display only.

Missing Entities is a very valuable report. It is generally run after most of the project design has been entered, or after most of the design for a particular entity or set of entities has been created. The report shows which parts of the design are undefined, and is limited to the relationships maintained by Excelerator.

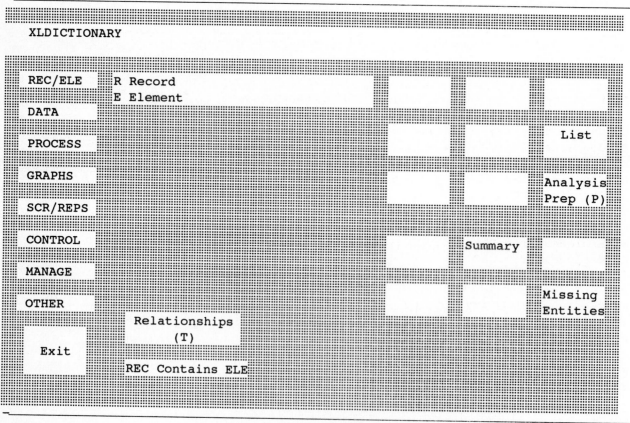

Figure 12.5 Relationship Action Screen

As design progresses, this report should be produced periodically to show design elements that need to be created. Since this report is for relationships, a vast amount of information may be obtained. Figure 12.6 shows an example produced for all **Record Contain Elements**.

You may reselect **Relationships** to obtain a different relationship for the same entity. To return to the entity action keypad, select the entity from the upper left portion of the screen, for example, Element.

SELECTED RELATIONSHIPS

The following are selected relationships and a brief explanation of them.

RECORD

REC Contains REC gives a list of all records that have data structures (sub records) within them.

REC Contained - In REC shows the data structures and the records they are contained within.

REC Contains ELE lists the records and elements found in each record.

REC Contains Any shows the records and anything they contain - data structures or elements.

ELEMENTS

Selecting Element from the top of the screen gives information about the elements in the system. Some of the relationships you can report on are:

ELE Contained - In REC lists each element and the records they are contained within.

ELE Contained - In SCD shows which elements are used in screen designs for prototyping.

ELE Contained - In RED shows which elements are used in reports designs for prototyping.

ELE Contained - In Access Keys Of DAS lists elements that are used as access keys of data stores.

```
Record Contains Missing Element                              Occ   Seq
------------------------------------------------------------ ---   ----
ADD ORDER                       SALESPERSON                  001   000
                                BRANCH                       001   000
CREDIT TRANSACTION              RETURN DATE                  001   000
                                INVOICE NUMBER               001   000
                                RETURN AMOUNT                001   000
INVOICE FILE                    INVOICE RECORD               001   000
INVOICE RECORD                  INVOICE DATE                 001   000
                                INVOICE NUMBER               001   000
                                INVOICE AMOUNT               001   000
PAYMENT TRANSACTION             PAYMENT DATE                 001   000
                                INVOICE NUMBER               001   000
                                PAYMENT AMOUNT               001   000
SALESPERSON                     SALESPERSON NAME             001   000
                                SALESPERSON TELEPHONE        001   000
                                SALESPERSON BRANCH           001   000
                                YTD SALES                    001   000
                                YTD COMMISSION               001   000
                                MONTH SALES                  001   000
                                MONTH COMMISSION             001   000
```

Figure 12.6 Example Of A Missing Entity Report

DATA CLASS OF ENTITIES

Select DATA from the left hand menu. The entities available are:

DAS	Data Store
DAE	Data Entity
DAF	Data Flow
TAB	Table of Codes
DAR	Data Relationship
DNR	Data N-Ary Relationship

These entities replace Record and Element on the XLDictionary screen. Select an entity and either an action or Relationships. For all the examples, select Relationships and choose one from the selector list. Enter a name as mentioned earlier.

Try using all names by pressing the enter key without an entry. Send the report to the printer or screen. Print your choice of missing entities or summary, or select List to view only. Experiment with various options and relationships to see which may be useful to yourself. Refer to Appendix C for the various classes of entities and Appendix E for a list of the relationships maintained by Excelerator.

Select Data Store, Relationship and **DAS Contained - In DFD**. This list shows the data stores and the data flow diagrams they are contained within.

Select Data Flow, then **DAF Sent By Data Store**. This lists a summary of which data flow come out of data stores.

Select Data Relationship and **DAR Contained-In DMD**. All the data relationships contained in the Data Model Diagrams are listed.

The same is true for selecting PROCESS, GRAPHS, SCR/REPS (Screens and Reports), CONTROL, MANAGE or OTHER from the XLDictionary menu. The cross-reference lists are too numerous to list in their entirety, but a few are shown below to give a feeling for the entities (the three letter codes) and the *type* of relationship, such as **Contained-In** or **Explodes-To**.

XLD CLASS	ENTITY	RELATIONSHIP
	MEANING (second line)	

PROCESS   Process   **PRC Explodes-to PPS**

Lists all processes that explode to Primitive Process Specifications.

PROCESS   Function   **FUN Contained-In STC**

Shows functions and the structure chart they are contained within. Sorted by function.

GRAPHS   Data Flow Diagram   **DFD Contains CTA**

Lists data flow diagrams and their control transforms.

GRAPHS   Data Model Diagram   **DMD Contains ANY**

The ANY entity refers to all the entities that may be contained in a relationship. In this case, the list shows data model diagrams on the left side (sorted). Either data entities or data relationships are on the right side, that is, all the entities contained in the data model diagram.

GRAPHS	State Transition Diagram	TRD Explodes-From CTA

Explodes-From shows all the child graphs (sorted) that explode from the parent graph. The above example shows all state transition diagrams that explode from control transforms. This is the reverse of the Explodes-To relationship.

SCR/REPS	Screen Design	SCD References ELE

The report shows screen designs and the XLDictionary elements used to create screen fields.

CONTROL	Signal	SIG Input-To TVA

The Signals that are input to transition vectors, shown on the transition vector description screen.

MANAGE	User Requirement	URQ Satisfied-By ANY

Provides a sorted list of user requirements, showing all entities that satisfy the user requirement. See Chapter 15 for details on management options.

OTHER	Entity List	ELS Contains ANY

Produces a report containing each entity list and all the entities on the list. This is an extremely valuable report. Chapter 14 covers the details of this important facility.

EXTENDED ANALYSIS AND REPORTING

The Extended Analysis feature of Excelerator provides very powerful analysis and reporting. The following reports provide different methods of analyzing the system design. These give a feeling for the many ways that Excelerator can list and report items stored in the XLDictionary, including all objects found on drawings.

These reports should be run after all the graphs and entities have been created, or at least assumed to have been created. Run the Missing Entities reports described previously along with the Undescribed Graph Entities, described in the appropriate chapters, to determine if the design is complete. Some of the Extended Analysis reports provide information on missing design components.

All the reports and matrices can be sent to the screen, printer, or a file for later printing. Select ANALYSIS, then **Extended Analysis**. An options screen is displayed, shown in

Figure 12.7. The first four options should be executed in the order listed. Record Content will analyze records and elements. After problems have been corrected, Key Validation will analyze records and data stores for problems with keys.

Data Model Validation will check the data model for problems and should be run next. Finally, execute Data Normalization after all other problems have been resolved.

RECORD CONTENT ANALYSIS

Select Record Content, then Execute. Choose REPORTS or MATRICES. REPORTS shows the information generated in a report format and MATRICES displays the information in a grid. A description of the reports and matrices follows.

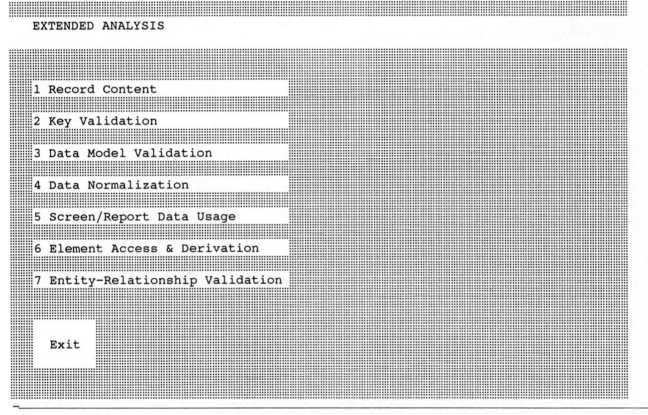

```
EXTENDED ANALYSIS


  1 Record Content

  2 Key Validation

  3 Data Model Validation

  4 Data Normalization

  5 Screen/Report Data Usage

  6 Element Access & Derivation

  7 Entity-Relationship Validation


    Exit
```

Figure 12.7 Extended Analysis Options

Select REPORTS and one of the following options:

Empty Records
Recursive Records
Equivalent Records
Subset Records
Similar Records
Partial Subset Records
ALL REPORTS

Empty Records shows records that contain no substructure records or elements, the record structure has not been defined. This should be run before any other analysis options, since these records must be defined.

Recursive Records lists all records that contain themselves at a lower level. The record structure would be in a lower level substructure.

Equivalent Records shows records that have the same lowest level contents, that is, the same elements when all records have been expanded. These may be redundant records. An example is shown in Figure 12.8.

Subset Records presents a list of records whose contents are a subset of another record.

Similar Records lists records that have a high percent of the same elements. It is like the equivalent records report, except not as exact. Enter a threshold percentage for the report, indicating how much of the record content needs to be identical for the records

```
DATE: 07-JAN-91                EQUIVALENT RECORDS           PAGE          1
TIME: 15:20                                            Excelerator/IS
PROJECT NAME: CUSTOMER

DESCRIPTION:    This report lists pairs of top-level Records with logically
                equivalent contents.  Records A and B have the same
                lowest-level contents, though they may group and order
                those contents differently.


RECORD A        IS EQUIVALENT TO    RECORD B
-----------------------------------------------------------------
|INSTRUCTOR COURSES           |STUDENT COURSES                  |
|ORDER RECORD                 |ORDER RECORD NEW                 |
|                             |                                 |
-----------------------------------------------------------------
```

Figure 12.8 Example Of An Equivalent Records Report

to be considered similar. The default is 75 percent.

Partial Subset Records shows records that have a high percentage of elements in common with other records. Again, enter a threshold percentage.

Select MATRICES. Available options are:

Record Contains Record (One Level)
Record Contains Element (One Level)
Basic Contents (All Levels)
Shared Elements Count
Percentage Overlap
ALL MATRICES

Record Contains Record (One level) shows which records contain which data structures (records in themselves). Refer to the example in Figure 12.9.

Record Contains Element shows records and their elements. A portion of this matrix is illustrated in Figure 12.10.

Basic Content (All Levels) presents records and their elements and structural records.
Shared Elements Count shows records plotted against each other. A count of shared elements, those in common to both records, is shown on the grid.

Percentage Overlap gives same information as Shared Elements Count, except the shared elements are shown as a percentage.

ALL MATRICES will put all the above matrices on one display screen (with scrolling) or a single report.

KEY VALIDATION

Select Key Validation, the second Extended Analysis option. This analyzes record keys and finds key discrepancies, both within data stores and between data stores and records. Included are records with keys missing, multiple keys, etc.

Unkeyed Records (One level) shows records for which no keys have been defined.

```
                            --------------------------------------------------
                            |R  |R  |R  |R  |R  |R  |R  |R  |R  |R  |R  |
                            |E  |E  |E  |E  |E  |E  |E  |E  |E  |E  |E  |
                            |C  |C  |C  |C  |C  |C  |C  |C  |C  |C  |C  |
                            |   |   |   |   |   |   |   |   |   |   |   |
                            |A  |L  |B  |C  |II |TI |CT |C  |FI |D  |IC |
                            |D  |I  |I  |U  |NN |RN |RR |U  |IN |A  |NO |
                            |D  |N  |L  |S  |VF |AF |EA |S  |NF |T  |SU |
                            |   |E  |L  |T  |OO |NO |DN |T  |AO |A  |TR |
                            |O  |   |I  |O  |IR |SR |IS |O  |NR |   |RS |
                            |R  |I  |N  |M  |CM |AM |TA |M  |CM |1  |UE |
                            |D  |T  |G  |E  |EA |CA | C |E  |IA |0  |CS |
                            |E  |E  |   |R  | T |TT | T |R  |AT |   |T  |
                            |R  |M  |F  |   | I |II | I |   |LI |   |O  |
                            |   |   |I  |A  | O |OO | O |M  | O |   |R  |
                            |   |   |L  |D  | N |NN | N |A  | N |   |   |
                            |   |   |E  |D  |   |   |   |S  |   |   |   |
                            |   |   |   |R  |   |   |   |T  |   |   |   |
                            |   |   |   |E  |   |   |   |E  |   |   |   |
                            |   |   |   |S  |   |   |   |R  |   |   |   |
                            |   |   |   |S  |   |   |   |   |   |   |   |
                            --------------------------------------------------
-----------------------------  ------------------------------------------------
|REC ADD ORDER             |  |   | R |   |   |   |   |   |   |   |   |   |
|--------------------------|  |---+---+---+---+---+---+---+---+---+---+---|
|REC LINE ITEM             |  |   |   |   |   |   |   |   |   |   |   |   |
|--------------------------|  |---+---+---+---+---+---+---+---+---+---+---|
|REC BILLING FILE          |  |   |   |   | R | R | R |   |   |   |   |   |
|--------------------------|  |---+---+---+---+---+---+---+---+---+---+---|
|REC CUSTOMER ADDRESS      |  |   |   |   |   |   |   |   |   |   |   |   |
|--------------------------|  |---+---+---+---+---+---+---+---+---+---+---|
|REC TRANSACTION           |  |   |   |   |   |   |   |   |   |   |   |   |
|INFORMATION               |  |   |   |   |   |   |   |   |   |   |   |   |
|--------------------------|  |---+---+---+---+---+---+---+---+---+---+---|
|REC CREDIT TRANSACTION    |  |   |   |   |   |   |   |   |   |   |   |   |
|--------------------------|  |---+---+---+---+---+---+---+---+---+---+---|
|REC CUSTOMER MASTER       |  |   |   |   | R |   |   |   |   | R |   |   |
|--------------------------|  |---+---+---+---+---+---+---+---+---+---+---|
-----------------------------  ------------------------------------------------
```

Figure 12.9 Example Of Record Contains Record Matrix

Record Contains Element (One Level)

Jan17 90 23:50:42 A-1

	ELE CUSTOMER NUMBER	ELE SALESPERSON	ELE BRANCH	ELE HOLD REASON	ELE ORDER TOTAL	ELE CUSTOMER NAME	ELE BRANCH NUMBER	ELE SALESPERSON NUMBER	ELE RETURN DATE	ELE INVOICE NUMBER	ELE RETURN AMOUNT
REC ADD ORDER	E	E	E	E	E						
REC BILLING FILE	E					E					
REC CUSTOMER ADDRESS											
REC CREDIT TRANSACTION	7						E	7	E	7	E
REC CUSTOMER MASTER	K					E	E	7			
REC INSTRUCTOR COURSES											
REC INVOICE FILE											
REC INVOICE RECORD	7						E	7		K	
REC ORDER ITEM RECORD											

Figure 12.10 Record Contains Element Matrix Example

```
-|--                                                                      --|-
  DATE: 18-JAN-90    MULTIPLE KEY RECORDS (ONE LEVEL)    PAGE 1
  TIME: 00:02                                       Excelerator/IS
  PROJECT NAME: DFD
  DESCRIPTION:    This report lists each Record with more than one key among its
  immediate contents. Asterisks indicate whether the Record contains multiple whole
  keys (K), repeated concatenated key values (1-9), or a combination of whole and
  concatenated keys (both K and 1-9).
                                          MULTIPLE KEY TYPE
  RECORD NAME                          |   K  | 1-9 |BOTH |
  -------------------------------------+------+-----+-----
  |CREDIT TRANSACTION                  |      |  *  |     |
  |CUSTOMER MASTER                     |      |     |  *  |
  |INVOICE RECORD                      |      |  *  |  *  |
  |PAYMENT TRANSACTION                 |      |  *  |     |
  |                                    |                  |
  -----------------------------------------------------
-|--                                                                      --|-
```

Figure 12.11   Multiple Key Records Report Example

Multiple Key Records (One Level) lists records with multiple keys or alternate indexes. Figure 12.11 is an example of this report.

Key elements (One Level) reports on each key and the records it is contained within. This is a very useful report for analyzing where the key elements are used and the effect of any proposed change to a key.

Foreign keys (All Levels) list each record and both the prime keys (**Type** is K) and any foreign keys, that is, keys of other records found as data on the given record.

Inherited keys shows which records get a key as a result of a data structure within the record containing a key.

Unkeyed Records (All levels) lists records that have no defined keys.

Data Store Exceptions reports on data stores and inherent problems, such as not exploding to a record, no key indicated, explodes to a record without a key, has a key conflict with the explosion record. This is a valuable report for analyzing your key elements.

Index Elements Exceptions shows data stores with a missing index or an index not a member of a record.

ALL REPORTS prints or displays all the above reports.

Selecting MATRICES gives the following options.

Record Contains Record (One level)
Record Contains Element
Basic Content (All Levels), all as described under Record Content.

Records in Data Stores shows which records are contained in which data stores.

Index elements in Data Stores cross-references indices and data stores they are contained within. This is a good overview of data stores and their key fields.

ALL MATRICES will put all the above matrices on one screen or report.

DATA NORMALIZATION

This feature helps to insure that the records are in the third normal form. Analysis is done on record keys and the Data Model Diagram. The analysis does not normalize the records for you, it only reports on errors in the design that prevent the records from being fully normalized. This option should be run late in analysis, after the design is complete.

Records, the Data Model Diagram, and Data Entities should be complete. Run Undescribed Graph Entities and Data Model Diagram Analysis first. Then use Record Content and Key Validation Analysis to determine any missing or contradictory information. Make corrections to the design before running the Data Normalization reports and matrices. Data Normalization has the following options available for reports:

Repeating Groups
Element Access Conflicts
Matching Key Records
Record Dependencies
Data Entity Exceptions
Data Model Relationships
DAR/Record Conflicts
ALL REPORTS

Repeating groups shows periodic groups (i.e. tables) that are within any of the records. Refer to Figure 12.12 for a sample report.

Elemental Access Conflicts lists each element found within several records, or redundant data. Elements shown are not key elements. Records analyzed are those that are described as normalized, that is, the **Normalized** field on the record description contains a **Y**.

```
DATE: 18-JAN-90          REPEATING GROUPS          PAGE    1
TIME: 00:16                                     Excelerator/IS
PROJECT NAME: DFD

DESCRIPTION:   This report identifies Records that violate 1st Normal Form by
containing Records and Elements that occur more than once. The report lists the
repeated contents.

 RECORD NAME             RECORDS/ELEMENTS REPEATED      | OCC | TYPE|
------------------------------------------------------+-----+-----
|ADD ORDER              |LINE ITEM                     | 008 |  R  |
|                       |                              |     |     |
|BILLING FILE           |INVOICE INFORMATION           | 100 |  R  |
|                       |TRANSACTION INFORMATION       | 100 |  R  |
|                       |INVOICE INFORMATION           | 100 |  R  |
|                       |TRANSACTION INFORMATION       | 100 |  R  |
|                       |                              |     |     |
|ORDER RECORD           |ITEM NUMBER                   | 010 |  E  |
|                       |QUANTITY ORDERED              | 010 |  E  |
|                       |QUANTITY SHIPPED              | 010 |  E  |
|                       |                              |     |     |
|ORDER RECORD NEW       |ORDER ITEMS                   | 010 |  R  |
|                                                                  |
-------------------------------------------------------------------
```

Figure 12.12 Repeating Groups Report Example

Matching Key Records lists which single record contain the whole key of another record. The key of both records is the same, and both are described as normalized. The records shown may be valid or they may be duplicate or similar records.

Record Dependencies shows records that are described as normalized and whose key is contained as an element of another record. These records have a one to many relationship that may be valid. Examine the records to see if the relationship is valid and make any corrections to the design.

Data Entity Exceptions provides a list of Data Entity problems that prevent further analysis. It lists the following:

The Data Entities do not have a record defined for them. Data Entity records that are not normalized (they do not contain a **Y** in the Normalized field). Those which have no keys. Data Entity records that have repeating groups. Ones that explode to a lower level record defined as a type **R** in a higher level record description (a structural record). Figure 12.13 shows an example of this report.

```
DATE: 18-JAN-90      DATA ENTITY EXCEPTIONS      PAGE    1
TIME: 00:20                               Excelerator/IS
PROJECT NAME: DFD
DESCRIPTION:   This report lists Data Entities that cannot be further analyzed.
Asterisks indicate whether each Data Entity explodes to no Record, to a Record not
flagged as Normalized, to a structural Record, to a Record with repeating groups,
or to a Record with no key.

                                   |       |REC  |      |    REC| REC
                                   |  NO   |NOT  |STRUC |    REP| NO
DATA ENTITY NAME                   |  REC  |NORML|REC   |  GROUP| KEY
----------------------------------------------------------------------
|COURSES                          |       | *   |      |       |      |
|STUDENTS                         |       | *   |      |       |      |
|TEXTBOOKS                        |       | *   |      |       |      |
|INSTRUCTORS                      |       | *   |      |       |      |
|                                 |       |     |      |       |      |
----------------------------------------------------------------------
```

Figure 12.13   Data Entity Exceptions Report Example

Data Model Relationships shows records that are described as normalized and explode from Data Entities. It provides relationship information, not design problems.

DAR/Record Conflicts shows records whose keys conflict with Data Relationships. It examines record keys and Data Model Diagram keys and reports on discrepancies.

The Matrices available for Data Normalization are:

Record Contains Record (One Level)
Record Contains Element (One Level)
Normalized Record Contents (All Levels)
Record Dependencies
Data Relationships
Data Entity Records
Data Entity Record Relationships
ALL MATRICES

Record Contains Record (One Level) is the same as described under Record Content Analysis.

Record Contains Element (One Level) is the same as described under Record Content Analysis.

Normalized Record Contents (All Levels) shows only normalized records and their elements, using the same format as Record Contains Element.

Record Dependencies displays records and their relation to other records, either one or many.

Data Relationships shows Data Entities and their relationship with each other, either one or many.

Data Entity Records displays Data Entities and the records they explode to.

Data Entity Record Relationships shows the records that Data Entities explode to and the relation between these records.

SCREEN/REPORT DATA USAGE

This feature analyzes prototype screens and reports and the corresponding elements found in the XLDictionary. The results may be used to determine redundant or duplicate screens and reports. Report and screen elements are presented.

The following reports are available:

Elements in Screen/Report Designs
Equivalent Screen/Report Designs
Subset Screen/Report Designs
ALL REPORTS

Elements in Screen/Report Designs lists each element and screens containing the element. This is an excellent report for viewing the impact of changes.

Equivalent Screen/Report Designs shows reports and screen designs that have the same elements, thus are equivalent. These may be a valid component of your design, as in the case of a valid change and invalid change report.

Subset Screen/Report Designs lists screens and reports that share the same elements. One screen or report contains a subset of the other screen or report's elements.

Two Matrices are available. They are:

Screen/Report Design Contents shows screens and reports and the elements found within the

```
                               -------------------------------------------------
                               |E  |E  |E  |E  |E  |E  |E  |E  |E  |E  |E  |
                               |L  |L  |L  |L  |L  |L  |L  |L  |L  |L  |L  |
                               |E  |E  |E  |E  |E  |E  |E  |E  |E  |E  |E  |
                               |   |   |   |   |   |   |   |   |   |   |   |
                               |C  |C  |S  |C  |S  |Z  |Z  |CT |SN |AC |C  |
                               |U  |U  |T  |I  |T  |I  |I  |UE |AU |CO |R  |
                               |S  |S  |R  |T  |A  |P  |P  |SL |LM |CD |E  |
                               |T  |T  |E  |Y  |T  |   |   |TE |EB |OE |D  |
                               |O  |O  |E  |   |E  |   |E  |OP |SE |U  |I  |
                               |M  |M  |T  |   |   |   |X  |MH |PR |N  |T  |
                               |E  |E  |   |   |   |   |P  |EO |E  |T  |   |
                               |R  |R  |   |   |   |   |A  |RN |R  |   |L  |
                               |   |   |   |   |   |   |N  | E |S  |S  |I  |
                               |N  |N  |   |   |   |   |S  |   |O  |T  |M  |
                               |U  |A  |   |   |   |   |I  |   |N  |A  |I  |
                               |M  |M  |   |   |   |   |O  |   |   |T  |T  |
                               |B  |E  |   |   |   |   |N  |   |   |U  |   |
                               |E  |   |   |   |   |   |   |   |   |S  |   |
                               |R  |   |   |   |   |   |   |   |   |   |   |
                               -------------------------------------------------
 ---------------------------   -------------------------------------------------
|SCD ADD CUSTOMER           |  | E | E | E | E | E | E | E | E | E | E | E |
|---------------------------|  |---+---+---+---+---+---+---+---+---+---+---|
|SCD ADD ORDER              |  | E |   |   |   |   |   |   |   | E |   |   |
|---------------------------|  |---+---+---+---+---+---+---+---+---+---+---|
|SCD CUSTOMER INQUIRY       |  | E | E | E | E | E | E | E | E | E | E | E |
|---------------------------|  |---+---+---+---+---+---+---+---+---+---+---|
|RED CUSTOMER REPORT        |  |   | E |   |   |   |   |   |   | E |   |   |
|---------------------------|  |---+---+---+---+---+---+---+---+---+---+---|
|RED NEW CUSTOMER           |  | E | E |   |   |   |   |   |   | E |   |   |
|REPORT                     |  |   |   |   |   |   |   |   |   |   |   |   |
 ---------------------------   -------------------------------------------------
```

Figure 12.14   Screen/Report Design Contents Matrix Example

screen or report, illustrated in Figure 12.14.

Screen/Report Design Shared Elements provides a cross-reference of all screens and reports and a count of the elements common to both.

ELEMENT ACCESS & DERIVATION

Elements Access and Derivation performs analysis on the elements that flow through a data flow diagram. The analysis follows elements in and out of processes and how they are used within data flow and records.

The following reports are available:

Unexploded Data Flows
Unprocessed Elements
Element Processing
Element Traceability
Misused Base Elements
Misused Derived Elements
ALL REPORTS

Unexploded Data Flows will list the data flow that do not explode to a record. Use this report early in analysis to list project work that needs completion.

Unprocessed Elements reports on elements that are not contained in any record. This report is excellent for analyzing what elements exist independent of any records. If you are keying elements in from JAD sessions or interviews, then later logically grouping them together to form records, this will show you elements omitted from record structures.

Element Processing shows data elements on the data flow diagram and the processes that have the data coming into or out of them. This can be done for either one element, a range of elements, or all elements. It also lists which elements are not described.

This report is very useful for tracking any proposed changes to an element or processes. It can be used to balance the data flow diagram processes. All base elements, those originally keyed, coming out of a process must enter the process. Only derived elements (those calculated or otherwise determined) may leave a process without entering it. This is a lengthy report which contains much information. Figure 12.15 shows an example of this report for only one element!

Element Traceability shows the elements found within records and data flows, and used by processes. This may be done for either one element, a range of elements, or all elements. Again a lengthy report, containing much valuable element and cross reference information. Record and process information is nicely indented for readability. Figure 12.16 shows an example for only one element.

```
DATE: 23-JAN-90          ELEMENT PROCESSING              PAGE     1
TIME: 00:41                                     Excelerator/IS    PROJECT
NAME: DFD

DESCRIPTION:    This report lists selected Elements and the Processes that use them.
                Entries in the Use column indicate whether Elements enter a Process
                (IN), leave a Process (OUT), or both enter and leave a Process (UPD).
                UPD stands for updated data.


ELEMENT NAME                    | USE | PROCESS(ES) USING THIS ELEMENT
--------------------------------+-----+-------------------------------
|BRANCH NUMBER                  | OUT |** not described **           |
|                               | UPD |1                             |
|                               | IN  |2                             |
|                               | OUT |3                             |
|                               | UPD |4                             |
|                               | IN  |5                             |
|                               | UPD |CUST LOGICAL 1                |
|                               | UPD |CUST LOGICAL 2                |
|                               | IN  |CUST LOGICAL 3                |
|                               | IN  |CUST LOGICAL 5                |
|                               | UPD |CUST LOGICAL 6                |
|                               | OUT |1.1                           |
|                               | OUT |1.2                           |
|                               | IN  |1.3                           |
|                               | IN  |1.4                           |
|                               | OUT |1.5                           |
|                               | UPD |1.6                           |
|                               | IN  |1.8                           |
|                               | OUT |1.2.2                         |
|                               | IN  |2.2                           |
|                               | OUT |3.3                           |
|                               |     |                              |
--------------------------------------------------------------------
```

Figure 12.15   Element Processing Partial Report - One Element

Misused Base Elements lists base elements, that is, those keyed as input into the system, which leave a process but do not enter the process. This is a potential output without corresponding input error. This is an extremely useful report for analyzing the correctness of element descriptions and processes. Also listed are elements that are not described in the XLDictionary. An example of this report is illustrated in Figure 12.17.

Misused Derived Elements lists elements that are derived, that is, calculated, but are not created by any process. Included are elements not described in the XLDictionary.

```
DESCRIPTION:     This report lists selected Elements along with the Records,
                 Data Flows and Processes that use them. Entries in the Use
                 column indicate whether Elements enter a Process (IN), leave
                 a Process (OUT), or both enter and leave a Process (UPD). UPD
                 stands for updated data.


ELEMENTS    |RECORDS     |DATA FLOWS |USE|PROCESSES
--------------------------------------------------------------------------
|ACCOUNT STATUS CODE                                                        |
|           CUSTOMER MASTER                                                  |
|           .             CUSTOMER MASTER                                    |
|           .             .               OUT:** not described **           |
|           .             .               UPD:CUST LOGICAL 1                 |
|           .             .               UPD:CUST LOGICAL 2                 |
|           .             .               IN :CUST LOGICAL 5                 |
|           .             .               UPD:CUST LOGICAL 6                 |
|           .             .               IN :1.4                            |
|           .             .               UPD:1.6                            |
|           .             .               IN :1.8                            |
|           .             .               IN :2.2                            |
|           .             .               OUT:3.3                            |
|           .             .               OUT:4.5                            |
|           .             .               IN :4.3                            |
|                                                                           |
--------------------------------------------------------------------------
```

Figure 12.16 Element Traceability Partial Report - One Element

ALL REPORTS gives all the above reports.

MATRICES has the following options, which provide a comprehensive view of data flow, elements, records and the processes they are used within.

Basic Contents (All Levels)
Data Flow Contents (One Level)
Data Flow Contents (All Levels)
Process Data Flows
Process Element Access
ALL MATRICES

```
DATE: 07-JAN-91          MISUSED BASE ELEMENTS              PAGE        1
TIME: 15:54                                                 Excelerator/IS
PROJECT NAME: CUSTOMER


DESCRIPTION:   This report lists Elements defined as base that are created by a
               Process. A base Element should not leave any Process it does not
               enter.


ELEMENT NAME     IS DERIVED BY        PROCESS NAME
----------------------------------------------------------------------
|CUSTOMER NUMBER                     |** not described **                |
|CUSTOMER NAME                       |** not described **                |
|BRANCH NUMBER                       |** not described **                |
|SALESPERSON NUMBER                  |** not described **                |
|RETURN DATE                         |1.1                                |
|                                    |                                   |
|INVOICE NUMBER                      |** not described **                |
|RETURN AMOUNT                       |1.1                                |
|STREET                              |** not described **                |
|CITY                                |** not described **                |
|STATE                               |** not described **                |
|                                    |                                   |
|ZIP                                 |** not described **                |
|ZIP EXPANSION                       |** not described **                |
|CUSTOMER TELEPHONE                  |** not described **                |
|ACCOUNT STATUS CODE                 |** not described **                |
|DATE OF LAST PURCHASE               |** not described **                |
|                                    |                                   |
|DATE OF LAST PAYMENT                |** not described **                |
|CREDIT LIMIT                        |** not described **                |
|INVOICE DATE                        |CUST LOGICAL 1                     |
|INVOICE AMOUNT                      |CUST LOGICAL 1                     |
|PAYMENT DATE                        |** not described **                |
|                                    |                                   |
|PAYMENT AMOUNT                      |** not described **                |
|                                    |                                   |
----------------------------------------------------------------------
```

Figure 12.17 Misused Base Elements Report Example

Basic Contents (All Levels) shows elements and records contained within other records.

Data Flow Contents (One Level) shows the records contained within data flow.

Data Flow Contents (All Levels) shows which elements and records are contained within data flow.

Process Data Flows shows which data flow are used by which processes. It provides a comprehensive view of the collection of data flow diagrams.

Process Element Access lists which elements and records are used by which processes.

ALL MATRICES will put all the matrices on one screen or report.

EXERCISES

1. Run the Where Used report for any record you have created.

2. Generate and print the Record Contains Record Matrix.

3. Generate and print the Record Contains Element Matrix.

4. Use the XLDICTIONARY option from the main menu to print the Elements Contained In Records report.

5. Use the XLDICTIONARY option from the main menu to print the Records Contained In Data Flow Diagram report.

6. Print the ELE Contained - In SCD report. What information does the report present to you?

7. Produce the DMD Contains ANY report. What summary information is presented?

8. Print the SCD References ELE report. How does this report compare to the information presented in Exercise number 6?

The following exercises use the analysis options found within the Extended Analysis feature.

9. Run the Equivalent Records report. Analyze the information being presented. Are all the records redundant? Should they be eliminated from the design?

10. Produce the report for Unkeyed Records (One Level). Do all the records listed represent errors in the design?

11. Print the Foreign keys (All Levels) report. How would you use this information in analyzing record design? In analyzing a data model diagram?

12. Run the Index Elements Exceptions report. What is the information telling you?

13. Produce the Index elements in Data Stores matrix. Examine the contents of the matrix and comment on the usefulness of the information.

14. Produce the Repeating Groups report. How would this report be useful in analyzing the design for normalized records? Which records are included on the report?

15. Produce the Record Dependencies report. How would the information be useful in

analyzing the file or data base design?

16. Print the Data Entity Records matrix. What information is being presented?

17. Run the Equivalent Screen/Report Designs report. How would this report be useful in analyzing the system design?

18. Print the Screen/Report Design Content matrix and make a comment on the usefulness of this matrix in analyzing the project.

19. Run the Misused Base Elements report. How can this report help you refine the system design?

20. Run the Misused Derived Elements report. How can this report help you refine the system design?

21. Produce the Data Flow Contents (All Levels) report. Make a comment on the usefulness of this report in analyzing the system design.

22. Print the Process Data Flows report. How would this report be used to analyze the system design?

23. Produce the Process Element Access report. How would the information be used?

13

CREATING CUSTOMIZED REPORTS

Chapter Goals:

> Learn how to use the Report Writer feature to create customized reports.
> Understand how to select entities and their attributes (fields) for determining report content.
> Know how to create report sequences.
> Understand the difference between report formats and how to use them.
> Know how to use the User-Defined format.
> Understand Excelerator reports and how to use the information.
> Know how to use the Screen Data Reporting feature for reporting on screen prototype data.

The Report Writer feature gives you the power to create standard or customized reports using XLDictionary entries. You can report on project progress and XLDictionary entities. As the project develops, the reports may be rerun to monitor change and developments. You would use it for creating reports that cannot be automatically generated by using the XLDictionary or Extended Analysis reporting features.

Report writer allows you to control the format of the reports and the sequence of the data within the reports. Entity list information may be custom printed using the Report Writer. There is a tremendous power and flexibility inherent in this feature.

To create (or change) a report, select **ANALYSIS** from the main menu and then **Report Writer**. Select Add to create a new report or modify to change an existing one. Key in the name of the report and press the <u>Tab</u> key. Be sure that the name is descriptive enough so that it may be easily selected from a collection of reports. When modifying, press enter for a selector list.

Enter the **XLD Type**. This is the three letter abbreviation for an entity or relationship stored in the XLDictionary. Since there are so many entities and relationships maintained by Excelerator (about 1440), it is fastest to key in the entity type, if known. If the type is not known, as for relationships, enter up to three letters followed by an asterisk (*). Excelerator presents a selector list of only the entities starting with the letter(s). Pressing the enter key will give a selector list of all the entities (see

Figure 13.1). The complete selector list is 21 pages long! Select one from the list.

A Report Definition Screen is displayed, shown in Figure 13.2. There are four choices plus Exit on the left: Ent List, Select, Sort, and Format. Entity List allows you to use a previously created selection list (which must correspond to the entity type entered with the report name). Chapter 14 provides information on the Entity List feature.

THE SELECT OPTION

The Select option allows you to choose various <u>attributes</u> or fields available for the specific XLDictionary type selected, the one originally entered with the report name. Choose **Select** and the attributes for the entity type are displayed. See Figure 13.3 for element (ELE) attributes.

```
XLD Type Selector List

    Entity name                        Code / 2nd Type

. . . . . . . . . . .    -   . . . . . . . . . .
DAF Has-Associated REF...............Reference Document
DAF Has-Associated TST. . . . . . . .Test
DAF Satisfies ERQ...................Engineering Requirement
DAF Satisfies URQ . . . . . . . . . .User Requirement
DAF Explodes-To ANY.................Any Entity Type
DAF Has-Associated ANY. . . . . . . .Any Entity Type
DAF Satisfies ANY...................Any Entity Type
DFD Has-Associated CAT. . . . . . . .Category
DFD Has-Associated CHG...............Change Request
DFD Has-Associated ELS. . . . . . . .Entity List
DFD Has-Associated ISS..............Issue
DFD Has-Associated NTE. . . . . . . .Note
DFD Has-Associated REF..............Reference Document
DFD Has-Associated TST. . . . . . . .Test
DFD Satisfies ERQ..................Engineering Requirement
DFD Satisfies URQ . . . . . . . . . .User Requirement
. . . . . . . . . . .    +   . . . . . . . . . . . . . . . .
```

Figure 13.1 Selector List for Entities

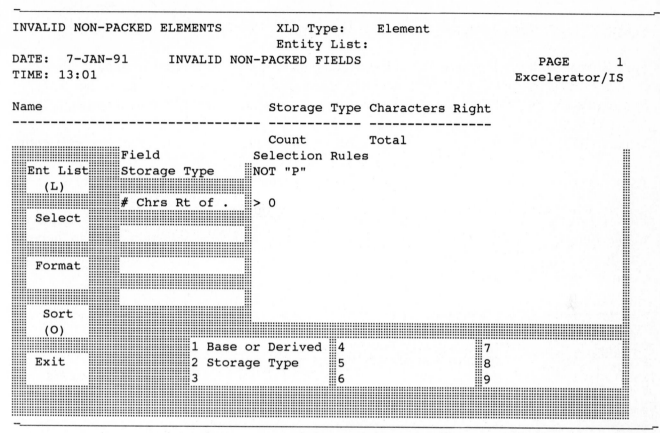

```
INVALID NON-PACKED ELEMENTS        XLD Type:      Element
                                   Entity List:
DATE:  7-JAN-91     INVALID NON-PACKED FIELDS                  PAGE      1
TIME: 13:01                                               Excelerator/IS


Name                                Storage Type  Characters Right
--------------------------------    ------------  ----------------
                                    Count         Total
                       Field        Selection Rules
  Ent List            Storage Type  NOT "P"
   (L)
                      # Chrs Rt of .  > 0
   Select


   Format



   Sort
   (O)
                      1 Base or Derived  4          7
   Exit               2 Storage Type     5          8
                      3                  6          9
```

Figure 13.2 Report Definition Screen

Select an attribute, for example, Name. Two **Rule** entry areas appear. If you want a group of entries all starting with the same characters, enter the characters followed by the wildcard "*" all in quotes. A second rule may be entered. When two rules are present, the AND operator connects them. Both conditions must be satisfied for the entity to be selected.

Rules follow the standard Excelerator format for conditions. Details are in Chapter 8, Data Dictionary. Some examples are:

Select Field	Rule	Meaning
Name	"CUST*"	Select all names beginning with the characters CUST
Name	NOT "*" OPT	Any blank names
# Chrs Rt of	> 0	Elements with characters to the right of the decimal point (see Figure 13.2)

Select Field	Rule	Meaning
Storage type	"B"	Elements with a storage type of binary
Storage type	NOT "P"	All storage types except "P" (see Figure 13.2)
Occurs (REC)	NOT = 1	All repeating groups, for the record (REC) entity
Assoc Type	"TST"	Find all elements with a test plan defined.

Press F3 when you are finished entering the rules for this attribute. An asterisk (*) is placed to the right of selected fields. Choose additional fields and their selection rules as needed for the report. When all the rules have been chosen, select the **....Complete....** option. Control returns to the selection menu on the left.

```
INVALID NON-PACKED ELEMENTS        XLD Type:     Element
                                   Entity List:
DATE:  7-JAN-91     INVALID NON-PACKED FIELDS                  PAGE      1
TIME: 13:01                                                    Excelerator/IS


Name                              Storage Type Characters Right
-------------------------------   ------------ ----------------
                                  Count        Total

 Ent List
   (L)                     Name              Base or Derived   Last Project
                           Alternate Name    Data Class        Locked By
   Select                  Definition        Source            Date Locked
                           Input Format      REQ Type          Lock Status
                           Output Format     Name-1            ....Complete....
   Format                  Edit Rules        Assoc Type
                           Storage Type    * Name-2
                           # Chrs Left of .  Description
   Sort                    # Chrs Rt of .  * Last Modified By
   (O)                     Default           Last Modify Date
                           Prompt            Number Changes
   Exit                    Column Header     Added By
                           Short Header      Date Added
Pick selection field and pick 'Complete' when finished
```

Figure 13.3 Attribute Selection Screen

SORT

Most reports have a specific sequence to make them easy to read and find information. The sort option allows you to specify major and minor sort sequences. Fields are sorted ascending in the ASCII sequence except dates, which sort in chronological order. Name is the default and is also the last sort field, if not previously selected. You may have up to nine sort fields, but a large number will take a long time to sort and use large amounts of disk space.

Select **Sort**. Choose the first sort sequence (the major sort field) and enter a **1** for the sort number. Select the next field, if needed. Enter a **2** for the sort number (intermediate sort field). Continue until all sort sequences have been established and then select ....**Complete**..... Figure 13.4 illustrates the sort selection screen. Base or Derived is the major sort sequence, Storage Type the minor. The sort sequences will be shown in the boxes numbered 1-9 on the bottom of the screen, shown in Figure 13.2.

THE REPORT FORMAT

The report format, or layout, must be defined. This format may be tailored to your individual or organizational needs or may be a standard Excelerator report.

There are 8 options available. User-Defined gives you the power to customize the report. The other options are standard Excelerator report formats, the same as obtained when reporting from the XLDictionary. These eight options are:

1.   **User-Defined.** This gives you the flexibility to define the report to any format desired. Use for entities and relationships.

2.   **Output.** This prints complete XLDictionary attributes for the selected entity.

3.   **Summary.** This report lists the entity and only two of the more important attributes, pre-selected by Excelerator. Use this report for entities and relationships.

4.   **List.** This option provides a display (no print available) of the entity or relationship. Only the entity name and one other important attribute, again pre-selected by Excelerator, will be shown.

5.   **Audit.** A report that shows the entity, dates and user who originally created, modified and locked the entity. One title line may be entered.

```
INVALID NON-PACKED ELEMENTS        XLD Type:    Element
                                   Entity List:
DATE:   7-JAN-91    INVALID NON-PACKED FIELDS          PAGE       1
TIME:  13:01                                          Excelerator/IS


Name                             Storage Type Characters Right
-------------------------------- ------------ ----------------
                                   Count       Total

  Ent List                        #               #                     #
   (L)             Name              Base or Derived  1 Last Project
                   Alternate Name    Data Class         Locked By
  Select           Definition        Source             Date Locked
                   Input Format      REQ Type           Lock Status
                   Output Format     Name-1             ....Complete....
  Format           Edit Rules        Assoc Type
                   Storage Type    2 Name-2
                   # Chrs Left of .  Description
   Sort            # Chrs Rt of .    Last Modified By
   (O)             Default           Last Modify Date
                   Prompt            Number Changes
  Exit             Column Header     Added By
                   Short Header      Date Added
Which sort field?
```

Figure 13.4 Report Layout Screen With Completed Entries

6.   **Expanded Output.** This report shows a complete list of relationships that explode from an entity. It takes a long time to generate the data, especially if wildcards (an asterisk) are included in the name for the selection criteria.

7.   **Where Used.** A report that shows where the entity is used, all it's relationships. This also may take a while to generate if using wild cards for the name selection.

8.   **Missing Entities.** This report lists entities referenced by other entities, which have not been defined. This option is for relationships only.

After choosing the report format, enter a title and press F3. Then select Exit and Save. No Save may be chosen if you have made any mistakes and wish to abandon or if you haven't made any changes.

Select **Execute** to run the report. Key in the name or press the enter key for a selector list when prompted for a name. For the printed reports, choose whether fields should be underlined. Then choose where the report should go: to a disk file, the screen or the printer.

THE USER-DEFINED FORMAT

To create a customized report, select **Format,** and **User-Defined**. The User-Defined screen is displayed. Refer to the example in Figure 13.5.

On the top is an area for the report layout to be displayed. Date, Time, Page number and the Excelerator version display by default. A horizontal menu selection line appears under the display area. The first line selection entry is Title. Select Title and key in up to two report title lines on the top of the screen. Press F3 to save.

In the center of the screen is a list of fields and column width defaults available for the selected entity (eg. REC or ELE). Select the attribute field for the first column, for example Name, from the list. Notice that it displays on the top of the screen. Good report design has, by convention, the major sort sequence on the leftmost column, followed by intermediate and

---

```
INVALID NON-PACKED ELEMENTS        XLD Type:    Element
                                   Entity List:
DATE:   7-JAN-91      INVALID NON-PACKED FIELDS                PAGE      1
TIME:  13:01                                               Excelerator/IS


Name                                 Storage Type Characters Right
------------------------------       ------------ -----------------
                                         Count         Total
              Title    Header  Width   Delete  <--||-->   Count   Total No Cnt/Tot
 Ent List
   (L)                       Name           32 Base or Derived 15 Last Project    16
                             Alternate Name 32 Data Class      32 Locked By       16
  Select                     Definition     60 Source          32 Date Locked     11
                             Input Format   25 REQ Type        08 Lock Status     11
                             Output Format  25 Name-1          32 ....Complete....
  Format                     Edit Rules     60 Assoc Type      10
                             Storage Type   12 Name-2          32
                             # Chrs Left of .16 Description     72
   Sort                      # Chrs Rt of . 14 Last Modified By16
   (O)                       Default        32 Last Modify Date16
                             Prompt         20 Number Changes  14
  Exit                       Column Header  47 Added By        16
                             Short Header   15 Date Added      10
Pick action or print field and pick 'Complete' when finished
```

Figure 13.5 The User-Defined Format Screen

---

minor sort sequences to the right.

Select a second field, Storage Type in this example. You are prompted for where you would like the field to be placed among the columns. The white screen area is the default location where the next column will be placed. Press the enter key or select the location to accept the default. This will be placed one space to the right of the previous column. You may select a format area above or below any already chosen column, indicated by a dashed line. The new field will be placed to the left of that column.

CHANGING THE DEFAULT
COLUMN HEADING AND WIDTH

The default column headings may be altered. Select **Header** from the line menu. Then select the column header you would like to change. Type in the new column header in the white entry area that displays. Keep in mind that the number of characters is limited to the number of hyphens shown under the column heading. Press enter when finished.

Example: Select Headers, then select # Chrs Rt of. Enter the new column heading **Chars. Right** and press the enter key.

To change the column width, select **Width** from the line menu, and a column from the report format display area. Type in the new width and press enter.

Example: Select Width and then select the Chars. Right column. Enter 16 for the width and press enter. Notice that the column width has been changed. Now select Header and Chars. Right. Type in **Characters Right** and press enter. This column heading would not fit in the old width of 14 characters.

Columns may be deleted by selecting Delete from the line menu. Any columns to the right of the deleted column are shifted left.

Since the full report may be 132 characters, the screen must be scrolled to show columns past column 80 (the screen width). Select the left arrow (<--) or the right arrow (-->) on the menu line to scroll the report format left or right.

The **Count** option will count the number of entries on the report. Select Count and select the column that the count should appear under when the report is printed.

Total will produce a total for numeric data fields. If a non-numeric field, such as Name, is selected, the total will be zero.

No Cnt/Tot will selectively delete counts and totals. Select No Cnt/Tot and the column that a count or total appears under. The count or total is removed.

When the format is finished, select **....Complete.....** Then select Exit and Save (or No Save to abandon). The report may be executed.

REPORT CONTROL

As the number of reports for a project increase, it is useful to know which reports are available and what is contained on each report. This is especially useful for teams of analysts where one person is creating the report and others need to view the information.
From the Report Writer action keypad, there are two useful reports and two corresponding inquiries available. **Summary Output** shows the report name, the title, and the entity type.

Output shows complete information on each report. Pressing the enter key when prompted for a Name Range will give a selector list. Selecting the first entry **. . All Entities on Selector List . .** will give details on all reports.

Selecting **List** displays the report names and titles on the screen.

Inspect provides detailed report information on the screen. Select Inspect and then enter a name (or press enter for a selector list). The report information is presented on three screens. Use PgUp and PgDn to scroll between the pages. Select Exit to leave the Report Writer feature.

SCREEN DATA REPORTING

The Screen Data Reporting feature allows you to produce reports using data files created by data entry screens. Thus data entered onto a screen may be selected, sorted and printed. This gives the ability to check your system design for report data being available from input screens and demonstrates design completeness.

Select **SCREENS & REPORTS** from the main menu. Select **Screen Data Reporting** from the options.

The standard Excelerator action keypad displays. Select Add, or Modify to change an existing report. Enter a name for the report and the data entry <u>file</u> name (eg. CUSTOMER MASTER) or press enter for a selector list of data entry files.

The Report Writer screen is displayed, illustrated in Figure 13.6. Three options plus Exit appear on the left.

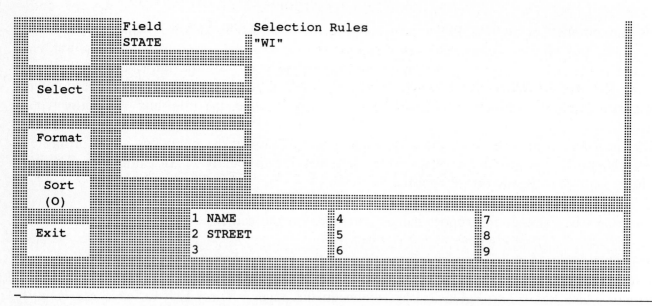

```
CUSTOMER REPORT FOR WISCONSIN       Screen Data: CUSTOMER MASTER

DATE:   7-JAN-91      REPORT OF ALL CUSTOMERS IN WISCONSIN        PAGE      1
TIME:  13:03                                                   Excelerator/IS

                                    Output


                     Field          Selection Rules
                     STATE          "WI"



        Select



        Format



         Sort
         (O)
                          1 NAME          4              7
        Exit              2 STREET        5              8
                          3               6              9
```

Figure 13.6 Report Writer For Screen Elements

Select, Sort, and **Format** are the same as described for the Report Writer feature. The major difference is that selection is for prototyping fields, rather than entity attributes.

SELECTION

Choose the **Select** option. A list of screen prototyping fields for this data entry file displays. Up to 5 may be selected. These may be printed or may only be used as selection criteria for records that contain the actual fields to be printed.

Select a desired field, eg. STATE. Two rule entry areas are displayed on the top of the screen. Enter the criteria for the report (eg. "WI" for all customers in Wisconsin). For a complete description of rule conditions, see Chapter 8, Data Dictionary.

Press F3 when the rule(s) have been entered. An asterisk appears to the right of the field. If dates are selected, the date rule must appear as the YYMMDD format. Select ....**Complete**.... or press the period (.) when finished.

EXERCISES

1. By Excelerator standards, only packed fields may have characters to the right of the decimal point. The following report lists all fields that have characters to the right of the decimal point and have a storage type other than packed. Refer to Figure 13.5.

   Select Add and then enter INVALID NON-PACKED ELEMENTS for the name and ELE for the entity type. Choose **Select** and the field **# Chrs Rt of ..** Enter **> 0** for the rule. Select **....Complete....**

   Select **Format** and **Summary Output**. Enter the title **Invalid Packed Fields**. Press F3 and then select Exit and Save.

   Select Execute and print the report.

   Select **Modify** and enter the name **INVALID NON-PACKED ELEMENTS**. Choose **Format,** then **Output**. Press F3, select Exit and Save.

   Select Execute and print the report.

2. Using the method outlined above, create a report that will show all elements without an input or output picture.

3. Produce a report that shows all records without keys defined on them.

4. Develop and print a report that shows all elements with edit rules that are blank.

5. Produce a list of all Table of Codes required to satisfy edit rules. Use the Element (ELE) entity and select Edit Rules. The Rule value should be "FROM*" indicating that a table is used for edit criteria. This is the only method of determining which Table of Codes entities are required and which elements they are used for.

6. Construct a screen data entry report for the Order Entry prototype created in Chapter 11. Include the customer number, salesperson number and branch. The title should be 'Customers Placing Orders'.

7.   Create a report for data entered for the Student Record Inquiry program, from the exercises in Chapter 11. The fields on the report should be:

        Student Number, Last Name, First Name, Grade Point Average, and Credits Earned.

8.   Create a report showing all elements with the **Source** area containing an entry. The criteria would be **NOT** " ". This lists all fields that should be included on input forms.

9.   Create a report showing all elements with the **Source** area containing a <u>single</u> entry. Use either the <u>New Employee Form</u> or <u>Student Registration Form</u>, added to the elements in Chapter 8. Include the element name, the input picture and the length. This report would show all elements, and their lengths, that need to be included on a specific source document.

10.   Produce a report showing all records which are not normalized. Check for a **Normalized** code of "N". Include a header "Records that are not normalized". List only the record name.

11.   Produce a list of all Processes that have a value "ON LINE". Include the Process number (the Name) and the process Label. The heading should be "On-line Process Listing".

12.   List all Processes that have a **Duration Value**, using an entry of **NOT** " ". Include the Process Name, Label, Duration Value and the Duration Type. This report would be useful for analyzing slow areas of the system for analyzing problems of response time or throughput.

13.   Print a report showing all manual processes. Select the **Manual or Computer** attribute for values of "M". This would be useful as a checklist for creating user procedure manuals.

14.   Produce a report listing data stores and their index elements. Create a title and include the data store name, label and index elements.

15.   Print a report showing all data stores and the records they explode to.

16.   Produce a list of all data stores and their total and average number of records.

14
ENTITY LISTS

SELECTING XLDICTIONARY DATA
FOR REPORTING AND EXPORT

Chapter Goals:

Understand what entity lists are.
Learn how to use create entity lists using a variety of methods.
Understand how to combine entity lists to form new lists.
Know how to use the entity lists to create reports and the difference between
    entity list reports and the Report Writer.
Understand how to use entity lists for transferring project information to other
    projects.

Entity List is a powerful feature of Excelerator that allows you to create lists of selected data stored within the XLDictionary. These lists provide a means for selecting entities and their data for exporting, importing and producing reports. You have full control over which entities or combination of entities are selected. An example would be to track the changes to the project, week by week or report on specific characteristics of data elements within the system.

An entity is any entry in the XLDictionary. Entity types (refer to Appendix B) are the general categories of Entities maintained by Excelerator. Each entity type has a three letter abbreviation, such as ELE (element), DAS (data store), REC (record) and so on. Entity lists may be formed from relationships. Some relationships examples are REC Contains ELE, DFD Contains PRO and REC Contains NTE.

The difference between the entity list feature and the report writer feature is that the report writer feature can use only one entity per report. Report Writer also saves the criteria for selecting data to be reported on. Thus when reports are generated using the Report Writer feature, the data on the reports changes from time to time, depending on the progress of the project.

Entity lists can report on entity types and a combination of entity types. Examples are ELE and CUSTOMER NUMBER, CUSTOMER NAME, and CURRENT BALANCE. An Entity List may be generated using several methods and, once created, remains unchanged unless modified. Thus an entity list would not change even though the project data may be changing. This can be a very useful method for reporting on the progress of a project.

An entity list contains only the *type* of entity and it's name. It uses these as an index to obtain full entity information from the XLDictionary. For any entity in the list, you can use the Browse key (F4) to view entities. It may be modified at this time, if desired, but use caution not to alter information vital to other parts of the system design.

An entity list may contain up to 134 entities. If you enter conditions that would create more than 134 entities, Excelerator prompts you for the name of a continuation list. Thus entity lists may be chained together. A second chained list may also be created by entering a name in the **Next Entity List** area. To view or modify the next chain, move the cursor to the Next Entity List area and press F4. Chains are handled as a single list for reporting and XLD Interface operations, however Delete and Output treat each list individually.

There are three options for creating an entity list. Four more options allow you to combine lists and there is one for reporting. These eight options are explained below.

To create or modify an entity list, select **Analysis** and then **Entity List**. Select Add (modify details will be covered later). An Entity List options screen displays providing 8 choices. These are briefly summarized here with details provided later. Refer to Figure 14.1.

1. **Screen Input** allows you to enter specific entity types and names using an input screen. This is useful for creating specific entity criteria for reporting or exporting certain parts of the system from a project.

2. **Union** creates an entity list by combining all the entities from two lists but without any duplicates.

   If entity list **1** = **AABBCC** and entity list **2** = **CCDDEE** then the union = **AABBCCDDEE**.

```
                                    1   Screen Input

                                    2   Union

                                    3   Intersection

                                    4   Difference

                                    5   Subtraction

                                    6   XLD Selection

                                    7   XLD Selection from List

                                    8   XLD Report Execution




Add how?
```

Figure 14.1   Entity List Options Screen

3.   **Intersection** selects entities that are common to two input entity lists.

        If entity list **1** = **AABBCC** and entity list **2** = **CCDDEE** then the intersection = **CC**.

4.   **Difference** gives all entities <u>not</u> in common to both lists.

        If entity list **1** = **AABBCC** and entity list **2** = **CCDDEE** then the difference = **AABBDDEE**.

5.   **Subtraction** compares two previously created entity lists and produces a resultant entity list of all entities on the first list that are not on the second list.

        If entity list **1** = **AABBCC** and entity list **2** = **CCDDEE** then list 1 subtract list 2 gives **AABB**.

6.   **XLD Selection** (Add only) allows you to choose specific entities using selector lists for entity types and selection rules for picking attributes within the entity type, similar

to selecting report criteria.

7.   **XLD Selection from List** selects a subset of entities from an existing entity list. Add creates a new list, modify overrides the existing list.

8.   **XLD Report Execution** (Add option only) allows you to create an entity list from previously created report selection criteria.

CREATING ENTITY LISTS

XLD REPORT EXECUTION

The easiest method of creating an entity list is from an already created report selection criteria. Select option number 8, XLD Report Execution. Key in the name of a report that has been previously created.

Example: Enter the name **NON PACKED DATA FIELDS WITH DEC** and press the enter key. A selector list of reports available will display. Select **INVALID NON-PACKED ELEMENTS**, created as a Report Writer exercise. A new entity list is created from previously established Report Writer selection criteria.

Select Inspect from the Entity List main menu. Press the enter key and select **NON PACKED DATA FIELDS WITH DEC** from the list. Notice the elements listed. Inspect provides a scroll region if more entries are available than fit on the screen. Press the down arrow to view more entities, the up arrow to show previous entities.

SCREEN INPUT

Select option number 1, Screen Input. An add entity list is displayed. The top two fields allow you to enter an alternate name and a definition. The **Next Entity List** entry is used to build another list linked to this one. Thus, if there are more entries in the list than will fit on the entry screen, the entities may be continued on another list. All linked lists are treated by Excelerator as one large, continuous list.

There are two columns for adding or modifying entities, illustrated in Figure 14.2. **Type** is the type of entity, eg. ELE, REC, DAS and so on, and may be mixed on the list. **Name** is the specific element name and cannot contain any wildcards (*). To delete an entry, places spaces in either the Type or Name Column and when saved, they will be removed from the list. Enter the type and names of the entities for the list. Press F3 when finished.

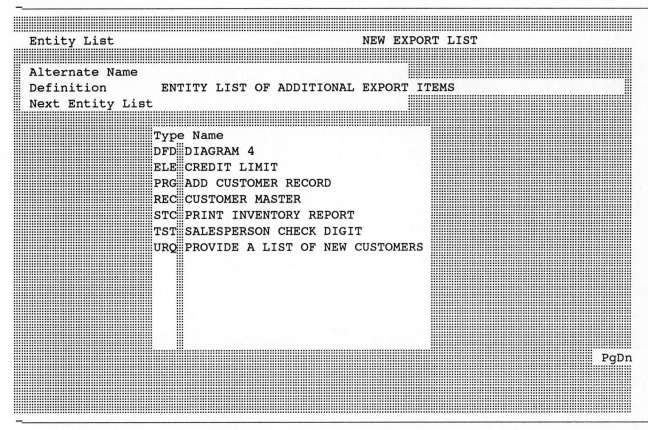

```
  Entity List                      NEW EXPORT LIST

  Alternate Name
  Definition          ENTITY LIST OF ADDITIONAL EXPORT ITEMS
  Next Entity List


              Type Name
              DFD DIAGRAM 4
              ELE CREDIT LIMIT
              PRG ADD CUSTOMER RECORD
              REC CUSTOMER MASTER
              STC PRINT INVENTORY REPORT
              TST SALESPERSON CHECK DIGIT
              URQ PROVIDE A LIST OF NEW CUSTOMERS




                                                               PgDn
```

Figure 14.2   Screen Input Entry Screen

XLD SELECTION

When a group of data with the same entity type is needed, XLD Selection (option 7) is an easy method for creating the list. Select XLD Selection and enter the name of the entity list. Press the <u>tab</u> key and enter the entity **Type**. Be sure to enter the type, since the selector list obtained by pressing the enter key is quite long. An attribute selection screen is displayed, illustrated in Figure 14.3.

Example: Enter the name BASE ELEMENTS. Press the tab key and enter ELE for the type. A selection screen displays, unique to the entity type. Figure 14.3 is an example for an element - type ELE. Selection is similar to that for the Report Writer feature. Choose the particular attribute or field and enter the condition(s). If 2 conditions are entered, both must be met for an entity to be selected (the **AND** connection).

XLD Type: ELE
Entity List: BASE ELEMENTS

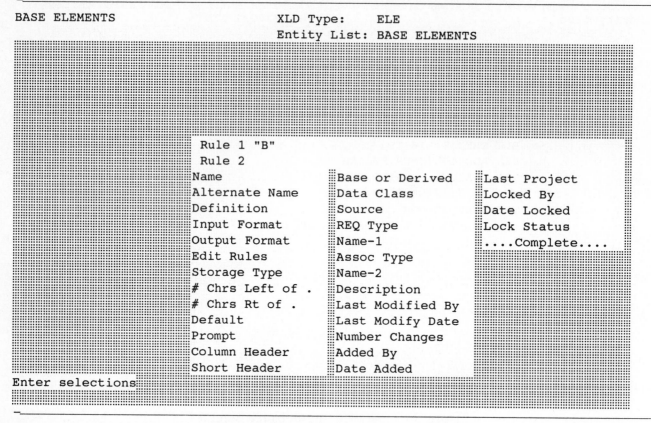

```
                     Rule 1 "B"
                     Rule 2
                     Name              Base or Derived    Last Project
                     Alternate Name    Data Class         Locked By
                     Definition        Source             Date Locked
                     Input Format      REQ Type           Lock Status
                     Output Format     Name-1             ....Complete....
                     Edit Rules        Assoc Type
                     Storage Type      Name-2
                     # Chrs Left of .  Description
                     # Chrs Rt of .    Last Modified By
                     Default           Last Modify Date
                     Prompt            Number Changes
                     Column Header     Added By
                     Short Header      Date Added
Enter selections
```

Figure 14.3 XLD Selection Screen

Example: Select **Base or Derived**. Enter "B" in rule 1, then press F3. An asterisk (*) appears to the right of the words "Base or Derived". Up to five entities per list may be chosen. Select **...Complete...** (or press the period) when finished. You will be prompted "OK to proceed? (Y/N)" If all your selections are correct, enter **Y**. If **N** is entered, you must start over at the action keypad. If **Y** is chosen, Excelerator will tell you how many entities were placed in the list.

Select Inspect from the action keypad. Press enter when prompted for a Name and choose the list just created. This allows you to verify the contents of the list: all elements that are Base.

Here is another example. This will be used later, in conjunction with the previous example. Select Add from the action keypad. Key in the name **ADD SCREEN FIELDS**. Press the tab for the entity type and enter **SC***. Select **SCD References ELE** for screen design references element. Refer to Figure 14.4.

```
XLD Type Selector List

  Entity name                         Code / 2nd Type

  Screen Data Entry . . . . . . . . . .SDE
  Screen Data Report...................SDR
  Screen Design . . . . . . . . . . . .SCD
  SCD Goes-To SCD......................Screen Design
  SCD References ELE. . . . . . . . . .Element
  SCD Run-By SDE.......................Screen Data Entry
  SCD Comes-From SCD. . . . . . . . . .Screen Design
```

Figure 14.4   Relation Selector List - SC*

Select **SCD Name** and enter **"ADD*"** for all screens starting with ADD and press F3. Select **...Complete...** (or press the period) when finished. Figure 14.5 shows the selection screen for this relationship. Enter **Y** if everything was entered correctly. Again, use Inspect to view the contents. Figure 14.6 shows the result of the inspect.

XLD SELECTION FROM LIST

XLD Selection from List allows you to create an entity list from one previously created. Select this option and enter the name **BASE ELEMENTS WITH DEFAULT VALUE**. Press the tab key (or down arrow) twice, key in ELE and press the enter key. A selector list of existing entity lists displays.

Select **BASE ELEMENTS**. A list now displays showing the available fields for elements. Select **Default** from the left column. Enter **NOT " "** for Rule 1 and press F3. Select **...Complete...** (or press the period) when finished, and use Inspect to view the contents. Figure 14.7 illustrates the selection screen.

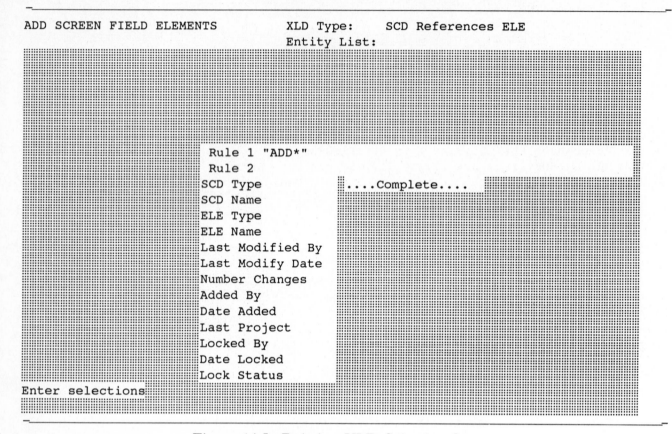

```
Rule 1 "ADD*"
Rule 2
SCD Type              ....Complete....
SCD Name
ELE Type
ELE Name
Last Modified By
Last Modify Date
Number Changes
Added By
Date Added
Last Project
Locked By
Date Locked
Lock Status
Enter selections
```

Figure 14.5 Relation XLD Selection Screen

COMBINING ENTITY LISTS

Entity lists may be combined to produce a vast amount of reports and unique combinations of project information. There are four methods of combining entity lists, as previously mentioned.

UNION

Union creates an entity list by combining all the entities from two lists but without any duplicates. Here's a simple example. Use XLD Selection to create a new list. Enter the name **NUMERIC BASE FIELDS**, press the tab key and enter ELE. Select **Input Format** and enter the criteria **"9*"** in Rule 1 for all field pictures that start with a "9", then press F3. Select **Base or Derived** and enter "B" in rule 1. Press F3 and select **...Complete....**

Select Inspect and enter the name NUMERIC BASE FIELDS to view the entity list.

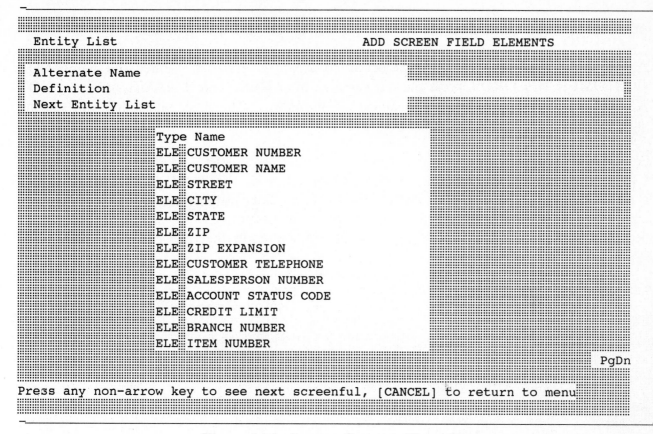

```
 Entity List                              ADD SCREEN FIELD ELEMENTS

 Alternate Name
 Definition
 Next Entity List

                 Type Name
                 ELE  CUSTOMER NUMBER
                 ELE  CUSTOMER NAME
                 ELE  STREET
                 ELE  CITY
                 ELE  STATE
                 ELE  ZIP
                 ELE  ZIP EXPANSION
                 ELE  CUSTOMER TELEPHONE
                 ELE  SALESPERSON NUMBER
                 ELE  ACCOUNT STATUS CODE
                 ELE  CREDIT LIMIT
                 ELE  BRANCH NUMBER
                 ELE  ITEM NUMBER
                                                                 PgDn

 Press any non-arrow key to see next screenful, [CANCEL] to return to menu
```

Figure 14.6 Inspect Screen - From List

Create the union entity list. This will combine all derived elements (which should be numeric) with the base numeric fields. Select Add, Union and enter the name **ALL NUMERIC FIELDS**. Press the tab key and enter the name NUMERIC BASE FIELDS when prompted for the Using List. Tab again and enter DERIVED ELEMENTS for the **And** List. You could also press enter for a selector list and choose the input entity lists. Figure 14.8 shows the name selection screen for the Union option. Excelerator will provide feedback on the entities selected. Use Inspect to view the elements on the final list.

INTERSECTION

Select Add and Intersection. This produces a list with elements in common to both input lists.

Example: Select Add and use XLD Selection to create a new list. Enter the name **RECS CONTAINING CUSTOMER NUMBER**, press the tab key and enter **REC**. Select **ELE/REC Name**. Enter "CUSTOMER NUMBER" in **Rule** 1, press F3 and select **...Complete...** (or press the period). This gives all records containing the customer number.

Again, select Add and use XLD Selection to create a new list. Enter the name **NOT CUSTOMER RECORDS,** press the tab key and enter **REC.** Select **NAME** and enter NOT "CUST*" in Rule 1, then press F3. Select **...Complete.....** This gives all records not starting with the text CUST.

Select Add and then Intersection. Key in the new name **RECS WITH C-N BUT NOT CUST,** press tab and enter the name RECS CONTAINING CUSTOMER NUMBER. Enter a second name of NOT CUSTOMER RECORDS. The resulting list contains all records containing the customer number but not starting with the text CUST. These records would use the customer number as a foreign key, able to randomly the read customer master file.

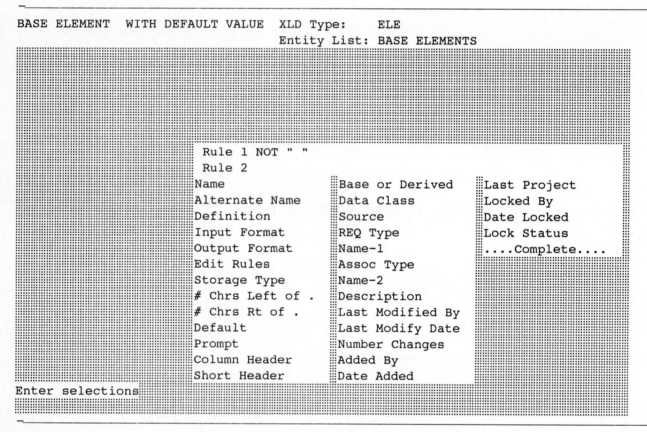

```
BASE ELEMENT  WITH DEFAULT VALUE  XLD Type:    ELE
                                   Entity List: BASE ELEMENTS


              Rule 1 NOT " "
              Rule 2
              Name            Base or Derived    Last Project
              Alternate Name  Data Class         Locked By
              Definition      Source             Date Locked
              Input Format    REQ Type           Lock Status
              Output Format   Name-1             ....Complete....
              Edit Rules      Assoc Type
              Storage Type    Name-2
              # Chrs Left of . Description
              # Chrs Rt of .  Last Modified By
              Default         Last Modify Date
              Prompt          Number Changes
              Column Header   Added By
              Short Header    Date Added
Enter selections
```

Figure 14.7   XLD Selection From List

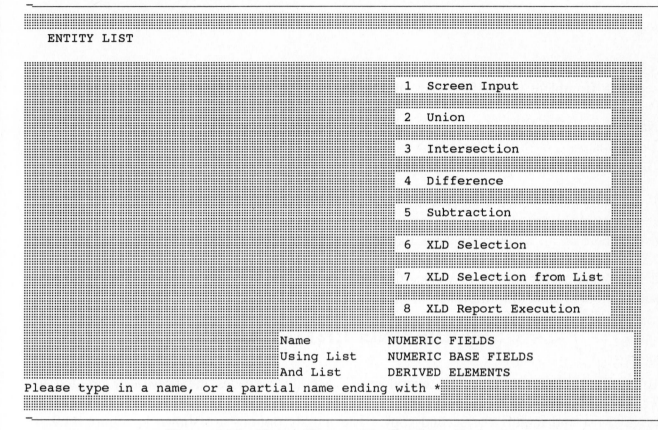

```
                                         1   Screen Input

                                         2   Union

                                         3   Intersection

                                         4   Difference

                                         5   Subtraction

                                         6   XLD Selection

                                         7   XLD Selection from List

                                         8   XLD Report Execution

                       Name          NUMERIC FIELDS
                       Using List    NUMERIC BASE FIELDS
                       And List      DERIVED ELEMENTS
Please type in a name, or a partial name ending with *
```

Figure 14.8   Union Feature To Combine Entity Lists

DIFFERENCE

Select Add and then Difference. This option gives all elements <u>not</u> in common to both entity lists.   Key in the name **BASE ELEMENTS - NO DEFAULT VALUE**.   Press enter and choose BASE ELEMENTS from the selector list.   Again, press enter and select BASE ELEMENTS WITH DEFAULT VALUE from the list presented.

Select Inspect, press the enter key and choose BASE ELEMENTS - NO DEFAULT VALUE from the selector list. Note that these elements are a subset of the base elements, with the characteristic of no default value.

SUBTRACTION

Select Add, then Subtraction. This produces a list of entities on the first list but not on the second. Complete in the following information:

Name   BASE ELEMENTS NOT ON INPUT SCREEN
Using List   BASE ELEMENTS
And List   ADD SCREEN FIELDS

Press enter and then use Inspect to view the contents. Base elements should be on input screens and this list shows all the base elements with add screens elements removed from the list. There is an assumption here that the screens to input new information all start with "ADD". Subtraction is a very useful method of monitoring the progress of a project. Create a list for a specific month or week. Create a similar list a month or week later. Then use subtraction to find the difference in data from one month or week to the next.

MODIFYING ENTITY LISTS

Entity lists may be modified in several ways. Modify overrides the previously created list. To keep the original list and make a modified list, use Copy to create a duplicate of the original list and modify the second copy. The modify options are shown in Figure 14.9.

Screen Input. Screen Input displays any previously created entity list. This is a scroll region. Press the down arrow to view more entries, the up arrow to scroll entries upward. Press F1 and the insert key to add a new entity to the middle of the list. Press F1 and the delete key to remove a line from the list.

Union. Union modifies the <u>first</u> list but keeps the second list. If you need to save first list, use Copy and modify the copy. Union may be used with the modify option if more than two lists need to be combined. Combine the first two lists and then modify, adding the next list.

Intersection. This may be used to create the intersection of any existing list with a second one.

Difference. Difference will modify a list with the information not in common with the first and second lists.

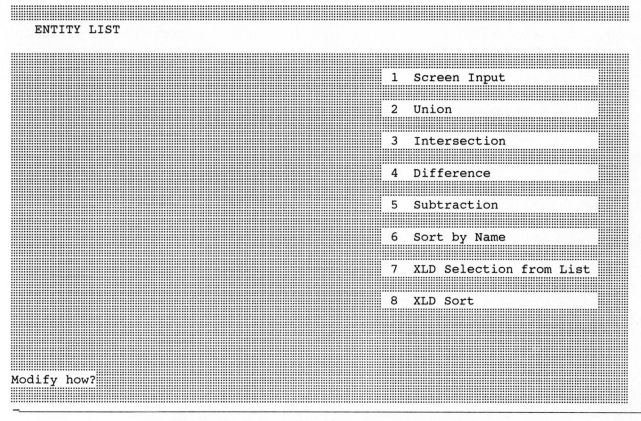

Figure 14.9 Modify Entity List Options Screen

Subtraction. Subtraction works similar to the other methods for combining lists. The first list is modified by subtrating elements on the second list from it.

Sort by Name. This option will take a list and sort it by the name of the entity. This is useful for entity lists that are created from screen input or by combining two lists. The output reports will have the entities in a sorted order for quickly locating of items. Select Sort by Name and press enter. Choose a name from the list and it will be sorted.

XLD Selection from List. Use this option as described for the Add action. The list may be modified with further selection criteria.

XLD Sort. This feature allows you to sort an entity list on any field on the list. This is also useful for entities created from screen input or by combining two lists. Enter an entity list name, press tab, and enter the type of entity. For mixed types, use **ANY**. Select a name from the list of fields presented. Enter a 1 for the first (major) sort field. Repeat for other sort sequences, using a number 2 for the second (minor) sort sequence, etc.

Select **...Complete...** or press the period, then enter **Y**. Figure 14.10 shows the sort selection screen used to arrange a list of entities to be exported to another project. The list was sorted by the entity *type*. Figure 14.11 presents the results obtained via the Inspect screen.

LIST, INSPECT,
SUMMARY OUTPUT, AND OUTPUT

These features are similar to those of the XLDictionary:

List shows the entity lists available.

Summary Output prints the names of available entity lists.

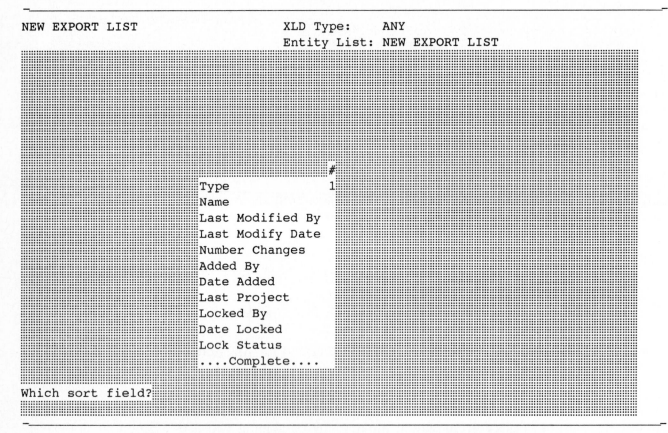

```
NEW EXPORT LIST                      XLD Type:    ANY
                                     Entity List: NEW EXPORT LIST




                                         #
                         Type            1
                         Name
                         Last Modified By
                         Last Modify Date
                         Number Changes
                         Added By
                         Date Added
                         Last Project
                         Locked By
                         Date Locked
                         Lock Status
                         ....Complete....

Which sort field?
```

Figure 14.10 XLD Selection Screen - Type Of ANY

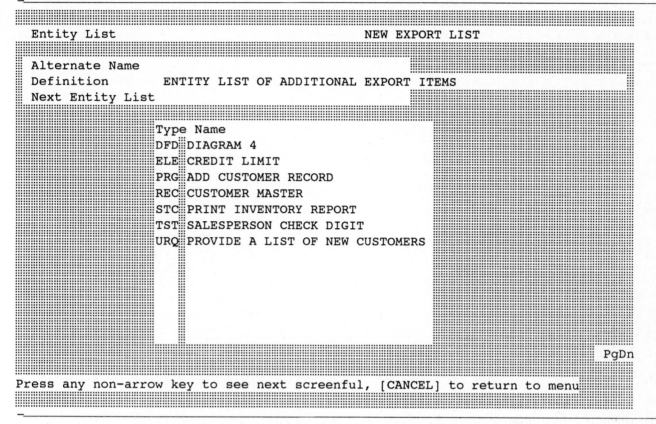

```
┌────────────────────────────────────────────────────────────────────┐
│  Entity List                          NEW EXPORT LIST                │
│                                                                      │
│  Alternate Name                                                      │
│  Definition        ENTITY LIST OF ADDITIONAL EXPORT ITEMS            │
│  Next Entity List                                                    │
│                                                                      │
│                    Type Name                                         │
│                    DFD DIAGRAM 4                                     │
│                    ELE CREDIT LIMIT                                  │
│                    PRG ADD CUSTOMER RECORD                           │
│                    REC CUSTOMER MASTER                               │
│                    STC PRINT INVENTORY REPORT                        │
│                    TST SALESPERSON CHECK DIGIT                       │
│                    URQ PROVIDE A LIST OF NEW CUSTOMERS               │
│                                                                      │
│                                                                      │
│                                                                      │
│                                                                      │
│                                                                      │
│                                                          PgDn        │
│                                                                      │
│  Press any non-arrow key to see next screenful, [CANCEL] to return to menu │
└────────────────────────────────────────────────────────────────────┘
```

Figure 14.11 Display Of Entity List Sorted By Entity Type

Inspect shows the contents of the entity list - the entity types and their names.

Output prints the contents of the entity list.

PRODUCING REPORTS OF ENTITY LIST DATA

Reports may be produced using the entity list names. These reports include the actual entity information, or *attributes* stored in the XLDictionary.

Select Execute from the action keypad. Enter a name, press the tab key, and enter an entity type. If you are unsure of the name, press the Tab key, and enter the entity type. Press enter and you will receive a selector screen of entity lists.

```
BASE ELEMENTS WITH DEFAULT VALUE  XLD Type:     ELE
                                  Entity List: BASE ELEMENTS WITH DEFAULT VALUE
DATE:  7-JAN-91                                                    PAGE      1
TIME: 13:20                                                   Excelerator/IS

                         1 User-Defined

                         2 Output

                         3 Summary

                         4 List

                         5 Audit

                         6 Expanded

                         7 Where Used

Which format?
```

Figure 14.12 Entity List Report Formats Available

The report format screen, shown in Figure 14.12, displays. Choose a format in the same manner described in Chapter 13, describing the Report Writer feature.

Example: Select Execute. Press the tab key and enter ELE. Press the enter key and select the name BASE ELEMENTS WITH DEFAULT VALUE from the list. Select the **Output** format. Key in the title **BASE ELEMENTS WITH A DEFAULT VALUE** on the top line and press F3. Reply **Y** to the prompt "OK to proceed? (Y/N)". Select the screen, printer or a file. A sample of the report is shown in Figure 14.13.

ENTITY LISTS USING RELATIONSHIPS

Entity lists may be created using relationships. This is very useful for printing or exporting selected groups of information. An example would be printing a list of elements that are components of a specific record. The following example illustrates the procedure for using relationships. Suppose that you need to print all the elements contained in the INVENTORY RECORD.

```
DATE:  7-JAN-91      BASE ELEMENTS WITH A DEFAULT VALUE               PAGE     1
TIME: 15:57                                                     Excelerator/IS

TYPE Element                            NAME ACCOUNT STATUS CODE

   Alternate Names ACCOUNT-STATUS-CODE


   Definition      A ONE DIGIT CODE TO REFLECT THE CUSTOMER'S STATUS

   Input Format    X
   Output Format   X
   Edit Rules      VALUES ARE "0" THRU "9"
   Storage Type    C
   Characters left of decimal 1   Characters right of decimal   0

   Default         0
   Prompt          STATUS CODE
   Column Header   STATUS CODE
   Short Header
   Base or Derived B
   Data Class
   Source          NEW CUSTOMER FORM


         Satisfies Requirement:                  Associated Entities:
  Type  Name                               Type  Name


                               Description


   Modified By   ALLEN            Date Modified  880719    # Changes  0
   Added By      ALLEN            Date Added     880719
   Last Project  DFD
   Locked By                      Date Locked    0         Lock Status
```

Figure 14.13 Sample Output - Entity List Report

Make the following choices:

Select: Add and XLD Selection

Name: INVENTORY RECORD ELEMENTS

Type: REC* This will provide a selector list of all relations starting with REC.

Select: REC Contains ELE

Choose: The Record Name field

Rule 1: Enter "INVENTORY RECORD" (including the quotation marks)
         Press F3

Select: ....Complete....
         Respond Y to the prompt **OK to proceed (Y/N)**

Select: Execute

Name: INVENTORY RECORD ELEMENTS

Type: ELE, for elements. This is necessary because the selector list contains only elements.
         The **Type** used when <u>creating</u> the list was REC Contains ELE, providing elements.

Select: A report type of **Output**

Enter: INVENTORY RECORD ELEMENTS for the report header.
         Press F3 and respond Y to the prompt. Select a file, the screen or printer for the
         report destination.

Figure 14.14 illustrates the entity list obtained when using REC Contains ELE.

THE XLDICTIONARY INTERFACE

EXPORTING AND IMPORTING
PROJECT INFORMATION

The XLD INTERFACE selection provides an easy method for transferring files to (export) and from (import) other projects. It may also be used to lock and unlock data. Locked data prevents others from modifying it. Figure 14.15 shows XLDictionary Interface options on the left.

There are several methods of selecting items to be exported. All data may be exported, or specific items may be chosen using Entity Lists or a selection screen. Items may be transferred to diskettes and then used on a different machine.

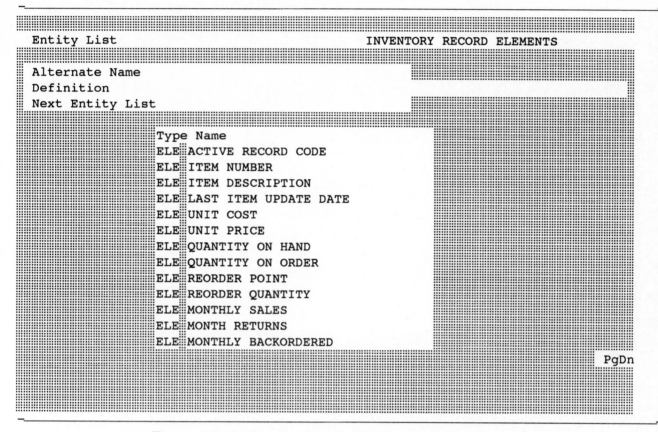

```
 Entity List                          INVENTORY RECORD ELEMENTS

 Alternate Name
 Definition
 Next Entity List

                    Type Name
                    ELE ACTIVE RECORD CODE
                    ELE ITEM NUMBER
                    ELE ITEM DESCRIPTION
                    ELE LAST ITEM UPDATE DATE
                    ELE UNIT COST
                    ELE UNIT PRICE
                    ELE QUANTITY ON HAND
                    ELE QUANTITY ON ORDER
                    ELE REORDER POINT
                    ELE REORDER QUANTITY
                    ELE MONTHLY SALES
                    ELE MONTH RETURNS
                    ELE MONTHLY BACKORDERED
                                                            PgDn
```

Figure 14.14   Entity List for Record Contains Element

Preview information may be obtained before the actual transfer of data occurs. This may be used for verification or stored on a file as an audit trail for the exported data.

EXPORTING PROJECT DATA

To transfer information, either from one project to another or as backup, select Export. Three options are available.

All will export complete project information.

Via Entity List uses a previously created entity list to select which information should be exported.   When this selection is choosen, you will be prompted to enter the name of the entity list.   Enter a name or press enter (or F4) to obtain a selection screen list of entity lists. Refer to Figure 14.15.

```
 ┌─────────────────────────────────────────────────────────────────────────┐
 ┊ DICTIONARY INTERFACE                                                      ┊
 └─────────────────────────────────────────────────────────────────────────┘

 ┌──────────────────┐      ┌─────────────────┐      ┌─────────────────┐
 │ 1 Export         │      │ All             │      │ Preview         │
 └──────────────────┘      └─────────────────┘      └─────────────────┘
   2 Import                  Via Entity List          Detailed Preview

   3 Lock                    Via Selection            Execute

   4 Unlock
                           BASE ELEMENT NOT ON INPUT SCREEN
   5 Export & Lock

   6 Import & Unlock

 Exit



 Transfer file:A:BASELENS

 Enter full path and filename, e.g. abc  \excel\demo\abc  a:abc  k:\share\abc
```

Figure 14.15   Export Screen

Via Selection gives a selection screen listing project type, name, and audit attributes. Select the attributes desired and choose ...Complete.... Refer to Figure 14.16.

Three additional choices are available.

Preview shows how *many* of each entity type will be exported.

Detailed Preview shows the actual entity types, names, and any messages that may pertain to the export (such as an entity locked by another user).

Execute starts the transfer of data. Press the enter key to accept the standard Excelerator format. Enter a file name, which may be on another disk drive (eg. A:CUSTPROJ) or within another subdirectory (eg. C:\TRANSFER\CUSTPROJ).

After the transfer has completed, Excelerator provides feedback on the number of entities transferred.

```
    Rule 1 "DFD"
    Rule 2
   Type
   Name
   Last Modified By
   Last Modify Date
   Number Changes
   Added By
   Date Added
   Last Project
   Locked By
   Date Locked
   Lock Status
   ....Complete....
Enter selections
```

Figure 14.16   Export Selection Screen

EXPORTING GROUPS OF PROJECT DATA

To export a group of related entities, such as a structure chart and all the functions, use an entity list based on relationships. The following procedure outlines how to create the entity list. This example is for a structure chart, INVENTORY REPORT and all it's functions.

Select: Add, then XLD Selection
Name: EXPORT INVENTORY REPORT STC
Type: STC*   (all relationships beginning with STC)
Select: STC Contains FUN
Select: STC Name
Rule 1:   "INVENTORY REPORT"
        Press F3 and select ....Complete....
        Press Y for OK to proceed (Y/N)

This provides an entity list of all <u>functions</u> on the structure chart. The structure chart must now be added to the list.

Select: Modify, then Screen Input
Name: EXPORT INVENTORY REPORT STC (or use a selector list)

    Select the first line of the entity list and press F1 and Ins simultaneously. This inserts a new line. Alternatively, you could add the structure chart to the end of the list.

Enter: STC for the **Type**
Enter: INVENTORY REPORT for the **Name** or press F4 with the cursor in the Name area for a selector list and choose the name.

    The list is now complete, it contains the structure chart and all it's functions. Figure 14.17 illustrates the final list.   Press F3 to save and use for the Export entity list.

IMPORTING

To transfer exported project information from another subdirectory or diskette, select Import. Enter the filename, including other subdirectories or drive letters where the file exists. You will be prompted to override all entries, etc. Respond appropriately for your situation. The import operation may be controlled using the same methods outlined for export, with the same preview options.

LOCKING AND UNLOCKING
XLDICTIONARY ENTITIES

XLDictionary entities may be locked and later unlocked. Locking provides a means of protecting information from alteration by other project users. This is useful to do when the entity - the record, element, process, etc. is complete; in it's final form. When entities are locked, only the project user, or a user setup as a type M for Master, can change the locked project data. The user responsible for locked data and the date locked will show in the audit attributes for the entity.

Export and Lock, and Import and Unlock, combine the export or import features and lock or unlock the entities.

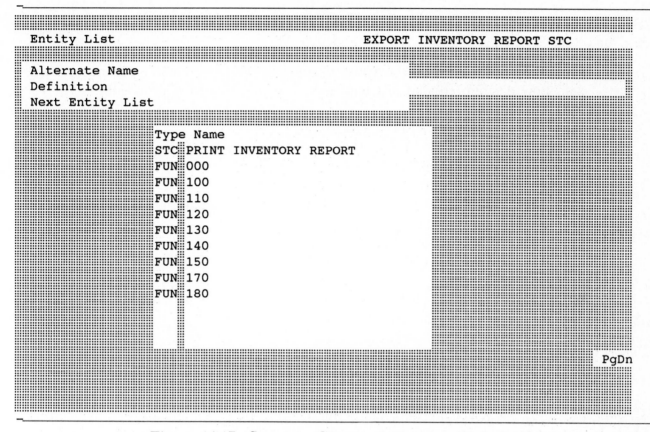

Figure 14.17 Structure Chart and Function Entity List

EXERCISES

1. Create an entity list used to export all entities for the Student Registration System data flow diagram created in Chapter 3. Use the following procedure:

    Select: Add and XLD Selection
    Name: REGISTRATION DFD EXPORT LIST
    Type: DFD Contains ANY (includes all DFD components)
    Select: DFD Name
    Rule 1:   REGISTRATION SYSTEM (use the actual name entered for the diagram)
                 Press F3 and select ....Complete....
                 Press Y (OK to proceed (Y/N) prompt)

    The entity list contains all the <u>components</u> on the data flow diagram. Next, add the data flow diagram to the list.

    Select: Modify, then Screen Input
    Name: REGISTRATION DFD EXPORT LIST (or use a selector list)

    Select the first line of the list and press F1 and Ins simultaneously.

    Enter: DFD for the **Type**
    Enter: REGISTRATION SYSTEM for the **Name** or press F4 with the cursor in the Name area and choose a name from the selector list.

    Press F3 to Save and print the list using Output.

2. Create a series of entity lists for all <u>graph</u> <u>descriptions</u>. Each list should be created using XLD Selection and the graph Type. Select the percent complete to be NOT 100. Use the Union feature to combine all lists. Produce a report showing all graphs that are not 100 percent complete.

3. Create the report described in this chapter called NON PACKED DATA FIELDS WITH DEC.

4. Create the entity list for the example BASE ELEMENTS WITH DEFAULT VALUE found in this chapter. Produce a report based on the list.

5.   Produce the entity list called NUMERIC BASE FIELDS. Use the Inspect option to view the contents.

6.   Use the entity list created in Exercise 1 and the export feature to lock the entities. View the entities with the XLDictionary Inspect feature. Then use the list to unlock the entities.

7.   Use the entity list created in Exercise 1 to export the entities to a diskette in drive A. Make sure that the diskette has been formatted <u>before</u> starting Excelerator.

8.   Create an entity list to export all entities created today. This feature is useful for creating quick project backup. Once a week perform a full export. Then create daily export files which are less time consuming to produce.

Select:	Add and XLD Selection
Name:	CURRENT DATE EXPORT LIST
Type:	ANY (this selects all entities)
Select:	Date Added
Rule 1:	Enter today's date as "YYMMDD" (including quote marks). Example: "910918" for September 18, 1991.

Press F3 and select ....Complete....
Press Y for OK to proceed (Y/N)

Print the resulting list.

9.   Create an entity list of all entities added this week. This could be used for export or for monitoring progress.

Select:	Add and XLD Selection
Name:	WEEKLY EXPORT LIST
Type:	ANY (this selects all entities)
Select:	Date Added
Rule 1:	Enter the starting date of the week using the **> "YYMMDD"** format.

Press F3 and select ....Complete....
Press Y for OK to proceed (Y/N)

Print the resulting list.

10.   Create an entity list of all entities created or modified in a given week. First, create the entity list described in Exercise 9. Next create the following entity list, containing all entities modified in the past week.

Select: Add and XLD Selection
Name: WEEKLY MODIFIED ENTITY LIST
Type: ANY (this selects all entities)
Select: Date Modified
Rule 1:   Enter the starting date of the week using the > "YYMMDD" format.

         Press F3 and select ....Complete....
         Press Y (OK to proceed (Y/N) prompt)

Next select **Modify** and **Union.** Enter the name WEEKLY EXPORT LIST. The **Using List** name is WEEKLY MODIFIED ENTITY LIST.

Print the resulting list. Remember, this list is stored using the name selected for the union, WEEKLY EXPORT LIST.

15

MANAGING EXCELERATOR PROJECTS

Chapter goals:

> Learn how to use Excelerator entities for managing projects.
> Understand associated entities and their effective use.
> Know how to link entities to user and engineering requirements.
> Learn how to create and use the Work Breakdown Structure diagram.
> Understand how to create project deliverables.
> Learn how to manage existing and new hardware required.

There are several important tools for managing a project. One of these is the group of entities collectively known as the associated entities. These collect information on a variety of subjects and are linked to almost any entity via description screens.

Another management tool is user and engineering requirements. User requirements specify the goals and objectives that must be accomplished. Engineering requirement are technical specifications necessary for implementing the user requirements.

A third management tool is the work breakdown structure. This option allows you to create a graph for managing the project workload, defining it in terms of specific deliverables.

There is an option for keeping track of the project users or clients and, finally, there is the System Device entity, used to keep track of hardware that either already exists or needs to be requisitioned. This entity is not under the Management XLDictionary class but serves well for organizing and reporting on hardware requirements.

These management tools will be discussed in detail.

ASSOCIATED ENTITIES

There are seven associated entities, which may be created, reported on, and linked with project graphs, processes, etc. using XLDictionary relationships. They are:

Category   **CAT** This entity is used to group several project entities together.

Change Request   **CHG** Use this to monitor changes that need to be made to the design and the progress of the changes.

Entity List   **ELS** This is described in Chapter 14.

Issue   **ISS** Any important problem or concern that needs resolution.

Note   **NTE** Any comment or general notation on a project entity.

Reference   **REF** Lists reference material information for any entity.

Test   **TST** Create effective test plans, either on a system, program or module level.

Associated entities may be created using either of two methods.

1.   Create, modify, etc. using the XLDictionary as described in Chapter 12. Select **XLDICTIONARY** from the main menu, then **MANAGE**. Proceed to add, modify, etc. any of the management entities. Figure 15.1 shows available menu options. This method is best when an associated entity exists on several screens or for creating the initial User Requirements. These may be created following a series of interviews or JAD (Joint Application Development) sessions.

2.   Create or modify from any entity description screen. Press PgDn on the description screen to display the Requirements and Associated Entities entry area. Enter the three letter entity type code and a name. You may press F4 with the cursor in the name area for a selector list. Once a name displays, press F4 with the cursor in the name field to describe the associated entity. Figure 15.2 illustrates this concept. This method is best for creating tests, issues, references, etc. for a specific entity.

Use the Entity List and Report Writer features to report on associated entity information and relationships.

```
XLDICTIONARY

REC/ELE      C Category                        Modify     Add        Delete
             G Change Request
DATA         D Deliverable
             E Engineering Requirement         Copy       Rename     List
PROCESS      I Issue
             N Note
GRAPHS       R Reference Document              Inspect               Analysis
             T Test                                                  Prep (P)
SCR/REPS     U User Requirement
             S User
CONTROL                                        Output     Summary    Audit
                                                                     (U)
MANAGE
                                              Expanded    Where
OTHER                                         (N)         Used

             Relationships
Exit            (T)                 Name
```

Figure 15.1   XLDictionary Menu For Project Management

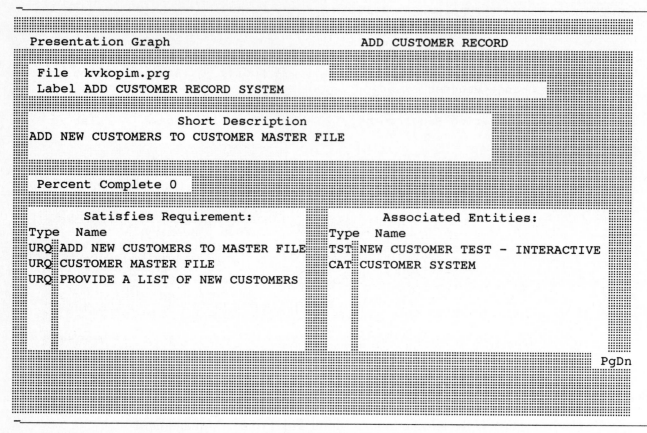

```
Presentation Graph                      ADD CUSTOMER RECORD

  File   kvkopim.prg
  Label  ADD CUSTOMER RECORD SYSTEM

                    Short Description
 ADD NEW CUSTOMERS TO CUSTOMER MASTER FILE


  Percent Complete 0

         Satisfies Requirement:              Associated Entities:
 Type   Name                           Type   Name
 URQ ADD NEW CUSTOMERS TO MASTER FILE   TST NEW CUSTOMER TEST - INTERACTIVE
 URQ CUSTOMER MASTER FILE               CAT CUSTOMER SYSTEM
 URQ PROVIDE A LIST OF NEW CUSTOMERS




                                                               PgDn
```

Figure 15.2 Associated Entities On A Description Screen

CATEGORY

The Category screen has only 3 fields on it: an alternate name, short description, and long description. Refer to the example in Figure 15.3. The category's power lies in selecting the Relationship option from the XLDictionary screen and reporting on which entities belong to the category. Use **CAT Associated-With Any** to report on all categories. Select Summary Report to view all entities within categories. Use Missing Entities to list all categories that haven't been defined.

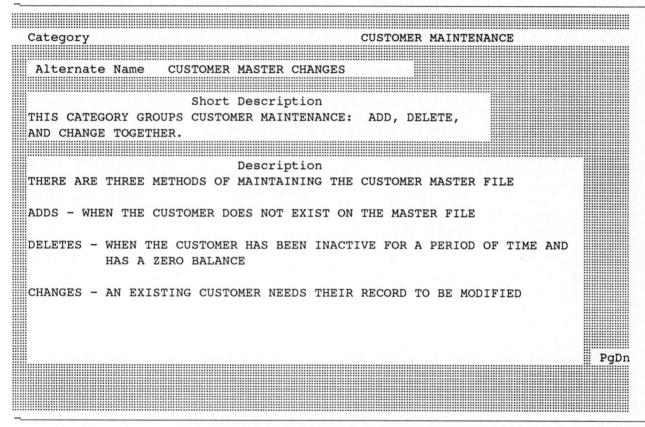

```
Category                              CUSTOMER MAINTENANCE

 Alternate Name    CUSTOMER MASTER CHANGES

                        Short Description
THIS CATEGORY GROUPS CUSTOMER MAINTENANCE:   ADD, DELETE,
AND CHANGE TOGETHER.


                         Description
THERE ARE THREE METHODS OF MAINTAINING THE CUSTOMER MASTER FILE

ADDS - WHEN THE CUSTOMER DOES NOT EXIST ON THE MASTER FILE

DELETES - WHEN THE CUSTOMER HAS BEEN INACTIVE FOR A PERIOD OF TIME AND
          HAS A ZERO BALANCE

CHANGES - AN EXISTING CUSTOMER NEEDS THEIR RECORD TO BE MODIFIED




                                                                PgDn
```

Figure 15.3 Category Description Screen

CHANGE REQUEST

The Change Request lets you keep track of required project changes and their progress. There are three screens for capturing change request information. The first, illustrated in Figure 15.4, provides general change request information.

A second screen, shown in Figure 15.5 to captures evaluation information.

The third Change request screen (Figure 15.6) is used to monitor implementation of the changes.

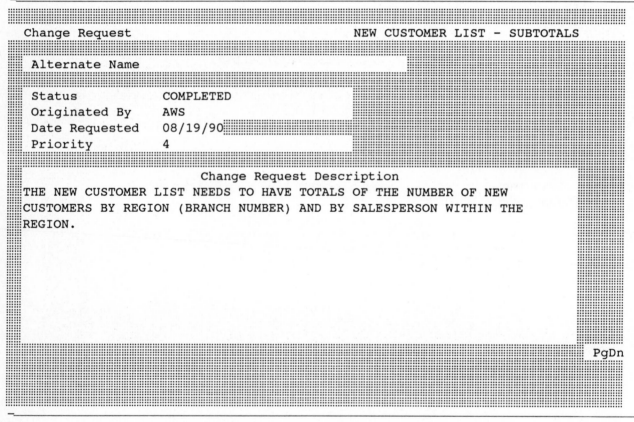

Figure 15.4 Change Request Description Screen

Use the Report Writer feature to list all change requests that are not fully implemented. Select all entities with the **Impl. Completed** date containing spaces.
Sort the report by priority to determine high and low priority actions. The reports may select all change requests with a specific priority or to be implemented by a particular analyst.

Reports may also be created summarizing evaluation and implementation effort. These may be used to estimate project costs. Sort the information by the implementation or evaluation analyst. Use the relationship **CHG Associated-With Any** to report on all change requests and entities to be changed.

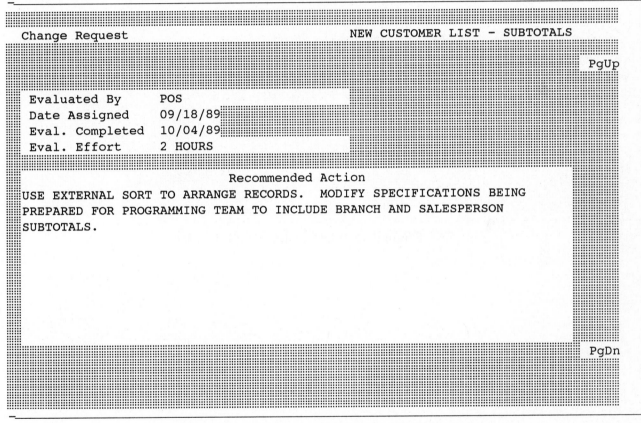

Figure 15.5 The Second Change Request Screen

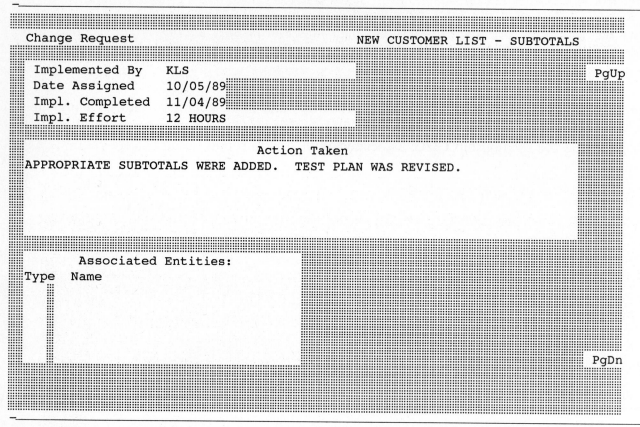

Figure 15.6 Change Request Implementation Screen

ISSUE

An issue is an important problem or consideration that needs resolution. This may concern a graph, data dictionary record or element, or any other entity. Two screens capture pertinent information, illustrated in Figures 15.7 and 15.8.

An Issue description and resolution dates are on the first screen. The action required to resolve the issue is on the second.

```
 Issue                                 CAPTURE LATE INFORMATION

   Alternate Name    TIMELINESS OF INFORMATION


   Responsibility    POS
   Priority          3
   Status            UNRESOLVED


   Date Raised                    01/07/90
   Planned Date of Resolution     06/30/90
   Expected Date of Resolution    06/30/90
   Actual Date of Resolution      00/00/00

                        Issue Description
 THERE IS SOME CONCERN OVER THE ACCURACY OF INFORMATION ON THE ANNUAL
 SALES REPORT.  RETURNS AND PAYMENTS ENTERED AFTER THE REPORT HAS BEEN
 RUN WILL NOT BE INCLUDED.  INITIAL RUN TIMING AND SUBSEQUENT RERUN
 TIMING NEED TO BE DETERMINED.


                                                                  PgDn
```

Figure 15.7   Issue Description Screen

Use the Report Writer feature to analyze and report on issues. List all issues with a Status of unresolved, sorted by Priority. Use the information to plan user interviews and strategy meetings aimed at resolving issues.

Other reports could list issues sorted by the analyst responsible for them. This may help to plan analyst workload.

Use the relationship **ISS Associated-With ANY** to report on all issues and their related entities. This relationship may be used with the report writer to list all outstanding issues sorted by entity. This is valuable since all the unresolved problems for a particular data flow diagram, for example, may be grouped together on a single report. Use the Missing Entities option to report all issues that are not defined but have been entered on entity description screens.

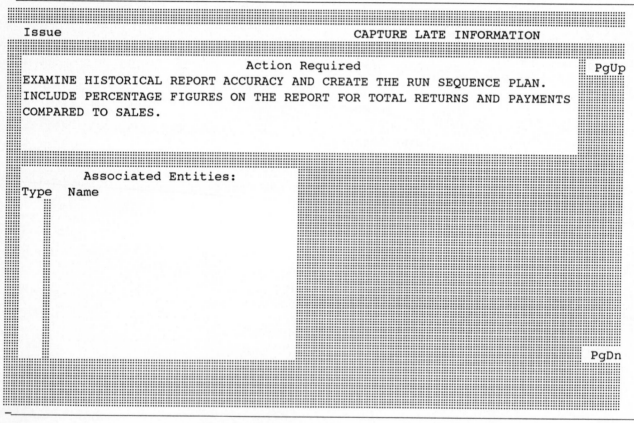

Figure 15.8 Issue Resolution Screen

NOTE

Use Note to create any comment or documentation on an entity or group of entities. The Note description screen contains an entry area for the text of the note. This is a scroll region and up to 60 lines may be entered. A continuation note may be attached if more lines are needed. Refer to the example in Figure 15.9.

As with other associated entities, all notes for a particular entity may be printed using the report writer.

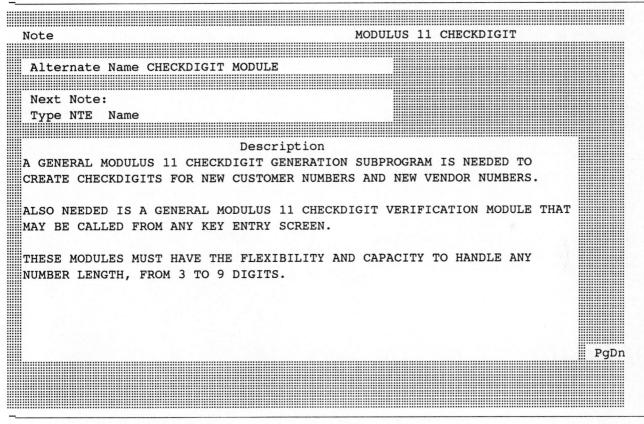

```
 Note                                    MODULUS 11 CHECKDIGIT

   Alternate Name CHECKDIGIT MODULE

   Next Note:
   Type NTE   Name

                          Description
 A GENERAL MODULUS 11 CHECKDIGIT GENERATION SUBPROGRAM IS NEEDED TO
 CREATE CHECKDIGITS FOR NEW CUSTOMER NUMBERS AND NEW VENDOR NUMBERS.

 ALSO NEEDED IS A GENERAL MODULUS 11 CHECKDIGIT VERIFICATION MODULE THAT
 MAY BE CALLED FROM ANY KEY ENTRY SCREEN.

 THESE MODULES MUST HAVE THE FLEXIBILITY AND CAPACITY TO HANDLE ANY
 NUMBER LENGTH, FROM 3 TO 9 DIGITS.



                                                                   PgDn
```

Figure 15.9   Note Description Screen

REFERENCE DOCUMENT

The Reference Document provides information to help an analyst or programmer understand technical or other details of the project. This entity does not contain the detailed information but lists where the information is located.

The document may be a book, with or without page references, a magazine or technical journal article. It may be company standards or policy, a set of tables, or any other material. The material may be printed or stored on electronic, magnetic, or optical media.

Refer to Figures 15.10 and 15.11 for the Reference Document Description screens. If the information is stored using electronic or magnetic media, enter a version and filename. Key in the location, whether electronic or a library. Press PgDn for the second screen and enter a description of the materials.

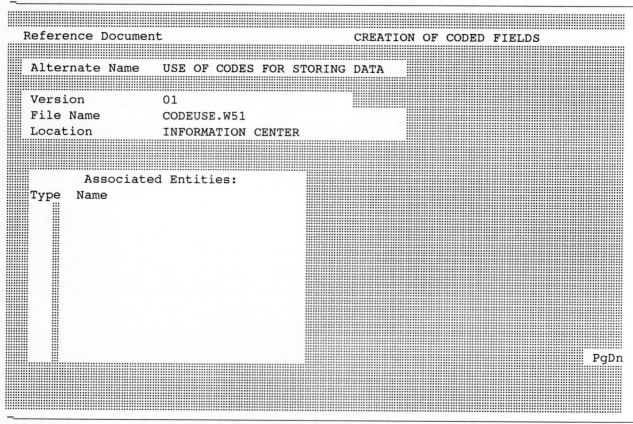

Figure 15.10 Reference Document Description Screen

Use the report writer to list all reference documents sorted by location. The report will provide a master index to all materials.

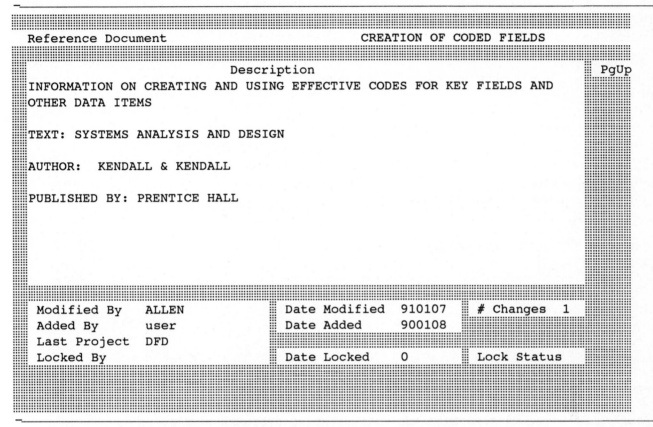

```
 Reference Document                    CREATION OF CODED FIELDS

                          Description                              PgUp
 INFORMATION ON CREATING AND USING EFFECTIVE CODES FOR KEY FIELDS AND
 OTHER DATA ITEMS

 TEXT: SYSTEMS ANALYSIS AND DESIGN

 AUTHOR:  KENDALL & KENDALL

 PUBLISHED BY: PRENTICE HALL




 Modified By    ALLEN        Date Modified  910107    # Changes  1
 Added By       user         Date Added     900108
 Last Project   DFD
 Locked By                   Date Locked    0          Lock Status
```

Figure 15.11   Reference Document Material Description Screen

TEST

Test allows you to create effective test plans, either on a system, program or module level. You may include details of test conditions and cases, test data, test plans or any other pertinent information.

Figure 15.12 is an example of the Test description screen. Enter the purpose for the test. The test type may contain several entries: Unit test, acceptance, beta test, gamma test, batch, or interactive. The test method should contain <u>how</u> you are going to test the entity. Test data, files, cases, etc. may be entered. The test description area may contain up to 30 lines describing test details.

Often Test entities may be created by Browsing (F4) from an entity description screen. This is good for modules, graph components, processes, primitive process specifications, etc. Since you are often working with detailed logic when creating the entities, you may be familiar with what would make for a successful test.

Use the report writer to list all tests sorted by entity. Examples are all tests for a given data flow diagram or structure chart. Tests may be selected or sorted by test type, such as all on-line tests.

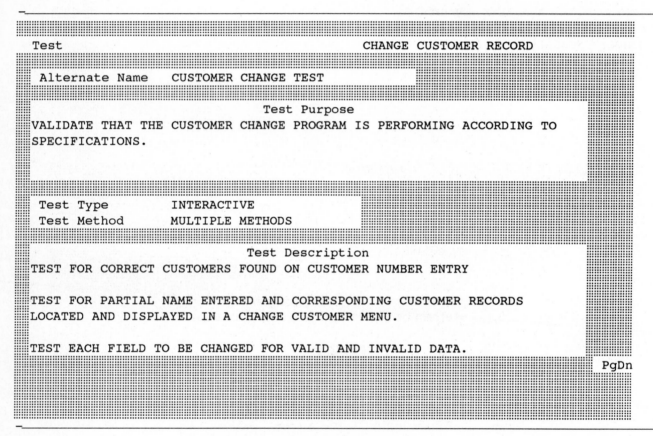

```
 Test                                    CHANGE  CUSTOMER  RECORD

   Alternate Name    CUSTOMER CHANGE TEST

                            Test Purpose
 VALIDATE THAT THE CUSTOMER CHANGE PROGRAM IS PERFORMING ACCORDING TO
 SPECIFICATIONS.



   Test Type          INTERACTIVE
   Test Method        MULTIPLE METHODS

                          Test Description
 TEST FOR CORRECT CUSTOMERS FOUND ON CUSTOMER NUMBER ENTRY

 TEST FOR PARTIAL NAME ENTERED AND CORRESPONDING CUSTOMER RECORDS
 LOCATED AND DISPLAYED IN A CHANGE CUSTOMER MENU.

 TEST EACH FIELD TO BE CHANGED FOR VALID AND INVALID DATA.
                                                                 PgDn
```

Figure 15.12 Test Description Screen

USER

The User management option provides a means of storing user information and entities related to their business expertise. These are the persons interviewed or those who participate in a JAD session.

On the User description screen, shown in Figure 15.13, enter any alternate name. If the user name refers to a department, the alternate name may be a key contact. It also may be used if the user has a preferred name to be called on an informal basis. Enter a definition for the department, if desired. Key in the user location - a department, building, room number, and so on.

In the **User Responsible For** region, enter the entity type and name for each entity the user is involved with. Press PgDn to enter further information.

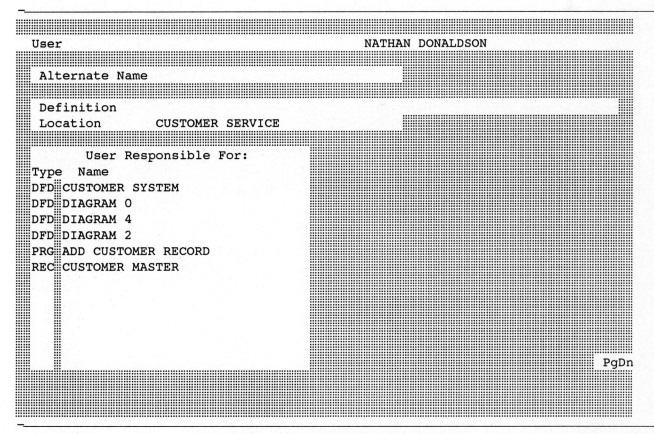

```
User                              NATHAN DONALDSON

  Alternate Name

  Definition
  Location        CUSTOMER SERVICE

          User Responsible For:
Type   Name
DFD  CUSTOMER SYSTEM
DFD  DIAGRAM 0
DFD  DIAGRAM 4
DFD  DIAGRAM 2
PRG  ADD CUSTOMER RECORD
REC  CUSTOMER MASTER

                                              PgDn
```

Figure 15.13 User Description Screen

On the second screen, illustrated in Figure 15.14, enter their phone number, and their title or position under User Designation. A description area is available for other information, such as key personnel working under the user, their supervisor, best times to contact them, their electronic mail ID, and so on.

Use the report writer to list all users and their telephone numbers creating a project phone directory. Use the relationship **USR Responsible-For ANY** to list all entities and the user responsible for them. Sort by entity type and name to group by entities. This shows each entity and all users involved with the entity and helps to schedule user meetings for problem resolution or to demonstrate prototypes.

MANAGING REQUIREMENTS

There are two requirement entities that may be created. These may be created either from entity description screens, as mentioned throughout this text, or by using the XLDictionary feature.

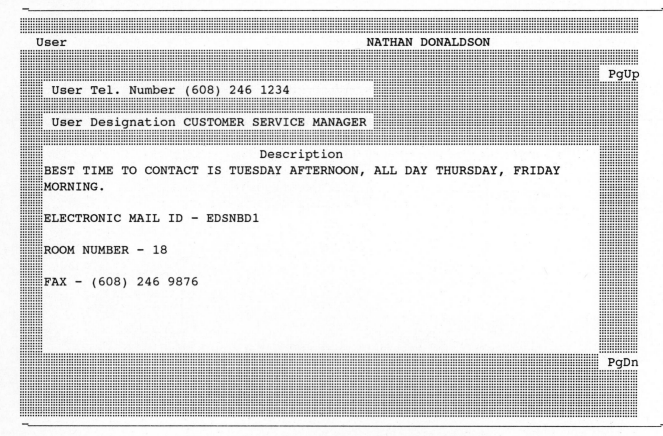

```
User                                    NATHAN DONALDSON

                                                                      PgUp
   User Tel. Number (608) 246 1234

   User Designation CUSTOMER SERVICE MANAGER

                           Description
  BEST TIME TO CONTACT IS TUESDAY AFTERNOON, ALL DAY THURSDAY, FRIDAY
  MORNING.

  ELECTRONIC MAIL ID - EDSNBD1

  ROOM NUMBER - 18

  FAX - (608) 246 9876



                                                                      PgDn
```

Figure 15.14 Second User Description Screen

USER REQUIREMENTS

User requirements are the needs of the system users that must be met. These are the final goals and products that the fully functional system must deliver. User requirements are usually determined early in the analysis stages. They might be the result of initial interviews, a series of JAD sessions, a problem definition, or the current system functions that are required in the new system. User requirements also may be the result of further analysis of the above mentioned items, or the analysis of early prototypes and resulting user feedback. They may evolve from the resolution of issues that arise as the analysis and design progresses and analysts become aware of necessary system modifications.

The User Requirement description screen is shown in Figure 15.15.

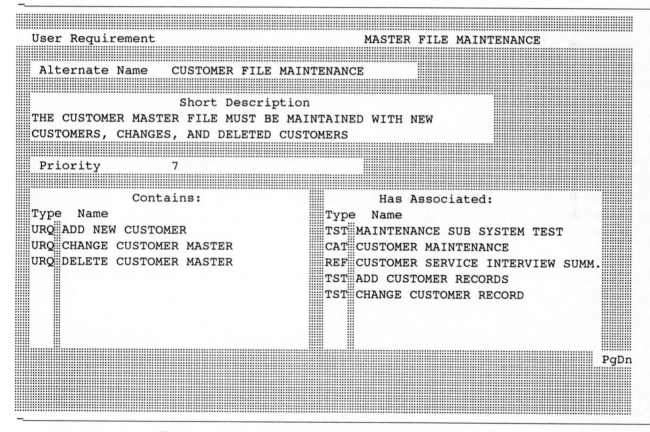

```
User Requirement                          MASTER FILE MAINTENANCE

    Alternate Name    CUSTOMER FILE MAINTENANCE

                       Short Description
    THE CUSTOMER MASTER FILE MUST BE MAINTAINED WITH NEW
    CUSTOMERS, CHANGES, AND DELETED CUSTOMERS

    Priority           7

            Contains:                          Has Associated:
    Type   Name                        Type   Name
    URQ ADD NEW CUSTOMER               TST MAINTENANCE SUB SYSTEM TEST
    URQ CHANGE CUSTOMER MASTER         CAT CUSTOMER MAINTENANCE
    URQ DELETE CUSTOMER MASTER         REF CUSTOMER SERVICE INTERVIEW SUMM.
                                       TST ADD CUSTOMER RECORDS
                                       TST CHANGE CUSTOMER RECORD

                                                                        PgDn
```

Figure 15.15 User Requirement Description Screen

Enter an optional alternate name and a short description. Key in a priority, using the methodology that is standard for your installation. Enter any User Requirements that this requirement expands to, which may be defined only as User Requirements (URQ). Complete any associated entities. Use REF to link the requirements to any specific documents, such as interview summaries, etc. from which the requirements were derived. Press PgDn to enter a longer description. When completed, press F3 to save and return.

Use the report writer to list all user requirements and the entities that satisfy the requirements. Use the Missing Entities option to list all undefined user requirements. These may be sorted by priority to help in planning the schedule of analysis activities.

ENGINEERING REQUIREMENTS

Engineering requirements show how the user requirements, the business needs, are to be implemented as physical system components. Examples would be specific files or data bases, screens, reports, etc. These may be derived from user requirements or may be determined directly from the user. Figure 15.16 shows the Engineering Requirement description screen.

Enter an alternate name and priority, if available. Key in a short description. The **Derived From:** area links Engineering Requirements back to User Requirements. The only entity type is USR. Enter the name, or, since the user requirements are usually defined first, press F4 with the cursor in the name field to obtain a selector list. The **Contains:** entry area is used to link this entity to further Engineering Requirements. Enter a type of ERQ and the name of any component Engineering Requirements. Press PgDn to enter any associated entities, and PgDn again to provide a longer description. Press F3 to save and return.

Use the report writer to list engineering requirements sorted by priority to help plan analyst workload.

```
┌─────────────────────────────────────────────────────────────────────┐
│ Engineering Requirement                    ADD CUSTOMER MASTER RECORD  │
│                                                                       │
│   Alternate Name    ADD CUSTOMER RECORD                               │
│                                                                       │
│   Priority              7                                             │
│                                                                       │
│                      Short Description                                │
│  CREATE ADD CUSTOMER ENTRY SCREENS                                    │
│                                                                       │
│                                                                       │
│           Derived From:                        Contains:             │
│  Type  Name                          Type  Name                       │
│  URQ MASTER FILE MAINTENANCE         ERQ RANDOM READ CUSTOMER MASTER   │
│  URQ ADD NEW CUSTOMER                                                 │
│                                                                       │
│                                                                       │
│                                                                       │
│                                                                       │
│                                                                  PgDn │
└─────────────────────────────────────────────────────────────────────┘
```

Figure 15.16 Engineering Requirement Description Screen

THE WORK BREAKDOWN STRUCTURE GRAPH

The Work Breakdown Structure is a hierarchy chart showing work components of the project. These are tasks that must be accomplished in order to complete the project. Start at the top of the diagram with the whole project and then define major tasks and secondary tasks. Each task is a project *deliverable*.

The deliverables, or work to be completed, may be exploded to create another child Work Breakdown Structure. The top rectangle of the <u>child</u> diagram should be identical with the rectangle on the parent diagram which explodes to the child diagram.

Figure 15.17 shows an example of a Work Breakdown Structure.

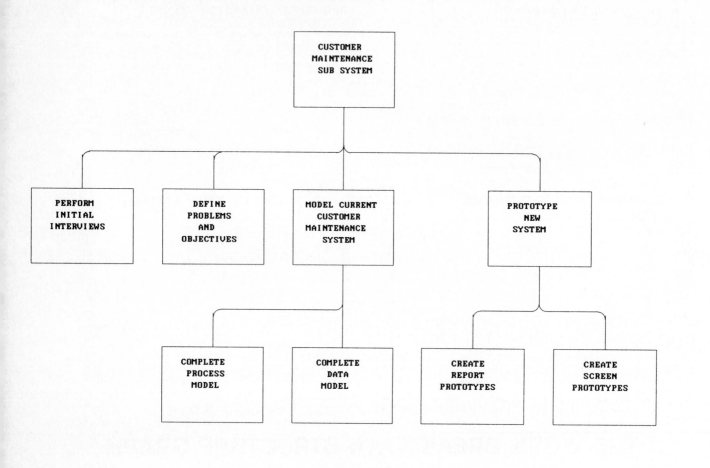

Figure 15.17   Work Breakdown Structure Example

CREATING THE
WORK BREAKDOWN STRUCTURE

Select GRAPHICS from the main menu, then Work Breakdown Structure.   Select Add to create or Modify to change.   Enter a name or press the enter key to obtain a selector list and choose a name.

Select PROFILE and use the following settings.   GRID, either FINE or SMALL,   LABEL MD, then COMPLETE and LAB ONLY.   Press the Esc key to save the settings.

Select OBJECT, a rectangle, and then choose areas on the drawing screen to place the rectangles. When all rectangles are placed, select CONNECT. Select the first rectangle, then the second. Some of the connections may go in or come out of the side of a rectangle, especially if the connecting rectangle is distance from the left or right or the first rectangle. If this is the case, select the profile option USERPORT before connecting or use the MOVE command to align the connections as desired.

Select LABEL to place text in the objects. Select each object and enter text in the pop-up window. Use tab to move to the second or third text lines. Press enter to complete the label.

DESCRIBING THE DELIVERABLES

Deliverables may be described in the XLDictionary. They can explode to any other graph - a Data flow diagram, structure chart, other work breakdown structure, etc. or any other entity, such as screen design or element.

```
Deliverable                           CREATE SCREEN PROTOTYPES

  Alternate Name    SCREEN PROTOTYPE PRODUCTION
  Label                   CREATE         SCREEN        PROTOTYPES

  Explodes To:
  Type WBS    Name CREATE SCREEN PROTOTYPES

                          Description
 THIS IS THE PARENT DELIVERABLE FOR THE SET OF SCREEN PROTOTYPES.    THERE
 ARE SEVERAL SCREENS THAT NEED TO BE DEVELOPED - ADD, DELETE, AND
 CHANGE.    THESE SHOULD BE PROTOTYPED AND REVIEWED UNTIL USER APPROVAL IS
 OBTAINED.    THEN USE THE TRANSFORM OPTION TO CREATE THE DATA DICTIONARY
 RECORDS AND ELEMENTS.    GENERATE TENTATIVE COBOL RECORD LAYOUTS FOR
 INITIAL REVIEW.



                                                                  PgDn
```

Figure 15.18 Deliverable Description Screen

Select DESCRIBE and the deliverable rectangle. On the deliverable description screen, shown in Figure 15.18, enter an optional alternate name and a label, if not previously created. If the deliverable explodes to another graph, enter the type and name of the graph. For existing graphs you may enter the **Type** and press F4 with the cursor in the name field for a selector list. Enter a description of the deliverable.

Press PgDn for a second screen, illustrated in Figure 15.19. This screen contains an area to track the deliverable components, those specific results of work to be done. Enter the type and name of the entity to be completed. Key in the name or other ID of the analyst or designer that will be completing the work. Enter a one letter code in the Status field indicating the progress of the work. Use **C** for completed, **S** for started, and blank for not started.

Use the Report Writer to list all work that has not been completed. List by analyst to manage workload.

```
 Deliverable                             CREATE SCREEN PROTOTYPES

 Type Deliverable Components        Assigned To        Status          PgUp
 SCD  ADD CUSTOMER                  POS                  C
 SCD  CHANGE CUSTOMER               KLS                  S
 SCD  DELETE CUSTOMER               NBD
 SCD  MAINTENANCE MENU              POS


 Project Plan Tasks               Start   End    Bus   Resource       %
 ID    Name                       Date    Date   Days  ID    Usage   Comp Stat


















 Task data supplied by Project Management Interface.  Output only.      PgDn
```

Figure 15.19 Deliverable Description - Second Screen

The bottom of the screen contains output information only and is used if your installation has ABT's Project Workbench interface. This software package updates Excelerator Deliverable entities with project information as the system design progresses.

Press PgDn for a third screen, shown in Figure 15.20. The **Tasks Updated** area information is also supplied by ABT's Project Workbench interface and may not be altered within Excelerator. Enter any requirements satisfied by this deliverable and associated entities. Press F3 to save and return to the drawing screen.

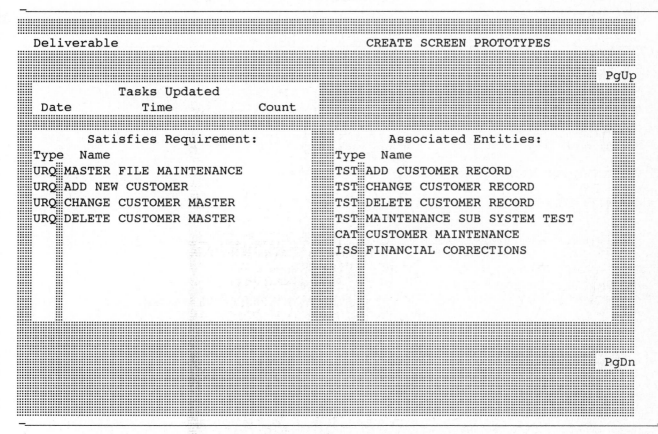

Figure 15.20 Deliverable Description - Third Screen

DESCRIBING THE
WORK BREAKDOWN STRUCTURE GRAPH

To describe the Work Breakdown Structure graph, select DESCRIBE and the graph name, located directly above the orientation map. The Work Breakdown Structure description screen, shown in Figure 15.21, is displayed. Enter a label for the graph, a short description, and the percent complete. Key in any requirements the graph satisfies and any associated entities. Press PgDn for a longer description entry area, if necessary. When finished, press F3 to save and return to the drawing screen.

If any Deliverable has an explosion path, you can select EXPLODE and the Deliverable. You may create the child diagram or view an existing diagram.

When finished, zoom to close up to review how the graph will print and make any necessary changes. Check your print setup and print when ready. Save your work, backup and exit (refer to Chapter 2).

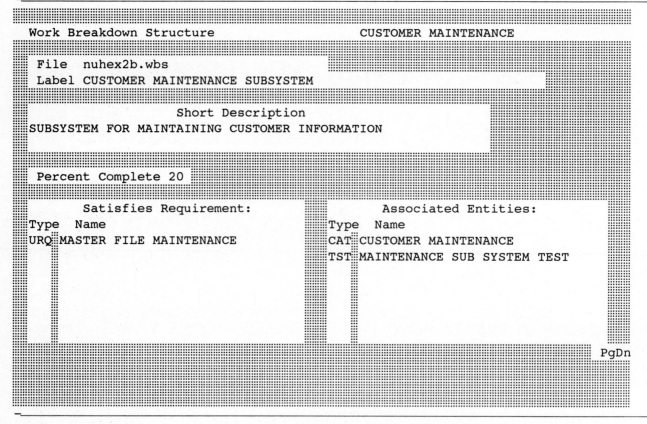

Figure 15.21 Work Breakdown Structure Description Screen

WORK BREAKDOWN STRUCTURE ANALYSIS

There are two analysis options for the Work Breakdown Structure graph. Select **ANALYSIS** and then **Graph Verification**. Choose the option **Undescribed Graph Entities** followed by **Work Breakdown Structure**. Select a destination: a file, the screen or the printer. This report shows which deliverables are not yet described in the XLDictionary.

The other report is the Graph Explosion Report which shows the relationship between the Work Breakdown Structure deliverables and the explosion entities linked via the Deliverable description screen. Select **ANALYSIS, Graph Summary Reports,** and **Work Breakdown Structure.** Enter the name of the graph or press the enter key for a selector list and choose a name. Key in the number of levels of explosion depth. Select a destination: a file, the screen or the printer.

MANAGING HARDWARE RESOURCES

The System Device entity may be used to manage hardware resources. This can be any hardware required by a process to perform it's work: mainframe terminals, microcomputers, printers, network servers, disk packs, and so on.

There are several ways to use this handy entity in a project. Use it as an inventory of existing equipment. The Report Writer can select specific hardware characteristics and report on all devices that match these criteria. An example would be all microcomputers that are IBM PS/2 models. The use of naming standards in the alternate name can help to facilitate inventory reporting.

Another use for this entity is to maintain a list of new equipment that needs to be purchased or leased for project implementation. This can be used to simplify ordering equipment in quantity and for selection and standardization.

DESCRIBING SYSTEM DEVICES

The System Device entity may be created in one of two methods. From the Structure Chart drawing screen, select OBJECT and then DEVICE. Place the system device on the graph in the same manner as all other objects. Select DESCRIBE and enter an ID. The graph name followed by an incremental number is presented as an ID. Press enter to accept or overtype with a more meaningful name.

The System Device may also be described by selecting XLDICTIONARY, then PROCESS, followed by System Device. Select Add to create or Modify to change.

The System Device description screen is shown in Figure 15.22.

Enter an optional alternate name. This may be the specific type of equipment. For purposes of analysis and reporting, you may wish to start the alternate name with micro, mini, or mainframe. This will allow you to select a class of devices when reporting. Key in a label, if it has not been previously created.

The system device may explode to another Structure Chart. If so, enter the name of the structure chart under the Explodes to: area.

Key in the following information. **Make** represents the manufacturer. **Space Requirement** describes the office space or footprint required for the equipment. Square footage or any other measurement may be entered. The **Model Number** describes the specific type of equipment. Enter the power requirement and the serial number. If the hardware is to be purchased, enter NEW for the serial number. This will allow you to produce reports on all equipment to be purchased for the project.

Location refers to the office area. **Vendor** is for the selling or leasing company. Fill in the operating system and whether the equipment is purchased or leased. **Protocol** refers to how the data is coded or other special protocol information. Key in any maintenance information and the data communications transfer rate (baud rate), if applicable.

The Connectivity group of entries refers to which devices may be connected to the equipment. The Attribute group allows you to list software used, special boards within a computer, hard disks or cards, and so on.

Press PgDn to enter any Associated Entities. Press PgDn again for a description area. Information entered here may be dates that the equipment must be purchased or installed, perhaps bid information, the number of units and specific locations, the sales representative for the vendor, phone numbers, or any other information.

Press F3 to save and return to the drawing screen or the XLDictionary.

```
 System Device                              CUSTOMER SERVICE WORKSTATION

  Alternate Name   MICRO IBM PS/2 SX55
  Label            CUSTOMER SERVICE WORKSTATION

  Explodes To:
  Type STC   Name


  Make             IBM              Space Requirement DESK
  Model Number     PS/2 SX55        Power Requirement STANDARD OUTLET
  Serial Number    009505882        Location          CLERICAL SUPPORT
  Vendor           SUPERVISION, INC. Operating System DOS 4.0
  Purchase/Lease   PURCHASED        Protocol          ASCII
  Maintenance      6 MONTHS         Transfer Rate     4800 BAUD


  Connectivity     RS-232           Attribute 1       dBASE III+
                   MONITOR - VGA    Attribute 2       WORDPERFECT
                   PRINT - HP LASERJET Attribute 3    FL78PC
                                    Attribute 4       CUST. INQUIRY
                                    Attribute 5       CUST. MAINTENANCE
                                                                   PgDn
```

Figure 15.22 System Device Description Screen

EXERCISES

1. Create the following user requirements:

   A. Item records used in the Inventory system need to be updated, including the following requirements. Note: create a higher level user requirement that contains points one through four as lower level requirements. Then define each requirement separately.

      1. Add new items received to the INVENTORY MASTER FILE.

      2. Update the QUANTITY ON HAND as shipments are received.

      3. Decrease the QUANTITY ON HAND of raw materials as products are manufactured.

      4. Changing the QUANTITY ON HAND to reflect loss, damage, etc.

   B. Inventory reports summarizing sales information need to be produced.

   C. Inventory item information should be available through screen inquiry.

2. Run the Missing Entities report for the relationship **ANY Associated With URQ**.

3. Create test plans for the processes on one of the data flow diagrams created in Chapter 3 or a structure chart created in Chapter 6.

4. Create Reference entities for texts used in your programming and systems analysis & design courses. Link these to data flow diagrams or structure charts you have created.

5. Create System Device entries for the microcomputer equipment that Excelerator is installed upon.

6. Create the Work Breakdown Structure shown in Figure 15.17. Define the deliverables.

7.   Create a Work Breakdown Structure for building the following Inventory System prototypes and describe the deliverables.

    A.   Reports.

        1.   Inventory backorder report.
        2.   Inventory reorder report.
        3.   Item sales summary.

    B.   Screens.

        1.   Add new item.
        2.   Change item information.
        3.   Delete item.
        4.   Update items received.
        5.   Item inquiry.

8.   Create User entities for your self and your teammates (if you are on a team) otherwise use several of your family members or classmates. If you are working on a project involving a real business problem within the community or school, create User entities for all contact persons.

16
PRODUCING PROJECT DOCUMENTATION

Chapter goals:

>   Understand the capabilities of the documentation feature.
>   Learn how to create and use a document graph.
>   Know how to describe document groups.
>   Know how to describe document fragments.
>   Learn how to verify the document graph.
>   Know how to batch produce documentation.
>   Understand how to link your word processor to Excelerator and access it from within Excelerator.

Documentation is a powerful feature that allows you to produce a complete document on the many diverse parts of a project. It has the capability to include Excelerator items as well as word processing text and DOS ASCII files into a single document. This feature also allows you to access word processing or project management software without exiting Excelerator.

Often graphs and analysis reports may take a long time to generate and print. The document production facility has the advantage of starting print operations and letting the process work automatically while you accomplish other tasks (or take a break!).

The Document Graph option allows you to create a hierarchal tree outline of the entire document, organizing chapters, sections, etc. Each part of the tree structure contains a graph, report, group of documents or other distinct part of the final document. It controls the order of material within the completed document.

Once the Document Graph is complete, use the Document Production facility to verify the Document Graph and that all items selected are available for inclusion in the document.

Changes may be made to the Document Graph and, when the final version is verified, the document may be produced. The output may be printed or saved on a file for printing later.

When accessing word processing or project management software from the Documentation feature, Excelerator transfers control to the software. After exiting the software package, control returns to the Excelerator Documentation menu.

CREATING THE DOCUMENT GRAPH

The first task is to create a document graph that controls which items print and the order they are printed. Select DOCUMENTATION from the main menu. A Documentation menu displays, illustrated in Figure 16.1. Select Documentation Graph and Add or Modify to change. Enter a name or press the enter key for a list of graphs already created and choose one from the list.

The drawing screen is displayed. Select PROFILE and then LABEL MD,

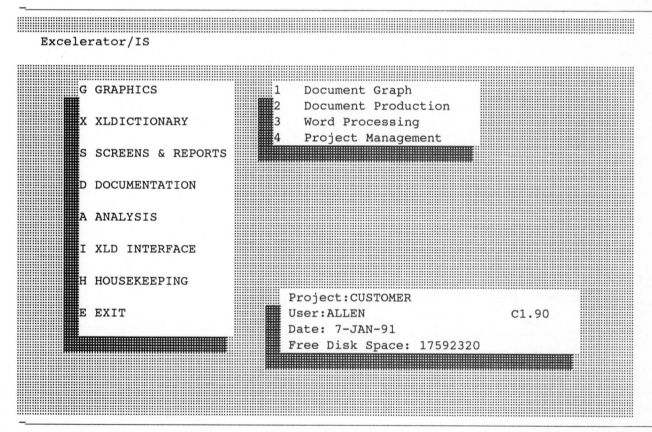

Figure 16.1   Documentation Menu Options

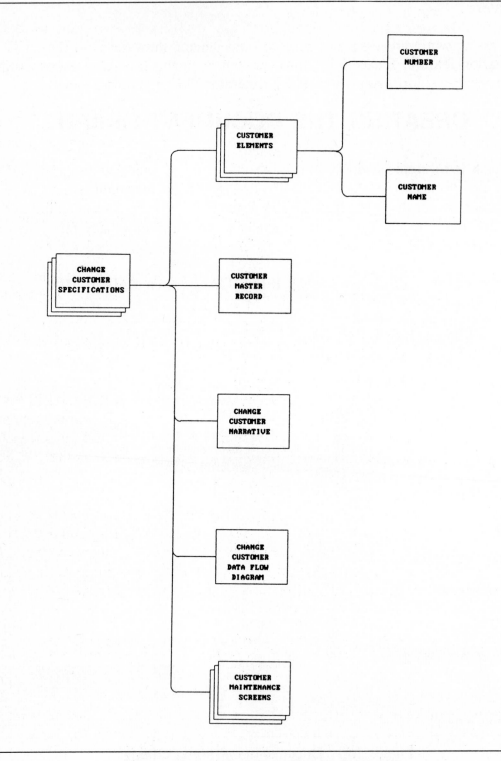

Figure 16.2 Document Graph Example

COMPLETE, and LAB ONLY. Press the Esc key to save the changes.

Select OBJECT, then either of two different types. DOCGROUP represents a group of documents and expands to several documents to the right of the symbol. FRAGMENT is an individual document. All document groups must expand to fragments. Refer to Figure 16.2 for a Document Graph example.

Select DOCGROUP and a location on the middle left side of the drawing screen. This group represents the overall documentation to be produced. Place other document groups where needed, usually toward the right. Select FRAGMENT and the locations to place the individual documents.

To connect objects, select CONNECT, the first object and then the second. Repeat for all connections.

To create labels for the objects, select LABEL. Choose the object and enter the text in the pop-up window. Use tab or arrow keys to create additional lines of text. Center the label and press the enter key when finished. Repeat for all objects.

DESCRIBING DOCUMENT GROUPS

The document groups and fragments must be described so that Excelerator will know what material to print. Select DESCRIBE and a Document Group. The graph name and a number (incremented for each object) is presented as a default. Press enter to accept or overtype with a meaningful name. The Document Group description screen is displayed, illustrated in Figure 16.3.

Enter a label, if not previously created. The **Filename** entry is used only if a Ventura Desktop Publishing file is to be printed. The **Suppress Output** field should be set to the default of **N**. Change it to **Y** only if you do not want this group of items to print. **Produce Outline** may be changed to **Y** if you would like an outline of the group as it prints. The description area is for comments. Press F3 to save and return. Repeat for all document groups.

DESCRIBING DOCUMENT FRAGMENTS

To describe document fragments, select DESCRIBE and a Document Fragment. The fragments specify individual items to print. Overtype the default ID that is presented, or press the enter key to accept. Figure 16.4 illustrates an example of the Document Fragment description screen. Enter a label, if not previously created, and a filename if using Ventura.

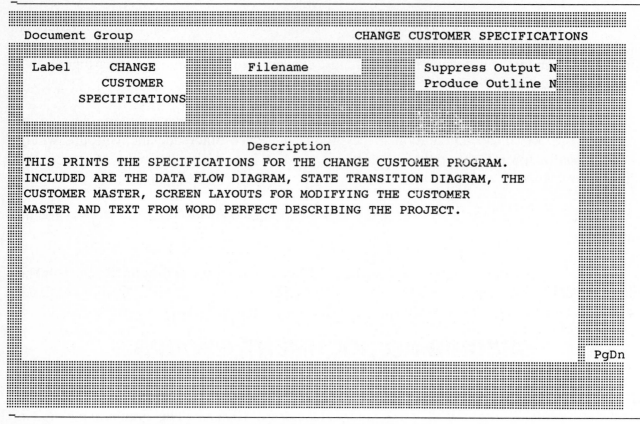

```
┌─────────────────────────────────────────────────────────────────┐
│ Document Group                    CHANGE CUSTOMER SPECIFICATIONS  │
│ ┌────────────────┐ ┌───────────────────┐ ┌────────────────────┐  │
│ │ Label    CHANGE│ │    Filename       │ │ Suppress Output  N │  │
│ │        CUSTOMER│ │                   │ │ Produce Outline  N │  │
│ │  SPECIFICATIONS│ │                   │ │                    │  │
│ └────────────────┘ └───────────────────┘ └────────────────────┘  │
│ ┌───────────────────────────────────────────────────────────┐    │
│ │                      Description                          │    │
│ │ THIS PRINTS THE SPECIFICATIONS FOR THE CHANGE CUSTOMER PROGRAM.│
│ │ INCLUDED ARE THE DATA FLOW DIAGRAM, STATE TRANSITION DIAGRAM, THE│
│ │ CUSTOMER MASTER, SCREEN LAYOUTS FOR MODIFYING THE CUSTOMER │    │
│ │ MASTER AND TEXT FROM WORD PERFECT DESCRIBING THE PROJECT.  │    │
│ │                                                           │    │
│ │                                                      PgDn │    │
│ └───────────────────────────────────────────────────────────┘    │
└─────────────────────────────────────────────────────────────────┘
```

Figure 16.3   Document Group Description Screen

The **Fragment Type** specifies what type of document is to be printed.   The entries may be:

A three letter entity code used throughout Excelerator.   Refer to Appendix B for a complete list of these codes and corresponding entities.

The exact name of a relationship type.   Refer to Appendix E for a complete listing.

A series of codes representing various analysis reports.   Refer to the Excelerator/IS manual titled Data & Reports, Appendix C, for a complete listing of these codes.

TXF for a text file, any ASCII file.

Any of the three letter entity codes representing a graph.   This will print the actual drawing rather than graph description screen information.   Refer to Appendix B for a complete list of these codes and the corresponding graphs.

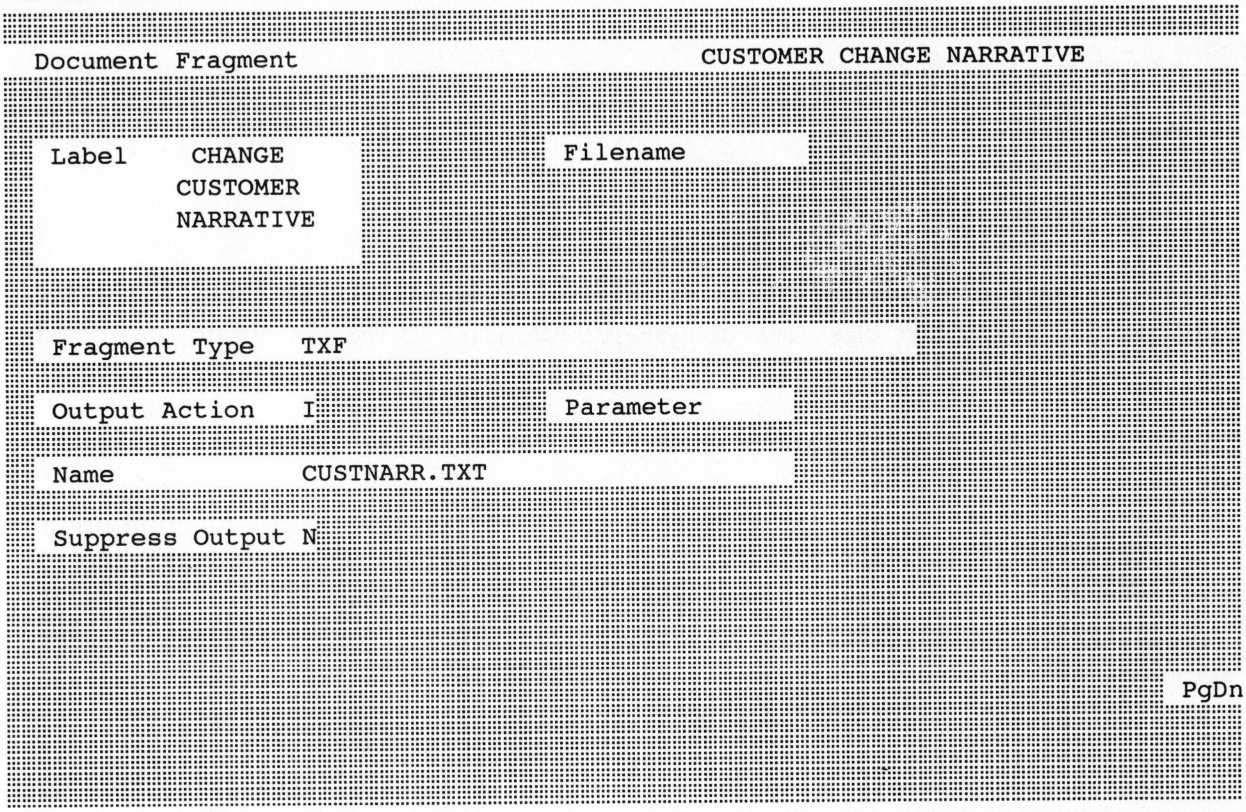

```
Document Fragment                              CUSTOMER CHANGE NARRATIVE

   Label      CHANGE                   Filename
              CUSTOMER
              NARRATIVE



   Fragment Type    TXF

   Output Action    I           Parameter

   Name             CUSTNARR.TXT

   Suppress Output N




                                                                      PgDn
```

Figure 16.4 Document Fragment Description Screen

The **Output Action** tells Excelerator the type of output to produce. This is how document production knows whether you are requesting a print of the graph description screen or the actual drawing. Most of the Output Action categories are the same as those used for XLDictionary reporting. The codes are:

I   Image, for graphs, screen and report designs, and all ASCII text files. This prints the drawing or screen design, not information *about* the drawing.

N   Expanded Output

M   Missing Entities

O   Output

S   Summary report

R   Report, used for Report Writer and Entity List output.

U   Audit

W   Where Used

X   Extended Analysis Matrix

The **Parameter** entry area is used by many of the analysis reports. Leave blank for entities, relationships, graphs and text files. For analysis reports, refer to the Excelerator/IS manual Data & Reports, Appendix C.

The **Name** field determines which entity, graph, etc. to print. Enter either:

A partial name followed by an asterisk (*) for a group of items that have a common prefix. This is a very powerful method for obtaining all graphs starting with a common name, all entities with the same beginning letters, etc. The use of naming standards is strongly recommended throughout Excelerator to simplify batch printing.

An asterisk (*) for all entities of the chosen type.

A complete name, for printing a specific item. You must enter the complete name when printing text files.

Place a **Y** in the **Suppress Output** field only if you do not want the fragment to print.

Press PgDn for a longer description entry area. Press F3 to save and return to the drawing screen. Repeat for all fragments. You may describe the Document Graph by selecting DESCRIBE and the graph name found directly above the orientation map.

When finished, zoom to close up to review how the graph will print and make any changes that are necessary. Check your print setup and print when ready. Save your work, backup and exit (see Chapter 2).

DOCUMENT PRODUCTION

To print a series of documents, select Document Production from the menu. Two options are available for printing.

1.   The whole graph.

2.   A Document Fragment. This provides a quick means for printing individual fragments.

On the action keypad, four choices are available:

Analysis Prep, which needs to be run after creating or modifying graphs. Select this option before you verify or produce documentation.

List shows available document graphs, groups or fragments.

Verify checks to see if the information entered on all the Document Fragment description screens is correct and the corresponding graphs, text, and other items exist. If errors occur, exit, modify the graph, change the Document Fragments if necessary, and rerun the Verify option.

Execute produces the documentation. Select a file or the printer as the final destination. If you select a file, Excelerator will present you with a system generated file name. Change the filename but <u>not</u> the extension of BAT. Excelerator creates a DOS batch file for easy printing.

To print a batch file, exit Excelerator and enter the batch file name at the DOS prompt. It will erase itself after the document has been printed.

ACCESSING WORD PROCESSING SOFTWARE

The third option on the Documentation menu is **Word Processing**, which provides a link to word processing software. This may be used to create documents related to project information or other text. Selecting this option runs your word processor. Upon exiting the word processor, control returns to the Documentation menu screen.

PROVIDING WORD PROCESSING
SOFTWARE LINKAGE

Before the word processing software may be used, Excelerator must know where the software resides, that is, what is the DOS path to the software and how to execute it. By default, Excelerator uses Microsoft Word, which may be changed to your word processing software.

To connect your word processor, exit Excelerator and change to the Excelerator subdirectory. Type **PATHMOD** at the DOS prompt and press the enter key. This executes the path modify program. The Pathmod menu screen is displayed. Select Modify and press the enter key for a name. A list of entries and file names displays. Select the plus (+) sign (or press enter) and choose **Word Processing** from the list.

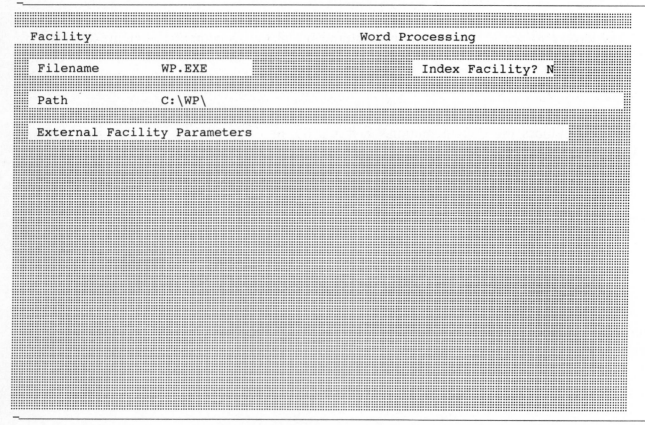

Figure 16.5 Pathmod Word Processing Modification Screen

The entry screen for modifying word processing is displayed, shown in Figure 16.5. Enter the filename to execute the word processing software, eg. **WP.EXE** for WordPerfect. Enter the DOS path: the drive and subdirectory where the software is located. An example would be **C:\WP**. Enter any External Facility Parameters or DOS line commands necessary to run the word processing software. Press F3 when finished to save and exit. Select Exit to return to DOS.

ACCESSING PROJECT MANAGEMENT SOFTWARE

The fourth option, Project Management, allows you to connect Excelerator to ABT's Project Workbench Advanced System Interface.

EXERCISES

1.   Create the Document Graph shown in Figure 16.2. Describe the document groups and fragments.

2.   Use the PATHMOD feature (run from the DOS prompt) to link your word processor to Excelerator.

3.   Create a test document by executing your work processor from within Excelerator. Enter your name and a paragraph explaining the features of the document production facility.

4.   Create a document graph to print some of the prototypes created in Chapter 11. Create a document fragment for the text created in Exercise number 3. Run the Verify option to make sure these documents exist and then print.

5.   Create a document graph to print any data flow diagram that you have created. Include the relationship REC Contains Any for one of the master files created.

17

EXPANDING THE POWER
EXCELERATOR INTERFACE PRODUCTS

Chapter goals:

> Learn about software that interfaces with Excelerator.
> Understand how to use Excelerator entities to generate program language
>   code.
> Understand the process involved in generating skeletal COBOL code.
> Learn how Micro Focus uses Excelerator output.
> Understand how re-engineering works with Design Recovery.
> Understand how the DB2 interface works.

Although Excelerator is extremely powerful by itself, there are many interface products that extend it's capabilities. These generate COBOL code, create DB2 tables, and build XLD entities from existing COBOL programs.

These products help to incorporate Excelerator over the full systems development life cycle. As CASE software progresses throughout the 1990's, we can expect this trend to continue, with an increasing number of products and enhancements.

For all the interface products, installation programs customize Excelerator, they add new options to the standard menu selections. The change may be reflected in the Excelerator logon screen. Customization of Excelerator requires obtaining installation diskettes and following the customization procedures prior to using the interface product.

CODE GENERATION

Excelerator will create COBOL program code for structure charts, functions, record layouts, report designs and screen designs. The code produced from structure charts is called *skeletal*, meaning that full procedure division code is not produced. Only paragraph names and the corresponding perform statements.

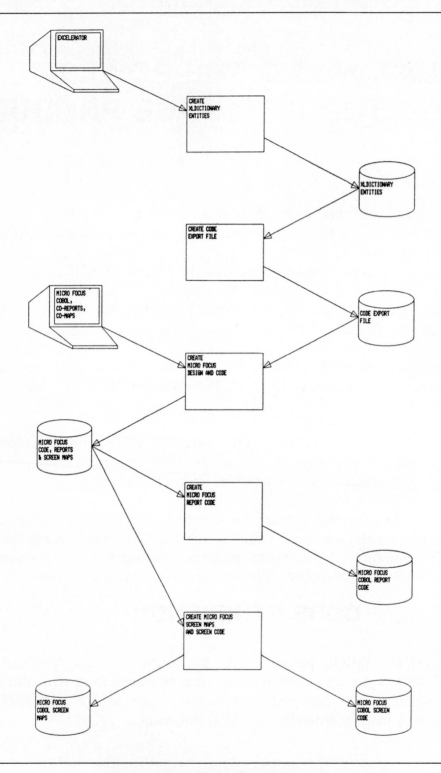

Figure 17.1   Code Generation Overview

GENERAL PROCEDURES

The first step in generating code is to create the Excelerator entities to be included in the resulting program. Examine the project and determine if you need report lines or screens. Draw the structure chart and describe the functions. Create records and describe the elements, using care to correctly define input and output formats and characteristics (character, packed or binary).

Next, create an entity list that will export the entities used for generating code. A special export function is available to transfer entities into a format for the Micro Focus interface. Excelerator creates one output file containing all exported entities.

The third step is to run the Micro Focus interface, which will transform Excelerator information into the format required for Micro Focus processing. Several files are created, one for each structure chart, record layout, screen and report.

The final step is to transform Micro Focus screens and reports into COBOL code and to merge the program sections together. Figure 17.1 illustrates the steps necessary to generate Micro Focus code from Excelerator entities. Each of these steps will be presented in detail.

ENTITY CONVERSION

Excelerator entities convert to the following Micro Focus components. Details about each entity follow.

Excelerator Entity	Micro Focus Component
Structure Chart	Skeletal COBOL program.
Function descriptions	Procedure division paragraph comments.
Records	COBOL data division copy entries.
Elements	Elementary fields, including pictures and usage.
Report designs	CO-Report design. Needs to be converted into code within Micro Focus.
Screen designs	CO-Maps screen design. Convert to code within Micro Focus.

STRUCTURE CHARTS AND FUNCTIONS

Structure charts should be drawn and the functions should be described. Label the functions clearly. Micro Focus will use the first thirty characters of the label, including spaces, for the COBOL section name. Labels are compressed to eliminate spaces and hyphens are inserted to separate words. The function ID is not included in the section name. To create section

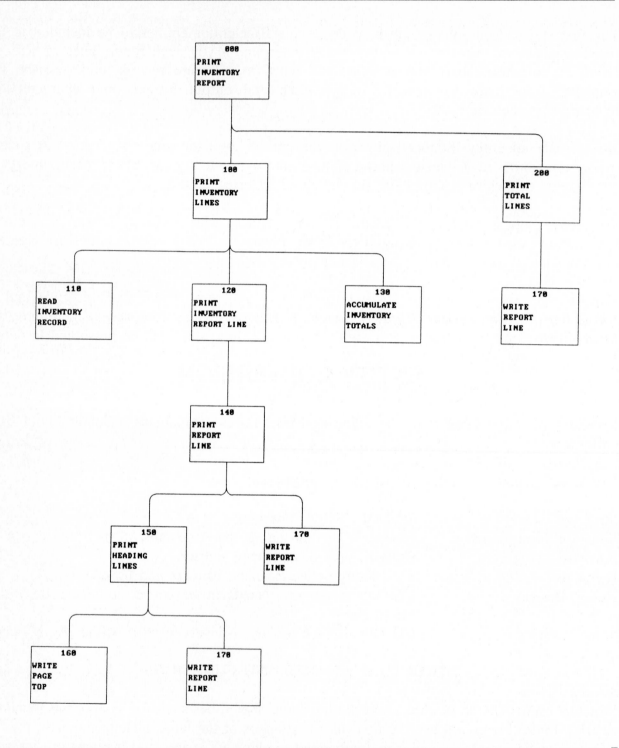

Figure 17.2 Produce Inventory Report Structure Chart

numbers, a good COBOL standard, include the function number as part of the label.

The conversion process generates code by analyzing the Y coordinate, or how high or low the functions are placed on the structure chart. This determines the order of the perform's in the COBOL program.

Figure 17.2 shows the structure chart for a simple program to print an inventory report. Inventory records are read and lines printed. Final totals accumulated and printed after all records are processed.

Each function is described in the XLDictionary, including entries in the description area on the second screen. Figure 17.3 illustrates the description for function 120, PRINT INVENTORY REPORT LINE. The description is written in COBOL code, using data names described as elements in the XLDictionary.

The skeletal code produced is shown in Figure 17.4. Notice that the PROGRAM-ID contains the first eight characters of the structure chart name, with spaces removed. All function

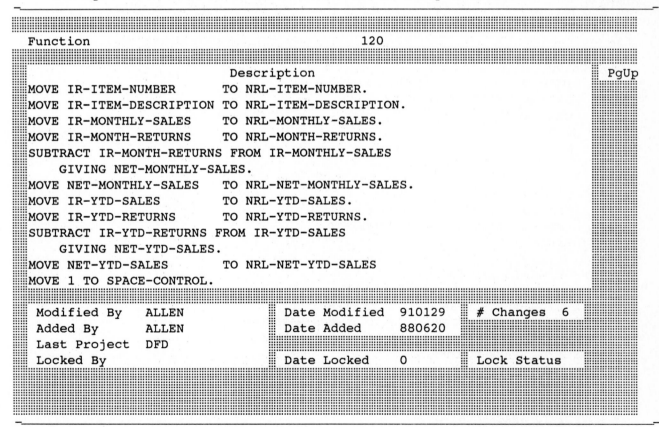

Figure 17.3   Description Screen - Function 120, Print Inventory Line

```
***********************************************************************
*
* SKELETON PROCEDURE DIVISION CREATED FROM AN EXCELERATOR
* STRUCTURE CHART AND PRODUCED BY THE MICRO FOCUS EXCELERATOR
* INTERFACE V1.0.17
*
***********************************************************************
 IDENTIFICATION DIVISION.
 PROGRAM-ID. PRINTINV.
 AUTHOR. XLINT.
 ENVIRONMENT DIVISION.
 CONFIGURATION SECTION.
 SOURCE-COMPUTER. IBM-PC.
 OBJECT-COMPUTER. IBM-PC.
 DATA DIVISION.
 FILE SECTION.
 WORKING-STORAGE SECTION.
 LINKAGE SECTION.
 PROCEDURE DIVISION.

 PRODUCE-INVENTORY-RE SECTION.

* OPEN INPUT  ITEM-FILE
* OPEN OUTPUT REPORT-LINE
      PERFORM   PRINT-INVENTORY-LI.
      PERFORM   PRINT-TOTAL-LI.
      CALL    "PRINTINV".
      STOP RUN.

 PRINT-INVENTORY-LI SECTION.

      PERFORM   READ-INVENTORY-RE.
      PERFORM   PRINT-INVENTORY-RE.
      PERFORM   ACCUMULATE-INVENTORY-TO.
      EXIT.

 PRINT-TOTAL-LI SECTION.

* MOVE TOTAL-MONTHLY-SALES     TO TL-MONTHLY-SALES.
* MOVE TOTAL-MONTH-RETURNS     TO TL-MONTH-RETURNS.
* MOVE TOTAL-NET-MONTHLY-SALES TO TL-NET-MONTHLY-SALES.
* MOVE 3 TO SPACE-CONTROL.
* MOVE TOTAL-YTD-SALES         TO TL-YTD-SALES.
* MOVE TOTAL-YTD-RETURNS       TO TL-YTD-RETURNS.
* MOVE TOTAL-NET-YTD-SALES     TO TL-NET-YTD-SALES.
* MOVE 2 TO SPACE-CONTROL.
      PERFORM   WRITE-REPORT-LI.
```

Figure 17.4 Skeletal Code For The Produce Inventory Report Structure Chart, Page 1

```
      EXIT.
      READ-INVENTORY-RE SECTION.

*  READ ITEM-FILE
*       AT END
*            MOVE 'Y' TO END-OF-FILE-SW.
*  IF NOT END-OF-FILE
*       ADD 1 TO RECORDS-READ.
        EXIT.

   PRINT-INVENTORY-RE SECTION.

*  MOVE IR-ITEM-NUMBER        TO NRL-ITEM-NUMBER.
*  MOVE IR-ITEM-DESCRIPTION TO NRL-ITEM-DESCRIPTION.
*  MOVE IR-MONTHLY-SALES      TO NRL-MONTHLY-SALES.
*  MOVE IR-MONTH-RETURNS      TO NRL-MONTH-RETURNS.
*  SUBTRACT IR-MONTH-RETURNS FROM IR-MONTHLY-SALES
*       GIVING NET-MONTHLY-SALES.
*  MOVE NET-MONTHLY-SALES     TO NRL-NET-MONTHLY-SALES.
*  MOVE IR-YTD-SALES          TO NRL-YTD-SALES.
*  MOVE IR-YTD-RETURNS        TO NRL-YTD-RETURNS.
*  SUBTRACT IR-YTD-RETURNS FROM IR-YTD-SALES
*       GIVING NET-YTD-SALES.
*  MOVE NET-YTD-SALES         TO NRL-NET-YTD-SALES
*  MOVE 1 TO SPACE-CONTROL.
        PERFORM   PRINT-REPORT-LI.
        EXIT.

   ACCUMULATE-INVENTORY-TO SECTION.

*  ADD IR-MONTHLY-SALES   TO TOTAL-MONTHLY-SALES.
*  ADD IR-MONTH-RETURNS   TO TOTAL-MONTH-RETURNS.
*  ADD NET-MONTHLY-SALES TO TOTAL-NET-MONTHLY-SALES.
*  ADD IR-YTD-SALES       TO TOTAL-YTD-SALES.
*  ADD IR-YTD-RETURNS     TO TOTAL-YTD-RETURNS.
*  ADD NET-YTD-SALES      TO TOTAL-NET-YTD-SALES.
        CALL    "ACCUMULA".
        EXIT.

   WRITE-REPORT-LI SECTION.

*  WRITE PRINT-AREA
*       AFTER ADVANCING SPACE-CONTROL LINES.
*  ADD SPACE-CONTROL TO LINE-COUNT.    WRITE PRINT-AREA
*       AFTER ADVANCING SPACE-CONTROL LINES.
*  ADD SPACE-CONTROL TO LINE-COUNT.    WRITE PRINT-AREA
*       AFTER ADVANCING SPACE-CONTROL LINES.
*  ADD SPACE-CONTROL TO LINE-COUNT.
```

Figure 17.4   Skeletal Code For The Produce Inventory Report Structure Chart, Page 2

```
        EXIT.
   PRINT-REPORT-LI SECTION.

 * IF LINE-COUNT IS GREATER THAN MAXIMUM-LINES
 * MOVE NEXT-REPORT-LINE TO PRINT-AREA
        PERFORM  PRINT-HEADING-LI.
        PERFORM  WRITE-REPORT-LI.
        EXIT.

   PRINT-HEADING-LI SECTION.

 * MOVE CURRENT-DATE TO REPORT-DATE
 * MOVE PAGE-NUMBER TO HDG1-PAGE-NUMBER
 * MOVE HEADING-LINE-1 TO PRINT-AREA.
 * MOVE HEADING-LINE-2 TO PRINT-AREA.
 * MOVE 2 TO SPACE-CONTROL.
 * MOVE HEADING-LINE-3 TO PRINT-AREA.
 * MOVE 1 TO SPACE-CONTROL.
 * MOVE 0 TO LINE-COUNT.
        PERFORM  WRITE-PAGE-TO.
        PERFORM  WRITE-REPORT-LI.
        EXIT.

   WRITE-REPORT-LI SECTION.

 * WRITE PRINT-AREA
 *      AFTER ADVANCING SPACE-CONTROL LINES.
 * ADD SPACE-CONTROL TO LINE-COUNT.    WRITE PRINT-AREA
 *      AFTER ADVANCING SPACE-CONTROL LINES.
 * ADD SPACE-CONTROL TO LINE-COUNT.
        EXIT.

   WRITE-PAGE-TO SECTION.

 * WRITE PRINT-AREA
 *      AFTER ADVANCING PAGE-TOP.
        EXIT.

   WRITE-REPORT-LI SECTION.

 * WRITE PRINT-AREA
 *      AFTER ADVANCING SPACE-CONTROL LINES.
 * ADD SPACE-CONTROL TO LINE-COUNT.
        EXIT.
```

Figure 17.4   Skeletal Code For The Produce Inventory Report Structure Chart, Page 3

names have spaces replaced with one hyphen and convert into COBOL sections. The code from function descriptions translates to procedure division paragraph comments.

Subordinate functions are placed lower in the program and the calling function has a matching PERFORM statement. Each section has an EXIT included as the last statement. Care was taken in the design of the function descriptions not to include any PERFORM statements, since these are generated.

RECORDS AND ELEMENTS

Each record converts into a separate COBOL record layout, described as a 01 level. To produce a more complete COBOL program, these must be copied into the skeletal program. Records were designed for the working storage area of the program, including switches, totals and print fields. These are not normally included in the data dictionary at a system level, since they are very program specific and are neither input nor output.

Record		INVENTORY RECORD			
Alternate Name					
Definition	%IR-%				
Normalized	N				
Name of Element or Record	Occ	Seq	Type	Sec-Keys	
ACTIVE RECORD CODE	1	0	E		
ITEM NUMBER	1	0	K		
ITEM DESCRIPTION	1	0	E	S	
LAST ITEM UPDATE DATE	1	0	E		
UNIT COST	1	0	E		
UNIT PRICE	1	0	E		
QUANTITY ON HAND	1	0	E		
QUANTITY ON ORDER	1	0	E		
REORDER POINT	1	0	E		
REORDER QUANTITY	1	0	E		
MONTHLY SALES	1	0	E		
MONTH RETURNS	1	0	E		
MONTHLY BACKORDERED	1	0	E		
YTD BACKORDERED	1	0	E		
					PgDn

Figure 17.5 Record Description For The Inventory Record

Each element within the record was carefully designed with the intent of generating COBOL code. Names should be limited to thirty characters, the maximum length for COBOL. Each element must contain an input picture or output picture and characteristic: character, packed or binary. Use a **V** in the picture to indicate the decimal point location.

If a prefix should precede each element data name, such as **IR-** for Inventory Record, include the prefix in the record definition, surrounded by percent signs, eg. **%IR-%**. The maximum prefix length is 16 characters. Figure 17.5 illustrates the records description for the Inventory Record and Figure 17.6 the resulting COBOL code.

```
*Record INVENTORY-RECORD Generated:   6-FEB-91
 01   INVENTORY-RECORD.
      05   IR-ACTIVE-RECORD-CODE          PIC X
                                VALUE 'A'.
      05   IR-ITEM-NUMBER                 PIC 9(8).
      05   IR-ITEM-DESCRIPTION            PIC X(25).
      05   IR-LAST-ITEM-UPDATE-DATE       PIC 9(6).
      05   IR-UNIT-COST                   PIC 9(4)V99
                   COMP-3.
      05   IR-UNIT-PRICE                  PIC 9(4)V99
                   COMP-3.
      05   IR-QUANTITY-ON-HAND            PIC 9(5)
                   COMP-3.
      05   IR-QUANTITY-ON-ORDER           PIC 9(5)
                   COMP-3.
      05   IR-REORDER-POINT               PIC 9(5)
                   COMP-3.
      05   IR-REORDER-QUANTITY            PIC 9(5)
                   COMP-3.
      05   IR-MONTHLY-SALES               PIC 9(5)V99
                   COMP-3.
      05   IR-MONTH-RETURNS               PIC 9(5)V99
                   COMP-3.
      05   IR-MONTHLY-BACKORDERED         PIC 9(5)
                   COMP-3.
      05   IR-YTD-BACKORDERED             PIC 9(5)
                   COMP-3.
      05   IR-YTD-SALES                   PIC 9(7)V99
                   COMP-3.
      05   IR-YTD-RETURNS                 PIC 9(7)V99
                   COMP-3.
      05   IR-VENDOR-NUMBER               PIC 9(6)
                                OCCURS 5 TIMES.
```

Figure 17.6 Inventory Record Generated COBOL Code

REPORT DESIGN

The SCREENS & REPORTS feature may be used to create report designs that convert to Micro Focus reports. The Micro Focus CO-Reports program translates these into COBOL code. When reports are created, build the heading lines and only one of each different detail line. A block of detail lines will <u>each</u> create a different 01 layout in the COBOL program. Each report is limited to 30 lines.

The report shown in Figure 17.7 contains the layout for the Inventory Report program. The generated code is shown in Figure 17.13.

99-99-99		INVENTORY COST REPORT					PAGE ZZ9
ITEM	ITEM DESCRIPTION	MONTH	MONTH	NET MONTH	YEAR TO DATE	YEAR TO DATE	NET YEAR TO
NUMBER		SALES	RETURNS	SALES	SALES	RETURNS	DATE SALES
99999999	XXXXXXXXXXXXXXXXXXXXXXXXX	ZZ,ZZ9.99	ZZ,ZZ9.99	ZZ,ZZZ.99	Z,ZZZ,ZZ9.99	Z,ZZZ,ZZ9.99	Z,ZZZ,ZZ9.99
	COMPANY TOTALS	Z,ZZZ,ZZ9.99	Z,ZZZ,ZZ9.99	Z,ZZZ,ZZ9.99	ZZZ,ZZZ,ZZ9.99	ZZZ,ZZZ,ZZ9.99	ZZZ,ZZZ,ZZ9.99
	RECORDS READ	ZZZZ9					

Figure 17.7 Inventory Report Design

SCREEN DESIGN

Screen designs transform into Micro Focus screens used within the CO-Maps facility. These screens may be used to create CICS basic map support (BMS) assembler code along with the corresponding COBOL code or MFS maps and COBOL.

The PRODUCE INVENTORY REPORT program contains no screens, but one is included as an example. The screen, illustrated in Figure 17.8, is used to add new items to the Inventory Master file. The CICS BMS assembler code is shown in Figure 17.15 and the corresponding CICS COBOL code is illustrated in Figure 17.16. Input pictures are used for data fields in the first COBOL layout and the whole screen layout is redefined to include output pictures. This provides a flexible approach to generating screen code, since the intent of the screen (either data entry or inquiry) is not known to the code generating program.

THE PROCEDURE FOR CODE GENERATION

The first step is to create the Excelerator entities used to generate code. These have been illustrated throughout this chapter. The report was created, showing the headers, one detail line, and footers. Complete records, working-storage work areas and elements have been entered. The structure chart was carefully drawn, conforming to the requirements for generating code. Function descriptions were written using COBOL syntax.

Step two is creating the export entity list. All code generating entities are included, illustrated in Figure 17.9. This list is used to export the entities in a format used by the Micro Focus interface.

The process is controlled by a special Excelerator export function, chosen from the Interface menu. Select **Interfaces** from the main menu and **COBOL/2 Interface**. Two options are available to transfer data to the Micro Focus interface. Option 1, **Export to File** uses an

```
 ___                                                                       __
|
|  INVSYS                  ADD INVENTORY ITEM                   INVU01
|  MM-DD-YY                                                     HH:MM
|
|  ITEM NUMBER        XXXXXXX
|
|  ITEM DESCRIPTION XXXXXXXXXXXXXXXXXXXXXXXX
|
|  UNIT COST         99999.99              UNIT PRICE        99999.99
|
|  QUANTITY ON HAND 99999                  QUANTITY ON ORDER 99999
|
|  REORDER POINT     99999                 REORDER QUANTITY  99999
|
|
|  VENDOR NUMBERS    XXXXX     XXXXX
|
|                    XXXXX     XXXXX
|
|                    XXXXX
|
|
|
|  XXXXXXXXXXXXXXXXXXXXXXXXX (OPERATOR MESSAGE) XXXXXXXXXXXXXXXXXXXXXXXXXXXXXXXXXX
|  XXXXXXXXXXXXXXXXXXXXXXXXX (ERROR MESSAGE) XXXXXXXXXXXXXXXXXXXXXXXXXXXXXXXXXX
|___                                                                       __|
```

Figure 17.8 Add Item Screen

entity list to create the export file. This file may be placed on diskette and taken to a different machine if Micro Focus is not on the same Microcomputer as Excelerator.

Option 2, **Automatic Export,** lets you select the entities, and then runs the Micro Focus Interface automatically.

Select Export to File. The export screen displays, providing options to control the file transfer. Refer to the example in Figure 17.10.

The **Use COBOL Prefix** option lets you select whether on not to include prefixes in front of record elements, such as **IR-.** A Yes/No selection will pop up. Select Yes to include prefixes in code data names.

The **Use Screen Data Maps** choice (Yes/No) determines whether to generate screen data maps for use in the Micro Focus CO-Maps feature. COBOL code for screen designs is always created.

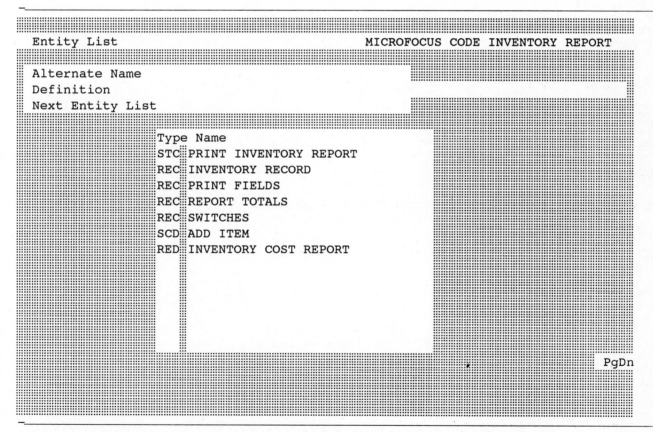

```
Entity List                                    MICROFOCUS CODE INVENTORY REPORT

   Alternate Name
   Definition
   Next Entity List

              Type Name
              STC PRINT INVENTORY REPORT
              REC INVENTORY RECORD
              REC PRINT FIELDS
              REC REPORT TOTALS
              REC SWITCHES
              SCD ADD ITEM
              RED INVENTORY COST REPORT




                                                                          PgDn
```

Figure 17.9 Entity List For Exporting Entities To Micro Focus

Alternate Name lets you use the Record's alternate name for the generated COBOL name. This provides flexibility when creating entities. The Alternate name may be created specifically for COBOL, while and the entity name may reflect user terminology.

Define Naming Mask lets you choose the characters in the entity name to be used as DOS filenames for the entities. You may choose the rightmost or leftmost characters in the entity name field and how many characters from the start or end of the field to skip before selecting naming characters. Any characters (such as spaces) that are not valid within a DOS file name are removed.

Execute begins the transfer process. A selector screen of entity lists is displayed. Choose each entity list containing export entities. This selector list differs from others in Excelerator. When an entry list is chosen, control does not return to the menu selection screen. Instead the selector list remains on the screen and other lists may be chosen. Press F3 when finished making choices and you will be prompted for a path and file name. Overtype the default name and press enter to start the transfer process. Select Exit when finished.

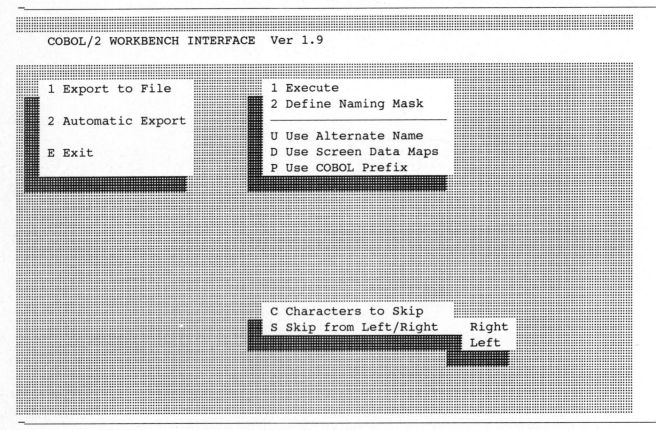

Figure 17.10   Export Screen For Transferring Entities To Micro Focus

The interface creates three DOS files, each with the export file name and an extension:

An output file with the DOS extension of **EXC**. This contains the transfer file.

A summary file containing counts of the exported entities. It has a DOS extension of **SUM**.

An error log listing any problems that prevent entities from being exported. The extension is **ERR**.

MICRO FOCUS CONVERSION

Exit Excelerator and run Micro Focus COBOL. Press F6, the Run option. Enter **XLINT** for the Micro Focus Excelerator Interface and the interface options screen is displayed. The bottom portion of this screen is shown in Figure 17.11 (the top part is blank). Menu options, chosen using function keys, display on the bottom of the screen. The line above the function key choices shows options that are set **on**.

These are indicated by text separated by a hyphen, for example, -structs- meaning that structure charts are to be converted into skeletal code. Pressing function keys *toggle* conversion options on or off. A toggle is similar to a button pressed once to turn a device on, such as a tape player, and pressed again to turn off. Pressing the function key once turns the option on, pressing again turns it off.

F2 changes the default path for locating files

F8 lets you change the system setup, such as the default path for files and whether to list conversion results to the screen or a file.

The toggle options available are:

F3 - create either CO Maps, Screens, Forms or no screen
F4 - create reports or not
F5 - create record layouts or not
F6 - transform structure charts to code or no conversion
F7 - confirm (file exists, override Y/N) when writing files that already exist.

```
Xlint————confirm—screen-list—Screens—reports—records—structs—Ins—Caps—Num—Scroll
F1=help F2=dir F3=scrns F4=repts F5=recs F6=strcts F7=confirm F8=sys-set  Escape
File C:\COBOL\                                                             Ctrl
```

Figure 17.11 Micro Focus Interface Options Screen

Press the toggles for your particular application. For the example, the PRODUCE INVENTORY REPORT uses reports, records and a structure chart. In addition, the sample screen design, ADD ITEM, is created for CO Maps.

When all the toggles are set, key the file name on the bottom of the screen and press enter. Conversion results will be displayed (unless they are sent to a file). Press Esc to exit to the main menu and Esc again to exit Micro Focus.

TRANSFORMING REPORT DESIGNS INTO COBOL CODE

Report designs convert into Micro Focus report designs, which may be used to generate COBOL code. Press F6 (Run) and enter COREPORT from within Micro Focus or enter CR at the DOS prompt to run the CO Reports program.

```
99-99-99                      INVENTORY COST REPORT


     ITEM          ITEM DESCRIPTION        MONTH           MONTH

     NUMBER                                SALES           RETURNS



     99999999    XXXXXXXXXXXXXXXXXXXXXXXXX   ZZ,ZZ9.99      ZZ,ZZ9.99



                          COMPANY TOTALS   Z,ZZZ,ZZ9.99   Z,ZZZ,ZZ9.99   Z,



                          RECORDS READ    ZZZZ9
Forming─INVENTOR─Text─Spaces─00────Line─01─Counter─001──Ins─Caps─Num────
F1=help F2=data-menu F3/F4=insert/delete-line F5=repeat-line F6=restore-line
F7=page-left F8=page-right F9=word-left F10=word-right   Alternate     Escape
```

Figure 17.12 Micro Focus Report Design screen

A Report Design screen is displayed. Figure 17.12 illustrates this screen showing the converted Excelerator INVENTORY REPORT. Press and hold the Alt key and tap F3 to load a report design. Then press F2 for a directory of *forms*, the Micro Focus name for report designs. Use the up and down arrows to select a name and press enter. Press enter again to load the form.

Review the form and press Alt and F5 to generate COBOL code. Press F2 from the options to initiate the process. A prompt will display asking if you wish to generate without saving. Reply Y for yes. Press the enter key to accept the default file name or overtype the name, if desired.

Lines will flash on the bottom of the screen showing generated code. When finished, press Esc and confirm Y to exit. The COBOL code will exist with an extension of **PD**. It may be copied into the program or printed. Figure 17.13 shows the COBOL code generated from the INVENTORY REPORT.

CREATING CICS MAPS AND COBOL CODE

The screen designs transform into Micro Focus screens and may be used with the CO-Maps program to create CICS or IMS code. The example in this section will focus on generating CICS code, but the same procedure is used for IMS code.

From the Micro Focus main menu, press F6 (run) and enter MAPS. You can run CO-Maps directly from DOS by entering MAPS. A menu selection screen displays, illustrated in Figure 17.14.

Move the down arrow until the light bar is over **Generation/Conversion** in the left column. With the light bar on **Generate BMS Macros** in the center column, press the enter key. Enter the name of the Micro Focus screen design created by the conversion process. You may also press F2 for a list of maps. Then move the light bar to the desired screen design and press the enter key.

The name used for the map in this example is ADDITEM. A default mapset name, ADDITEM.BMS, is presented. Press enter or overtype with a new name. Press the enter key and the Assembler map will be created. Figure 17.15 is the complete map for the ADD ITEM screen.

Press F4 to move the light bar down to the **Generate BMS Cobol Copy** option. Press the enter key and the previous mapset name will display. Press enter to accept or overtype to change. The filename for the COBOL code is presented. The name for the sample screen is ADDITEM.CPY (for copy). Press enter to accept or overtype to change. Figure 17.16 is

```
   01   PRT-INVENTOR-01.
        03   FILLER                          PIC X(0001) VALUE SPACE.
        03   FILLER                          PIC X(0008) VALUE '99-99-9
 -      '9'.
        03   FILLER                          PIC X(0022) VALUE SPACE.
        03   FILLER                          PIC X(0021) VALUE 'INVENTO
 -      'RY COST REPORT'.
        03   FILLER                          PIC X(0022) VALUE SPACE.
        03   FILLER                          PIC X(0008) VALUE 'PAGE ZZ
 -      '9'.
   01   PRT-INVENTOR-03.
        03   FILLER                          PIC X(0003) VALUE SPACE.
        03   FILLER                          PIC X(0004) VALUE 'ITEM'.
        03   FILLER                          PIC X(0010) VALUE SPACE.
        03   FILLER                          PIC X(0004) VALUE 'ITEM'.
        03   FILLER                          PIC X(0001) VALUE SPACE.
        03   FILLER                          PIC X(0011) VALUE 'DESCRIP
 -      'TION'.
        03   FILLER                          PIC X(0011) VALUE SPACE.
        03   FILLER                          PIC X(0005) VALUE 'MONTH'.
        03   FILLER                          PIC X(0009) VALUE SPACE.
        03   FILLER                          PIC X(0005) VALUE 'MONTH'.
        03   FILLER                          PIC X(0008) VALUE SPACE.
        03   FILLER                          PIC X(0003) VALUE 'NET'.
        03   FILLER                          PIC X(0001) VALUE SPACE.
        03   FILLER                          PIC X(0005) VALUE 'MONTH'.
        03   FILLER                          PIC X(0005) VALUE SPACE.
        03   FILLER                          PIC X(0004) VALUE 'YEAR'.
        03   FILLER                          PIC X(0001) VALUE SPACE.
        03   FILLER                          PIC X(0002) VALUE 'TO'.
        03   FILLER                          PIC X(0001) VALUE SPACE.
        03   FILLER                          PIC X(0004) VALUE 'DATE'.
        03   FILLER                          PIC X(0005) VALUE SPACE.
        03   FILLER                          PIC X(0004) VALUE 'YEAR'.
        03   FILLER                          PIC X(0001) VALUE SPACE.
        03   FILLER                          PIC X(0002) VALUE 'TO'.
        03   FILLER                          PIC X(0001) VALUE SPACE.
        03   FILLER                          PIC X(0004) VALUE 'DATE'.
        03   FILLER                          PIC X(0006) VALUE SPACE.
        03   FILLER                          PIC X(0003) VALUE 'NET'.
        03   FILLER                          PIC X(0001) VALUE SPACE.
        03   FILLER                          PIC X(0004) VALUE 'YEAR'.
        03   FILLER                          PIC X(0001) VALUE SPACE.
        03   FILLER                          PIC X(0002) VALUE 'TO'.
```

Figure 17.13   COBOL Code Generated From The Inventory Report, Page 1

```
01   PRT-INVENTOR-04.
     03   FILLER                              PIC X(0002) VALUE SPACE.
     03   FILLER                              PIC X(0006) VALUE 'NUMBER'
     .
     03   FILLER                              PIC X(0036) VALUE SPACE.
     03   FILLER                              PIC X(0005) VALUE 'SALES'.
     03   FILLER                              PIC X(0008) VALUE SPACE.
     03   FILLER                              PIC X(0007) VALUE 'RETURNS
-    ''.
     03   FILLER                              PIC X(0009) VALUE SPACE.
     03   FILLER                              PIC X(0005) VALUE 'SALES'.
     03   FILLER                              PIC X(0011) VALUE SPACE.
     03   FILLER                              PIC X(0005) VALUE 'SALES'.
     03   FILLER                              PIC X(0011) VALUE SPACE.
     03   FILLER                              PIC X(0007) VALUE 'RETURNS
-    ''.
     03   FILLER                              PIC X(0008) VALUE SPACE.
     03   FILLER                              PIC X(0004) VALUE 'DATE'.
     03   FILLER                              PIC X(0001) VALUE SPACE.
     03   FILLER                              PIC X(0005) VALUE 'SALES'.
01   PRT-INVENTOR-06.
     03   FILLER                              PIC X(0001) VALUE SPACE.
     03   INVENTOR-06-001                     PIC 9(0008).
     03   FILLER                              PIC X(0004) VALUE SPACE.
     03   INVENTOR-06-002                     PIC X(0025).
     03   FILLER                              PIC X(0005) VALUE SPACE.
     03   FILLER                              PIC X(0009) VALUE 'ZZ,ZZ9.
-    '99'.
     03   FILLER                              PIC X(0005) VALUE SPACE.
     03   FILLER                              PIC X(0009) VALUE 'ZZ,ZZ9.
-    '99'.
     03   FILLER                              PIC X(0005) VALUE SPACE.
     03   FILLER                              PIC X(0009) VALUE 'ZZ,ZZZ.
-    '99'.
     03   FILLER                              PIC X(0005) VALUE SPACE.
     03   FILLER                              PIC X(0012) VALUE 'Z,ZZZ,Z
-    'Z9.99'.
     03   FILLER                              PIC X(0005) VALUE SPACE.
     03   FILLER                              PIC X(0012) VALUE 'Z,ZZZ,Z
-    'Z9.99'.
     03   FILLER                              PIC X(0005) VALUE SPACE.
     03   FILLER                              PIC X(0012) VALUE 'Z,ZZZ,Z
-    'Z9.99'.
```

Figure 17.13   COBOL Code Generated From The Inventory Report, Page 2

```
01   PRT-INVENTOR-08.
        03   FILLER                          PIC X(0024) VALUE SPACE.
        03   FILLER                          PIC X(0007) VALUE 'COMPANY
   -     ''.
        03   FILLER                          PIC X(0001) VALUE SPACE.
        03   FILLER                          PIC X(0006) VALUE 'TOTALS'
         .
        03   FILLER                          PIC X(0002) VALUE SPACE.
        03   FILLER                          PIC X(0012) VALUE 'Z,ZZZ,Z
   -     'Z9.99'.
        03   FILLER                          PIC X(0002) VALUE SPACE.
        03   FILLER                          PIC X(0012) VALUE 'Z,ZZZ,Z
   -     'Z9.99'.
        03   FILLER                          PIC X(0002) VALUE SPACE.
        03   FILLER                          PIC X(0012) VALUE 'Z,ZZZ,Z
   -     'Z9.99'.
        03   FILLER                          PIC X(0003) VALUE SPACE.
        03   FILLER                          PIC X(0014) VALUE 'ZZZ,ZZZ
   -     ',ZZ9.99'.
        03   FILLER                          PIC X(0003) VALUE SPACE.
        03   FILLER                          PIC X(0014) VALUE 'ZZZ,ZZZ
   -     ',ZZ9.99'.
        03   FILLER                          PIC X(0003) VALUE SPACE.
        03   FILLER                          PIC X(0014) VALUE 'ZZZ,ZZZ
   -     ',ZZ9.99'.
  01   PRT-INVENTOR-10.
        03   FILLER                          PIC X(0024) VALUE SPACE.
        03   FILLER                          PIC X(0007) VALUE 'RECORDS
   -     ''.
        03   FILLER                          PIC X(0001) VALUE SPACE.
        03   FILLER                          PIC X(0004) VALUE 'READ'.
        03   FILLER                          PIC X(0004) VALUE SPACE.
        03   FILLER                          PIC X(0005) VALUE 'ZZZZ9'.
```

Figure 17.13   COBOL Code Generated From The Inventory Report, Page 3

the full CICS COBOL code for the ADD ITEM screen. Press Esc to exit CO-Maps.

```
┌──────────────────────────────────────────────────────────────────────┐
│        Innovative Solutions CICS/BMS - IMS/MFS Screen Development System │
├──────────────────────────────────────────────────────────────────────┤
│                                                                        │
│   Function                        Option                               │
│                                                                        │
│   Mapset Processing              ┌──────────────────────────────────┐  │
│   Map Processing                 │ Generate BMS Macros              │  │
│   Field Processing               │ Generate MFS Macros              │  │
│   Generation/Conversion          │ Generate BMS Cobol Copy          │  │
│   Maps Utilities                 │ Generate MFS Cobol Copy          │  │
│                                  │ Generate Micro Focus Copy        │  │
│                                  │ Convert BMS Macros               │  │
│                                  │ Convert Forms Definition         │  │
│                                  │                                  │  │
│                                  └──────────────────────────────────┘  │
│                                                                        │
│                                                                        │
│                                                                        │
│                                                                        │
│ ═Generate═BMS═Cobol═Copybook═════════════════════════════════════════ │
│ F1=help  F2=Directory  Escape                                          │
│ Enter Mapset ADDITEM then press enter                                  │
└──────────────────────────────────────────────────────────────────────┘
```

Figure 17.14   Screen Generation Menu Selection Screen

COMBINING CODE INTO THE FINAL PROGRAM

The code generated by Excelerator and Micro Focus is placed in several DOS files. Each structure chart, record, screen and report create a separate file. These must be combined to create the final COBOL program. If the functions have been described with COBOL logic, the asterisks must be removed from procedure division paragraphs. The final skeletal program code is shown in Figure 17.18.

Any missing code must be added to create the final compilable program. Enter any selects, file descriptions, additional working-storage entries and procedure division code. The looping modules will need to have the PERFORM changed to a PERFORM UNTIL. PERFORM statements will need to be moved to proper locations within other generated code.

Report data names as well as report line names must be changed to those referenced in the Procedure division. Common structure chart functions (functions located in several places with the same ID) may generate extra paragraphs which need to be deleted.

```
ADDITEM   DFHMSD TYPE=&&SYSPARM
ADDITEM   DFHMDI SIZE=(  ,  )
          DFHMDF POS=(01,02),                                                    X
                 LENGTH=078,                                                     X
                 INITIAL='INVSYS                        ADD  INVENTORY  ITEX
                 M                              INVU01'
DATE      DFHMDF POS=(02,01),                                                    X
                 HILIGHT=REVERSE,                                                X
                 LENGTH=008,                                                     X
                 PICOUT='Z9-99-99'
HOURS     DFHMDF POS=(02,74),                                                    X
                 HILIGHT=REVERSE,                                                X
                 LENGTH=002,                                                     X
                 PICOUT='Z9'
          DFHMDF POS=(02,76),                                                    X
                 LENGTH=001,                                                     X
                 INITIAL=':'
MINUTES   DFHMDF POS=(02,77),                                                    X
                 HILIGHT=REVERSE,                                                X
                 LENGTH=002,                                                     X
                 PICOUT='Z9'
          DFHMDF POS=(04,01),                                                    X
                 LENGTH=011,                                                     X
                 INITIAL='ITEM NUMBER'
ITEM-NU   DFHMDF POS=(04,18),                                                    X
                 HILIGHT=REVERSE,                                                X
                 LENGTH=008,                                                     X
                 PICOUT='9(8)',                                                  X
                 PICIN='9(8)'
          DFHMDF POS=(06,01),                                                    X
                 LENGTH=016,                                                     X
                 INITIAL='ITEM DESCRIPTION'
ITEM-DE   DFHMDF POS=(06,18),                                                    X
                 HILIGHT=REVERSE,                                                X
                 LENGTH=025,                                                     X
                 PICOUT='X(25)',                                                 X
                 PICIN='X(25)'
          DFHMDF POS=(08,01),                                                    X
                 LENGTH=009,                                                     X
                 INITIAL='UNIT COST'
```

Figure 17.15   Complete CICS BMS Map For The Add Item Screen, Page 1

```
UNIT-CO  DFHMDF POS=(08,18),                                X
               HILIGHT=REVERSE,                             X
               LENGTH=007,                                  X
               PICOUT='Z,ZZZ.99',                           X
               PICIN='9(4)V99'
         DFHMDF POS=(08,46),                                X
               LENGTH=010,                                  X
               INITIAL='UNIT PRICE'
UNIT-PR  DFHMDF POS=(08,64),                                X
               HILIGHT=REVERSE,                             X
               LENGTH=007,                                  X
               PICOUT='Z,ZZZ.99',                           X
               PICIN='9(4)V99'
         DFHMDF POS=(10,01),                                X
               LENGTH=016,                                  X
               INITIAL='QUANTITY ON HAND'
QUANTIT  DFHMDF POS=(10,18),                                X
               HILIGHT=REVERSE,                             X
               LENGTH=005,                                  X
               PICOUT='ZZZZ9',                              X
               PICIN='9(5)'
         DFHMDF POS=(10,46),                                X
               LENGTH=017,                                  X
               INITIAL='QUANTITY ON ORDER'
QUANTIT  DFHMDF POS=(10,64),                                X
               HILIGHT=REVERSE,                             X
               LENGTH=005,                                  X
               PICOUT='ZZZZ9',                              X
               PICIN='9(5)',                                X
               INITIAL='0       '
         DFHMDF POS=(12,01),                                X
               LENGTH=013,                                  X
               INITIAL='REORDER POINT'
REORDER  DFHMDF POS=(12,18),                                X
               HILIGHT=REVERSE,                             X
               LENGTH=005,                                  X
               PICOUT='ZZZZ9',                              X
               PICIN='9(5)'
         DFHMDF POS=(12,46),                                X
               LENGTH=016,                                  X
               INITIAL='REORDER QUANTITY'
```

Figure 17.15 Complete CICS BMS Map For The Add Item Screen, Page 2

```
REORDER    DFHMDF POS=(12,64),                                        X
                  HILIGHT=REVERSE,                                    X
                  LENGTH=005,                                         X
                  PICOUT='ZZZZ9',                                     X
                  PICIN='9(5)'
           DFHMDF POS=(15,01),                                        X
                  LENGTH=014,                                         X
                  INITIAL='VENDOR NUMBERS'
VENDOR-    DFHMDF POS=(15,18),                                        X
                  HILIGHT=REVERSE,                                    X
                  LENGTH=006,                                         X
                  PICOUT='9(6)',                                      X
                  PICIN='9(6)'
VENDOR-    DFHMDF POS=(15,28),                                        X
                  HILIGHT=REVERSE,                                    X
                  LENGTH=006,                                         X
                  PICOUT='9(6)',                                      X
                  PICIN='9(6)'
VENDOR-    DFHMDF POS=(17,18),                                        X
                  HILIGHT=REVERSE,                                    X
                  LENGTH=006,                                         X
                  PICOUT='9(6)',                                      X
                  PICIN='9(6)'
VENDOR-    DFHMDF POS=(17,28),                                        X
                  HILIGHT=REVERSE,                                    X
                  LENGTH=006,                                         X
                  PICOUT='9(6)',                                      X
                  PICIN='9(6)'
VENDOR-    DFHMDF POS=(19,18),                                        X
                  HILIGHT=REVERSE,                                    X
                  LENGTH=006,                                         X
                  PICOUT='9(6)',                                      X
                  PICIN='9(6)'
OPERATO    DFHMDF POS=(23,01),                                        X
                  HILIGHT=REVERSE,                                    X
                  LENGTH=079,                                         X
                  PICOUT='X(79)',                                     X
                  INITIAL='PRESS PF1 FOR HELP, PF3 TO EXIT            X
                  '
ERROR-M    DFHMDF POS=(24,01),                                        X
                  HILIGHT=REVERSE,                                    X
                  LENGTH=077,                                         X
                  PICOUT='X(77)'
           DFHMSD TYPE=FINAL
           END
```

Figure 17.15   Complete CICS BMS Map For The Add Item Screen, Page 3

```
01   ADDITEMI.
     05   CURRENT DATEL                        PIC S9(4) COMP.
     05   CURRENT DATEF                        PIC X(01).
     05   FILLER REDEFINES CURRENT DATEF.
          10   CURRENT DATEA                   PIC X(01).
     05   CURRENT DATEI                        PIC X(008).
     05   HOURSL                               PIC S9(4) COMP.
     05   HOURSF                               PIC X(01).
     05   FILLER REDEFINES HOURSF.
          10   HOURSA                          PIC X(01).
     05   HOURSI                               PIC X(002).
     05   MINUTESL                             PIC S9(4) COMP.
     05   MINUTESF                             PIC X(01).
     05   FILLER REDEFINES MINUTESF.
          10   MINUTESA                        PIC X(01).
     05   MINUTESI                             PIC X(002).
     05   ITEM NUMBERL                         PIC S9(4) COMP.
     05   ITEM NUMBERF                         PIC X(01).
     05   FILLER REDEFINES ITEM NUMBERF.
          10   ITEM NUMBERA                    PIC X(01).
     05   ITEM NUMBERI                         PIC 9(8).
     05   ITEM DESCRIPTIONL                    PIC S9(4) COMP.
     05   ITEM DESCRIPTIONF                    PIC X(01).
     05   FILLER REDEFINES ITEM DESCRIPTIONF.
          10   ITEM DESCRIPTIONA               PIC X(01).
     05   ITEM DESCRIPTIONI                    PIC X(25).
     05   UNIT COSTL                           PIC S9(4) COMP.
     05   UNIT COSTF                           PIC X(01).
     05   FILLER REDEFINES UNIT COSTF.
          10   UNIT COSTA                      PIC X(01).
     05   UNIT COSTI                           PIC 9(4)V99.
     05   UNIT PRICEL                          PIC S9(4) COMP.
     05   UNIT PRICEF                          PIC X(01).
     05   FILLER REDEFINES UNIT PRICEF.
          10   UNIT PRICEA                     PIC X(01).
     05   UNIT PRICEI                          PIC 9(4)V99.
     05   QUANTITY ON HANDL                    PIC S9(4) COMP.
     05   QUANTITY ON HANDF                    PIC X(01).
     05   FILLER REDEFINES QUANTITY ON HANDF.
          10   QUANTITY ON HANDA               PIC X(01).
     05   QUANTITY ON HANDI                    PIC 9(5).
     05   QUANTITY ON ORDERL                   PIC S9(4) COMP.
     05   QUANTITY ON ORDERF                   PIC X(01).
     05   FILLER REDEFINES QUANTITY ON ORDERF.
          10   QUANTITY ON ORDERA              PIC X(01).
     05   QUANTITY ON ORDERI                   PIC 9(5).
```

Figure 17.16 Complete COBOL Program For The Add Item Screen, Page 1

```
05   REORDER POINTL                        PIC S9(4) COMP.
05   REORDER POINTF                        PIC X(01).
05   FILLER REDEFINES REORDER POINTF.
     10   REORDER POINTA                   PIC X(01).
05   REORDER POINTI                        PIC 9(5).
05   REORDER QUANTITYL                     PIC S9(4) COMP.
05   REORDER QUANTITYF                     PIC X(01).
05   FILLER REDEFINES REORDER QUANTITYF.
     10   REORDER QUANTITYA                PIC X(01).
05   REORDER QUANTITYI                     PIC 9(5).
05   VENDOR NUMBERL                        PIC S9(4) COMP.
05   VENDOR NUMBERF                        PIC X(01).
05   FILLER REDEFINES VENDOR NUMBERF.
     10   VENDOR NUMBERA                   PIC X(01).
05   VENDOR NUMBERI                        PIC 9(6).
05   VENDOR NUMBERL                        PIC S9(4) COMP.
05   VENDOR NUMBERF                        PIC X(01).
05   FILLER REDEFINES VENDOR NUMBERF.
     10   VENDOR NUMBERA                   PIC X(01).
05   VENDOR NUMBERI                        PIC 9(6).
05   VENDOR NUMBERL                        PIC S9(4) COMP.
05   VENDOR NUMBERF                        PIC X(01).
05   FILLER REDEFINES VENDOR NUMBERF.
     10   VENDOR NUMBERA                   PIC X(01).
05   VENDOR NUMBERI                        PIC 9(6).
05   VENDOR NUMBERL                        PIC S9(4) COMP.
05   VENDOR NUMBERF                        PIC X(01).
05   FILLER REDEFINES VENDOR NUMBERF.
     10   VENDOR NUMBERA                   PIC X(01).
05   VENDOR NUMBERI                        PIC 9(6).
05   VENDOR NUMBERL                        PIC S9(4) COMP.
05   VENDOR NUMBERF                        PIC X(01).
05   FILLER REDEFINES VENDOR NUMBERF.
     10   VENDOR NUMBERA                   PIC X(01).
05   VENDOR NUMBERI                        PIC 9(6).
05   OPERATOR MESSAGEL                     PIC S9(4) COMP.
05   OPERATOR MESSAGEF                     PIC X(01).
05   FILLER REDEFINES OPERATOR MESSAGEF.
     10   OPERATOR MESSAGEA                PIC X(01).
05   OPERATOR MESSAGEI                     PIC X(079).
05   ERROR MESSAGEL                        PIC S9(4) COMP.
05   ERROR MESSAGEF                        PIC X(01).
05   FILLER REDEFINES ERROR MESSAGEF.
     10   ERROR MESSAGEA                   PIC X(01).
05   ERROR MESSAGEI                        PIC X(077).
```

Figure 17.16   Complete COBOL Program For The Add Item Screen, Page 2

```
01  ADDITEMO  REDEFINES ADDITEMI.
    05  FILLER                      PIC X(03).
    05  CURRENT DATEO               PIC Z9-99-99.
    05  FILLER                      PIC X(03).
    05  HOURSO                      PIC Z9.
    05  FILLER                      PIC X(03).
    05  MINUTESO                    PIC Z9.
    05  FILLER                      PIC X(03).
    05  ITEM NUMBERO                PIC 9(8).
    05  FILLER                      PIC X(03).
    05  ITEM DESCRIPTIONO           PIC X(25).
    05  FILLER                      PIC X(03).
    05  UNIT COSTO                  PIC Z,ZZZ.99.
    05  FILLER                      PIC X(03).
    05  UNIT PRICEO                 PIC Z,ZZZ.99.
    05  FILLER                      PIC X(03).
    05  QUANTITY ON HANDO           PIC ZZZZ9.
    05  FILLER                      PIC X(03).
    05  QUANTITY ON ORDERO          PIC ZZZZ9.
    05  FILLER                      PIC X(03).
    05  REORDER POINTO              PIC ZZZZ9.
    05  FILLER                      PIC X(03).
    05  REORDER QUANTITYO           PIC ZZZZ9.
    05  FILLER                      PIC X(03).
    05  VENDOR NUMBERO              PIC 9(6).
    05  FILLER                      PIC X(03).
    05  VENDOR NUMBERO              PIC 9(6).
    05  FILLER                      PIC X(03).
    05  VENDOR NUMBERO              PIC 9(6).
    05  FILLER                      PIC X(03).
    05  VENDOR NUMBERO              PIC 9(6).
    05  FILLER                      PIC X(03).
    05  VENDOR NUMBERO              PIC 9(6).
    05  FILLER                      PIC X(03).
    05  OPERATOR MESSAGEO           PIC X(79).
    05  FILLER                      PIC X(03).
    05  ERROR MESSAGEO              PIC X(77).
```

Figure 17.16 Complete COBOL Program For The Add Item Screen, Page 3

```
***********************************************************************
*
* SKELETON PROCEDURE DIVISION CREATED FROM AN EXCELERATOR
* STRUCTURE CHART AND PRODUCED BY THE MICRO FOCUS EXCELERATOR
* INTERFACE V1.0.17
*
***********************************************************************
 IDENTIFICATION DIVISION.
 PROGRAM-ID. PRINTINV.
 AUTHOR. XLINT.
 ENVIRONMENT DIVISION.
 CONFIGURATION SECTION.
 SOURCE-COMPUTER. IBM-PC.
 OBJECT-COMPUTER. IBM-PC.
 DATA DIVISION.
 FILE SECTION.
 WORKING-STORAGE SECTION.

*Record SWITCHES Generated:   6-FEB-91
 01   SWITCHES.
      05   END-OF-FILE-SW               PIC X.


*Record PRINT-FIELDS Generated:   6-FEB-91
 01   PRINT-FIELDS.
      05   SPACE-CONTROL                PIC 9
                      COMP      VALUE 1.
      05   MAXIMUM-LINES                PIC 99
                      COMP.
      05   LINE-COUNT                   PIC 99
                      COMP.
      05   PAGE-NUMBER                  PIC 999
                      COMP-3.
*Record REPORT-TOTALS Generated:   6-FEB-91
 01   REPORT-TOTALS.

      05   TOTAL-MONTHLY-SALES          PIC 9(7)V99
                      COMP-3.
```

Figure 17.17 Complete Generated COBOL Code - Produce Inventory Report Program, Page 1

```
          05  TOTAL-MONTH-RETURNS              PIC 9(7)V99
                         COMP-3.
          05  TOTAL-NET-MONTHLY-SALES          PIC 9(7)V99
                         COMP-3.
          05  TOTAL-YTD-SALES                  PIC 9(9)V99
                         COMP-3.
          05  TOTAL-YTD-RETURNS                PIC 9(9)V99
                         COMP-3.
          05  TOTAL-YTD-NET-SALES              PIC 9(9)V99
                         COMP-3.
     *Record INVENTORY-RECORD Generated:  6-FEB-91
      01  INVENTORY-RECORD.
          05  IR-ACTIVE-RECORD-CODE            PIC X
                                  VALUE 'A'.
          05  IR-ITEM-NUMBER                   PIC 9(8).
          05  IR-ITEM-DESCRIPTION              PIC X(25).
          05  IR-LAST-ITEM-UPDATE-DATE         PIC 9(6).
          05  IR-UNIT-COST                     PIC 9(4)V99
                         COMP-3.
          05  IR-UNIT-PRICE                    PIC 9(4)V99
                         COMP-3.
          05  IR-QUANTITY-ON-HAND              PIC 9(5)
                         COMP-3.
          05  IR-QUANTITY-ON-ORDER             PIC 9(5)
                         COMP-3.
          05  IR-REORDER-POINT                 PIC 9(5)
                         COMP-3.
          05  IR-REORDER-QUANTITY              PIC 9(5)
                         COMP-3.
          05  IR-MONTHLY-SALES                 PIC 9(5)V99
                         COMP-3.
          05  IR-MONTH-RETURNS                 PIC 9(5)V99
                         COMP-3.
          05  IR-MONTHLY-BACKORDERED           PIC 9(5)
                         COMP-3.
          05  IR-YTD-BACKORDERED               PIC 9(5)
                         COMP-3.
          05  IR-YTD-SALES                     PIC 9(7)V99
                         COMP-3.
          05  IR-YTD-RETURNS                   PIC 9(7)V99
                         COMP-3.
          05  IR-VENDOR-NUMBER                 PIC 9(6)
                                  OCCURS 5 TIMES.
```

Figure 17.17 Complete Generated COBOL Code - Produce Inventory Report Program, Page 2

```
    01   HEADING-LINE1.
         03   FILLER                         PIC X(0001) VALUE SPACE.
         03   HDG1-DATE                      PIC X(0008) VALUE '99-99-9
-    '9'.
         03   FILLER                         PIC X(0022) VALUE SPACE.
         03   FILLER                         PIC X(0021) VALUE 'INVENTO
-    'RY COST REPORT'.
         03   FILLER                         PIC X(0022) VALUE SPACE.
         03   FILLER                         PIC X(0008) VALUE 'PAGE'.
         03   HDG1-PAGE                      PIC XX9.
    01   HEADING-LINE2.
         03   FILLER                         PIC X(0003) VALUE SPACE.
         03   FILLER                         PIC X(0004) VALUE 'ITEM'.
         03   FILLER                         PIC X(0010) VALUE SPACE.
         03   FILLER                         PIC X(0004) VALUE 'ITEM'.
         03   FILLER                         PIC X(0001) VALUE SPACE.
         03   FILLER                         PIC X(0011) VALUE 'DESCRIP
-    'TION'.
         03   FILLER                         PIC X(0011) VALUE SPACE.
         03   FILLER                         PIC X(0005) VALUE 'MONTH'.
         03   FILLER                         PIC X(0009) VALUE SPACE.
         03   FILLER                         PIC X(0005) VALUE 'MONTH'.
         03   FILLER                         PIC X(0008) VALUE SPACE.
         03   FILLER                         PIC X(0003) VALUE 'NET'.
         03   FILLER                         PIC X(0001) VALUE SPACE.
         03   FILLER                         PIC X(0005) VALUE 'MONTH'.
         03   FILLER                         PIC X(0005) VALUE SPACE.
         03   FILLER                         PIC X(0004) VALUE 'YEAR'.
         03   FILLER                         PIC X(0001) VALUE SPACE.
         03   FILLER                         PIC X(0002) VALUE 'TO'.
         03   FILLER                         PIC X(0001) VALUE SPACE.
         03   FILLER                         PIC X(0004) VALUE 'DATE'.
         03   FILLER                         PIC X(0005) VALUE SPACE.
         03   FILLER                         PIC X(0004) VALUE 'YEAR'.
         03   FILLER                         PIC X(0001) VALUE SPACE.
         03   FILLER                         PIC X(0002) VALUE 'TO'.
         03   FILLER                         PIC X(0001) VALUE SPACE.
         03   FILLER                         PIC X(0004) VALUE 'DATE'.
         03   FILLER                         PIC X(0006) VALUE SPACE.
         03   FILLER                         PIC X(0003) VALUE 'NET'.
         03   FILLER                         PIC X(0001) VALUE SPACE.
         03   FILLER                         PIC X(0004) VALUE 'YEAR'.
         03   FILLER                         PIC X(0001) VALUE SPACE.
         03   FILLER                         PIC X(0002) VALUE 'TO'.
```

Figure 17.17   Complete Generated COBOL Code - Produce Inventory Report Program, Page 3

```
01   HEADING-LINE3.
     03   FILLER                              PIC X(0002) VALUE SPACE.
     03   FILLER                              PIC X(0006) VALUE 'NUMBER'.
     03   FILLER                              PIC X(0036) VALUE SPACE.
     03   FILLER                              PIC X(0005) VALUE 'SALES'.
     03   FILLER                              PIC X(0008) VALUE SPACE.
     03   FILLER                              PIC X(0007) VALUE 'RETURNS.
     03   FILLER                              PIC X(0009) VALUE SPACE.
     03   FILLER                              PIC X(0005) VALUE 'SALES'.
     03   FILLER                              PIC X(0011) VALUE SPACE.
     03   FILLER                              PIC X(0005) VALUE 'SALES'.
     03   FILLER                              PIC X(0011) VALUE SPACE.
     03   FILLER                              PIC X(0007) VALUE 'RETURNS
-    ''.
     03   FILLER                              PIC X(0008) VALUE SPACE.
     03   FILLER                              PIC X(0004) VALUE 'DATE'.
     03   FILLER                              PIC X(0001) VALUE SPACE.
     03   FILLER                              PIC X(0005) VALUE 'SALES'.
01   NEXT-REPORT-LINE.
     03   FILLER                              PIC X(0001) VALUE SPACE.
     03   NRL-ITEM-NUMBER                     PIC 9(0008).
     03   FILLER                              PIC X(0004) VALUE SPACE.
     03   NRL-ITEM-DESCRIPTION                PIC X(0025).
     03   FILLER                              PIC X(0005) VALUE SPACE.
     03   NRL-MONTHLY-SALES                   PIC ZZ,ZZ9.99.
     03   FILLER                              PIC X(0005) VALUE SPACE.
     03   NRL-MONTH-RETURNS                   PIC ZZ,ZZ9.99.
     03   FILLER                              PIC X(0005) VALUE SPACE.
     03   NRL-NET-MONTHLY-SALES               PIC ZZ,ZZZ.99.
     03   FILLER                              PIC X(0005) VALUE SPACE.
     03   NRL-YTD-SALES                       PIC Z,ZZZ,ZZ9.99.
     03   FILLER                              PIC X(0005) VALUE SPACE.
     03   NRL-YTD-RETURNS                     PIC Z,ZZZ,ZZ9.99.
     03   FILLER                              PIC X(0005) VALUE SPACE.
     03   NRL-NET-YTD-SALES                   PIC Z,ZZZ,ZZ9.99.
```

Figure 17.17 Complete Generated COBOL Code - Produce Inventory Report Program, Page 4

```
   01   FINAL-TOTAL-LINE.
        03   FILLER                              PIC X(0024) VALUE SPACE.
        03   FILLER                              PIC X(0007) VALUE 'COMPANY.
        03   FILLER                              PIC X(0001) VALUE SPACE.
        03   FILLER                              PIC X(0006) VALUE 'TOTALS'.
        03   FILLER                              PIC X(0002) VALUE SPACE.
        03   TL-MONTHLY-SALES                    PIC Z,ZZZ,ZZ9.99.
        03   FILLER                              PIC X(0002) VALUE SPACE.
        03   TL-MONTH-RETURNS                    PIC Z,ZZZ,ZZ9.99.
        03   FILLER                              PIC X(0002) VALUE SPACE.
        03   TL-NET-MONTHLY-SALES                PIC Z,ZZZ,ZZ9.99.
        03   FILLER                              PIC X(0003) VALUE SPACE.
        03   TL-YTD-SALES                        PIC ZZZ,ZZZ,ZZ9.99.
        03   FILLER                              PIC X(0003) VALUE SPACE.
        03   TL-YTD-RETURNS                      PIC ZZZ,ZZZ,ZZ9.99.
        03   FILLER                              PIC X(0003) VALUE SPACE.
        03   TL-YTD-NET-SALES                    PIC ZZZ,ZZZ,ZZ9.99.
   01   FINAL-TOTAL-LINE2.
        03   FILLER                              PIC X(0024) VALUE SPACE.
        03   FILLER                              PIC X(0007) VALUE 'RECORDS
 -      ''.
        03   FILLER                              PIC X(0001) VALUE SPACE.
        03   FILLER                              PIC X(0004) VALUE 'READ'.
        03   FILLER                              PIC X(0004) VALUE SPACE.
        03   TL-RECORDS-READ                     PIC ZZZZ9.

   LINKAGE SECTION.
   PROCEDURE DIVISION.

   PRODUCE-INVENTORY-RE SECTION.

        OPEN INPUT  ITEM-FILE
        OPEN OUTPUT REPORT-LINE
        PERFORM  PRINT-INVENTORY-LI
           UNTIL END-OF-FILE.
        PERFORM  PRINT-TOTAL-LI.
        CLOSE INPUT  ITEM-FILE
        CLOSE OUTPUT REPORT-LINE
        STOP RUN.
```

Figure 17.17   Complete Generated COBOL Code - Produce Inventory Report Program, Page 5

```
PRINT-INVENTORY-LI SECTION.
     PERFORM   READ-INVENTORY-RE.
    IF NOT END-OF-FILE
        PERFORM   PRINT-INVENTORY-RE
        PERFORM   ACCUMULATE-INVENTORY-TO.


PRINT-TOTAL-LI SECTION.

        MOVE TOTAL-MONTHLY-SALES      TO TL-MONTHLY-SALES.
        MOVE TOTAL-MONTH-RETURNS      TO TL-MONTH-RETURNS.
        MOVE TOTAL-NET-MONTHLY-SALES  TO TL-NET-MONTHLY-SALES.
        MOVE TOTAL-YTD-SALES          TO TL-YTD-SALES.
        MOVE TOTAL-YTD-RETURNS        TO TL-YTD-RETURNS.
        MOVE TOTAL-NET-YTD-SALES      TO TL-NET-YTD-SALES.
        MOVE FINAL-TOTAL-LINE         TO PRINT-AREA.
        MOVE 3 TO SPACE-CONTROL.
        PERFORM   WRITE-REPORT-LI.
        MOVE RECORDS-READ             TO TL-RECORDS-READ.
        MOVE FINAL-TOTAL-LINE2         TO PRINT-AREA.
        MOVE 2 TO SPACE-CONTROL.
        PERFORM   WRITE-REPORT-LI.


READ-INVENTORY-RE SECTION.
     READ ITEM-FILE
         AT END
             MOVE 'Y' TO END-OF-FILE-SW.
     IF NOT END-OF-FILE
         ADD 1 TO RECORDS-READ.


PRINT-INVENTORY-RE SECTION.
        MOVE IR-ITEM-NUMBER        TO NRL-ITEM-NUMBER.
        MOVE IR-ITEM-DESCRIPTION   TO NRL-ITEM-DESCRIPTION.
        MOVE IR-MONTHLY-SALES      TO NRL-MONTHLY-SALES.
        MOVE IR-MONTH-RETURNS      TO NRL-MONTH-RETURNS.
        SUBTRACT IR-MONTH-RETURNS FROM IR-MONTHLY-SALES
            GIVING NET-MONTHLY-SALES.
        MOVE NET-MONTHLY-SALES     TO NRL-NET-MONTHLY-SALES.
        MOVE IR-YTD-SALES          TO NRL-YTD-SALES.
        MOVE IR-YTD-RETURNS        TO NRL-YTD-RETURNS.
        SUBTRACT IR-YTD-RETURNS FROM IR-YTD-SALES
            GIVING NET-YTD-SALES.
        MOVE NET-YTD-SALES         TO NRL-NET-YTD-SALES.
        MOVE NEXT-REPORT-LINE      TO PRINT-AREA.
        MOVE 1 TO SPACE-CONTROL.
        PERFORM   PRINT-REPORT-LI.
```

Figure 17.17   Complete Generated COBOL Code - Produce Inventory Report Program, Page 6

```
      ACCUMULATE-INVENTORY-TO SECTION.

            ADD IR-MONTHLY-SALES   TO TOTAL-MONTHLY-SALES.
            ADD IR-MONTH-RETURNS   TO TOTAL-MONTH-RETURNS.
            ADD NET-MONTHLY-SALES TO TOTAL-NET-MONTHLY-SALES.
            ADD IR-YTD-SALES       TO TOTAL-YTD-SALES.
            ADD IR-YTD-RETURNS     TO TOTAL-YTD-RETURNS.
            ADD NET-YTD-SALES      TO TOTAL-NET-YTD-SALES.

      PRINT-REPORT-LI SECTION.

            IF LINE-COUNT IS GREATER THAN MAXIMUM-LINES
                MOVE NEXT-REPORT-LINE TO PRINT-AREA
                PERFORM   PRINT-HEADING-LI.
            PERFORM   WRITE-REPORT-LI.

      PRINT-HEADING-LI SECTION.

            MOVE CURRENT-DATE TO REPORT-DATE
            MOVE PAGE-NUMBER TO HDG1-PAGE-NUMBER
            MOVE HEADING-LINE-1 TO PRINT-AREA.
            PERFORM   WRITE-PAGE-TO.
            MOVE HEADING-LINE-2 TO PRINT-AREA.
            MOVE 2 TO SPACE-CONTROL.
            PERFORM   WRITE-REPORT-LI.
            MOVE HEADING-LINE-3 TO PRINT-AREA.
            MOVE 1 TO SPACE-CONTROL.
            PERFORM   WRITE-REPORT-LI.
            MOVE 0 TO LINE-COUNT.

      WRITE-PAGE-TO SECTION.

            WRITE PRINT-AREA
                AFTER ADVANCING PAGE-TOP.
            EXIT.

      WRITE-REPORT-LI SECTION.

            WRITE PRINT-AREA
                AFTER ADVANCING SPACE-CONTROL LINES.
            ADD SPACE-CONTROL TO LINE-COUNT.
```

Figure 17.17   Complete Generated COBOL Code - Produce Inventory Report Program, Page 7

RE-ENGINEERING WITH DESIGN RECOVERY

You may be thinking that it takes a lot of effort to generate COBOL code. It may seem so at first, but why re-enter code that can be derived from the system design. This provides consistency between the project dictionary and the computer programs that implement the design.

There is another equally important reason for using the design for creating program code. This is an Index Technology product called Design Recovery. This product will enable you to create XLDictionary entities from existing programs. COBOL programs are transformed into entities, the design may be modified, and program code re-generated. The process is illustrated in Figure 17.18

It is easy to see the benefits of this approach to maintenance work. There is no need to manually create diagrams, records and so on. The XLDictionary entities may be used to analyze the system and produce documentation. Additional features may be added to the design and resulting code. Screens may be modified and reviewed by users before re-generating code for the final product.

ENTITY CREATION

Computer programs are transformed into the following entities:

Program component	XLDictionary entity
COBOL program	Structure chart
File section	Records and elements
Working Storage	Records and elements
Linkage Section	Records and elements
Procedure Division Paragraphs	Function descriptions
CICS/BMS (Basic Mapping Support) source code	Screen designs

| IMS/MFS (Message Format Services) | Screen designs |
| IMS Data Model Diagrams | Data model diagrams |

DESIGN ANALYSIS

As you can see, this is a powerful tool for creating entities from existing code. The next step is to analyze the existing programs. Along with the analysis features presented in Chapter 12, there are several additional reports available.

Two reports identify unused code that exists in programs. This is usually due to maintenance modifications over the life of the program and should be removed from the new program. One report will list all unreferenced paragraphs in the procedure division. Another lists all unreferenced data division names.

A Data Assignment Report lists all data fields and the operations that assign values to them.

The File I/O Report shows file usage in the program.

The Cyclic Complexity Report calculates the number of logic paths in a program. It provides a measure of how complex the program structure is. This can be used to help plan workload.

THE DB2 INTERFACE

Index Technology has an interface to transfer entities into the DB2 environment. As with other add on products, the DB2 interface customizes Excelerator, adding options. The interface has the ability to transfer existing DDL directly into the XLDictionary.

Eight additional entities are added to Excelerator. These allow you to create the physical design of the database from logical design. Code may be generated in COBOL, C, PL/1 and BASIC for table and view definitions. SQL/DDL, CREATE, COMMENT ON and DECLARE statements may be generated.

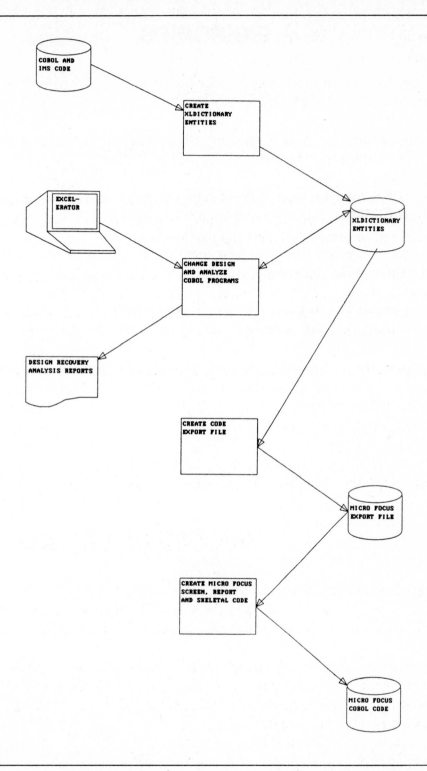

Figure 17.18   Design Recovery Overview

EXERCISES

You will need the Excelerator and Micro Focus interface products as well as a copy of Micro Focus Workbench to do these exercises.

1.   Use any previously created structure chart to generate skeletal procedure division code. Print the resulting code.

2.   Create CICS code for any of the screen designs you have created. Print the BMS map and COBOL code for the screen.

3.   Use a report design that you have created to generate report definition layouts. Generate and print the resulting code.

4.   Create function descriptions for the structure chart used in Exercise 1. Export the structure chart and the functions. Generate and print the resulting code.

5.   Create record layouts and define all the elements for the structure chart used in Exercise 1. Generate COBOL code for the records. Merge it with the previously generated program code.

APPENDIX A

CONTROL AND FUNCTION KEYS

F1   Special function shift key

F2   Help

F3   Save current text entry and return

F4   Browse - move to other screens defining further   related
                entities for your current screen

End   End of line

Home   Beginning of line

PgUp   Display previous screen

PgDn   Display next screen

Ins   Toggle between insert and overstrike mode

Tab   Go to the next field

Shift & Tab   Go to the previous field

Backspace   Delete preceding character

Delete   Delete character at the cursor

Escape   Cancel

Enter   Carriage return (or select if at a menu screen)

F1 & +   Go to the next word

F1 & -   Go to the previous word

F1 & Tab   Go to field following your current region

F1 & Home	Go to field preceding your current region
F1 & ↑	Go to the first field on the screen
F1 & ↓	Go to the last field on the screen
F1 & PgUp	Display previous screenful within text scrolling block
F1 & PgDn	Display next screenful within text scrolling block
F1 & Ins	Insert a line above current line
F1 & Backspace	Delete line from the beginning to the cursor
F1 & End	Delete remaining line to the right
F1 & Delete	Delete the entire line

In addition to these function key assignments, there are also special assignments when performing screen and report prototyping.

APPENDIX B

ENTITY TYPES - NAMES AND ABBREVIATIONS

Entity Name	Entity Code	XLDictionary Class
Category	CAT	Manage
Change Request	CHG	Manage
Control Flow	CTF	Control
Control Store	CSA	Control
Control Table	CTT	Control
Control Transformation	CTA	Control
Data Entity	DAE	Data
Data Flow	DAF	Data
Data Flow Diagram	DFD	Graphs
Data Model Diagram	DMD	Graphs
Data N-Ary Relationship	DNR	Data
Data Relationship	DAR	Data
Data Store	DAS	Data
Deliverable	DEL	Manage
Document Fragment	DOF	Other
Document Graph	DCG	Graphs
Document Group	DOC	Other

Entity Name	Entity Code	XLDictionary Class
Element	ELE	Rec/Ele
Engineering Requirement	ERQ	Manage
Entity List	ELS	Other
Entity-Relationship Diagram	ERA	Graphs
External Entity	EXT	Process
Function	FUN	Process
Issue	ISS	Manage
Module	MOD	Process
Note	NTE	Manage
Presentation Graph	PRG	Graphs
Presentation Graph Connection	PGC	Process
Presentation Graph Object	PGO	Process
Primitive Process Specification	PPS	Process
Process	PRC	Process
Prompt	PRM	Control
Record	REC	Rec/Ele
Reference Document	REF	Manage
Report	REP	Other

Entity Name	Entity Code	XLDictionary Class
Report Design	RED	Scr/Reps
Screen Data Entry	SDE	Scr/Reps
Screen Data Report	SDR	Scr/Reps
Screen Design	SCD	Scr/Reps
Signal	SIG	Control
State	STA	Control
State Transition Diagram	TDR	Graphs
Structure Chart	STC	Graphs
Structure Diagram	STD	Graphs
Structure Graph Connection	SGC	Process
Structured Decision Table	SDT	Control
System Device	SDV	Process
Table Of Codes	TAB	Data
Test	TST	Manage
Transition Vector	TVA	Control
User	USR	Manage
User Requirement	URQ	Manage
Work Breakdown Structure	WBS	Graphs

APPENDIX C

XLDICTIONARY CLASSES

XLDictionary Class	Entity Code	Entity Name
REC/ELE	REC	Record
	ELE	Element
DATA	DAS	Data Store
	DAE	Data Entity
	DAF	Data Flow
	TAB	Table of Codes
	DAR	Data Relationship
	DNR	Data N-Ary Relationship
PROCESS	PRC	Process
	FUN	Function
	SDV	System Device
	EXT	External Entity
	MOD	Module
	PGO	Presentation Graph Object
	SGC	Structure Graph Connection
	PGC	Presentation Graph Connection
	PPS	Primitive Process Specification
GRAPHS	DFD	Data Flow Diagram
	STC	Structure Chart
	DMD	Data Model Diagram
	ERA	Entity-Relationship Diagram
	TRD	State Transition Diagram
	STD	Structure Diagram
	PRG	Presentation Graph
	WBS	Work Breakdown Structure
	DCG	Document Graph

XLDictionary Class	Entity Code	Entity Name
SCR/REPS	RED	Report Design
	SCD	Screen Design
	SDE	Screen Data Entry
	SDR	Screen Data Report
CONTROL	CSA	Control Store
	CTA	Control Transformation
	CTF	Control Flow
	PRM	Prompt
	SIG	Signal
	CTT	Control Table
	SDT	Structured Decision Table
	STA	State
	TVA	Transition Vector
MANAGE	CAT	Category
	CHG	Change Request
	DEL	Deliverable
	ERQ	Engineering Requirement
	ISS	Issue
	NTE	Note
	REF	Reference Document
	TST	Test
	URQ	User Requirement
	USR	User
OTHER	DOC	Document Group
	DOF	Document Fragment
	REP	Report
	ELS	Entity List

APPENDIX D

EXCELERATOR LIMITS

This is a listing of selected Excelerator limits. Refer to the Excelerator Facilities & Functions Reference Guide, Appendix C for a complete listing.

Objects on a graph	75
Connections on a graph	150
Explosion levels	10
Fields in a Report Design	600
Fields in a Screen Design	200
Elements & records in a record	115
Codes in a table of codes	100
Entities in an Entity List	134
Levels per browse	7
Users per project	25

APPENDIX E

XLDICTIONARY RELATIONSHIPS

Use this relationship summary to explore the available reports and missing information that may be generated. These may be used for project documentation, to monitor project progress and determine work that is not yet complete.

Some of the relationship types are shown below. This list includes only the more common relationships and is not a complete list. The relationships that only occur for one or two entities are included in the complete index and their meaning is often clear from the context with which they are used.

Associated-With, Has-Associated refer to the entities that are used to manage the project. These supply supplemental information but are not a child diagram or any other subset of the design.

Child-Of, Parent-Of refer to an entity that would expand from or to another entity.

Connected-By, Connects, Connects-To refers to the connections that are found on a graph.

Contained-In, Contains refer to which entities are contained in a graph or which graphs contain other entities.

Explodes-From, Explodes-To shows which entities explode to or are exploded from other entities.

Received-By, Receives shows which entities receive other entities as input.

Satisfied-By, Satisfies shows which engineering or user requirements are satisfied by which entities.

Sends, Sends-To, Sent-By refers to which entities send information to other entities, the opposite of receives.

ANY refers to several different entities that may be combined in one report. For example, records may contain structural records and elements. REC Contains ANY produces a report that shows both records and elements contained within higher level records.

Entity name   Code / 2nd Type

```
ANY Associated-With CHG..............Change Request
ANY Associated-With CSA             Control Store
ANY Associated-With CTA..............Control Transformation
ANY Associated-With CTF             Control Flow
ANY Associated-With CTT..............Control Table
ANY Associated-With DAE             Data Entity
ANY Associated-With DAF..............Data Flow
ANY Associated-With DAR             Data Relationship
ANY Associated-With DAS..............Data Store
ANY Associated-With DCG             Document Graph
ANY Associated-With DEL..............Deliverable
ANY Associated-With DFD             Data Flow Diagram
ANY Associated-With DMD..............Data Model Diagram
ANY Associated-With DNR             Data N-Ary Relationship
ANY Associated-With ELE..............Element
ANY Associated-With ERA             Entity-Relationship Diagram
ANY Associated-With ERQ..............Engineering Requirement
ANY Associated-With EXT             External Entity
ANY Associated-With FUN..............Function
ANY Associated-With ISS             Issue
ANY Associated-With MOD..............Module
ANY Associated-With NTE             Note
ANY Associated-With PGC..............Presentation Graph Conn.
ANY Associated-With PGO             Presentation Graph Object
ANY Associated-With PPS..............Primitive Process Spec.
ANY Associated-With PRC             Process
ANY Associated-With PRG..............Presentation Graph
ANY Associated-With PRM             Prompt
ANY Associated-With REC..............Record
ANY Associated-With SDT             Structured Decision Table
ANY Associated-With SDV..............System Device
ANY Associated-With SGC             Structure Graph Connection
ANY Associated-With SIG..............Signal
ANY Associated-With STA             State
ANY Associated-With STC..............Structure Chart
ANY Associated-With STD             Structure Diagram
ANY Associated-With TRD..............State Transition Diagram
ANY Associated-With TST             Test
ANY Associated-With TVA..............Transition Vector
ANY Associated-With URQ             User Requirement
ANY Associated-With WBS..............Work Breakdown Structure
ANY Child-Of DAS                    Data Store
ANY Child-Of DOC....................Document Group
ANY Child-Of DOF                    Document Fragment
ANY Child-Of FUN....................Function
```

```
Entity name          Code / 2nd Type

ANY Child-Of SDV....................System Device
ANY Constant-In PPS                 Primitive Process Spec.
ANY Contained-In CTT................Control Table
ANY Contained-In DCG                Document Graph
ANY Contained-In DEL................Deliverable
ANY Contained-In DFD                Data Flow Diagram
ANY Contained-In DMD................Data Model Diagram
ANY Contained-In ELS                Entity List
ANY Contained-In ERA................Entity-Relationship Diagram
ANY Contained-In PRG                Presentation Graph
ANY Contained-In REC................Record
ANY Contained-In STC                Structure Chart
ANY Contained-In STD................Structure Diagram
ANY Contained-In TRD                State Transition Diagram
ANY Contains DAE....................Data Entity
ANY Contains DAS                    Data Store
ANY Contains FUN....................Function
ANY Contains SGC                    Structure Graph Connection
ANY Explodes-From CSA...............Control Store
ANY Explodes-From CTA               Control Transformation
ANY Explodes-From CTF...............Control Flow
ANY Explodes-From DAE               Data Entity
ANY Explodes-From DAF...............Data Flow
ANY Explodes-From DAS               Data Store
ANY Explodes-From DEL...............Deliverable
ANY Explodes-From FUN               Function
ANY Explodes-From PGC...............Presentation Graph Conn.
ANY Explodes-From PGO               Presentation Graph Object
ANY Explodes-From PRC...............Process
ANY Has-Associated ISS              Issue
ANY Has-Associated NTE..............Note
ANY Has-Associated REF              Reference Document
ANY Has-Associated TST..............Test
ANY Has-Input SIG                   Signal
ANY Input-To PPS....................Primitive Process Spec.
ANY Output-From TVA                 Transition Vector
ANY Parent-Of DAS...................Data Store
ANY Parent-Of DOC                   Document Group
ANY Parent-Of DOF...................Document Fragment
ANY Parent-Of FUN                   Function
ANY Parent-Of SDV...................System Device
ANY Participates-In DNR             Data N-Ary Relationship
ANY Passed-As-Control-Via SGC.......Structure Graph Connection
ANY Passed-As-Data-Via SGC          Structure Graph Connection
ANY Produced-By PPS.................Primitive Process Spec.
ANY Prompted-By TVA                 Transition Vector
ANY Received-By CSA.................Control Store
```

Entity name   Code / 2nd Type

```
ANY Received-By CTA                 Control Transformation
ANY Received-By DAS.................Data Store
ANY Received-By EXT                 External Entity
ANY Received-By PRC.................Process
ANY Receives CTF                    Control Flow
ANY Receives DAF....................Data Flow
ANY Receives-From CSA               Control Store
ANY Receives-From CTA...............Control Transformation
ANY Receives-From DAS               Data Store
ANY Receives-From EXT...............External Entity
ANY Receives-From PRC               Process
ANY Receives SGC....................Structure Graph Connection
ANY References ELE                  Element
ANY Related-To DAE..................Data Entity
ANY Related-To DAE                  Data Entity
ANY Related-To DNR..................Data N-Ary Relationship
ANY Related-To DNR                  Data N-Ary Relationship
ANY Related-With ANY................Any Entity Type
ANY Related-With ANY                Any Entity Type
ANY Responsibility-Of USR           User
ANY Returned-As-Control-Via SGC.....Structure Graph Connection
ANY Returned-As-Data-Via SGC        Structure Graph Connection
ANY Satisfied-By CSA................Control Store
ANY Satisfied-By CTA                Control Transformation
ANY Satisfied-By CTF................Control Flow
ANY Satisfied-By CTT                Control Table
ANY Satisfied-By DAE................Data Entity
ANY Satisfied-By DAF                Data Flow
ANY Satisfied-By DAR................Data Relationship
ANY Satisfied-By DAS                Data Store
ANY Satisfied-By DCG................Document Graph
ANY Satisfied-By DEL                Deliverable
ANY Satisfied-By DFD................Data Flow Diagram
ANY Satisfied-By DMD                Data Model Diagram
ANY Satisfied-By DNR................Data N-Ary Relationship
ANY Satisfied-By ELE                Element
ANY Satisfied-By ERA................Entity-Relationship Diagram
ANY Satisfied-By EXT                External Entity
ANY Satisfied-By FUN................Function
ANY Satisfied-By MOD                Module
ANY Satisfied-By PGC................Presentation Graph Conn.
ANY Satisfied-By PGO                Presentation Graph Object
ANY Satisfied-By PPS................Primitive Process Spec.
ANY Satisfied-By PRC                Process
ANY Satisfied-By PRG................Presentation Graph
ANY Satisfied-By PRM                Prompt
```

Entity name   **Code / 2nd Type**

ANY Satisfied-By REC.................Record
ANY Satisfied-By SDT   Structured Decision Table
ANY Satisfied-By SDV.................System Device
ANY Satisfied-By SGC   Structure Graph Connection
ANY Satisfied-By SIG.................Signal
ANY Satisfied-By STA   State
ANY Satisfied-By STC.................Structure Chart
ANY Satisfied-By STD   Structure Diagram
ANY Satisfied-By TRD.................State Transition Diagram
ANY Satisfied-By TST   Test
ANY Satisfied-By TVA.................Transition Vector
ANY Satisfied-By WBS   Work Breakdown Structure
ANY Satisfies ERQ....................Engineering Requirement
ANY Satisfies URQ   User Requirement
ANY Sends CTF........................Control Flow
ANY Sends DAF   Data Flow
ANY Sends SGC........................Structure Graph Connection
ANY Sends-To CSA   Control Store
ANY Sends-To CTA.....................Control Transformation
ANY Sends-To DAS   Data Store
ANY Sends-To EXT.....................External Entity
ANY Sends-To PRC   Process
ANY Sent-By CSA......................Control Store
ANY Sent-By CTA   Control Transformation
ANY Sent-By DAS......................Data Store
ANY Sent-By EXT   External Entity
ANY Sent-By PRC......................Process

CAT - Catagory

CAT Associated-With ANY   Any Entity Type
CAT Associated-With CHG..............Change Request
CAT Associated-With CSA   Control Store
CAT Associated-With CTA..............Control Transformation
CAT Associated-With CTF   Control Flow
CAT Associated-With CTT..............Control Table
CAT Associated-With DAE   Data Entity
CAT Associated-With DAF..............Data Flow
CAT Associated-With DAR   Data Relationship
CAT Associated-With DAS..............Data Store
CAT Associated-With DCG   Document Graph
CAT Associated-With DEL..............Deliverable
CAT Associated-With DFD   Data Flow Diagram
CAT Associated-With DMD..............Data Model Diagram
CAT Associated-With DNR   Data N-Ary Relationship
CAT Associated-With ELE..............Element
CAT Associated-With ERA   Entity-Relationship Diagram

```
Entity name          Code / 2nd Type

CAT Associated-With ERQ..............Engineering Requirement
CAT Associated-With EXT              External Entity
CAT Associated-With FUN..............Function
CAT Associated-With ISS              Issue
CAT Associated-With MOD..............Module
CAT Associated-With NTE              Note
CAT Associated-With PGC..............Presentation Graph Conn.
CAT Associated-With PGO              Presentation Graph Object
CAT Associated-With PPS..............Primitive Process Spec.
CAT Associated-With PRC              Process
CAT Associated-With PRG..............Presentation Graph
CAT Associated-With PRM              Prompt
CAT Associated-With REC..............Record
CAT Associated-With REF              Reference Document
CAT Associated-With SDT..............Structured Decision Table
CAT Associated-With SDV              System Device
CAT Associated-With SGC..............Structure Graph Connection
CAT Associated-With SIG              Signal
CAT Associated-With STA..............State
CAT Associated-With STC              Structure Chart
CAT Associated-With STD..............Structure Diagram
CAT Associated-With TRD              State Transition Diagram
CAT Associated-With TST..............Test
CAT Associated-With TVA              Transition Vector
CAT Associated-With URQ..............User Requirement
CAT Associated-With WBS              Work Breakdown Structure
```

CHG - Change Request

```
CHG Associated-With ANY..............Any Entity Type
CHG Associated-With CSA              Control Store
CHG Associated-With CTA..............Control Transformation
CHG Associated-With CTF              Control Flow
CHG Associated-With CTT..............Control Table
CHG Associated-With DAE              Data Entity
CHG Associated-With DAF..............Data Flow
CHG Associated-With DAR              Data Relationship
CHG Associated-With DAS..............Data Store
CHG Associated-With DCG              Document Graph
CHG Associated-With DEL..............Deliverable
CHG Associated-With DFD              Data Flow Diagram
CHG Associated-With DMD..............Data Model Diagram
CHG Associated-With DNR              Data N-Ary Relationship
CHG Associated-With ELE..............Element
CHG Associated-With ERA              Entity-Relationship Diagram
CHG Associated-With ERQ..............Engineering Requirement
```

Entity name	Code / 2nd Type

CHG Associated-With EXT   External Entity
CHG Associated-With FUN..............Function
CHG Associated-With ISS   Issue
CHG Associated-With MOD..............Module
CHG Associated-With PGC   Presentation Graph Conn.
CHG Associated-With PGO..............Presentation Graph Object
CHG Associated-With PPS   Primitive Process Spec.
CHG Associated-With PRC..............Process
CHG Associated-With PRG   Presentation Graph
CHG Associated-With PRM..............Prompt
CHG Associated-With REC   Record
CHG Associated-With SDT..............Structured Decision Table
CHG Associated-With SDV   System Device
CHG Associated-With SGC..............Structure Graph Connection
CHG Associated-With SIG   Signal
CHG Associated-With STA..............State
CHG Associated-With STC   Structure Chart
CHG Associated-With STD..............Structure Diagram
CHG Associated-With TRD   State Transition Diagram
CHG Associated-With TST..............Test
CHG Associated-With TVA   Transition Vector
CHG Associated-With URQ..............User Requirement
CHG Associated-With WBS   Work Breakdown Structure
CHG Has-Associated ANY..............Any Entity Type
CHG Has-Associated CAT   Category
CHG Has-Associated NTE..............Note
CHG Has-Associated REF   Reference Document

CSA - Control Store

CSA Contained-In DFD................Data Flow Diagram
CSA Explodes-To ANY   Any Entity Type
CSA Explodes-To CTT.................Control Table
CSA Explodes-To SIG   Signal
CSA Has-Associated ANY..............Any Entity Type
CSA Has-Associated CAT   Category
CSA Has-Associated CHG..............Change Request
CSA Has-Associated ELS   Entity List
CSA Has-Associated ISS..............Issue
CSA Has-Associated NTE   Note
CSA Has-Associated REF..............Reference Document
CSA Has-Associated TST   Test
CSA Receives ANY....................Any Entity Type
CSA Receives CTF   Control Flow
CSA Receives DAF....................Data Flow
CSA Receives-From ANY   Any Entity Type
CSA Receives-From CSA...............Control Store

Entity name	Code / 2nd Type	

CSA Receives-From CTA   Control Transformation
CSA Receives-From DAS...............Data Store
CSA Receives-From EXT   External Entity
CSA Receives-From PRC...............Process
CSA Satisfies ANY   Any Entity Type
CSA Satisfies ERQ...................Engineering Requirement
CSA Satisfies URQ   User Requirement
CSA Sends ANY.......................Any Entity Type
CSA Sends CTF   Control Flow
CSA Sends DAF.......................Data Flow
CSA Sends-To ANY   Any Entity Type
CSA Sends-To CSA....................Control Store
CSA Sends-To CTA   Control Transformation
CSA Sends-To DAS....................Data Store
CSA Sends-To EXT   External Entity
CSA Sends-To PRC....................Process

CTA - Control Transformation

CTA Contained-In DFD   Data Flow Diagram
CTA Explodes-To SDT.................Structured Decision Table
CTA Explodes-To TRD   State Transition Diagram
CTA Has-Associated CAT..............Category
CTA Has-Associated CHG   Change Request
CTA Has-Associated ELS..............Entity List
CTA Has-Associated ISS   Issue
CTA Has-Associated NTE..............Note
CTA Has-Associated REF   Reference Document
CTA Has-Associated TST..............Test
CTA Prompted-By TVA   Transition Vector
CTA Receives ANY....................Any Entity Type
CTA Receives-From ANY   Any Entity Type
CTA Receives-From CSA...............Control Store
CTA Receives-From CTA   Control Transformation
CTA Receives-From DAS...............Data Store
CTA Receives-From EXT   External Entity
CTA Receives-From PRC...............Process
CTA Satisfies ANY   Any Entity Type
CTA Satisfies ERQ...................Engineering Requirement
CTA Satisfies URQ   User Requirement
CTA Sends ANY.......................Any Entity Type
CTA Sends-To ANY   Any Entity Type

Entity name   Code / 2nd Type

CTF - Control Flow

CTF Contained-In DFD.................Data Flow Diagram
CTF Explodes-To ANY   Any Entity Type
CTF Explodes-To CTT..................Control Table
CTF Explodes-To PRM   Prompt
CTF Explodes-To SIG..................Signal
CTF Has-Associated ANY   Any Entity Type
CTF Has-Associated CAT...............Category
CTF Has-Associated CHG   Change Request
CTF Has-Associated ELS...............Entity List
CTF Has-Associated ISS   Issue
CTF Has-Associated NTE...............Note
CTF Has-Associated REF   Reference Document
CTF Has-Associated TST...............Test
CTF Received-By ANY   Any Entity Type
CTF Received-By CSA..................Control Store
CTF Received-By CTA   Control Transformation
CTF Received-By DAS..................Data Store
CTF Received-By EXT   External Entity
CTF Received-By PRC..................Process
CTF Satisfies ANY   Any Entity Type
CTF Satisfies ERQ....................Engineering Requirement
CTF Satisfies URQ   User Requirement
CTF Sent-By ANY......................Any Entity Type
CTF Sent-By CSA   Control Store
CTF Sent-By CTA......................Control Transformation
CTF Sent-By DAS   Data Store
CTF Sent-By EXT......................External Entity
CTF Sent-By PRC   Process

CTT - Control Table

CTT Contained-In CTT.................Control Table
CTT Contains ANY   Any Entity Type
CTT Contains CTT.....................Control Table
CTT Contains SIG   Signal
CTT Explodes-From ANY................Any Entity Type
CTT Explodes-From CSA   Control Store
CTT Explodes-From CTF................Control Flow
CTT Has-Associated ANY   Any Entity Type
CTT Has-Associated CAT...............Category
CTT Has-Associated CHG   Change Request
CTT Has-Associated ELS...............Entity List
CTT Has-Associated ISS   Issue
CTT Has-Associated NTE...............Note
CTT Has-Associated REF   Reference Document

Entity name   Code / 2nd Type

```
CTT Has-Associated TST...............Test
CTT Input-To PPS                     Primitive Process Spec.
CTT Produced-By PPS..................Primitive Process Spec.
CTT Satisfies ANY                    Any Entity Type
CTT Satisfies ERQ....................Engineering Requirement
CTT Satisfies URQ                    User Requirement
```

DAE - Data Entity

```
DAE Contained-In ANY.................Any Entity Type
DAE Contained-In DMD                 Data Model Diagram
DAE Contained-In ERA.................Entity-Relationship Diagram
DAE Explodes-To ANY                  Any Entity Type
DAE Explodes-To DMD..................Data Model Diagram
DAE Explodes-To ERA                  Entity-Relationship Diagram
DAE Explodes-To REC..................Record
DAE Has-Associated ANY               Any Entity Type
DAE Has-Associated CAT...............Category
DAE Has-Associated CHG               Change Request
DAE Has-Associated ELS...............Entity List
DAE Has-Associated ISS               Issue
DAE Has-Associated NTE...............Note
DAE Has-Associated REF               Reference Document
DAE Has-Associated TST...............Test
DAE Is-1st-Participant-In DAR        Data Relationship
DAE Is-2nd-Participant-In DAR........Data Relationship
DAE Participates-In DNR              Data N-Ary Relationship
DAE Related-To ANY...................Any Entity Type
DAE Related-To ANY                   Any Entity Type
DAE Related-To DAE...................Data Entity
DAE Related-To DAE                   Data Entity
DAE Related-To DNR...................Data N-Ary Relationship
DAE Related-To DNR                   Data N-Ary Relationship
DAE Satisfies ANY....................Any Entity Type
DAE Satisfies ERQ                    Engineering Requirement
DAE Satisfies URQ....................User Requirement
```

DAF - Data Flow

```
DAF Contained-In DFD                 Data Flow Diagram
DAF Explodes-To ANY..................Any Entity Type
DAF Explodes-To DMD                  Data Model Diagram
DAF Explodes-To ELE..................Element
DAF Explodes-To ERA                  Entity-Relationship Diagram
DAF Explodes-To REC..................Record
DAF Explodes-To STD                  Structure Diagram
```

Entity name   **Code / 2nd Type**

DAF Has-Associated ANY...............Any Entity Type
DAF Has-Associated CAT   Category
DAF Has-Associated CHG...............Change Request
DAF Has-Associated ELS   Entity List
DAF Has-Associated ISS...............Issue
DAF Has-Associated NTE   Note
DAF Has-Associated REF...............Reference Document
DAF Has-Associated TST   Test
DAF Received-By ANY..................Any Entity Type
DAF Received-By CSA   Control Store
DAF Received-By CTA..................Control Transformation
DAF Received-By DAS   Data Store
DAF Received-By EXT..................External Entity
DAF Received-By PRC   Process
DAF Satisfies ANY....................Any Entity Type
DAF Satisfies ERQ   Engineering Requirement
DAF Satisfies URQ....................User Requirement
DAF Sent-By ANY   Any Entity Type
DAF Sent-By CSA......................Control Store
DAF Sent-By CTA   Control Transformation
DAF Sent-By DAS......................Data Store
DAF Sent-By EXT   External Entity
DAF Sent-By PRC......................Process

DAR - Data Relationship

DAR Contained-In DMD   Data Model Diagram
DAR Has-1st-Participant DAE..........Data Entity
DAR Has-2nd-Participant DAE   Data Entity
DAR Has-Associated ANY...............Any Entity Type
DAR Has-Associated CAT   Category
DAR Has-Associated CHG...............Change Request
DAR Has-Associated ELS   Entity List
DAR Has-Associated ISS...............Issue
DAR Has-Associated NTE   Note
DAR Has-Associated REF...............Reference Document
DAR Has-Associated TST   Test
DAR Satisfies ANY....................Any Entity Type
DAR Satisfies ERQ   Engineering Requirement
DAR Satisfies URQ....................User Requirement

DAS - Data Store

DAS Child-Of ANY   Any Entity Type
DAS Child-Of DAS.....................Data Store
DAS Child-Of FUN   Function
DAS Child-Of SDV.....................System Device

Entity name	Code / 2nd Type
DAS Contained-In ANY	Any Entity Type
DAS Contained-In DFD..................	Data Flow Diagram
DAS Contained-In STC	Structure Chart
DAS Explodes-To ANY..................	Any Entity Type
DAS Explodes-To DMD	Data Model Diagram
DAS Explodes-To ERA..................	Entity-Relationship Diagram
DAS Explodes-To REC	Record
DAS Has-Access-Key ELE...............	Element
DAS Has-Associated ANY	Any Entity Type
DAS Has-Associated CAT...............	Category
DAS Has-Associated CHG	Change Request
DAS Has-Associated ELS...............	Entity List
DAS Has-Associated ISS	Issue
DAS Has-Associated NTE...............	Note
DAS Has-Associated REF	Reference Document
DAS Has-Associated TST...............	Test
DAS Parent-Of ANY	Any Entity Type
DAS Parent-Of DAS....................	Data Store
DAS Parent-Of FUN	Function
DAS Parent-Of SDV....................	System Device
DAS Receives ANY	Any Entity Type
DAS Receives CTF.....................	Control Flow
DAS Receives DAF	Data Flow
DAS Receives-From ANY................	Any Entity Type
DAS Receives-From CSA	Control Store
DAS Receives-From CTA................	Control Transformation
DAS Receives-From DAS	Data Store
DAS Receives-From EXT................	External Entity
DAS Receives-From PRC	Process
DAS Receives SGC.....................	Structure Graph Connection
DAS Satisfies ANY	Any Entity Type
DAS Satisfies ERQ....................	Engineering Requirement
DAS Satisfies URQ	User Requirement
DAS Sends ANY........................	Any Entity Type
DAS Sends CTF	Control Flow
DAS Sends DAF........................	Data Flow
DAS Sends SGC	Structure Graph Connection
DAS Sends-To ANY.....................	Any Entity Type
DAS Sends-To CSA	Control Store
DAS Sends-To CTA.....................	Control Transformation
DAS Sends-To DAS	Data Store
DAS Sends-To EXT.....................	External Entity
DAS Sends-To PRC	Process

```
Entity name          Code / 2nd Type

DCG - Document Graph

DCG Contains ANY.....................Any Entity Type
DCG Contains DOC                     Document Group
DCG Contains DOF.....................Document Fragment
DCG Has-Associated ANY               Any Entity Type
DCG Has-Associated CAT...............Category
DCG Has-Associated CHG               Change Request
DCG Has-Associated ELS...............Entity List
DCG Has-Associated ISS               Issue
DCG Has-Associated NTE...............Note
DCG Has-Associated REF               Reference Document
DCG Has-Associated TST...............Test
DCG Satisfies ANY                    Any Entity Type
DCG Satisfies ERQ....................Engineering Requirement
DCG Satisfies URQ                    User Requirement

DEL - Deliverable

DEL Child-Of DEL.....................Deliverable
DEL Contained-In WBS                 Work Breakdown Structure
DEL Contains ANY.....................Any Entity Type
DEL Explodes-To ANY                  Any Entity Type
DEL Has-Associated ANY...............Any Entity Type
DEL Has-Associated CAT               Category
DEL Has-Associated CHG...............Change Request
DEL Has-Associated ELS               Entity List
DEL Has-Associated ISS...............Issue
DEL Has-Associated NTE               Note
DEL Has-Associated REF...............Reference Document
DEL Has-Associated TST               Test
DEL Parent-Of DEL....................Deliverable
DEL Satisfies ANY                    Any Entity Type
DEL Satisfies ERQ....................Engineering Requirement
DEL Satisfies URQ                    User Requirement

DFD - Data Flow Diagram

DFD Contains ANY.....................Any Entity Type
DFD Contains CSA                     Control Store
DFD Contains CTA.....................Control Transformation
DFD Contains CTF                     Control Flow
DFD Contains DAF.....................Data Flow
DFD Contains DAS                     Data Store
DFD Contains EXT.....................External Entity
DFD Contains PRC                     Process
DFD Explodes-From PRC................Process
```

Entity name	Code / 2nd Type	
DFD Has-Associated ANY		Any Entity Type
DFD Has-Associated CAT		Category
DFD Has-Associated CHG		Change Request
DFD Has-Associated ELS		Entity List
DFD Has-Associated ISS		Issue
DFD Has-Associated NTE		Note
DFD Has-Associated REF		Reference Document
DFD Has-Associated TST		Test
DFD Satisfies ANY		Any Entity Type
DFD Satisfies ERQ		Engineering Requirement
DFD Satisfies URQ		User Requirement

DMD – Data Model Diagram

DMD Contains ANY		Any Entity Type
DMD Contains DAE		Data Entity
DMD Contains DAR		Data Relationship
DMD Explodes-From ANY		Any Entity Type
DMD Explodes-From DAE		Data Entity
DMD Explodes-From DAF		Data Flow
DMD Explodes-From DAS		Data Store
DMD Has-Associated ANY		Any Entity Type
DMD Has-Associated CAT		Category
DMD Has-Associated CHG		Change Request
DMD Has-Associated ELS		Entity List
DMD Has-Associated ISS		Issue
DMD Has-Associated NTE		Note
DMD Has-Associated REF		Reference Document
DMD Has-Associated TST		Test
DMD Satisfies ANY		Any Entity Type
DMD Satisfies ERQ		Engineering Requirement
DMD Satisfies URQ		User Requirement

DNR – Data N-Ary Relationship

DNR Contained-In ERA		Entity-Relationship Diagram
DNR Explodes-To REC		Record
DNR Has-Associated ANY		Any Entity Type
DNR Has-Associated CAT		Category
DNR Has-Associated CHG		Change Request
DNR Has-Associated ELS		Entity List
DNR Has-Associated ISS		Issue
DNR Has-Associated NTE		Note
DNR Has-Associated REF		Reference Document
DNR Has-Associated TST		Test
DNR Has-Participant ANY		Any Entity Type

Entity name	Code / 2nd Type

DNR Has-Participant DAE   Data Entity
DNR Has-Participant DNR..............Data N-Ary Relationship
DNR Participates-In DNR   Data N-Ary Relationship
DNR Related-To ANY...................Any Entity Type
DNR Related-To ANY   Any Entity Type
DNR Related-To DAE...................Data Entity
DNR Related-To DAE   Data Entity
DNR Related-To DNR...................Data N-Ary Relationship
DNR Related-To DNR   Data N-Ary Relationship
DNR Satisfies ANY...................Any Entity Type
DNR Satisfies ERQ   Engineering Requirement
DNR Satisfies URQ...................User Requirement

DOC - Document Group

DOC Child-Of ANY   Any Entity Type
DOC Child-Of DOC....................Document Group
DOC Child-Of DOF   Document Fragment
DOC Contained-In DCG................Document Graph
DOC Parent-Of ANY   Any Entity Type
DOC Parent-Of DOC...................Document Group
DOC Parent-Of DOF   Document Fragment

DOF - Document Fragment

DOF Child-Of ANY....................Any Entity Type
DOF Child-Of DOC   Document Group
DOF Child-Of DOF....................Document Fragment
DOF Contained-In DCG   Document Graph
DOF Parent-Of ANY...................Any Entity Type
DOF Parent-Of DOC   Document Group
DOF Parent-Of DOF...................Document Fragment

ELE - Element

ELE Access-Key-Of DAS   Data Store
ELE Constant-In PPS.................Primitive Process Spec.
ELE Contained-In REC   Record
ELE Explodes-From DAF...............Data Flow
ELE Has-Associated ANY   Any Entity Type
ELE Has-Associated CAT..............Category
ELE Has-Associated CHG   Change Request
ELE Has-Associated ELS..............Entity List
ELE Has-Associated ISS   Issue
ELE Has-Associated NTE..............Note
ELE Has-Associated REF   Reference Document

Entity name   Code / 2nd Type

ELE Has-Associated TST...............Test
ELE Input-To PPS   Primitive Process Spec.
ELE Passed-As-Control-Via SGC........Structure Graph Connection
ELE Passed-As-Data-Via SGC   Structure Graph Connection
ELE Produced-By PPS..................Primitive Process Spec.
ELE Referenced-By ANY   Any Entity Type
ELE Referenced-By RED................Report Design
ELE Referenced-By SCD   Screen Design
ELE Returned-As-Control-Via SGC......Structure Graph Connection
ELE Returned-As-Data-Via SGC   Structure Graph Connection
ELE Satisfies ANY....................Any Entity Type
ELE Satisfies ERQ   Engineering Requirement
ELE Satisfies URQ....................User Requirement

ELS - Entity List

ELS Associated-With ANY   Any Entity Type
ELS Associated-With CSA..............Control Store
ELS Associated-With CTA   Control Transformation
ELS Associated-With CTF..............Control Flow
ELS Associated-With CTT   Control Table
ELS Associated-With DAE..............Data Entity
ELS Associated-With DAF   Data Flow
ELS Associated-With DAR..............Data Relationship
ELS Associated-With DAS   Data Store
ELS Associated-With DCG..............Document Graph
ELS Associated-With DEL   Deliverable
ELS Associated-With DFD..............Data Flow Diagram
ELS Associated-With DMD   Data Model Diagram
ELS Associated-With DNR..............Data N-Ary Relationship
ELS Associated-With ELE   Element
ELS Associated-With ERA..............Entity-Relationship Diagram
ELS Associated-With EXT   External Entity
ELS Associated-With FUN..............Function
ELS Associated-With MOD   Module
ELS Associated-With PGC..............Presentation Graph Conn.
ELS Associated-With PGO   Presentation Graph Object
ELS Associated-With PPS..............Primitive Process Spec.
ELS Associated-With PRC   Process
ELS Associated-With PRG..............Presentation Graph
ELS Associated-With PRM   Prompt
ELS Associated-With REC..............Record
ELS Associated-With SDT   Structured Decision Table
ELS Associated-With SDV..............System Device
ELS Associated-With SGC   Structure Graph Connection
ELS Associated-With SIG..............Signal

Entity name	Code / 2nd Type	

ELS Associated-With STA   State
ELS Associated-With STC..............Structure Chart
ELS Associated-With STD   Structure Diagram
ELS Associated-With TRD..............State Transition Diagram
ELS Associated-With TVA   Transition Vector
ELS Associated-With WBS..............Work Breakdown Structure
ELS Comes-From ELS   Entity List
ELS Contains ANY.....................Any Entity Type
ELS Goes-To ELS   Entity List
ELS Processed-By REP.................Report

ERA - Entity-Relationship Diagram

ERA Contains ANY   Any Entity Type
ERA Contains DAE.....................Data Entity
ERA Contains DNR   Data N-Ary Relationship
ERA Explodes-From ANY................Any Entity Type
ERA Explodes-From DAE   Data Entity
ERA Explodes-From DAF................Data Flow
ERA Explodes-From DAS   Data Store
ERA Has-Associated ANY...............Any Entity Type
ERA Has-Associated CAT   Category
ERA Has-Associated CHG...............Change Request
ERA Has-Associated ELS   Entity List
ERA Has-Associated ISS...............Issue
ERA Has-Associated NTE   Note
ERA Has-Associated REF...............Reference Document
ERA Has-Associated TST   Test
ERA Satisfies ANY....................Any Entity Type
ERA Satisfies ERQ   Engineering Requirement
ERA Satisfies URQ....................User Requirement

ERQ - Engineering Requirement

ERQ Contained-In ERQ   Engineering Requirement
ERQ Contains ERQ.....................Engineering Requirement
ERQ Derived-From URQ   User Requirement
ERQ Has-Associated ANY...............Any Entity Type
ERQ Has-Associated CAT   Category
ERQ Has-Associated CHG...............Change Request
ERQ Has-Associated ISS   Issue
ERQ Has-Associated NTE...............Note
ERQ Has-Associated REF   Reference Document
ERQ Has-Associated TST...............Test
ERQ Satisfied-By ANY   Any Entity Type
ERQ Satisfied-By CSA.................Control Store
ERQ Satisfied-By CTA   Control Transformation

Entity name	Code / 2nd Type

ERQ Satisfied-By CTF.................Control Flow
ERQ Satisfied-By CTT   Control Table
ERQ Satisfied-By DAE.................Data Entity
ERQ Satisfied-By DAF   Data Flow
ERQ Satisfied-By DAR.................Data Relationship
ERQ Satisfied-By DAS   Data Store
ERQ Satisfied-By DCG.................Document Graph
ERQ Satisfied-By DEL   Deliverable
ERQ Satisfied-By DFD.................Data Flow Diagram
ERQ Satisfied-By DMD   Data Model Diagram
ERQ Satisfied-By DNR.................Data N-Ary Relationship
ERQ Satisfied-By ELE   Element
ERQ Satisfied-By ERA.................Entity-Relationship Diagram
ERQ Satisfied-By EXT   External Entity
ERQ Satisfied-By FUN.................Function
ERQ Satisfied-By MOD   Module
ERQ Satisfied-By PGC.................Presentation Graph Conn.
ERQ Satisfied-By PGO   Presentation Graph Object
ERQ Satisfied-By PPS.................Primitive Process Spec.
ERQ Satisfied-By PRC   Process
ERQ Satisfied-By PRG.................Presentation Graph
ERQ Satisfied-By PRM   Prompt
ERQ Satisfied-By REC.................Record
ERQ Satisfied-By SDT   Structured Decision Table
ERQ Satisfied-By SDV.................System Device
ERQ Satisfied-By SGC   Structure Graph Connection
ERQ Satisfied-By SIG.................Signal
ERQ Satisfied-By STA   State
ERQ Satisfied-By STC.................Structure Chart
ERQ Satisfied-By STD   Structure Diagram
ERQ Satisfied-By TRD.................State Transition Diagram
ERQ Satisfied-By TST   Test
ERQ Satisfied-By TVA.................Transition Vector
ERQ Satisfied-By WBS   Work Breakdown Structure

EXT - External Entity

EXT Contained-In DFD.................Data Flow Diagram
EXT Has-Associated ANY   Any Entity Type
EXT Has-Associated CAT...............Category
EXT Has-Associated CHG   Change Request
EXT Has-Associated ELS...............Entity List
EXT Has-Associated ISS   Issue
EXT Has-Associated NTE   Note
EXT Has-Associated REF...............Reference Document
EXT Has-Associated TST   Test

Entity name	Code / 2nd Type
EXT Receives ANY.......................	Any Entity Type
EXT Receives CTF	Control Flow
EXT Receives DAF.......................	Data Flow
EXT Receives-From ANY	Any Entity Type
EXT Receives-From CSA................	Control Store
EXT Receives-From CTA	Control Transformation
EXT Receives-From DAS................	Data Store
EXT Receives-From EXT	External Entity
EXT Receives-From PRC................	Process
EXT Satisfies ANY	Any Entity Type
EXT Satisfies ERQ.....................	Engineering Requirement
EXT Satisfies URQ	User Requirement
EXT Sends ANY..........................	Any Entity Type
EXT Sends CTF	Control Flow
EXT Sends DAF..........................	Data Flow
EXT Sends-To ANY	Any Entity Type
EXT Sends-To CSA......................	Control Store
EXT Sends-To CTA	Control Transformation
EXT Sends-To DAS......................	Data Store
EXT Sends-To EXT	External Entity
EXT Sends-To PRC......................	Process

FUN - Function

FUN Child-Of ANY	Any Entity Type
FUN Child-Of DAS......................	Data Store
FUN Child-Of FUN	Function
FUN Child-Of SDV......................	System Device
FUN Contained-In ANY	Any Entity Type
FUN Contained-In STC.................	Structure Chart
FUN Contained-In STD	Structure Diagram
FUN Explodes-To ANY..................	Any Entity Type
FUN Explodes-To MOD	Module
FUN Explodes-To STC..................	Structure Chart
FUN Explodes-To STD	Structure Diagram
FUN Has-Associated ANY..............	Any Entity Type
FUN Has-Associated CAT	Category
FUN Has-Associated CHG..............	Change Request
FUN Has-Associated ELS	Entity List
FUN Has-Associated ISS..............	Issue
FUN Has-Associated NTE	Note
FUN Has-Associated REF..............	Reference Document
FUN Has-Associated TST	Test
FUN Parent-Of ANY....................	Any Entity Type
FUN Parent-Of DAS	Data Store
FUN Parent-Of FUN....................	Function

Entity name   **Code / 2nd Type**

```
FUN Parent-Of SDV                System Device
FUN Receives SGC.................Structure Graph Connection
FUN Satisfies ANY                Any Entity Type
FUN Satisfies ERQ................Engineering Requirement
FUN Satisfies URQ                User Requirement
FUN Sends SGC....................Structure Graph Connection
```

ISS - Issue

```
ISS Associated-With ANY          Any Entity Type
ISS Associated-With CSA..........Control Store
ISS Associated-With CTA          Control Transformation
ISS Associated-With CTF..........Control Flow
ISS Associated-With CTT          Control Table
ISS Associated-With DAE..........Data Entity
ISS Associated-With DAF          Data Flow
ISS Associated-With DAR..........Data Relationship
ISS Associated-With DAS          Data Store
ISS Associated-With DCG..........Document Graph
ISS Associated-With DEL          Deliverable
ISS Associated-With DFD..........Data Flow Diagram
ISS Associated-With DMD          Data Model Diagram
ISS Associated-With DNR..........Data N-Ary Relationship
ISS Associated-With ELE          Element
ISS Associated-With ERA..........Entity-Relationship Diagram
ISS Associated-With ERQ          Engineering Requirement
ISS Associated-With EXT..........External Entity
ISS Associated-With FUN          Function
ISS Associated-With MOD..........Module
ISS Associated-With PGC          Presentation Graph Conn.
ISS Associated-With PGO..........Presentation Graph Object
ISS Associated-With PPS          Primitive Process Spec.
ISS Associated-With PRC..........Process
ISS Associated-With PRG          Presentation Graph
ISS Associated-With PRM..........Prompt
ISS Associated-With REC          Record
ISS Associated-With SDT..........Structured Decision Table
ISS Associated-With SDV          System Device
ISS Associated-With SGC..........Structure Graph Connection
ISS Associated-With SIG          Signal
ISS Associated-With STA..........State
ISS Associated-With STC          Structure Chart
ISS Associated-With STD..........Structure Diagram
ISS Associated-With TRD          State Transition Diagram
ISS Associated-With TST..........Test
ISS Associated-With TVA          Transition Vector
```

Entity name   **Code / 2nd Type**

ISS Associated-With URQ.............User Requirement
ISS Associated-With WBS   Work Breakdown Structure
ISS Has-Associated ANY.............Any Entity Type
ISS Has-Associated CAT   Category
ISS Has-Associated CHG.............Change Request
ISS Has-Associated NTE   Note
ISS Has-Associated REF.............Reference Document

MOD – Module

MOD Explodes-From FUN   Function
MOD Has-Associated ANY.............Any Entity Type
MOD Has-Associated CAT   Category
MOD Has-Associated CHG.............Change Request
MOD Has-Associated ELS   Entity List
MOD Has-Associated ISS.............Issue
MOD Has-Associated NTE   Note
MOD Has-Associated REF.............Reference Document
MOD Has-Associated TST   Test
MOD Satisfies ANY..................Any Entity Type
MOD Satisfies ERQ   Engineering Requirement
MOD Satisfies URQ..................User Requirement

NTE – Note

NTE Associated-With ANY   Any Entity Type
NTE Associated-With CHG.............Change Request
NTE Associated-With CSA   Control Store
NTE Associated-With CTA.............Control Transformation
NTE Associated-With CTF   Control Flow
NTE Associated-With CTT.............Control Table
NTE Associated-With DAE   Data Entity
NTE Associated-With DAF.............Data Flow
NTE Associated-With DAR   Data Relationship
NTE Associated-With DAS.............Data Store
NTE Associated-With DCG   Document Graph
NTE Associated-With DEL.............Deliverable
NTE Associated-With DFD   Data Flow Diagram
NTE Associated-With DMD.............Data Model Diagram
NTE Associated-With DNR   Data N-Ary Relationship
NTE Associated-With ELE.............Element
NTE Associated-With ERA   Entity-Relationship Diagram
NTE Associated-With ERQ.............Engineering Requirement
NTE Associated-With EXT   External Entity
NTE Associated-With FUN.............Function
NTE Associated-With ISS   Issue

Entity name	Code / 2nd Type	

NTE Associated-With MOD..............Module
NTE Associated-With PGC   Presentation Graph Conn.
NTE Associated-With PGO..............Presentation Graph Object
NTE Associated-With PPS   Primitive Process Spec.
NTE Associated-With PRC..............Process
NTE Associated-With PRG   Presentation Graph
NTE Associated-With PRM..............Prompt
NTE Associated-With REC   Record
NTE Associated-With SDT..............Structured Decision Table
NTE Associated-With SDV   System Device
NTE Associated-With SGC..............Structure Graph Connection
NTE Associated-With SIG   Signal
NTE Associated-With STA..............State
NTE Associated-With STC   Structure Chart
NTE Associated-With STD..............Structure Diagram
NTE Associated-With TRD   State Transition Diagram
NTE Associated-With TST..............Test
NTE Associated-With TVA   Transition Vector
NTE Associated-With URQ..............User Requirement
NTE Associated-With WBS   Work Breakdown Structure
NTE Comes-From NTE..................Note
NTE Goes-To NTE   Note
NTE Has-Associated ANY..............Any Entity Type
NTE Has-Associated CAT   Category
NTE Has-Associated REF..............Reference Document

PGC - Presentation Graph Connection

PGC Connects PGO   Presentation Graph Object
PGC Contained-In PRG................Presentation Graph
PGC Explodes-To ANY   Any Entity Type
PGC Has-Associated ANY..............Any Entity Type
PGC Has-Associated CAT   Category
PGC Has-Associated CHG..............Change Request
PGC Has-Associated ELS   Entity List
PGC Has-Associated ISS..............Issue
PGC Has-Associated NTE   Note
PGC Has-Associated REF..............Reference Document
PGC Has-Associated TST   Test
PGC Received-By PGO.................Presentation Graph Object
PGC Satisfies ANY   Any Entity Type
PGC Satisfies ERQ...................Engineering Requirement
PGC Satisfies URQ   User Requirement
PGC Sent-By PGO....................Presentation Graph Object

Entity name   Code / 2nd Type

PGO - Presentation Graph Object

```
PGO Connected-By PGC                 Presentation Graph Conn.
PGO Connects-To PGO..................Presentation Graph Object
PGO Connects-To PGO                  Presentation Graph Object
PGO Contained-In PRG.................Presentation Graph
PGO Explodes-To ANY                  Any Entity Type
PGO Has-Associated ANY...............Any Entity Type
PGO Has-Associated CAT               Category
PGO Has-Associated CHG...............Change Request
PGO Has-Associated ELS               Entity List
PGO Has-Associated ISS...............Issue
PGO Has-Associated NTE               Note
PGO Has-Associated REF...............Reference Document
PGO Has-Associated TST               Test
PGO Receives-From PGO................Presentation Graph Object
PGO Receives PGC                     Presentation Graph Conn.
PGO Satisfies ANY....................Any Entity Type
PGO Satisfies ERQ                    Engineering Requirement
PGO Satisfies URQ....................User Requirement
PGO Sends PGC                        Presentation Graph Conn.
PGO Sends-To PGO.....................Presentation Graph Object
```

PPS - Primitive Process Specification

```
PPS Explodes-From PRC                Process
PPS Has-Associated ANY...............Any Entity Type
PPS Has-Associated CAT               Category
PPS Has-Associated CHG...............Change Request
PPS Has-Associated ELS               Entity List
PPS Has-Associated ISS...............Issue
PPS Has-Associated NTE               Note
PPS Has-Associated REF...............Reference Document
PPS Has-Associated TST               Test
PPS Has-Input ANY....................Any Entity Type
PPS Has-Input CTT                    Control Table
PPS Has-Input ELE....................Element
PPS Has-Input REC                    Record
PPS Has-Input SIG....................Signal
PPS Produces ANY                     Any Entity Type
PPS Produces CTT.....................Control Table
PPS Produces ELE                     Element
PPS Produces REC.....................Record
PPS Produces SIG                     Signal
PPS Satisfies ANY....................Any Entity Type
PPS Satisfies ERQ                    Engineering Requirement
PPS Satisfies URQ....................User Requirement
```

Entity name   **Code / 2nd Type**

PPS Uses-Constant ANY   Any Entity Type
PPS Uses-Constant ELE...............Element
PPS Uses-Constant REC   Record

PRC - Process

PRC Contained-In DFD...............Data Flow Diagram
PRC Explodes-To ANY   Any Entity Type
PRC Explodes-To DFD...............Data Flow Diagram
PRC Explodes-To PPS   Primitive Process Spec.
PRC Explodes-To PRG...............Presentation Graph
PRC Explodes-To STC   Structure Chart
PRC Explodes-To STD...............Structure Diagram
PRC Has-Associated ANY   Any Entity Type
PRC Has-Associated CAT.............Category
PRC Has-Associated CHG   Change Request
PRC Has-Associated ELS.............Entity List
PRC Has-Associated ISS   Issue
PRC Has-Associated NTE.............Note
PRC Has-Associated REF   Reference Document
PRC Has-Associated TST.............Test
PRC Prompted-By TVA   Transition Vector
PRC Receives ANY...................Any Entity Type
PRC Receives CTF   Control Flow
PRC Receives DAF...................Data Flow
PRC Receives-From ANY   Any Entity Type
PRC Receives-From CSA..............Control Store
PRC Receives-From CTA   Control Transformation
PRC Receives-From DAS..............Data Store
PRC Receives-From EXT   External Entity
PRC Receives-From PRC..............Process
PRC Satisfies ANY   Any Entity Type
PRC Satisfies ERQ..................Engineering Requirement
PRC Satisfies URQ   User Requirement
PRC Sends ANY......................Any Entity Type
PRC Sends CTF   Control Flow
PRC Sends DAF......................Data Flow
PRC Sends-To ANY   Any Entity Type
PRC Sends-To CSA...................Control Store
PRC Sends-To CTA   Control Transformation
PRC Sends-To DAS...................Data Store
PRC Sends-To EXT   External Entity
PRC Sends-To PRC...................Process

Entity name   Code / 2nd Type

PRG - Presentation Graph

PRG Contains ANY   Any Entity Type
PRG Contains PGC.....................Presentation Graph Conn.
PRG Contains PGO   Presentation Graph Object
PRG Explodes-From PRC...............Process
PRG Has-Associated ANY   Any Entity Type
PRG Has-Associated CAT..............Category
PRG Has-Associated CHG   Change Request
PRG Has-Associated ELS..............Entity List
PRG Has-Associated ISS   Issue
PRG Has-Associated NTE..............Note
PRG Has-Associated REF   Reference Document
PRG Has-Associated TST..............Test
PRG Satisfies ANY   Any Entity Type
PRG Satisfies ERQ...................Engineering Requirement
PRG Satisfies URQ   User Requirement

PRM - Prompt

PRM Explodes-From CTF...............Control Flow
PRM Has-Associated ANY   Any Entity Type
PRM Has-Associated CAT..............Category
PRM Has-Associated CHG   Change Request
PRM Has-Associated ELS..............Entity List
PRM Has-Associated ISS   Issue
PRM Has-Associated NTE..............Note
PRM Has-Associated REF   Reference Document
PRM Has-Associated TST..............Test
PRM Output-From TVA   Transition Vector
PRM Satisfies ANY...................Any Entity Type
PRM Satisfies ERQ   Engineering Requirement
PRM Satisfies URQ...................User Requirement

REC - Record

REC Constant-In PPS   Primitive Process Spec.
REC Contained-In REC................Record
REC Contains ANY   Any Entity Type
REC Contains ELE....................Element
REC Contains REC   Record
REC Explodes-From ANY...............Any Entity Type
REC Explodes-From DAE   Data Entity
REC Explodes-From DAF...............Data Flow
REC Explodes-From DAS   Data Store
REC Explodes-From DNR...............Data N-Ary Relationship
REC Explodes-From SGC   Structure Graph Connection

Entity name	Code / 2nd Type

REC Has-Associated ANY...............Any Entity Type
REC Has-Associated CAT   Category
REC Has-Associated CHG...............Change Request
REC Has-Associated ELS   Entity List
REC Has-Associated ISS...............Issue
REC Has-Associated NTE   Note
REC Has-Associated REF...............Reference Document
REC Has-Associated TST   Test
REC Input-To PPS.....................Primitive Process Spec.
REC Passed-As-Control-Via SGC   Structure Graph Connection
REC Passed-As-Data-Via SGC...........Structure Graph Connection
REC Produced-By PPS   Primitive Process Spec.
REC Returned-As-Control-Via SGC......Structure Graph Connection
REC Returned-As-Data-Via SGC   Structure Graph Connection
REC Satisfies ANY....................Any Entity Type
REC Satisfies ERQ   Engineering Requirement
REC Satisfies URQ....................User Requirement

RED - Report Design

RED References ELE   Element

REF - Reference Document

REF Associated-With ANY..............Any Entity Type
REF Associated-With CHG   Change Request
REF Associated-With CSA..............Control Store
REF Associated-With CTA   Control Transformation
REF Associated-With CTF..............Control Flow
REF Associated-With CTT   Control Table
REF Associated-With DAE..............Data Entity
REF Associated-With DAF   Data Flow
REF Associated-With DAR..............Data Relationship
REF Associated-With DAS   Data Store
REF Associated-With DCG..............Document Graph
REF Associated-With DEL   Deliverable
REF Associated-With DFD..............Data Flow Diagram
REF Associated-With DMD   Data Model Diagram
REF Associated-With DNR..............Data N-Ary Relationship
REF Associated-With ELE   Element
REF Associated-With ERA..............Entity-Relationship Diagram
REF Associated-With ERQ   Engineering Requirement
REF Associated-With EXT..............External Entity
REF Associated-With FUN   Function
REF Associated-With ISS..............Issue
REF Associated-With MOD   Module

Entity name	Code / 2nd Type

REF Associated-With NTE..............Note
REF Associated-With PGC   Presentation Graph Conn.
REF Associated-With PGO..............Presentation Graph Object
REF Associated-With PPS   Primitive Process Spec.
REF Associated-With PRC..............Process
REF Associated-With PRG   Presentation Graph
REF Associated-With PRM..............Prompt
REF Associated-With REC   Record
REF Associated-With SDT..............Structured Decision Table
REF Associated-With SDV   System Device
REF Associated-With SGC..............Structure Graph Connection
REF Associated-With SIG   Signal
REF Associated-With STA..............State
REF Associated-With STC   Structure Chart
REF Associated-With STD..............Structure Diagram
REF Associated-With TRD   State Transition Diagram
REF Associated-With TST..............Test
REF Associated-With TVA   Transition Vector
REF Associated-With URQ..............User Requirement
REF Associated-With WBS   Work Breakdown Structure
REF Has-Associated CAT..............Category

REP - Report

REP Processes ELS   Entity List

SCD - Screen Design

SCD Comes-From SCD..................Screen Design
SCD Goes-To SCD   Screen Design
SCD References ELE..................Element
SCD Run-By SDE   Screen Data Entry

SDE - Screen Data Entry

SDE Reported-By SDR.................Screen Data Report
SDE Runs SCD   Screen Design

SDR - Screen Data Report

SDR Reports-On SDE.................Screen Data Entry

SDT - Structured Decision Table

SDT Explodes-From CTA   Control Transformation
SDT Has-Associated ANY..............Any Entity Type
SDT Has-Associated CAT   Category

Entity name   **Code / 2nd Type**

SDT Has-Associated CHG...............Change Request
SDT Has-Associated ELS   Entity List
SDT Has-Associated ISS...............Issue
SDT Has-Associated NTE   Note
SDT Has-Associated REF...............Reference Document
SDT Has-Associated TST   Test
SDT Satisfies ANY...................Any Entity Type
SDT Satisfies ERQ   Engineering Requirement
SDT Satisfies URQ...................User Requirement

SDV - System Device

SDV Child-Of ANY   Any Entity Type
SDV Child-Of DAS....................Data Store
SDV Child-Of FUN   Function
SDV Child-Of SDV....................System Device
SDV Contained-In STC   Structure Chart
SDV Explodes-To STC.................Structure Chart
SDV Has-Associated ANY   Any Entity Type
SDV Has-Associated CAT..............Category
SDV Has-Associated CHG   Change Request
SDV Has-Associated ELS..............Entity List
SDV Has-Associated ISS   Issue
SDV Has-Associated NTE..............Note
SDV Has-Associated REF   Reference Document
SDV Has-Associated TST..............Test
SDV Parent-Of ANY   Any Entity Type
SDV Parent-Of DAS...................Data Store
SDV Parent-Of FUN   Function
SDV Parent-Of SDV...................System Device
SDV Receives SGC   Structure Graph Connection
SDV Satisfies ANY...................Any Entity Type
SDV Satisfies ERQ   Engineering Requirement
SDV Satisfies URQ...................User Requirement
SDV Sends SGC   Structure Graph Connection

SGC - Structure Graph Connection

SGC Contained-In ANY................Any Entity Type
SGC Contained-In STC   Structure Chart
SGC Contained-In STD................Structure Diagram
SGC Explodes-To REC   Record
SGC Has-Associated ANY..............Any Entity Type
SGC Has-Associated CAT   Category
SGC Has-Associated CHG..............Change Request
SGC Has-Associated ELS   Entity List

Entity name	Code / 2nd Type
SGC Has-Associated ISS..............Issue	
SGC Has-Associated NTE	Note
SGC Has-Associated REF..............Reference Document	
SGC Has-Associated TST	Test
SGC Passes-Control ANY..............Any Entity Type	
SGC Passes-Control ELE	Element
SGC Passes-Control REC..............Record	
SGC Passes-Data ANY	Any Entity Type
SGC Passes-Data ELE..................Element	
SGC Passes-Data REC	Record
SGC Received-By ANY..................Any Entity Type	
SGC Received-By DAS	Data Store
SGC Received-By FUN..................Function	
SGC Received-By SDV	System Device
SGC Returns-Control ANY..............Any Entity Type	
SGC Returns-Control ELE	Element
SGC Returns-Control REC..............Record	
SGC Returns-Data ANY	Any Entity Type
SGC Returns-Data ELE..................Element	
SGC Returns-Data REC	Record
SGC Satisfies ANY....................Any Entity Type	
SGC Satisfies ERQ	Engineering Requirement
SGC Satisfies URQ....................User Requirement	
SGC Sent-By ANY	Any Entity Type
SGC Sent-By DAS......................Data Store	
SGC Sent-By FUN	Function
SGC Sent-By SDV......................System Device	

SIG - Signal

SIG Contained-In CTT	Control Table
SIG Explodes-From ANY................Any Entity Type	
SIG Explodes-From CSA	Control Store
SIG Explodes-From CTF................Control Flow	
SIG Has-Associated ANY	Any Entity Type
SIG Has-Associated CAT..............Category	
SIG Has-Associated CHG	Change Request
SIG Has-Associated ELS..............Entity List	
SIG Has-Associated ISS	Issue
SIG Has-Associated NTE..............Note	
SIG Has-Associated REF	Reference Document
SIG Has-Associated TST..............Test	
SIG Input-To ANY	Any Entity Type
SIG Input-To PPS....................Primitive Process Spec.	
SIG Input-To TVA	Transition Vector

Entity name   **Code / 2nd Type**

SIG Output-From TVA.................Transition Vector
SIG Produced-By PPS   Primitive Process Spec.
SIG Satisfies ANY....................Any Entity Type
SIG Satisfies ERQ   Engineering Requirement
SIG Satisfies URQ....................User Requirement

STA - State

STA Contained-In TRD   State Transition Diagram
STA Explodes-To TRD.................State Transition Diagram
STA Has-Associated ANY   Any Entity Type
STA Has-Associated CAT..............Category
STA Has-Associated CHG   Change Request
STA Has-Associated ELS..............Entity List
STA Has-Associated ISS   Issue
STA Has-Associated NTE..............Note
STA Has-Associated REF   Reference Document
STA Has-Associated TST..............Test
STA Receives TVA   Transition Vector
STA Satisfies ANY...................Any Entity Type
STA Satisfies ERQ   Engineering Requirement
STA Satisfies URQ...................User Requirement
STA Sends TVA   Transition Vector
STA Transitions-From STA............State
STA Transitions-To STA   State

STC - Structure Chart

STC Contains ANY....................Any Entity Type
STC Contains DAS   Data Store
STC Contains FUN....................Function
STC Contains SDV   System Device
STC Contains SGC....................Structure Graph Connection
STC Explodes-From ANY   Any Entity Type
STC Explodes-From FUN...............Function
STC Explodes-From PRC   Process
STC Explodes-From SDV...............System Device
STC Has-Associated ANY   Any Entity Type
STC Has-Associated CAT..............Category
STC Has-Associated CHG   Change Request
STC Has-Associated ELS..............Entity List
STC Has-Associated ISS   Issue
STC Has-Associated NTE..............Note
STC Has-Associated REF   Reference Document
STC Has-Associated TST..............Test
STC Satisfies ANY   Any Entity Type

Entity name   **Code / 2nd Type**

STC Satisfies ERQ....................Engineering Requirement
STC Satisfies URQ   User Requirement

STD - Structure Diagram

STD Contains ANY.....................Any Entity Type
STD Contains FUN   Function
STD Contains SGC.....................Structure Graph Connection
STD Explodes-From ANY   Any Entity Type
STD Explodes-From DAF................Data Flow
STD Explodes-From FUN   Function
STD Explodes-From PRC................Process
STD Has-Associated ANY   Any Entity Type
STD Has-Associated CAT...............Category
STD Has-Associated CHG   Change Request
STD Has-Associated ELS...............Entity List
STD Has-Associated ISS   Issue
STD Has-Associated NTE..............Note
STD Has-Associated REF   Reference Document
STD Has-Associated TST..............Test
STD Satisfies ANY   Any Entity Type
STD Satisfies ERQ...................Engineering Requirement
STD Satisfies URQ   User Requirement

TAB - Table Of Codes

TAB Comes-From TAB...................Table of Codes
TAB Goes-To TAB   Table of Codes

TRD - State Transition Diagram

TRD Contains ANY.....................Any Entity Type
TRD Contains STA   State
TRD Contains TVA.....................Transition Vector
TRD Explodes-From ANY   Any Entity Type
TRD Explodes-From CTA................Control Transformation
TRD Explodes-From STA   State
TRD Has-Associated ANY..............Any Entity Type
TRD Has-Associated CAT   Category
TRD Has-Associated CHG..............Change Request
TRD Has-Associated ELS   Entity List
TRD Has-Associated ISS..............Issue
TRD Has-Associated NTE   Note
TRD Has-Associated REF..............Reference Document
TRD Has-Associated TST   Test
TRD Satisfies ANY...................Any Entity Type
TRD Satisfies ERQ   Engineering Requirement
TRD Satisfies URQ...................User Requirement

Entity name   **Code / 2nd Type**

TST - Test

TST Associated-With ANY   Any Entity Type
TST Associated-With CSA.............Control Store
TST Associated-With CTA   Control Transformation
TST Associated-With CTF.............Control Flow
TST Associated-With CTT   Control Table
TST Associated-With DAE.............Data Entity
TST Associated-With DAF   Data Flow
TST Associated-With DAR.............Data Relationship
TST Associated-With DAS   Data Store
TST Associated-With DCG.............Document Graph
TST Associated-With DEL   Deliverable
TST Associated-With DFD.............Data Flow Diagram
TST Associated-With DMD   Data Model Diagram
TST Associated-With DNR.............Data N-Ary Relationship
TST Associated-With ELE   Element
TST Associated-With ERA.............Entity-Relationship Diagram
TST Associated-With ERQ   Engineering Requirement
TST Associated-With EXT.............External Entity
TST Associated-With FUN   Function
TST Associated-With MOD.............Module
TST Associated-With PGC   Presentation Graph Conn.
TST Associated-With PGO.............Presentation Graph Object
TST Associated-With PPS   Primitive Process Spec.
TST Associated-With PRC.............Process
TST Associated-With PRG   Presentation Graph
TST Associated-With PRM.............Prompt
TST Associated-With REC   Record
TST Associated-With SDT.............Structured Decision Table
TST Associated-With SDV   System Device
TST Associated-With SGC.............Structure Graph Connection
TST Associated-With SIG   Signal
TST Associated-With STA.............State
TST Associated-With STC   Structure Chart
TST Associated-With STD.............Structure Diagram
TST Associated-With TRD   State Transition Diagram
TST Associated-With TVA.............Transition Vector
TST Associated-With URQ   User Requirement
TST Associated-With WBS.............Work Breakdown Structure
TST Has-Associated ANY   Any Entity Type
TST Has-Associated CAT.............Category
TST Has-Associated CHG   Change Request
TST Has-Associated ISS.............Issue
TST Has-Associated NTE   Note
TST Has-Associated REF.............Reference Document
TST Satisfies ANY   Any Entity Type

Entity name	Code / 2nd Type	

TST Satisfies ERQ...................Engineering Requirement
TST Satisfies URQ   User Requirement

TVA - Transition Vector

TVA Contained-In TRD................State Transition Diagram
TVA Has-Associated ANY   Any Entity Type
TVA Has-Associated CAT..............Category
TVA Has-Associated CHG   Change Request
TVA Has-Associated ELS..............Entity List
TVA Has-Associated ISS   Issue
TVA Has-Associated NTE..............Note
TVA Has-Associated REF   Reference Document
TVA Has-Associated TST..............Test
TVA Has-Input SIG   Signal
TVA Has-Output ANY..................Any Entity Type
TVA Has-Output PRM   Prompt
TVA Has-Output SIG..................Signal
TVA Prompts ANY   Any Entity Type
TVA Prompts CTA.....................Control Transformation
TVA Prompts PRC   Process
TVA Received-By STA.................State
TVA Satisfies ANY   Any Entity Type
TVA Satisfies ERQ...................Engineering Requirement
TVA Satisfies URQ   User Requirement
TVA Sent-By STA.....................State

URQ - User Requirement

URQ Contained-In URQ   User Requirement
URQ Contains URQ....................User Requirement
URQ Derives ERQ   Engineering Requirement
URQ Has-Associated ANY..............Any Entity Type
URQ Has-Associated CAT   Category
URQ Has-Associated CHG..............Change Request
URQ Has-Associated ISS   Issue
URQ Has-Associated NTE..............Note
URQ Has-Associated REF   Reference Document
URQ Has-Associated TST..............Test
URQ Satisfied-By ANY   Any Entity Type
URQ Satisfied-By CSA................Control Store
URQ Satisfied-By CTA   Control Transformation
URQ Satisfied-By CTF................Control Flow
URQ Satisfied-By CTT   Control Table
URQ Satisfied-By DAE................Data Entity
URQ Satisfied-By DAF   Data Flow
URQ Satisfied-By DAR................Data Relationship
URQ Satisfied-By DAS   Data Store

Entity name	Code / 2nd Type	
URQ Satisfied-By DCG	....	Document Graph
URQ Satisfied-By DEL		Deliverable
URQ Satisfied-By DFD	....	Data Flow Diagram
URQ Satisfied-By DMD		Data Model Diagram
URQ Satisfied-By DNR	....	Data N-Ary Relationship
URQ Satisfied-By ELE		Element
URQ Satisfied-By ERA	....	Entity-Relationship Diagram
URQ Satisfied-By EXT		External Entity
URQ Satisfied-By FUN	....	Function
URQ Satisfied-By MOD		Module
URQ Satisfied-By PGC	....	Presentation Graph Conn.
URQ Satisfied-By PGO		Presentation Graph Object
URQ Satisfied-By PPS	....	Primitive Process Spec.
URQ Satisfied-By PRC		Process
URQ Satisfied-By PRG	....	Presentation Graph
URQ Satisfied-By PRM		Prompt
URQ Satisfied-By REC	....	Record
URQ Satisfied-By SDT		Structured Decision Table
URQ Satisfied-By SDV	....	System Device
URQ Satisfied-By SGC		Structure Graph Connection
URQ Satisfied-By SIG	....	Signal
URQ Satisfied-By STA		State
URQ Satisfied-By STC	....	Structure Chart
URQ Satisfied-By STD		Structure Diagram
URQ Satisfied-By TRD	....	State Transition Diagram
URQ Satisfied-By TST		Test
URQ Satisfied-By TVA	....	Transition Vector
URQ Satisfied-By WBS		Work Breakdown Structure

USR - User

USR Responsible-For ANY	....	Any Entity Type

WBS - Work Breakdown Structure

WBS Contains DEL		Deliverable
WBS Has-Associated ANY	....	Any Entity Type
WBS Has-Associated CAT		Category
WBS Has-Associated CHG	....	Change Request
WBS Has-Associated ELS		Entity List
WBS Has-Associated ISS	....	Issue
WBS Has-Associated NTE		Note
WBS Has-Associated REF	....	Reference Document
WBS Has-Associated TST		Test
WBS Satisfies ANY	....	Any Entity Type
WBS Satisfies ERQ		Engineering Requirement
WBS Satisfies URQ	....	User Requirement

INDEX

Selector list 9
        Entities 38
        Processes 51
        Relationships 211, 236
        Screen design 186
Shared Elements Count matrix
        219
Signal
        Describing 63
        Transition vector 171
Similiar Records report 218
SIZE 83
Sort
        Modifying, Entity list
        259
        Report writer 239
State Transition Diagram 40,
        165
        Analysis 174
        Creating 165
        Describing 167
        Level balancing 177
        Syntax errors 172
States
        Describing 169
Storage type 129
Structure chart 86
        Describing 91
        Describing objects 88
        Symbols 92
Structure charts
        Code generation 315
Structure Diagrams 94
        Symbols 94
Subset Records report 218
Subset Screen/Report Designs
        report 226
Subtraction
        Creating, Entity list
        258
        Entity list 249
        Modifying, Entity list
        259
Summary Report 206, 243
        Relationships 212
        Report Writer 239
SYMBOL 92
SYSLABEL 14
System device

Creating entity 297
        For managing hardware 297
System flowcharts 101
        Objects 102
SYSTPORT 11
Table of codes 131
        Printing 132
Test entity 285
Text
        Blocks 83
        Placing on the drawing 83
Text file, from word processing
        4306
TITLE 84
Title block 84
Total, Report Writer 242
Transform 201
        Update options 201
Transition vector
        Describing 170
TXT BLK 83
Undescribed Graph Entities
        Data model diagram 161
        Entity-relationship diagram
        161
        State transition diagram 174
        Work breakdown structure graph
        297
Unexploded Data Flows report 228
Union
        Creating, Entity list 254
        Entity list 248
        Modifying, Entity list 258
Unkeyed Records (All levels) report
        222
Unkeyed Records (One level) report
        219
Unlocking XLDictionary entities 268
Unprocessed Elements report 228
User Defined report 239
User requirement 38, 89
User requirements 130, 289
        Creating 289
User, information on 287
USERPORT 11
        Procedure 88
USRLABEL 14
VIEW 42